I0105210

Interdependent Yet Intolerant

Interdependent Yet Intolerant

Native Citizen–Foreign Migrant Violence

and Global Insecurity

Robert Mandel

Stanford University Press
Stanford, California

Stanford University Press
Stanford, California

©2021 by the Board of Trustees of the Leland Stanford Junior University. All rights reserved.

Scripture quotations taken from The Holy Bible, New International Version® NIV®. Copyright © 1973 1978 1984 2011 by Biblica, Inc. TM. Used by permission. All rights reserved worldwide.

No part of this book may be reproduced or transmitted in any form or by any means, electronic or mechanical, including photocopying and recording, or in any information storage or retrieval system without the prior written permission of Stanford University Press.

Printed in the United States of America on acid-free, archival-quality paper

Library of Congress Cataloging-in-Publication Data

Names: Mandel, Robert, author.
Title: Interdependent yet intolerant : native citizen-foreign migrant violence and global insecurity / Robert Mandel.
Description: Stanford, California : Stanford University Press, 2021. | Includes bibliographical references and index.
Identifiers: LCCN 2020045309 (print) | LCCN 2020045310 (ebook) | ISBN 9781503614796 (cloth) | ISBN 9781503628199 (paperback) | ISBN 9781503628205 (ebook)
Subjects: LCSH: Emigration and immigration—Social aspects. | Violence. | Hate crimes. | Xenophobia. | Globalization. | Emigration and immigration—Government policy.
Classification: LCC JV6225 .M365 2021 (print) | LCC JV6225 (ebook) | DDC 362.89/91—dc23
LC record available at https://lccn.loc.gov/2020045309
LC ebook record available at https://lccn.loc.gov/2020045310

Cover illustration: Matt Wuerker

Typeset by Newgen North America in 10/14 Minion Pro

Notable Quotations

"If a man be gracious and courteous to strangers, it shows he is a citizen of the world."

—Francis Bacon, sixteenth- to seventeenth-century British philosopher, statesman, and lawyer

"A simple way to take measure of a country is to look at how many want in . . . and how many want out."

—Tony Blair, twentieth- to twenty-first-century British prime minister

"There is, however, a limit at which forbearance ceases to be a virtue."

—Edmund Burke, eighteenth-century Irish-born British statesman and political philosopher

"If we cannot end now our differences, at least we can make the world safe for diversity."

—John Fitzgerald Kennedy, twentieth-century U.S. president

"A nation that cannot control its borders is not a nation."

—Ronald Reagan, twentieth-century U.S. president

"Every immigrant who comes here should be required within five years to learn English or leave the country."

—Theodore Roosevelt, twentieth-century U.S. president

"We cannot bring ourselves to believe it possible that a foreigner should in any respect be wiser than ourselves."

—Anthony Trollope, nineteenth-century British novelist

"Do not judge, or you too will be judged."

—Matthew 7:1, New International Version

"For we were all baptized by one spirit so as to form one body—whether Jews or Gentiles, slave or free. . . ."

—1 Corinthians 12:13, New International Version

Table of Contents

List of Figures

Acknowledgments

This is my sixteenth book, the twelfth in a series I have authored analyzing twenty-first-century global security controversies. All of this work aims to challenge, refine, or tweak conventional assumptions. Regarding this study's topic, most international relations analysts typically embrace the value of the foreign, seeing it as contributing to the world's rich interwoven tapestry, but many people in the world view outsiders and their values as frightening and deeply unsettling, vastly preferring the comfort of familiar homegrown traditions. So it has been fascinating to undertake a study where perspectives differ so sharply and fervently within and across societies.

This topic posed more of a challenge than most for me because of the huge scope of relevant literature and the high degree of divisive emotionalism embedded in it. Despite my concerted efforts to provide an impartial analysis of central controversies, some readers may think they spot bias on one side or another. To those concerned, all I can say is that I have tried my best to provide balanced analysis to shed new light on truly thorny issues.

I am deeply indebted to my undergraduate student research assistant Madison Thomas for all her amazingly excellent work on this project. I am also incredibly grateful to Alan Harvey, the superb editor-in-chief of Stanford University Press, for his wonderful shepherding of this manuscript toward publication. However, I alone take full responsibility for any disarming distortions or egregious errors found here.

I wish to dedicate this book to the unfortunate victims of violence—both foreign migrants and native citizens—based on intolerance, and to open-minded scholars, practitioners, and policy makers who seek fair and sensitive ways to analyze its causes, consequences, and cures. My hope is that this effort will somehow end up helping to move the world toward peaceful coexistence.

Interdependent Yet Intolerant

Introduction

WE LIVE IN A WORLD breeding contradictory impulses endangering global peace and stability. On the one hand, international communication and transportation have led us to become more aware of and interdependent with each other than ever before, providing many with unprecedented opportunities to interact positively with diverse people, goods, services, and ideas. On the other hand, rapid unpredictable changes in way of life linked to the influx of foreign people and ideas have often negatively induced discomfort, fear, anger, and intolerance. Living within such highly interconnected but yet divided multicultural settings—where internal and external frictions have become increasingly intertwined—can be deeply unsettling, with established patterns of behavior continuously subject to significant challenge. In many ways, the central global paradox has been, as nationalism expert Andreas Wimmer points out, that "inclusion according to the universal ideals of the Enlightenment was bound up with new forms of exclusion based on the principle of ethnicity and nationhood."[1] Despite growing interconnectedness, "the need for separation, for distinguishing among 'us,' 'we,' and 'the others,'" has seemed to intensify.[2] The implications of such a volatile global setting include that no single party—individual, group, or state—can rest complacent and confident that it can totally successfully determine its own fate, and, when failure does occur, it may be more attractive to demonize outsiders as scapegoats than to take responsibility for disappointments encountered.

A fundamental expectation-reality gap characterizes this unstable global predicament, and it is perhaps surprising to some that the contradictory impulses have not yet been reconciled. Regarding this dysfunctional gap, insufficient attention has been devoted to broadly analyzing how native-foreigner tensions can be emerging within a world where so many espouse a liberal international order, with a particularly glaring omission being examination of when, how, and why the enlightened cooperative values vocalized by much of the global community encounter societal rejection so spirited that violence ensues.

Provocative Central Thrust

From a security viewpoint, this book conceptually and empirically explores the circumstances when intolerance is most likely to escalate between native citizens and foreign migrants, and when such intolerance is likely to become sufficiently extreme as to lead to violence and global insecurity. Based on an analysis of twelve twenty-first-century global case studies of intrasocietal violence between native citizens and foreign migrants, this study concludes that—rather than breeding mutual tolerance through increased contact, homogenized tastes, and technology, and enlightened values—interdependence and globalization operating within today's liberal international order counterintuitively can help to stimulate boomerang effects in the opposite direction. The multifaceted roots of ensuing violence include (1) foreign immigration pressures overwhelming host states' willingness to take people in; (2) bottom-up cultural and economic frustrations; (3) a populist, nationalist, tribalist, and xenophobic backlash by those wanting to preserve the status quo in the face of external pressure to change; and (4) political leaders and media outlets amplifying existing discontents and divisive enemy images. In accordance with case study insights, this study suggests detailed policy recommendations about how to manage intrasocietal violence between natives and foreigners in an interdependent world. This volume addresses the responsibility and means for fixing these problems; debunks popular myths surrounding violence perpetrators, including that they are all far-right native citizens motivated by a single form of intolerance; and highlights the dangers of fortress mentalities, societal polarization, security outsourcing, and tolerance hypocrisy. Throughout, this study explicitly attempts to remain impartial in exploring native-foreigner relations, resisting the temptation to engage in emotional passionate support of one side or the other. Finally, this investigation concludes by urging societies to rethink predominant notions of national identity and control.

Fears of the unexpected, unfamiliar, and unknown have ancient roots, but many observers expected them to fade in the modern high-contact setting. Instead, such apprehensions have flourished in recent years, leading to more visible and more deadly cross-group intolerance within societies. Past optimistic hope has frequently given way to present pessimistic dread, reflecting a sometimes desperate desire to protect natives' status quo or to protect foreigners' basic rights. This distressing pattern associates with increasingly highly skewed asymmetrical interdependence relationships; growing internal and external economic inequality between haves and have-nots; loss in local distinctive identity and control; and growing misunderstandings between natives and foreigners. The outcome has encompassed escalating pressures to change border access to maintain homeland security.

Friction that may sometimes become violent frequently occurs between pressures of integration and fragmentation, unifying and dividing the fabric of the international community. The net effect can be profound insecurity:

> Many people feel that everything familiar to them is being threatened, that they are being confronted with decisions, cultural artifacts and the presence among them of persons, all coming from outside their familiar and trusted sphere. They seek security by trying to exclude the forces and people that are doing this to them. Most affected are those whose own working lives give them little control in any case, and who are accustomed to the security that comes from the enforcement of rules that exclude troubling diversity.[3]

The pervasive sense of insecurity has led many people to question the value of mutual acceptance, often replaced by a desire for alien exclusion. Both national governments and international institutions have encountered difficulties in attempting to manage this kind of volatile predicament. When the insecure mass public recognizes national governments' inability to restore among those living within their national borders a firm sense of societal safety, distrust of state political institutions may escalate, leading in many cases to citizens resorting to private security to provide their protection and even on occasion to using coercion to preserve local identities and to safeguard cherished belief systems.

This topic necessitates exploration of several fundamental security questions. Why do cross-country contact, interdependence, and globalization not foster consistently more global understanding and acceptance? What explains the widespread existence of cross-national fear and hatred given vast improvement in communication and transportation technologies? How can primordial populist, nativist, tribalist, and xenophobic sentiments thrive in a modern interconnected world? In what circumstances does the greatest international vulnerability to such fear and hatred and resulting coercive disruptions exist?

When are an inward focus among native-born citizens on protecting their own lifestyle and among foreign migrant communities on protecting their own rights most dangerous to individual, state, and global security? When are related intra-state cultural and economic intolerance-oriented frictions most likely to translate into interstate tensions? Why would politicians and media outlets choose to amplify mass public intolerance? In a world full of diverse and distinctive firmly held beliefs, loyalties, and practices, finding better ways to answer and address these complex security questions seems vital for global peace and stability.

Analytical Scope

This book covers human, state, and global security causes, consequences, and cures of native-foreigner violence because intolerance tensions fundamentally affect people's sense of safety from harm, given that both native citizens and foreign migrants perceive that such tensions directly affect their ability to survive and thrive. The focus here is on the security implications of intolerance—when it turns violent—for that is when cross-group prejudice seems most dangerous. This investigation's geographical scope is explicitly global, encompassing native-foreigner interactions not confined to one country or one region, because native-foreigner intolerance has differing manifestations in differing parts of the world. Moreover, such frictions' security impacts are not locationally insular—just confined to domestic society—for they tend to seep over national and regional borders because of cross-boundary ties among both perpetrators and victims. This study covers exclusively twenty-first-century incidents, for that is when native-foreigner intolerance under a liberal international order seems to have hit a critical boiling point. The emphasis here is only on intolerance between native citizens and foreign migrants—not on human rights violations, white nationalism/supremacy movements, racist bigotry, religious shunning, or homophobia—because pernicious native-foreigner confrontations appear to have the greatest potential to significantly heighten global rather than just local insecurity.

Broad Security Implications

The issues addressed here associate with several wider global security concerns. These include (1) the emergence of domestic and transnational challenges to the global status quo, despite the presumed durability of the liberal international order, the state system, and national sovereignty; (2) the intensifying Western/

non-Western and Global North/Global South value divides, despite assumptions that the growth and spread of international interaction stimulate global understanding; (3) the rising attractiveness of populist political leaders playing to a mass public audience frustrated by foreign influences and loss of local identity, despite the presumed internationalist thinking emanating from cross-state interdependence and globalization; (4) the increasing state tendency to restrict foreign immigration, despite the premise that openness to foreign goods and services should stimulate receptivity to foreign ideas and foreign labor; (5) the growing mass public cynicism about national governments' ability to protect the safety of those living within a country's borders and their way of life, despite the presumption that the spread of democracy should stimulate more effective ways to track and fulfill these citizens' needs; and (6) the persistence of global anarchy incorporating a resurgence of "might makes right" behavior by nonstate groups, despite the assumption that the growth and spread of enlightened international norms should stimulate global civility.

1

Intensifying Global Interdependence

INTERDEPENDENCE AND GLOBALIZATION reflect the growing speed, breadth, and intensity of international interconnectedness, where cross-national transactions are less constrained by national sovereignty and state boundaries. Accelerating these trends are rapid advances in communication, transportation, and information processing. Although the opportunities and dangers surrounding these globalizing forces seem generally understood, over time a glaring global gap has emerged between interdependence expectations and intolerance realities, summarized in Figure 1.1.

Experts agree that economic, political, and cultural interdependence and globalization among states and among groups within states are on the rise. Indeed, "jet airplanes, cheap telephone service, email, computers, huge oceangoing vessels, instant capital flows, all these have made the world more interdependent than ever."[1] Given accelerated global connectivity and transnationalism, now "there is a sense that we are more closely linked globally than ever before."[2]

However, the security consequences of interdependence and globalization are decidedly mixed:

> Like Damocles' sword, this global interconnectivity both strengthens us and moderates us at the same time. We are strengthened because we are better connected to others than ever before and thus capable of spreading the seeds of liberty and opportunity to populations that yearn for it and where the lack of it is still being justified. We are moderated by this interconnectivity because others can more easily exploit the seams and turn our freedoms against us to infect with vitriolic propaganda that violently radicalizes populations across this interconnected web.[3]

INTERDEPENDENCE EXPECTATIONS WITHIN THE LIBERAL INTERNATIONAL ORDER

Increased contact breeds mutual understanding, openness, and tolerance
Homogenization of tastes, technology, and values reduces cultural clashes
Cross-national interactions stimulate cosmopolitanism
Spreading enlightened democratic values eradicates primordial hatreds
Transactions freed from border barriers foster concern for the common good
A growing sense of global civility facilitates a universal moral code

INTOLERANCE REALITIES CHARACTERIZING MUCH OF TODAY'S WORLD

Protective desire to return to a benevolent status quo by focusing on one's own well-being
Realization of amplified highly skewed interdependence relationships
Growing internal/external economic inequality between haves and have-nots
Perceived loss in local distinctive identity and national control
Antagonism toward foreign migrants, often associated with criminals/terrorists
Escalating pressures to restrict border access to maintain homeland security

FIGURE 1.1: Interdependence Expectations Versus Intolerance Realities

Interconnectedness provides the opportunity for either peaceful cooperation or hostile interpenetration. Perhaps the key danger here is a magnified sense of societal vulnerability: one's cherished cultural and economic lifestyle can be disrupted by unexpected external supply fluctuations, reflecting, for example, an undersupply of desired cross-border transfers of goods and services or an oversupply of unwanted cross-border transfers of foreign immigrants. In the long run, interdependence may intensify anxieties about both loss of identity and loss of control.

High Interdependence Expectations

Today's liberal international order has interdependence as one of its central pillars.[4] For decades, many advocates have voiced positive progressive expectations about the enlightened liberal international world order. This system, within which interdependence operates, "enshrines the idea of tolerance"[5] and purports to maximize respect for differences—"as children of the Enlightenment, we believe the expansion of knowledge and material progress goes hand in hand with improvements in human behavior and moral progress."[6] These high expectations usually focus on the following controversial central elements: increased contact breeds mutual understanding, openness, and tolerance; homogenization of tastes, technology, and values reduces cultural clashes; cross-national interactions stimulate cosmopolitanism; spreading enlightened democratic values eradicates primordial hatreds; transactions freed from border barriers foster concern for the common good; and a growing sense of global civility facilitates a universal moral code. Key underlying global hopes have included higher cultural sensitivity and empathy among differing societies; higher economic living standards and better products and services for everyone; more people becoming compassionately aware of others located in different parts of the world without access to survival needs or experiencing violence or political persecution; more political leaders coming under close scrutiny about how they respond to the needs of those living within their countries; and thus a larger proportion of the world's population becoming free from want and fear. Most broadly, interdependence is supposed to reduce the probability of war and promote durable peace because of the huge losses entailed by interrupting constructive flows across national boundaries,[7] with the underlying assumption that force would rarely be used when complex interdependence prevails under globalization.[8] Prominent global order analysts Daniel Deudney and John Ikenberry confidently predict that "as long as interdependence—economic, security-related, and environmental—continues to grow, peoples and governments everywhere will be compelled to work together to solve problems or suffer grievous harm; by necessity, these efforts will build on and strengthen the institutions of the liberal order."[9]

Dashed Interdependence Dreams

In stark contrast to the optimistic liberal international order expectations about interdependence and globalization promoting mutual respect and civil interaction, much of the world has experienced a highly visible backlash. This largely bottom-up populist backlash—which is neither distinctly American nor distinctly Western—is by native citizens angry about the growing economic inequality and unwanted cultural change prompted through globalization,[10] with both globalized elites and foreign migrants held responsible for ongoing lifestyle disruptions. Economically, international free trade policies have a long tradition of producing job displacement and inequality,[11] and in the end, as globalization expert Joseph Stiglitz notes, "globalization has resulted in some—even possibly a majority—of citizens being worse off."[12] Exacerbating this outcome was the 2008 global financial crisis, which revealed the fragility of the global economic system and "opened up a window of opportunity for challengers to the political status quo."[13] Culturally, the growth in dissident populism reflects a widespread nostalgic desire to find "a bulwark against long-term processes of value change"[14] often negatively associated with foreign dependence and the entrance of foreign immigrants. Within the United States, although some citizens fail to recognize it because they "have lived inside the bubble of the liberal world order so long,"[15] a widespread concern has emerged that interdependence increases the chances for Americans to become hapless victims of political instability and socioeconomic problems in other countries.[16] Within Western Europe, although the interdependence-oriented European Union (EU) "was intended to quash nationalist tensions in Europe," "it may have exacerbated them"—the flood of Middle Eastern and North African immigrants attempting to enter the region resulted in populist uprisings across the continent protesting the policies of the EU and supportive national governments.[17] While some negative reactions to globalization and interdependence are doubtlessly groundless or overblown, many people all over the world seem convinced that these trends are responsible for both their current misery and their future decline.

Even many traditional supporters of interdependence and globalization now slowly but surely have begun to admit that they have not delivered on their lofty promises and have contributed to tensions within and across societies and to pervasive frustration and resentment about their underperformance. Now globalization's discontents—which began in developing countries—have become truly worldwide: rather than experiencing higher economic living standards, people "have seen their jobs destroyed and their lives become more insecure," and rather than experiencing greater cultural tolerance and empathy, people have "felt increasingly powerless against forces beyond their control" and "seen their democracies undermined" and "their cultures eroded."[18] Instead of reducing the chances of war, "the interpenetration of societies is the driving force behind many current conflicts."[19] In the Global North, the election to high political office of aggressively nationalistic leaders and the challenge to the EU represented by the 2016 British Brexit referendum are key elements of the globalization backlash.[20] In the Global South, the conversion of economies into export platforms has spawned resentment of increasing dependence, and the rapid rate of technological change has made it difficult for resource-strapped countries to keep pace. Intrasocietal cultural and economic antagonisms appear to be intensifying and to be stimulating greater skepticism about the desirability of global interconnectedness, at least partially due to globalized elites' shortsighted mismanagement of interdependence and globalization processes in recent decades. Mass public fears have flourished about the resulting cultural, economic, and political instability. Although some analysts view interdependence as a purely international cross-state phenomenon and native citizen–foreign migrant tensions as a purely local domestic phenomenon, the intolerance associated with both are deeply intertwined: interdependence and globalization pressures can make it much more difficult for each state to prevent its domestic native-foreigner frictions from generating transnational shock waves and spreading to other countries, in the process magnifying the destabilizing impact of any local trauma by increasing its negative global repercussions.

Absence Of Stable Interdependence Prerequisites

For international interdependence to work properly, a system of formal and informal rules designed both to lower transaction costs and to regulate cross-border transfers is needed.[21] However, today many unruly parties—such as transnational terrorists and transnational criminals—can move easily across countries, choosing to operate in those with the most distracted, inept, or corruptible authority structures incapable of enforcing global rules or even societal norms. Such disruptive forces, using covert and hard-to-interpret signals, can then thrive and expand into effective transnational operations because of their ability to bypass the rigidities of sovereignty. Decreased understanding of—or compliance to—the set of rules-of-the-game in international relations appears to exist.[22] In the absence of a uniform global ruleset consistently voiced and followed, each party seems freer to behave and interpret communication according to its own idiosyncratic premises. The increasing popularity of moral relativism can make any thrust promoting a more coherent set of interpretation norms or rules of the game—especially by the West—run the risk of being identified with the most virulent forms of cultural imperialism. In this way of thinking, many observers see establishing more universal rules as being akin to an anti-democratic quashing of everyone's ability to experience independent empowerment. For disenfranchised states and nonstate groups, the very notion of rules of the game in today's world is reminiscent of an era when they felt that they had to sacrifice autonomy in foreign policy for a quite arbitrary world order. Furthermore, for many disadvantaged parties unable to move up the global hierarchy, violating the rules of the game can seem to be a means of escaping from a stifling and humiliating status quo, a system whose premises they feel powerless to influence.[23] Those who do not want to play by the rules, including rogue states, terrorist groups, and criminal organizations, know that it is extremely difficult for major powers to exert effective long-run pressure on them, and indeed much of these noncompliant parties' status appears to derive from their ability to misinterpret or flagrantly thwart the major powers' rules of the game and to get away with it without suffering devastating consequences. Unlike during some past historical periods, core powers cannot set the rules of the game by themselves, at least in part because of their lack of universally recognized global legitimacy and their reluctance to coerce unwilling parties into compliance, increasing these powers' vulnerability to disruption.[24] Moreover, with notions of "hard facts" or compromise often disparaged, powerful states cannot be compelled to obey these rules as long as they believe that "doing so is not in their interest."[25]

For interdependence among states and among groups within states to be most stable, durable, and resilient, it is ideally roughly reciprocal, so that each interdependent party has a similar level of reliance on the others. However, in today's world, global interdependence is usually skewed and asymmetrical, so that a powerful country or dominant group is in the "driver's seat" because it is more powerful than others or is less dependent on others than they are on it. Skewed interdependence dramatically alters the range of options—expanding some and contracting others—from which political leaders and private citizens get to choose how to follow their own beliefs and practices, and this pattern can generate significant resentment. Within societies, such skewed interdependence can transform the relative bargaining power of some groups whose contributions are considered vital and nonsubstitutable over other groups whose contributions are considered more superfluous or easily substitutable. Across countries, Stiglitz concludes that "the winners from globalization had increased power to shape globalization to benefit themselves at the expense of others," and "some countries (poor developing countries) can become effectively dependent on the goodwill of others."[26] The result has been a debilitating erosion of indigenous control, with dependent Global South states worrying that Global North countries have the power to dictate what transpires within their societies. Frustration can emerge when poor countries perceive largely one-way dependence on rich countries[27]—over time, it can become unbearable for a subordinate party to realize that it has become permanently disadvantaged in an asymmetric relationship from which it cannot escape, in which dominant parties feel unconstrained to maximize their success and its suffering.

Rising Interdependence-Induced Antagonism Toward Elites

When considering mass public irritations surrounding globalization and interdependence, significant internal and international antagonism toward socioeconomic elites is evident. Although the focus here is exclusively on friction between native citizens and foreign migrants because that kind of turmoil is most likely to lead to violence, controversies surrounding mass-elite tensions include (1) the means by which interdependence and globalization have contributed to burgeoning mass public resentment and distrust of global elites; (2) the perceived links among global elites, cosmopolitanism, and international migration; and (3) the underlying logic behind why mass-elite tensions have not generally resulted in violence.

How Interdependence and Globalization Induce Mass-Elite Tensions

Considering first interdependence-induced mass public resentment of socio-economic elites, the bulk of the gains from globalization have gone to those at the top.[28] Often political and corporate elites living in large urban areas within the Global North have been the direct beneficiaries of the fruits of interdependence and globalization, while the rural poor within both the Global North and the Global South find their living conditions deteriorating. The elite targets of popular cynicism and resentment are wide-ranging, including "big business, big banks, multinational corporations, media pundits, elected politicians and government officials, intellectual elites and scientific experts, and the arrogant and privileged rich."[29] If an organization is wealthy, successful, and transnational, then it is automatically suspect. Within Europe, widespread rebellion has occurred "against a cosmopolitan European elite that is allegedly out of touch with the concerns of the average Pole, Hungarian, Italian, Greek, German or Briton":[30] for example, during a key October 2016 speech, British prime minister Theresa May acknowledged that "today, too many people in positions of power behave as though they have more in common with international elites than with the people down the road, the people they employ, the people they pass on the street."[31] Around the world, there is a yearning for politicians with a decidedly more local focus—"people hunger for leaders and policymakers committed to serving and protecting their own, giving preference and offering better opportunities to the neediest among them rather than the neediest elsewhere."[32]

Turning to interdependence-induced mass public distrust of elites, recently many private citizens have lost faith in the ability of those in charge to channel the impacts of interdependence and globalization in ways that enhance their well-being. Many citizens are skeptical about their safety, their states' ability to protect them, and their states' prioritization of their protection; in the long run, such cynicism can lower expectations, so that the most vulnerable weak, poor, and marginalized people feel they have no control over their lives and are constantly exposed to miserable conditions. This confidence deficit between the population at large and the elites centers on questions of national identity.[33] For many people, this distrust is a direct function of feeling "betrayed" and "victimized" by these elites:

> In the process of adaptation to the New Global World Order, there has been a fundamental breakdown of trust and communication between elites and the general population. The pressures of adaptation to the new globalised world are particularly directed at those who do not fit in to the new international knowledge based economy, the unskilled and the low-skilled. The overall discourse of adaptation and competitive adjustment has a strong bias against the lower middle class and non-academic professionals. This bias is one of the root causes for populist resentment and revolt. Policy and political elites are selling and producing insecurity and uncertainty, instead of showing security and stable leadership in a world of flux.[34]

Such elite behavior is often seen as intentional, sinister, and deceptive. Although normally such a loss of trust could be addressed and remedied through extensive mutual communication, the gap in interests, values, modes of expression, and reference points has grown so large between the masses and the elites that resolution seems highly unlikely.

Perceived Links Among Global Elites, Cosmopolitanism, and International Migration

Looking first at the interdependence-induced links between global elites and cosmopolitanism, elites' embrace of globalist values has deep roots. Elaborate transnational networks regularly bring elite professionals together from all over the world, producing an economic, cultural, and political elite with parallel educational backgrounds and extensively networked personal and professional contacts, and this homogenized interaction has created what Deudney and Ikenberry call "an increasingly common identity and culture—a powerful sense that 'we' constitutes more than the traditional community of the nation-state."[35] This common identity—in which homogeneity rather than heterogeneity prevails—reveals how the premises of cosmopolitanism usually differ sharply from those of multiculturalism. These increasingly integrated elites "advocate, without much historical or sociological reflection, their 'brave new world' of the bright, well-educated, entrepreneurial and highly mobile," while in contrast such "a future world of globalisation, open borders, free flows of people, lifelong-learning in the knowledge-based society is a nightmare world for nonelites, the 'losers of globalisation.'"[36]

While becoming increasingly enthralled with the virtues of globalized integration, cultural and economic elites often perversely look down their noses at their own societies. Elites' "high-and-mighty" attitude, often characterized as "self-hate,"[37] involves antagonistically seeing their own country's history as checkered, "oppressive and outdated."[38] In similar fashion, when reacting to strong emotional patriotism for one's own country, "for most political thinkers and elites in the developed West, nationalism is a dangerous, divisive, illiberal impulse that should be treated with skepticism or even outright disdain."[39] Because of their fervent belief that the liberal international order is critical for global peace and prosperity,[40] the primary fear of many Western elites is the fall of this order, as they worry that the emotional intensity of the growing anti-globalization backlash against it could be so severe as to lead "to a wholesale retreat from globalization."[41] This perspective is patently self-serving, with little consideration of how this order and the associated globalization and interdependence have ended up benefiting the few at the expense of the many.

Considering next the interdependence-induced links between global elites and international migration, observers often see the these ties as a direct function of converging economic self-interest:

> In essence, nativism argues that the out-group and the elite are joined in their cause to displace the people truly from here. This seems to be due to countervailing interests: the industry and elite, on the one hand, need immigrants to do the work and/or want to abide by the fundamental values enshrined in the nation's founding documents. The nativist "common" man, on the other hand, sees them as a threat to his/her future and job opportunities.[42]

Populist anger against foreign migrants often links tightly to elite support for interdependence and globalization, with intense criticism voiced about "perfidious elites who coddle undeserving out-groups—immigrants and minorities—while treating the nation's true people with contempt."[43] Cas Mudde, an expert on populism, asserts that "mass immigration is presented as a willing plot of (inter)national politicians, business leaders, and trade union leaders to strengthen their own position at the expense of the average citizen," and that "the elite (seen as a homogenous corrupt entity) are accused of covering up the real costs of immigration and of muffling the people through antidiscrimination laws and political correctness."[44] For example, in 2015 a German intelligence officer noted ironically that "we are producing extremists through immigration," as "mainstream civil society is radicalizing because the majority don't want migration and they are being forced by the political elite."[45] Thus dissatisfied native citizens create a powerful hybrid enemy image combining intrusive foreign migrants at home and arrogant international elites flourishing under interdependence and globalization within the distrusted liberal international order.

Why Mass-Elite Tensions Have Generally Remained Nonviolent

While native citizen–foreign migrant tensions often become violent, mass-elite tensions generally have not done so. Although many native citizens equally blame foreign migrants and globalized elites for ongoing cultural and economic woes, they tend to vent their violent rage at the weaker of these two:

> All contemporary xenophobic movements, from Donald Trump in the USA and [Marine] Le Pen in France to Geert Wilders in the Netherlands and Norbert Hofer in Austria, link their attacks on immigrants and refugees to those on the national elites implicated in the financial crisis. In turn, some protest movement that began as non-xenophobic opponents of elites, like il Movimento Cinque Stelle in Italy, find that they can get more traction if they include resentment of refugees in their rhetoric. Groups like UKIP in the UK or Alternative für Deutschland, which started life as critics of the European Union, have found success by responding to fears around immigrants and Muslims. The challenge to powerful elites is hereby made safe, because it is enfolded in attacks on the weaker symbols of globalization. One might be frightened to kick a strong man, but one might kick what one believes to be his dog.[46]

So foreign migrants suffer because of the clash between globalist cosmopolitans and xenophobic nationalists.

Rising Interdependence-Induced Mass Migration Across Borders

Interdependence and globalization facilitate the desire of people to move across national borders (including regular immigrants as well as refugees and asylum seekers) by increasing their awareness of better opportunities elsewhere, facilitating their escape from persecution and conflict, making dramatic lifestyle improvements possible from relocation by widening the global rich-poor gap, and enhancing foreign friends and relatives' ability to facilitate relocation by the existence of transnational advocacy networks. Although human migration across locations has always occurred, the modern ties between interdependence and migration merit special attention because now the interconnections between transnational connectivity and migration are becoming increasingly impactful.[47]

Today over 3 percent of the world's population lives outside their country of origin,[48] constituting a direct challenge to host countries' cultural and economic status quo. The United Nations (UN) High Commissioner for Refugees estimates that globally the number of refugees in the world has increased by almost 4.7 million—about 45 percent—during the last five years.[49] In 2015, what the European Commission (EC) called the "largest global humanitarian crisis" of our time[50] occurred, and by the end of that year 1.3 million migrants had applied for asylum in the European Union, Norway, and Switzerland."[51] Globally, migration has increased at a far greater rate than anticipated,[52] catching many states unprepared to receive them and many foreign migrants unprepared to make needed adjustments.

Although lowering cross-national barriers was intended mainly to amplify the global spread of goods, services, and information, interdependence and globalization have expedited destitute people's yearning to find a new home. The International Organization for Migration has even announced that "the rising tide of people crossing frontiers is among the most reliable indicators of the intensity of globalization."[53] This pattern reveals a key inconsistency in liberal internationalist norms: the global community views cross-border flows of people in a radically more restrictive way[54] than cross-border flows of goods and services. Unlike receptivity to temporary tourists, "the specter of the long term mass transfer of desperate (and frequently undesired) humans across state boundaries associates with a uniquely acute sense of peacetime threat to sovereignty in the current international system":[55]

> The nation-state is understood as an internally fluid but externally bounded space, as a space of free social and geographical mobility, in both vertical and horizontal dimensions. But geographical mobility is understood as sharply bounded. There is free mobility within but not between nation-states. . . . Mobility within nation-states is facilitated and seen as normal, even desirable (in that it contributes to the smooth functioning of labor and housing markets, and to cultural homogenization), but mobility between nation-states is hindered and seen as anomalous.[56]

From an economic standpoint, the transnational mobility of capital is much higher than the transnational mobility of labor, reinforcing global inequalities[57] because while capital investors could choose the optimal global locations to maximize returns, labor was largely fixed in location, placing workers at a decided bargaining disadvantage.[58] From a cultural standpoint, although transnational identity communities have emerged,[59] the transnational mobility of ideas and beliefs is much higher than the transnational mobility of adherents, potentially limiting artificially people's ability to live with those sharing common values. In contrast, globalization and interdependence pressures have failed to restrict national governments' autonomy to impose border controls.[60] Therefore, many of the world's workers have been prevented from following international jobs or joining family and friends abroad because of border access restrictions. Moreover, even if workers could follow the money, liberal international norms seem to underestimate the strength and durability of distinctive cultural attachments, framing the mass movement of foreign workers into and out of societies as disruptive to existing identity and community functioning. Regardless of any liberal internationalist aspirations for borders more open to migration, the glaring inconsistency in practice, with smooth cross-border movement for commodities but not for people, is viewed as hypocritical by much of the world, reducing the credibility of liberal internationalist rhetoric and values. While for the mass public the globalization of goods, services, and information has "produced their share of pain and rejection," its reaction to "the globalization of people" has turned out to be much "stronger, more visceral, and more emotional."[61]

Causes and Consequences of Interdependence-Induced Migration

Finding themselves in a decidedly interdependent situation, native citizens and foreign immigrants hold markedly different expectations. Based on their lengthy residence within their societies granting them a perhaps exaggerated sense of their legitimate right to an undisrupted life, native citizens usually anticipate that their national governments will find effective ways to restrict the influx of foreign migrants, vetting them properly prior to permission to enter the country; to monitor admitted immigrants carefully once they cross the border; to assimilate and integrate foreign migrants smoothly into domestic society; and to shield the native lifestyle from newcomers intentionally or unintentionally generating significant disruption to the presumed benevolent status quo. In contrast, based on the hardships they have encountered in travel and their perhaps overly glowing images of destination country conditions, foreign migrants usually anticipate that host countries' national governments will find effective ways to ensure their safety, protect their basic rights, respect their human dignity and their distinctive cultural traditions, and provide them with opportunities for adjustment so they can find employment and a secure life. Within most countries, there is no forum through which such contrasting expectations can be expressed, discussed, or reconciled amicably, and recent foreign immigrants all too often encounter shattered hopes in terms of overly rosy host state images and unrealistic reasons for leaving their home countries.

Causes of Interdependence-Induced Migration

In terms of "push" elements driving would-be migrants to leave their country, globalization makes people more aware of opportunities elsewhere and makes it more likely that they will try to pursue these opportunities because of ubiquitous globalized production systems and transnational migration networks. To escape persecution, displacement of refugees and asylum seekers can stem from both civil wars and oppressive violent extremism not in conflict zones,[62] as overall ethnic conflict can be both a cause and consequence of refugee flows.[63] To find improved economic opportunity, because interdependence and globalization specifically amplify awareness of global inequality, they can help to induce those in dire straits or at the bottom of the international pecking order to seek to migrate elsewhere for a better life; radio, television, and Internet-based social media have increased impoverished workers' awareness of the huge wage differentials between rich and poor countries, enhancing these workers' desire to migrate.[64] According to a 2016 World Bank report, people migrating from the poorest countries to advanced industrial societies on average gained fifteen times as much income, enrolled twice as much in school, and experienced one sixteenth as much child mortality.[65]

In terms of "pull" elements driving the Global North to need foreign migrants, interdependence has increased awareness of the marked demographic imbalances producing—particularly within Europe—a need for young foreign workers:

> The demographic pressures of an aging population created demand for all kinds of workers: on farms, in manufacturing, in construction, and in services. As a result, men and women workers have come from less-developed countries in

Asia and Africa, as well as from the former socialist countries of Eastern and Central Europe. They came legally and illegally, often tolerating very low wages, poor living and working conditions, and constant insecurity in the hope of somehow raising their own living standards and remitting something to households back home.[66]

The type of work done by foreign migrants could potentially help host societies, as especially undocumented migrants focus on jobs no native citizen would want to undertake:[67]

Europe needs migrants. Its working-age population is declining, while the number of pensioners that European workers need to support is soaring as the postwar baby-boom generation retires en masse. Young, hardworking, tax-paying newcomers would be a shot in the arm for Europe's senescent economies. They would help spread the huge burden of public debt over more shoulders, to the benefit of the existing population. They can do tough jobs that young Europeans with higher aspirations spurn, like picking fruit and caring for the elderly. Many have valuable skills that can be put to good use, in hospitals, in engineering, or in computing. Others are likely to become entrepreneurs.[68]

Thus, while migrants deemed to be illegal may not pay taxes, many legitimate private native businesses—even within some countries whose national governments have severe anti-immigrant policies—have encouraged lax law enforcement toward undocumented workers precisely because they provide cheap labor and can help reduce production costs to keep profits high and prices low of goods and services in high demand globally.

Consequences of Interdependence-Induced Migration

Interdependence-induced migration could ideally promote global security. This positive outcome seems logical, given the nature of the "push" and "pull" elements and the seemingly reasonable premise that those with the stamina, drive, and perseverance to make the often perilous voyage between their home state and their desired host state would be creative and energetic positive contributors to the welfare of host states.[69] Increased awareness of what is going on elsewhere in the world, stimulated both by advances in communication and transportation and by the entrance of foreigners into a society, makes native residents more cognizant of their interdependence, potentially improving their capacity to organize without consideration of territorial barriers.[70] Although news of foreign suffering could desensitize people to human misery half-way around the world[71] if they pessimistically believed it was unchangeable, increasing people's awareness of faraway traumas likely to have cross-border spillover effects could conceivably stimulate receptivity to cross-national caring and consultation.

However, interdependence-induced migration also can spread perceived economic, cultural, and political insecurity, and regardless of its actual impact it has aroused considerable emotional anxiety within host states. Intense resentment appears to be the most common host society reaction to foreign immigrants.[72] Notably, it has become painfully evident that multicultural contact has increased at a far more rapid rate than multicultural tolerance or sensitivity. The influx of often unwanted foreign migrants introduces cultural and economic insecurity fears revolving around an unanticipated and crippling disruption in domestic lifestyle: economically, a huge influx of migrants may enhance competition for scarce jobs, economic resources, and social services; culturally, divisive antagonistic ethnic, cultural, religious, or linguistic forces may emerge within the host society.[73] When migrant communities are large and growing, and when they have their own schools, newspapers, cultural organizations, and places of worship, native citizens may readily see them as a cultural threat.[74] Because of continuing perceived tensions between the economic need for migrant labor and the cultural disruption emanating from the presence of foreigners,[75] many people have begun to fear that "the cost of greater 'economic integration' would be greater 'social disintegration.'"[76] From a political standpoint, societal worries persist that "refugees will seek to dictate the host country's policies toward the sending country"[77] and that "immigrants increase risk of terrorism."[78] Sizable migration flows seem to have their most dramatic security impacts on state capacity when the national government is weak or failing before the foreign newcomers' arrival.[79]

These anxiety-laden reactions by native citizens to the influx of foreign migrants seem unlikely to promote any increased mutual understanding between newcomers and long-standing residents, and instead appear prone to increase tensions between the two groups by stimulating intolerance. Often native citizens create images of foreigners quite different from their self-image (termed *contrast projection*), start resenting the newcomers, and then through superficial contact develop negative stereotypes of them and begin to dislike them, often feeling that the foreigners should have stayed at home and never come.[80] Similarly, often foreign migrants' resentment toward native citizens due to

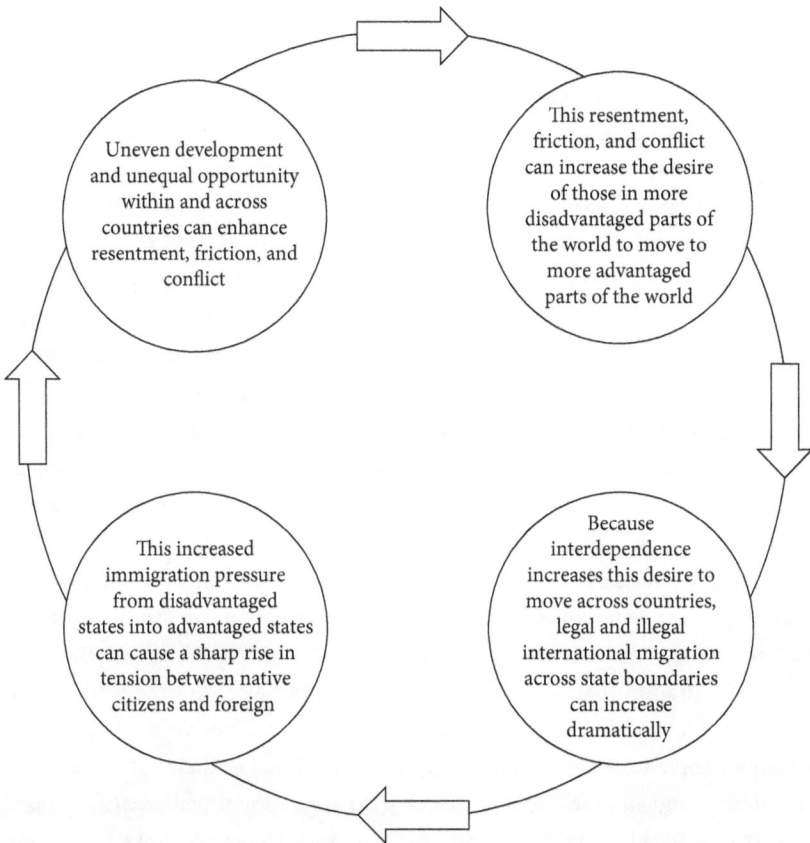

FIGURE 1.2: Interdependence-Intolerance Cycle

second-class discriminatory treatment within host societies seems likely to increase over time. A resulting interdependence-intolerance cycle can persist, shown in Figure 1.2: interdependence and globalization can enhance uneven development internationally, thus producing global inequality and associated resentment, friction, and conflict; this resentment, friction, and conflict can then increase the desire of those in disadvantaged parts of the world (largely in the Global South) to move to more advantaged parts of the world (largely in the Global North); then more people will find a way legally and illegally to change where they live; and finally, increased immigration pressure from disadvantaged into advantaged states can result in uneven development and unequal opportunities within and across countries, enhancing resentment and friction and causing a sharp rise in intolerance between native citizens and foreign migrants.[81] This resulting deepening intolerance could trigger a new wave of resentment, friction, and conflict, repeating the cycle and causing it to intensify.

Through migration, interdependence and globalization have induced a multidirectional impact on national identity. Enticing foreigners with differing values to move across national borders may increase native citizens' apprehensions about the distinctiveness of their societies and about the sluggishness of migrant assimilation. On the one hand, interdependence and globalization seem to have "deeply weakened many communities" by enhancing inequalities, expanding management-worker divides, and furthering outsourcing of jobs.[82] Native citizens often see the unanticipated influx of alien values and the rapid growth of non-native populations within their societies as endangering their own belief system. Some national politicians fear that interdependence-induced migration will eradicate their countries' core identities: for example, Marine Le Pen, in her first campaign speech in her attempt to become French president, "equated globalization with 'Islamic fundamentalism,' since 'both are working to make our nation disappear'";[83] following her victory in the election's first round, she warned that "the main thing at stake in this election is the rampant globalisation that is endangering our civilisation."[84] On the other hand, interdependence and globalization may actually help to revive local cultures,[85] causing people to become more focused on what makes their culture special, distinctive, and unique[86] and reinforcing feelings of national identification.[87] The strong backlash against economic and social change—linked to interdependence and globalization and perceived as highly disruptive[88]—can nudge societies toward "resistance identities" reinforcing existing ethnic, religious, or national divides:[89] the reinvigoration of national identity can thus constitute a direct counterthrust against globalizing influences.[90] By blurring common conceptual demarcations,[91] an influx of foreign migrants can also challenge the traditional ways in which national identity, sovereignty, and control have associated with citizenship.[92]

Different dimensions of interdependence and globalization may create distinct security challenges regarding national control. Considering economic interdependence and globalization, while free market economics has assumed that the most efficient world would have no barriers to global transactions, in practice—as both native citizens' and foreign migrants' vocal frustrations and demands for job protection demonstrate—these globalized forces underestimate the demands for localized control. Regarding political inter-dependence and globalization, while many observers have assumed that peace and civility would result from increased cross-national interactions, in practice these globalized forces not only have fundamentally weakened states in terms of diminishing central governments' abilities to be the sole determinant of what transpires within their boundaries but also—as native citizens' fearful reactions to foreign migrants demonstrate—have opened the door to the possibility of "alternative governance" allowing distinctive groups within society to take advantage of existing grievances to push their own agendas by taking control and providing their own security completely independent from state-sponsored protection.[93] From the perspective of sovereign states' claims to politically determine "what and who enters or leaves national territory," human smugglers and illegal migrants are framed as "forces or disorder and danger."[94] Concluding with cultural interdependence and globalization, while many analysts have assumed that the smooth global spread of common values and beliefs would ensue, in practice—as foreign migrants' domestic impacts demonstrate—these globalized forces overestimate the fungibility of culture and underestimate the persistence of local identities, with largely homogenous societies often transforming into more multicultural societies[95] at a far faster rate than affected communities can handle.

While interdependence advocates expected that the response to foreigners and foreign ideas would be fluid adjustment, enhanced cooperation, and compassionate receptivity, instead major security challenges have emerged about how some form of stabilizing control can be maintained in the face of the clash between the local and the global. Even when foreign ideas and practices are widely recognized as superior, integrating them into some societies may be quite painful. Moreover, "although the forces of globalization have reduced some of the divisive effects of boundaries between states, they have also encouraged new divisions among national groups within states."[96] Thus resurfacing local clashes augment the insecurity-promoting impacts of local-global antagonisms.

Growing extremist exclusionism within societies may manifest itself in a couple of distinct ways, reinforcing closure toward outsiders. Culturally, "globalization's foundations are rotting away, spawning parochialism, nativism and xenophobia."[97] Contrary to popular belief, many "social problems commonly discussed as racial, ethnic or class phenomena are, in essence, outcomes of the struggle of outsider and established groups that have become interdependent."[98] Economically, by making production and employment more transnational, necessary to reach global consumers of goods and services, interdependence and globalization have led to internationally intensifying competition, and this outside pressure has resulted in the upsurge of a "new protectionism,"[99] reflecting growing domestic nationalist pressures to safeguard native producers' advantages. When external pressures appear to be pernicious and uncontrollable, involving forces one cannot understand demanding changes one perceives as both radical and unacceptable, a national desire to turn inward seems natural. One consequence of this inward turn is an increased likelihood of deciding foreign migrants' acceptability based largely on their likely compliance with native norms,[100] making any migrants' rights totally contingent on their speedy assimilation, acceptance of national beliefs, and transformed state loyalty.[101]

Interdependence-induced migration opens up broader security questions: (1) the value of state-centered citizenship versus cross-national, transnational, or global citizenship;[102] (2) the closely related values of civic identity versus ethnic identity, debating whether ancestry, language, and customs matter in membership in a society;[103] and (3) the value of unity-oriented assimilation versus separatism-oriented multiculturalism as a way of integrating foreign newcomers into society.[104] The first question challenges conventional citizenship notions,[105] introducing thorny controversies about both who should be considered a full-fledged citizen with associated rights and who should have the legitimate authority to set requirements for national citizenship. The second question challenges whether loyalty, heritage, or even who provides one's basic needs ought to form the basis of—or even play a significant role in—one's primary identity. The third question challenges whether either assimilation or multiculturalism would be appropriate within societies with intractable native-foreign antagonisms. Ironically, despite some sweeping claims, no allegedly security-enhancing alternative—state-centered/cross-border citizenship, civic/ethnic identity, or assimilation/multiculturalism—has empirically demonstrated any indisputable historical global track record producing genuine global peaceful tolerance.

2 Deepening Native-Foreigner Intolerance

CONTRIBUTING TO THE GLOBAL increase in intolerance between native citizens and foreign migrants has been rising nationalism, xenophobia, and tribalism; deep cultural and economic grievances; and politician and media manipulation. Within societies, each amplifies existing antagonistic native-foreigner divides, undermining civil discourse and mutual acceptance of differences. In their most extreme forms, the resulting emotions can sometimes lead to anarchic "might makes right" thinking, "eye for an eye" retaliation, and exclusionary isolationism.

The concepts of nationalism, nativism, ethnocentrism, xenophobia, and tribalism, often used in confusing or inconsistent ways, overlap with each other but have distinctive nuances. Figure 2.1 identifies the key nationalism-xenophobia differences, based on well-established traditions for distinguishing in-group favoritism from out-group hostility.[1] While nationalism and xenophobia might be considered "opposite sides of the same coin," each can occur without the other;[2] when both sentiments are present, one usually takes precedence over the other in determining decisions and actions. Ethnocentrism and tribalism are closely related to nationalism but reflect a more explicitly cultural rather than political focus. Nativism, a term the American Know Nothing Party originated back in the 1840s emphasizing exclusively birthplace as the basis for citizenship, is closely linked to ethnic nationalism, where ancestry is the key determinant of national identity.[3] Figure 2.2 sheds more light on relevant distinctions by contrasting nationalism, xenophobia, and tribalism to their polar opposites. Cultural and economic frustrations may either develop and flourish independently or be causes or consequences of nationalism, nativism,

NATIONALISM	XENOPHOBIA
Internally oriented attitudes and behaviors	Externally oriented attitudes and behaviors
Native-born over non-native-born privileging	Domestic citizens over foreigners privileging
Obsessive in-group favoritism	Intense fear of strangers and outsiders
Ethnocentric feelings of superiority	Disdain for those from other countries
Pride in traditional status quo	Apprehension about alien-induced change
Lifestyle disruption focus	Security threat focus
Tribalist self-absorption	Fixation on the threat from the other
Domestic cultural cleavage widening	International political cleavage widening

FIGURE 2.1: Nationalism Versus Xenophobia

ethnocentrism, xenophobia, or tribalism. Seeing one's own group as superior does not invariably associate with fear of outsiders; and being paranoid about foreigners does not invariably associate with seeing one's own state or society as superior. Whatever the level of existing tensions, politicians and media outlets often exploit them for their own purposes.

Rising Nationalism

Nationalism is an internally oriented set of attitudes and behaviors, reflecting an essentially political means to preserve identity:[4] one recognizes oneself as part of a political community of people emphasizing primarily shared ideological beliefs and allegiances, frequently reflecting in-group favoritism and ethnocentric feelings of superiority toward outsiders.[5] Nationalism's polar opposite is internationalism, which is more broadly "based on a positive appreciation of being enriched by engagement with other cultures"[6] and countries. Embedded in nationalism is an "us versus them" distinction, pitting a given group's identity against outside groups, which are typically framed as threatening.[7] In a globalized world, nationalistic state leaders face an international dilemma—they must engage in crucial interactions with the outside world, which at the same time is viewed as a source of instability;[8] within countries, nationalistic group leaders face an identical dilemma in interactions with contending domestic groups. The global spread of nationalism and populism has largely been mutually reinforcing,[9] and recently populists have "proudly claimed the mantle of nationalism, promising to defend the interests of the majority against immigrant minorities and out-of-touch elites."[10]

Antagonism toward interdependence-induced migration is a typical means through which nationalism is promoted. Ethnic nationalists have especially focused on the threat posed by foreigners permanently entering their societies:[11]

Nationalism-Internationalism Continuum

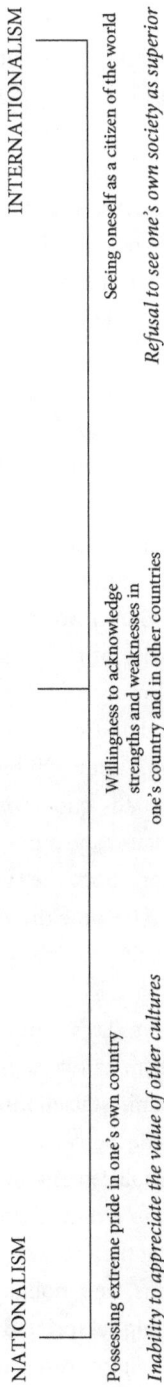

NATIONALISM ——————————————————— INTERNATIONALISM

Possessing extreme pride in one's own country
Inability to appreciate the value of other cultures

Willingness to acknowledge strengths and weaknesses in one's country and in other countries

Seeing oneself as a citizen of the world
Refusal to see one's own society as superior

Xenophobia-Outside Trust Continuum

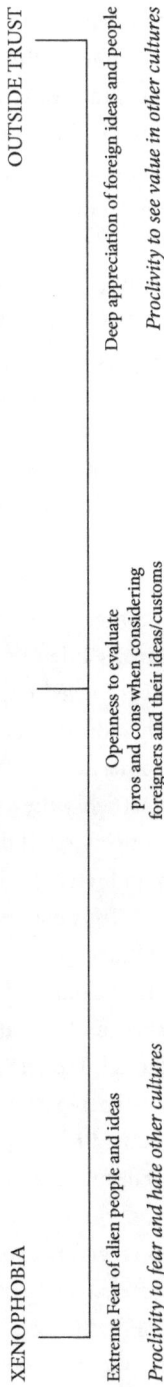

XENOPHOBIA ——————————————————— OUTSIDE TRUST

Extreme Fear of alien people and ideas
Proclivity to fear and hate other cultures

Openness to evaluate pros and cons when considering foreigners and their ideas/customs

Deep appreciation of foreign ideas and people
Proclivity to see value in other cultures

Tribalism-Outside Caring Continuum

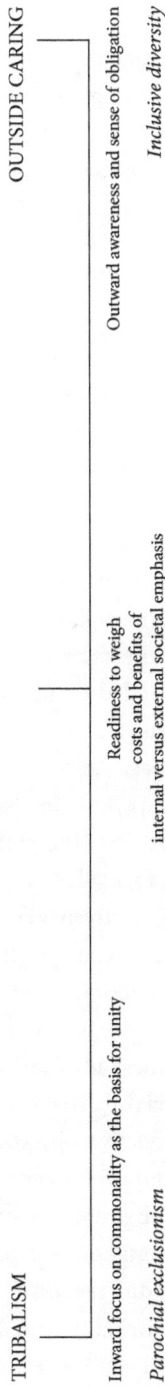

TRIBALISM ——————————————————— OUTSIDE CARING

Inward focus on commonality as the basis for unity
Parochial exclusionism

Readiness to weigh costs and benefits of internal versus external societal emphasis

Outward awareness and sense of obligation
Inclusive diversity

FIGURE 2.2: Intolerance-Promoting Movements and Their Polar Opposites

they view immigrants crossing national borders as challenging national ideologies staunchly defend "the territorial and ethnic boundedness of the national
entity."[12] In many ways, nationalism thrives in today's world precisely because
exposure to large numbers of foreign immigrants can induce citizens to engage in reflection about the distinctive characteristics of their national identity
and ultimately underscore its importance.[13] Because, as discussed earlier, the
entrance of foreign migrants into a society automatically raises issues about
national identity and national control, the connection between foreign immigration and intensifying nationalism seems to be exceedingly tight.

Ideally, nationalism could constructively provide citizens a sense of belonging, giving their lives broader purpose, raising their morale, and making them
feel secure, understood, and approved. Nationalism could foster stabilizing
unity during times of crisis, keeping a state together and promoting willingness to make sacrifices, including in extreme cases a willingness to die for one's
country. In the view of nationalism expert Andreas Wimmer, "nationalism is
not an irrational sentiment that can be banished from contemporary politics
through enlightened education"; rather, "it is one of the modern world's foun-
dational principles" in which citizens "identify with the idea of the nation as
an extended family whose members owed one another loyalty and support"
because of "a sense of mutual obligation and shared political destiny."[14] Nationalists' reactive focus is on the domestic societal well-being: they exhibit tremendous pride in trying to protect what they see as the status quo—wishing
to revert to a "pre-globalization conception of the nation-state" and a nostalgic
return to a golden age[15]—with high levels of self-absorption about the success
and distinctiveness of their society. Thus nationalism could become the essential glue keeping each nation-state together and smoothly functioning regardless of internal or external security challenges.

However, the harsh realities surrounding nationalism in today's world challenge these idealistic hopes. Although moderate nationalism can certainly be
beneficial, extreme nationalism or hyper-patriotism can manifest itself through
unproductive obsession with country pride, protecting the perceived status
quo, and overblown fears about cultural and economic displacement and decline.[16] Extreme nationalists can be so resistant to change, so afraid of cultural
contamination, and so defensive in reacting to outsiders that they may see even
minor differences in language, dress, interpersonal norms, and holidays as
deeply irritating and as strengthening the "sense of belonging" associated with
nationalism:[17] when confronting outsiders seen as increasingly threatening,

sometimes nationalistic "natives vehemently defend everyday practices, banal linguistic forms, and national symbols."[18] Such extreme nationalists may be wary about global trends, viewing world events as relatively unpredictable, and may deeply resent the perceived loss of control over what occurs in their land. Moreover, they tend to be cynically suspicious and distrustful that news they receive is intentionally tainted by covert influence from unreliable globalized sources not sharing their values or secretly conspiring to undermine their patriotism. They have great loyalty to their country, but not necessarily to their national government—frequently, if a state government does not pursue an agenda that supports extreme nationalists' concerns, and if it diverts state resources away from protecting native citizens, these nationalists can become quite upset and may vehemently oppose the existing regime and attempt to change its political leadership.

Extreme nationalism seems most likely to emerge under certain identifiable conditions. Nationalist fervor frequently escalates when societal unrest results from the erosions of local identities,[19] often by globalizing forces. This pattern can be accentuated when foreign migrants differ visibly—racially, ethnically, or religiously—from native citizens and when there is no preexisting robust context for societal integration of foreigners. Moreover, this kind of nationalism rises when a group perceives that it has inadequate capacities to provide an effective response to a critical outside threat, such as when traditional institutions appear to be collapsing or not satisfying people's basic needs and no readily effective substitutes are available.[20] In such circumstances, participation in a nationalist group is explicitly designed to restore people's sense of safety,[21] often through some form of exclusionary intolerance. Such participation can provide comforting meaning to insecure and frustrated people facing dramatic change perceived as dangerous, such as declining employment, rapidly escalating urbanization, and growing criminalization of the economy.[22] These changes can be perceptually linked to a large foreign migrant influx—populist nationalists are more successful at exploiting existing societal cleavages when sizable immigration highlights the globalization shock.[23]

This large foreign migrant influx can cause nationalist resentment of outsiders to explode into conflict, sometimes even involving intra-societal violence:

> Perhaps the trouble starts with the sense of difference we all feel between "us" and "them." Any time people can make a distinction between those who belong to their own collective grouping—be it tribe, state, or nation—and other

groups with which they cannot identify easily, they have laid the foundation for conflict. It is all too easy for a group to slide from recognizing that it is different from other groups to believing that it is superior to them.[24]

When country pride, narrowly focused patriotism, and profound faith in one's group's inherent superiority become too extreme, destabilizing violent turmoil between the in-group and the out-group seems imminent. Because nationalism may arise by exploiting anxieties and insecurities associated with globalization and interdependence,[25] emotional fear and hatred frequently seem more likely than rational cost-benefit analysis to dominate political decision making, enhancing the possibilities for impulsive violence.[26]

Partially because of fervent nationalism's common association with hostility, self-centeredness, condescension, intolerance, and rejectionism, the international community's prejudice against it has recently intensified:

> Nationalism has a bad reputation today. It is, in the minds of many educated Westerners, a dangerous ideology. Some acknowledge the virtues of patriotism, understood as the benign affection for one's homeland; at the same time, they see nationalism as narrow-minded and immoral, promoting blind loyalty to country over deeper commitments to justice and humanity.[27]

Many observers particularly in the West tend to label traditional nationalism as primitive, premodern, or "backward-looking."[28] In this regard, two special targets of intense global community disdain are nativism and ethnic nationalism, both of which are globally resurgent.[29] This common disparagement of nationalism manifests itself both in uncomfortable relations with highly nationalist states and in enthusiastic approval for states endorsing the liberal international order, interdependence and globalization, and cross-national free-flowing ideas, information, goods, services, and capital.[30] In recent decades, the gap between the perspectives of members of the international community who consider themselves to be enlightened and progressive and those espousing extreme nationalism has widened, as "a deepening fault line seems to divide cosmopolitans and nationalists, advocates of 'drawbridge down' and 'drawbridge up.'"[31] This increasingly intractable gap has significantly impeded mutual communication, understanding, and cooperation within and across countries.

Rising Xenophobia

Xenophobia is an externally oriented set of attitudes and behaviors reflecting amplified fear of foreigners, extending nationalism's privileging of native citizens within one's country to extreme disdain for those from other countries.[32] The polar opposite of xenophobic rejection is outside trust, entailing a welcoming attitude toward those from other places. As one form of backlash against interdependence and globalization, xenophobia involves powerful negative emotions—particularly fear and hatred[33]—toward strangers, usually encompassing "every type and level of antipathy toward aliens, their institutions, and their ideas."[34] Over time, such negative feelings become extremely difficult to change because viewing one's own group as heroic and outsiders as demonic tends to become increasingly reinforced (through selective attention) over time, to the point where "grievances are enshrined and other groups are portrayed as inherently vicious and aggressive."[35] Xenophobia places a major emphasis on foreigners' political, economic, and cultural differences constituting in and of themselves a major threat to the integrity and cohesion of domestic society, for regardless of foreigners' intent the mere presence of such sharp disparities signals danger to xenophobes.

Interdependence and globalization play a major role in giving rise to xenophobia, for just as with nationalism, the induced increased movement of people across national boundaries can intensify tense interactions between native citizens and people from other countries. Because international migration is the most "controversial" dimension of globalization,[36] as well as the most "intrusive and disruptive," it "can give rise to fear, racism, and xenophobia."[37] Unless a base level of cross-national and cross-cultural understanding and compassion exists, xenophobic frustration then develops about local societal changes perceived as both detrimental and dangerous. Resulting xenophobic policies become obsessed with the other, containing or minimizing the alien, and a constant paranoid sense of outside threat.

Xenophobia answers the question of how to preserve nationalist status quo ideals, by pointing to foreigners and foreign ideas as the exclusive source of challenge to the primacy or purity of the homeland way of life. Thus xenophobes provide a simple and easy-to-understand cure for everything that ails you and your society—keep aliens out. Because fact-checking about intolerant slurs is difficult, xenophobes usually feel empowered to say whatever they want about foreigners. When cultural and economic trends are not going well and seem to be beyond local control, xenophobes can provide an immediate, definitive, and viscerally satisfying explanation that provides a ready outlet for frustration and avoids the difficult but necessary possibility of any critical self-examination by native citizens about their own behavior or about their own government's actions.

Domestic xenophobia tends to widen international political cleavages. Such rejectionist popular attitudes can trigger exclusionary policies where national governments' calculus becomes decidedly more anti-foreigner, meaningful communication between different groups erodes, and eventually global alliances—with governments of foreign migrants' home countries—disintegrate. Through xenophobia's focus on fear of the unknown, due to the belief that everyone outside one's society poses key dangers, it is extremely difficult for a xenophobic society to exhibit sustained contentment and long-term confidence about its ability alone to confront successfully outside challenges, a handicap that proves to be particularly painful when the society in question is highly externally dependent for basic needs. Unfortunately for xenophobes, within an interdependent world full of key cross-national transactions, it is extremely difficult for xenophobic states' citizens or government officials to find ways to cocoon themselves from continuous exposure to foreigners and foreign ideas, even if most foreign migrants are kept out.

Xenophobia seems most likely to emerge when a society experiences dramatic undesired change, identity challenges, and control loss. Unpredictability in these elements erodes any sense of citizen security, particularly among those unable to readily adjust to major transformations. Perceived escalation in cross-national permeable border threat enhances such mass public fear, supported and maintained through the psychologically constricting process of focusing on dire worst-case assumptions. Once created, it becomes hard to step out of this closed-minded antagonistic mind-set, promoting a mutual negative self-fulfilling prophecy in which no action is interpreted positively among opposing antagonists.

A notable illustration of this pattern was the spring 2020 global spread of the coronavirus pandemic. As soon as the worldwide crisis emerged, several political groups in the United States, the United Kingdom, Italy, Spain, Greece, France, and Germany latched onto it to promote anti-immigrant xenophobic conspiracy notions demonizing refugees and foreigners; on May 8, 2020, UN secretary-general António Guterres warned that "the pandemic continues to unleash a tsunami of hate and xenophobia, scapegoating and scare-mongering."[38] Moreover, even within China the coronavirus triggered an upsurge of nationalism and xenophobia—although the Chinese government denounced xenophobic harassment of Asians overseas and foreign border closings when most of those affected were Chinese nationals, afterward it characterized foreigners as public health risks, corralled many foreign residents into forced quarantines, and barred virtually all foreigners from entering the country.[39] More generally, xenophobia is a "familiar symptom of viral outbreaks" due to the fear engendered: discrimination against foreigners escalated during the 1853 yellow fever outbreak in the United States, the 2003 SARS epidemic, and the 2014 Ebola outbreak, a pattern caused World Health Organization director-general Tedros Adhanom Ghebreyesus to comment that "stigma, to be honest, is more dangerous than the virus itself."[40]

A large influx of foreign migrants can directly stimulate native citizens' xenophobic fears, particularly about the specter of stark demographic changes potentially challenging their controlling position in society:

> Some academics . . . have warned that unchecked Latino immigration is bringing with it alien cultural values. . . . Maybe the real fear is more visceral than that. Maybe it's that you don't have to extrapolate immigration and fertility rates very far into the future to see an America in which minorities—Hispanic, African, and Asian American—are a majority.[41]

Such underlying fears run deep, and seem likely to escalate intrasocietal tensions as foreigners become scapegoats for any real or imagined domestic problems surrounding economic, political, and cultural upheaval, including disease, crime, overpopulation, land degradation, or any significant disruption to the cherished comfortable lifestyles of the indigenous population.[42] For xenophobes, focusing on foreign migrants seems particularly tantalizing as a vehicle for maximizing native citizen apprehensions. Rightly or wrongly, much of the Global North increasingly sees the permanent influx of foreigners as a liability rather than an asset, with growing hostility toward open borders and the entry of immigrants. Once a state's citizenry becomes much more aware of its substantial dependence on foreign people and countries,[43] intolerant anger at the loss of national control may increase. Xenophobia can readily lead to pressure to fortify borders and to coercively enforce anti-foreigner state regulations to curtail migrant entry, beliefs, practices, and freedoms.

Native citizens often become xenophobic because they fear tangible personal losses attributed to the influx of foreign immigrants, with a particular Global North concern about the specter of hordes of unsanctioned aliens from the Global South engulfing advanced industrialized societies to escape misery in their home states:

> Apparent losers may include domestic workers who are (or believe they are) affected by competition from migrants, or citizens who feel that their way of life or even identity is being threatened. It does not matter whether these claims

are empirically true; they fit into a clear and compelling narrative, in which immigrants are portrayed as villains. Such a narrative, as we have seen, is a very effective mobilization tool in the hands of cynical politicians.[44]

Amplified by the proximity of distinctive foreigner needs, domestic citizens may feel scarcity, divisiveness, and loss of control within their societies. Much of this sense of threat appears to originate at the grassroots level, as a mass influx of foreigners can send bottom-up shock waves through affected communities, with national governments often bearing most of the brunt of widespread anti-immigrant populist fears.

Native citizens' xenophobic fear, hatred, and sense of threat regarding foreign migrants living within their societies appear generally to be much greater than that regarding foreigners living in other countries:

> According to the inner logic of . . . distinctively modern discourses of exclusion, the strangers within the national territory are even more dangerous than the ones lurking on the other side of the frontiers; they form the demonised fifth column secreted within one's own group. While the stranger "out there" has become the object of systematised negative stereotyping and the enemy of nationalist wars, the stranger within has become the target of the various waves of xenophobia that have swept most Western countries since the end of the nineteenth century.[45]

As social psychologist Ralph White pointed out decades ago when identifying the "traitors in our midst" enemy image[46] (exemplified within the United States by the 1692–1693 Salem witch trials and by the early-1950s McCarthy-era fear of domestic communists), fearing a group within one's own society can be far more intense and socially disruptive because it can call into question a country's own national identity.

Regardless of what percentage of each society's population is xenophobic, and despite the passage of anti-hate-speech laws in many societies, in recent years it has become more globally acceptable to be highly vocal about xenophobic sentiments. During the 2015–2016 European refugee crisis, citizens' sense of panic, vulnerability, and helplessness about unsanctioned migrants incited comments like "the barbarians have breached the gates, "Europe is being overrun," and "our civilization and our prosperity are at risk."[47] Moreover, "the fear of being overwhelmed by difference runs through much of the discourse," with talk of "open doors" or "open windows" needing to be "secured" or "closed," and metaphors of "flood" suggesting "a fear that the unspecified European mainstream could be 'overwhelmed' or 'inundated,' and 'drown' as a consequence."[48] After this crisis and following one million asylum seekers arriving in Germany, in that country "intolerance—particularly xenophobia—is seemingly becoming less socially taboo as it is normalized in political discourse"; and recently within the United States, xenophobic "intolerance and hateful rhetoric are also gaining more traction and public airing."[49] Today anti-foreign-Muslim-migrant rhetoric is more common than ever in Western countries, and anti-Western rhetoric is more common than ever in Muslim countries. In much of the world, xenophobic groups have been able to exert undue political influence though clever use of Internet-based social media to spread hate and fear of foreigners (often by spreading false rumors about foreign migrants' transgressions) to recruit supporters.[50] Thus despite global interdependence, technological advances, and global communication, it seems pretty much as likely today as was the case in the ancient past that a typical person might encounter xenophobic rhetoric on a regular basis.

The high frequency of such exposure to inflammatory emotional expression can desensitize native citizens to the demeaning implications of such discriminatory sentiments, and simultaneously can induce such citizens to tolerate these condescending remarks as a regular part of normal discourse, even as such rhetoric continues to be extremely hurtful to the targets of intolerance. In a related manner, if domestic violent acts by xenophobic native citizens against foreign migrants occur and are widely publicized on a regular basis, then desensitization regarding harm to people and property can ensue, as native citizens assume that this disruptive pattern is just the new norm: for example, the South African legacy of social violence has been associated with significant evidence that desensitization is growing in response to such xenophobic brutality.[51]

The prelude to the 2016 Brexit decision to leave the EU nicely illustrates the increased acceptability of vocalizing xenophobic intolerance. The campaign was "mired by scaremongering"[52] and thus far was "the UK's most divisive, hostile, negative and fear-provoking of the 21st century,"[53] reflecting a discourse of "xenophobia and hatred."[54] Three nasty metaphors dominated news coverage of foreign migrants—"migrants as water ('floodgates,' 'waves'), as animals or insects ('flocking,' 'swarming') or as an invading force."[55] This emotional predicament vividly shows how government complacency about popular support for the liberal internationalist status quo can be quite dangerous when extremist xenophobia—palpable fears about losing one's job, cultural identity, and way of life—is flourishing: British political leaders were inattentive to the rise within their own country of political parties obsessed with restoring the country's autonomy by attracting support from nationalist, populist, and xenophobic segments of society.[56] Since 2016, such anti-internationalist sentiments have certainly not subsided within the United Kingdom, perhaps best signaled by the selection of Boris Johnson—one of the biggest supporters of leaving the EU—as the country's prime minister in July 2019.

Growing xenophobia has led to the rise of highly influential anti-immigrant political parties (especially from the far right), which have gained a greater voice in national governments within many of the world's democracies. Several Western European countries exhibited this pattern even before the 2015–2016 refugee crisis:

> Right-wing and anti-immigration political parties—the Northern League in Italy, the Flemish Blok in Belgium, the Danish People's Party in Denmark, the National Front in France, the British National Party in the UK, the Movimiento Social Republicano (MSR) Español in Spain, the National Renewal Party in Portugal, and so on—have increased their vote shares in all recent elections in Europe. In Hungary, the far-right party Jobbik entered Parliament for the first time in April 2010, after getting 17 percent of the vote, just behind the former ruling party the socialists, who received 19 percent. In France, regional elections in March 2010 saw electoral revival for the overtly racist National Front. In the Netherlands, the anti-immigration Freedom Party performed very well in elections in June 2010, more than tripling the number of seats it held.[57]

In 2017, across Europe xenophobia affected several crucial political elections—in Austria, France, Germany, and the Netherlands, some key candidates for political office campaigned on the premise that foreign migrants should be blamed for citizens' cultural and economic frustrations.[58]

Overall, the entrance of outsiders into a society generating native citizen xenophobia can lead to four key insecurity impacts:[59] (1) a cultural threat, including perceived erosion in a society's sense of identity and growing ethnic, racial, religious, linguistic, or ideological tensions;(2) a political threat, including increased perceived risks of crime, terrorism, and regime instability; (3) an economic threat, including perceived increases in competition and displacement by foreign workers and in economic burdens in providing education, health care, or other social services; and (4) a military threat, including perceived challenges to a country's territorial integrity as paranoid states escalate armaments and fortify their borders out of fear of future foreign intrusion, causing neighbors to follow suit due to their worries about offensive threat. Negative historical experiences with foreigners may enhance this emotional insecurity.[60]

Rising Tribalism

Tribalism represents the ultimate in a self-centered insular focus emphasizing commonality as the basis for unity. Operating with a "birds of a feather flock together" mentality, tribalism has people of the same ethnicity, religion, or race cluster in totally separate communities. While nationalism reflects common political beliefs, tribalism reflects common background. As explained in Figure 2.3, a patchwork of separatist tribalist enclaves is emerging around the globe, "more than able to hold their own in the brave new world of the Internet."[61] Tribalism is explicitly anti-assimilation, seeking to protect each group's distinctive lifestyle and beliefs, based on the premise that extensive contact and interaction with other groups would dilute and ultimately erode distinctive cultural identity. Tribalism is the polar opposite of outside caring, reflecting the broader societal awareness and sense of responsibility embedded in globalism. A *New York Times* columnist characterizes the emerging battle as being between "the modernizing, barrier-breaking sweep of globalization and the tribal reaction to it, which lies in the assertion of religious, national, linguistic, racial or ethnic identity against the unifying technological tide."[62] Benjamin Barber colorfully calls this a clash between "the forces of Jihad and the forces of McWorld"— "the one driven by parochial hatreds, the other by universalizing markets, the one re-creating ancient subnational and ethnic borders from within, the other making national borders porous from without."[63] Tribalist groups maintain cohesion through a separatist mentality unconcerned about outsiders, impeding constructive cross-community intermingling.

The impulse toward tribalism is universal, even if not evident everywhere. Although individuals and groups reverting to traditional patterns of affiliation— often in tribal form[64]—is often linked to poor indigenous communities in the Global South, tribalist enclaves also exist in the Global North, where "the wealthy move to private gated communities and travel to well protected shopping malls, both fitted with high walls, strong gates, CCTV and patrolled by private security guards."[65] For example, a patchwork of often-fortified mono-ethnic neighborhoods exists in several major East Coast American cities:

> As the more prosperous players plug into a global economy . . . they retreat into secure enclaves protected by private security forces—a process former U.S.

EXPANDING NATIVISM STRESSING IN-GROUP SUPERIORITY

Declining sense of responsibility to broader community
Increasing privileging of one's own group's status and well-being

---

RISING TRIBALISM AND ETHNIC ENCLAVES

Insular focus on management of own affairs and provision of own protection
Little caring about outsiders—or caring about them only enough to keep them out

---

PROGRESSION IN BOTH THE GLOBAL NORTH AND THE GLOBAL SOUTH

Wealthy moving to private gated communities patrolled by private security guards
Poor marginalized communities relying on gangs to maintain order in urban ghettos

---

MAGNIFIED SEPARATISM BETWEEN NATIVES AND FOREIGNERS

New immigrants staying in national/ethnic enclaves with similar cultures/languages
Host states allowing national/ethnic enclaves to be culturally segregated from the natives

---

INCREASING INTOLERANT INSECURITY

Voluntary or involuntary tribalist separation promoting societal discrimination
Enclaves held together by external isolation and fear are potential cauldrons of violence

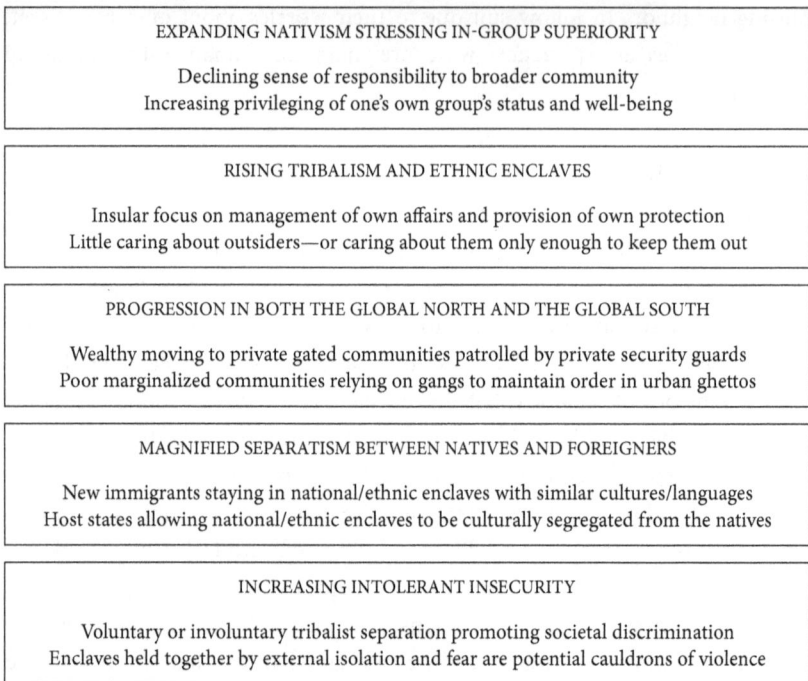

FIGURE 2.3: Emerging Tribalist Enclaves

Secretary of Labor Robert Reich called the "secession of the successful." Marginalized communities have essentially done the same thing, using a different kind of private security force—the gang—to maintain order in the global cities' multiplying and expanding ghettos.[66]

Within Western Europe, governments and migrants share a consensus about the viability of tribalism:

New immigrants are more likely to remain within enclaves of individuals from countries with cultures and linguistic dialects similar to their own, than they are to venture into environments where they may feel socially uncomfortable. Western European nations have been happy to oblige, allowing sections within urban areas (and in some cases, entire cities) to become culturally segregated from the host nation population. This inclination has been difficult to reverse, as multiculturalism has long been considered "politically correct"—those who question its value have been labeled "racist" (and yes, "xenophobic").[67]

While like-minded people of common origin may feel quite comfortable nestled within such cocoons, the broader consequences for cross-group relations can be decidedly dangerous.

This "separate but presumed equal" approach can destabilize national societies. Growing exclusivist communities may define their self-interest narrowly in terms of enhancing their power relative to that of other communities, with no broader statewide sense of obligation. When foreign migrants live together in relative isolation, their understanding of overarching national norms within the host state is stymied, their desire to assimilate is reduced, and they may be induced to try to establish a separate satellite nation representative of the traditions and values of their home rather than their host country.

Tribalist enclaves may specifically amplify societal discrimination and polarization. Although such arrangements can certainly foster strong and vibrant senses of community, identity, and in-group solidarity, Barber notes that it also sometimes "guarantees parochialism and is grounded in exclusion."[68] When a diverse society falls prey to tribalism, societal instability can ensue and sometimes lead to violence. This volatility appears to be especially likely if tribalist enclaves are characterized by extreme economic insecurity[69] and are based on extreme cultural fear of outsiders.[70] Once such tribalist enclaves become an established pattern, they are extremely hard to dissolve, given that people everywhere fiercely defend their right to choose with whom they live and commingle.

Rising Cultural Frustrations

Ancient hatreds between long-standing neighboring societal groups[71] obviously predate the advent of modern interdependence and globalization and the associated mass cross-border migration of people, and these sentiments can promote intolerance without these globalized influences. Such deep-seated primordial cultural antagonisms can persist within and across countries, shaped by "an unchanging geography, shared history and experiences, and often by spiritual and ideological beliefs that defy modern reason," as "nations travel along deep and broad ruts in which they have been traveling for hundreds of years."[72] Moreover, an emphasis on culture can often associate with exclusion rather than inclusion, causing protective policies to have in many instances negative security consequences.[73] Within divided societies, debates have been raging for centuries about the virtues of existing cultural identities and the legitimacy of existing territorial control, and such controversies persist. Despite external pressures from liberal international order and interdependence and globalization processes, profound resentment of differences continues in such societies, enhanced by strong racist sentiments in some places and by strong religious sentiments in others.[74]

While the West largely appreciates the benefits from interdependence and globalization, much of the non-Western world has long been frustrated about their implications, going back to the age of colonization—seeing them as inherently endangering local cultures, promoting cultural and economic imperialism, and weakening states.[75] Such globalized forces can make it much more difficult for any group within a society to maintain a unique and distinctive identity, and states can no longer exert dominant cultural control.[76] A constant effort occurs within many premodern societies to resist ever-escalating external globalization and interdependence conformity pressures, and the need for this never-ending resistance is deeply unsettling to those who are absolutely convinced that the preservation of their culture and some level of autonomy is an inherent right and is illegitimately directly threatened by outside forces.

Rising Economic Frustrations

Intrasocietal economic tensions similarly need not be due to external interdependence and globalization pressures or to the mass migration of people across borders. For example, internally dysfunctional economic structure or poor political leadership alone can cause economic recessions and widening income gaps. Victims of unexpected economic hardships usually are impatient for improvements because of the growing global obsession with immediate material self-gratification.[77] The growing worldwide rich-poor gap can generate seething cross-group antagonisms that can become quite destabilizing: in the thirty years prior to 2002, the income share of the poorest fifth of the world's population fell from 2.3 percent to 1 percent, while that of the richest fifth grew from 70 percent to 86 percent.[78] Hardest hit within the Global North are communities relying on manufacturing and blue-collar workers in low-tech product manufacturing: "workers in American and Western European factory towns found themselves in competition with Chinese electronics assemblers, Indian call center employees and auto factory workers in Eastern Europe, Mexico and beyond,"[79] but the decline in manufacturing employment may be due more to automation than to globalization.[80] Within the Global South, many citizens, experiencing record unemployment rates at least partly due to inefficient domestic production, increasingly complain about their poverty and global inequality[81] with the Global North.

The likelihood of intolerance arising between native citizens and foreign migrants rises when these citizens' and migrants' sense of economic distress escalates because governments undertake little effective remedial action to cope with ensuing changes within the domestic economy, leaving them to suffer ever-deepening economic woes. Many of these economic problems may be unrelated to the entrance of foreigners, instead, for example, reflecting investment decisions by multinational corporations or economic jolts within other countries. Strong native citizen anger about their economic misery, combined with foreign migrant anger about their own lack of economic opportunity, can foster enduring economic instability.

Rising Politician and Media Intolerance Manipulation

Both public and private sources readily manipulate existing antagonisms in a way that inflames intolerance between native citizens and foreign migrants. Over the centuries, propaganda expertise has been increasingly refined and used to fuel hostile emotions amplifying popular indignation about alleged harmful disruptions to their lifestyle.[82] The temptation to engage in mass public manipulation regarding social tolerance issues is equally present, using different kinds of tools, in democratic and authoritarian societies.

Both national politicians and media outlets can manipulate mass public opinion in differing directions, producing multiple forms of intolerance while at the same time increasing their popularity. Regarding political leaders, typically nationalist populist politicians scapegoat foreigners for any ongoing societal problems, increasing the hysteria and intolerance among native citizens toward immigrants. However, at the same time, more globally oriented politicians may downplay any threat from the influx of foreign migrants and aggressively paint anyone as xenophobic who wishes to tighten border controls or who is opposed to greater international or cross-group interaction and exchange, increasing societal intolerance toward them. For example, in a June 2017 speech in Canada constituting a thinly veiled attack on President Donald Trump and his supporters, former U.S. president Barack Obama bashed the "extreme nationalism and xenophobia and the politics of 'us-versus-them,'" which he said could lead to "intolerance and tribalism and organizing ourselves along ethnic lines" due to a self-centered insistence that "what's good for me and my immediate people is all that matters," with "no obligations beyond our borders."[83] Regarding media outlets, similar multidirectional manipulation is evident. Typically, nationalist populist media use sensationalist coverage of shocking incidents to create outrage against foreigners, increasing intolerance of natives toward migrants. However, at the same time, more globally oriented media minimize coverage of foreign migrant threat and instead maximize coverage of nativist violence toward foreign migrants and underrepresented minorities, thereby increasing intolerance toward citizens who may genuinely think their identity is under attack. For example, attracting significant negative national media attention was the Minutemen vigilante group's patrolling of twenty-three miles of Arizona's southern border with Mexico in April–May 2005 to keep illegal migrants out, and Democratic front-runner Hillary Clinton's smearing in March 2016 of her opponent Bernie Sanders in the presidential race because she claimed that he supported that nativist organization (even though the vigilante group had disintegrated years earlier and Sanders had simply voted for a bill preventing the Department of Homeland Security from providing foreign governments with information on American organized volunteer civilian action groups).[84] Thus, because of politician and media manipulation, one side promotes underestimation of nativist threat and overestimation of migrant threat, while the other side promotes overestimation of nativist threat and underestimation of migrant threat. Either type of distortion can inflame native-foreigner tensions.

The global rise of nationalist populism facilitates both directions of successful target intolerance manipulation. Since many populists do not operate on the basis of evidence-based arguments, outside manipulation can be employed without limits. On the one hand, it is relatively easy through manipulation to trigger nationalist populist fervor, demonstrated by U.S. president Donald Trump's 2017 foreign security policies (reflecting exaggerated fears of national decline) and the 2016 British Brexit vote (reflecting exaggerated fears of sovereignty loss and illegal migrants).[85] On the other hand, it is relatively easy through manipulation to condemn nationalist populism, shown by a typical thrust claiming that "once in power, most nationalist populists don't actually work to take back control on the people's behalf, as they promised to do; instead, they perform a sort of nationalist pantomime of largely symbolic gestures."[86] Manipulation by either political leaders or media outlets—potentially creating new resentments or exacerbating existing ones—seems to be most effective in today's world when using populists' confirmation bias to reinforce strongly held preconceived images held by natives or foreigners about security fears and identity aspirations.

Politicians' Inflammation of Intolerance

Political leaders have had a wide berth to engage in manipulation: they may misrepresent threats from nativist or foreign groups so as to desensitize citizens to real dangers, make citizens alarmed over nothing, or even sometimes promote the image if not the reality of tolerance and acceptance. The dominant pattern is that politicians use manipulation to promote native citizen intolerance of foreign migrants; this pattern occurs because, given widespread mass citizen frustration, politicians see no downside to reassuring natives that these problems are not their fault but rather due to alien meddling. However, occasionally national leaders go in the opposite direction; for example, in response to the rise of nativism in Europe, several national and local governments spent millions of dollars to initiate pro–multicultural tolerance initiatives.[87]

Because even within democratic societies with diverse information sources, the mass public has no way to credibly independently verify whether a foreign migrant threat is real or concocted, native citizens often feel that they have no choice but to believe what politicians tell them. These leaders rarely shy away from embellishment of antagonisms to achieve their desired ends—"if politicians do anything well, it is to fan the flames of *Chicken Little* hysteria; they have an innate talent for scaring neurotic people who are prone to believe whatever government tells them about potential threats."[88] Placed in the hands of political demagogues, inculcating widespread citizen fear in response to carefully framed threat is an amazingly powerful tool to garner widespread support for state policies.

Attempts to manipulate the mass public seem most likely to occur when political leaders need to portray aggressive actions as defensive or to deflect mass public attention away from their own policy failures, incompetence, corruption, or responsibility for social or economic decline. Among the manipulation tools that political leaders possess, impassioned public speeches seem to be particularly effective—such speeches are usually driven more by political "rhetoric and ideology" than by evidence,[89] amplifying mass public xenophobia.[90] Extremist politicians may mobilize support among frustrated native citizens either by identifying their misery source as interdependence and globalization pressures[91] or by trying to connect the threat of terrorism and violence directly to migration.[92]

Sometimes political leaders attempt to open citizens up to foreign conspiratorial interpretations to facilitate this manipulation. The mass public is then led to conclude that what they think is the root of domestic problems is illusory, and that the real cause is something more hidden, complex, and nefarious. In leading citizens along this conspiratorial path, politicians can make it appear as if easy solutions exist to remedy complex domestic problems. Using preexisting fear and hatred, these leaders may choose to whip up mass populations into frenzied violence-generating bloodlust.

Mass Media's Inflammation of Intolerance

Private mass media (including traditional print and broadcast media and Internet-based social media) possess equal power to distort native citizen and foreign migrant perceptions. The dominant global pattern where national media provide upsetting intolerance-enhancing coverage amplifying public outrage focuses on "'bad news' about migration."[93] However, regarding host society native-migrant relations, it would be way too simple to argue that national media convey a single message;[94] while "some outlets are overwhelmingly negative, ignoring the positive contributions many migrants make to their host communities, others are overwhelmingly positive, ignoring the negative impacts immigration can have."[95] Lately, in several countries noticeably more positive coverage of foreign migrants has emerged.[96]

Aside from the pursuit of advertising revenues and larger audiences, mass media may be motivated by a desire to judge foreign immigrants through "national narratives and the perceived interests of the state."[97] Several studies find that across societies national media coverage of migration issues increases their societal importance and can affect resulting state policies.[98] Internet-based social media sites have generally not provided more balanced intolerance-reducing coverage than traditional mass media; today many websites (1) pretend to be independent information providers while secretly being controlled by public or private parties prone to manipulate the mass public for either economic profit or political gain,[99] and (2) allow for unlimited contributors to express inadequately curated sentiments, thus potentially providing outlets for extremist views that would never make it into traditional print and broadcast media.

Mass media outlets often perpetuate negative stereotypes inflaming antagonisms between native citizens and foreign migrants. Media propaganda may depict foreign migrants or nativist populists as so consistently dangerous that there is little need to further understanding. Given the increase in the global acceptability of vocalizing intolerance, "media coverage can also remove migrants metaphorically from the population altogether through dehumanizing language," such as through "casting migration as a form of natural disaster (often a flood) or migrants as animals, especially insects ('swarms')."[100] On the one hand, populists can benefit because mass media choose to adopt "their framing and rhetoric, with the effect of ratifying and amplifying their messages";[101] on the other hand, demeaning media portrayal of nativist populists can severely damage their image. Regardless, mass media can stimulate violent conflict by publicizing cross-group grievances.[102]

Mass media's selective coverage furthers this manipulation. Commonly, mass media tend to focus more on violent areas and less on peaceful cooperative multicultural societies,[103] and the result may exacerbate intolerance of nativists and foreigners.[104] For example, when stories about the mass influx of foreigners and their economic and cultural disruption within societies dominate the media, "members of the host environment feel jittery based on the belief that these newcomers will diminish their opportunities to earn a decent living," take their jobs, and contaminate their culture, and then "resentment grows, animosity follows, and the end point is often violent."[105] Media outlets may underreport, soft-pedal, explain as reasonable, or outright ignore certain stakeholder initiatives, such as modest, subtle, and conciliatory gestures, while overreporting and exaggerating others, such as aggressive, belligerent, and extremist actions.[106]

Politician and Media Promotion of Enemy Images

Fostering fear and hate requires a clear target, readily provided in the case of nativist-foreigner tensions. Fear generates enemies because of the desire to protect oneself against sources of danger (defensive), while hatred generates enemies because of the desire to punish sources of discontent (offensive). The enemy concept has deep roots, with many societies defining their security in terms of overcoming an enemy, harking back to the idea of a nemesis in religion and folklore; identifying an outside counterforce promoting negative ends, against which one heroically struggles, has been across time and place a key element in the formation of societal identity. Enemy images tend to become reciprocal, enhancing the possibility of action-reaction cycles between natives and foreigners. A typical escalation sequence,[107] shown in Figure 2.4, goes from fear and hatred, to enemy image creation, and finally to taking hostile violent actions.

MOVEMENT FROM TRANQUILITY TO VIOLENCE

Developing Hostile Attitudes

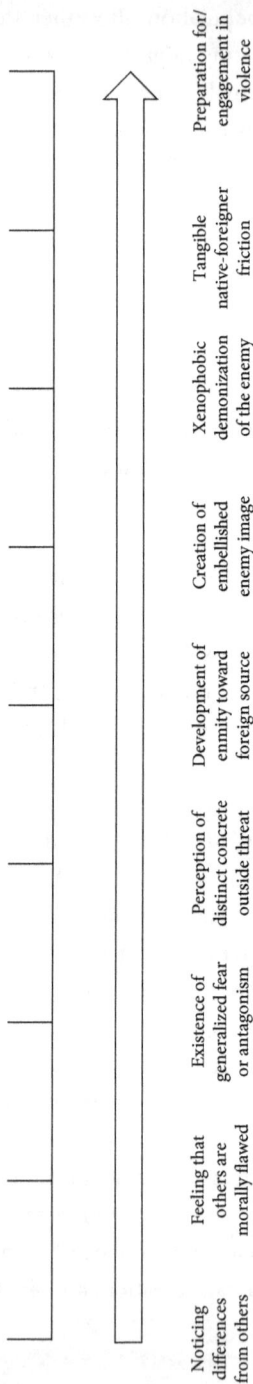

Undertaking Hostile Actions

| Noticing differences from others | Feeling that others are morally flawed | Existence of generalized fear or antagonism | Perception of distinct concrete outside threat | Development of enmity toward foreign source | Creation of embellished enemy image | Xenophobic demonization of the enemy | Tangible native-foreigner friction | Preparation for/ engagement in violence |

EMOTIONAL PROGRESSION FROM ACCEPTANCE/TOLERANCE TO REJECTION/INTOLERANCE

FIGURE 2.4: Fear/Hatred, Enemy Images, and Violent Intolerance

Often enemy image manipulators assign a nonredeemable demonic character to their chosen targets:

> The image of the enemy is fear-filled as no other is, since no one attributes calculable ways of behavior to the foe, but, on the contrary, expects any manner of enormity from him. Though he be animalistic in being without human emotions and reason, he is thought to be capable of treachery, recklessness, and blood lust to superhuman extent. Based as it is on ignorance and primitive dread, this image prevents those who hold it from any reasonable calculation of the enemy's actual strength or weakness.[108]

Thus an enemy image can attribute evil or degenerate motives to targets: the inherent intangibility of such negative motivation often requires that it "be given flesh and location," but in doing so it almost automatically becomes "beyond redemption, beyond discourse, beyond comprehension and understanding" to those opposing it.[109] Even in the modern world, this kind of demonization can lead to genocide,[110] sometimes entailing complete dehumanization of other groups and complete desensitization to their suffering. A sense of public dread can result, where those affected are subject to depression, paranoia, edginess, impaired ability to think, hypochondria, and hysteria,[111] ultimately crippling one's economy and societal infrastructure. Such cases may induce no sense of any commonality between oneself and one's enemy, exemplified by portrayals of foreigners as being subhuman because of antagonistic relationships reflecting grudges persisting over centuries.

Once formed, foreign enemy images have usually proven to be extremely resistant to change:

> Since an enemy is seen as a threat to national survival, to change his image involves dropping one's guard—that is, acting as if he could be trusted. All life experience teaches that in the face of a serious conflict of interest, real or illusory, this is very risky, especially when there is no one to turn to for protection or redress should one's trust prove to have been unjustified. The enemy may be frightening, but the thought of dropping one's guard is more so.[112]

What normally happens after such enemy image formation is that threat targets assume that dangers emerging from an adversary are severe and escalating: the underlying presumptions—especially if enemy intolerance is high—are that its intentions are unwavering and hostile and that it cannot be significantly reformed or rehabilitated.

Having a strong enemy image can readily be portrayed by its facilitators as security-promoting, and indeed many Global North and Global South countries have used it to help forge common internal identities. The allegedly beneficial constructive psychological and political enemy image functions[113] include being a scapegoat for internal woes, providing a rationale for a desired military buildup, fostering a politically unifying crusade, inducing smug satisfaction about one's own superiority, and creating a strong "don't mess with me" global image. National governments lacking high levels of mass public support or tangible domestic or international success may often intentionally turn citizens' attention toward an enemy as a distracting way to set everything right again. Emphasizing the security dangers posed by identified groups helps to sustain both national identity and national government legitimacy.[114] Those within an enemy-focused society may develop increased trust in their own authority structure, crystallize their own cultural beliefs, sharpen their sense of policy focus and mission, and tie security expenditures directly to the identified threat. What unifies such societies thus becomes less internal commonality of beliefs or widespread pride in accomplishments and instead simply universal fear or hatred of the threatening group or country. Out of this perverse syndrome, a fulfilling sense of societal purification can emerge.

3 Intolerance-Based Violence and Global Insecurity

INTOLERANCE STRONGLY LINKS to cross-cultural violence,[1] promoting societal instability and disruption to the status quo.[2] Although many empirical studies suggest that undocumented immigration resulting from interdependence and globalization does not increase societal violence,[3] and that over the centuries global violence has steadily decreased because of cross-group interconnectivity and understanding,[4] the narrower contention here is simply that sometimes tensions between native citizens and foreign migrants can culminate in mutual brutality, labeled "intolerance-based violence." Exploration seems absolutely vital of its typical progression, its general nature, its paradoxes, states' management deficiencies, mass public cynicism about state management, and its human, state, and global insecurity consequences.

Under the umbrella of broad identity-based hate violence, within societies key differences exist between that perpetrated toward locals versus outsiders, shown in Figure 3.1. Regarding discriminatory violence directed toward long-standing domestic minorities, a primary cause is the majority population seeing its lifestyle eroding; a common trigger is the growth in culturally distinct minority populations seen as insufficiently assimilating into society and as being potential criminals; a pervasive impediment to acceptance is racial or religious differences, with both sides thinking they have a reasonably high understanding of the other because they have lived in the same society so long; violence perpetrators tend to be long-standing bigots and nativists; the probability of generating cross-state tensions is low; and the usual policy reaction is promoting legislation accelerating internal discrimination and tribalism. Regarding intolerance-based violence directed toward recent foreign immigrants, a primary cause is the domestic entrance of people and values seen as alien; a common trigger is the growth in culturally distinct minority immigrants seen as insufficiently assimilating into society and as being potential terrorists; a pervasive impediment to acceptance is domestic-foreign differences, with both sides recognizing that they have abysmally low understanding of the other due to their recent juxtaposition; violence perpetrators tend to be displaced xenophobes; the probability of generating cross-state tensions is high; and the usual policy reactions are promoting legislation restricting external border access. The similarities between violence targeting locals versus foreigners are that both reflect fear of control loss and moral breakdown, are cathartic outlets for pent-up frustrations about undesired change, and stimulate pushes for protection of a presumed beneficial status quo. Violence against locals can sometimes be just as domestically disruptive as that against foreigners. For example, considering just a two-month period, on March 15, 2019, at the Al Noor mosque and the Linwood Islamic Centre in Christchurch, New Zealand, a twenty-eight-year-old self-proclaimed racist killed around 49 worshippers and wounded over 20 others in the worst mass shooting in New Zealand history;[5] on April 21, 2019, in Colombo, Sri Lanka, a series of bombs targeting Christian churches and high-end hotels killed hundreds of people;[6] and on April 27, 2019, at the Chabad of Poway synagogue in Escondido, California, during Passover, a gunman used a semiautomatic rifle to kill a Jewish worshipper and wound the rabbi and two others.[7]

Domestic intolerance-based violence also differs from transnational terrorist violence, as summarized in Figure 3.2. Regarding terrorist violence, a primary cause is alienation with the dominant system values and structure; the immediate objective is radical political change in national governments; the long-run goal is overturning the political status quo; the main target is state ideology and leadership; the violence perpetrators are disaffected foreign political or religious ideologues; and the usual policy reaction is state offensive initiation of external punitive military action. Regarding intolerance-based violence, a primary cause is entrance of people seen as alien into one's society; the immediate objective is radical cultural shifts restoring societal integrity; the long-run goal is protection of natives' imagined status quo or foreigners' imagined basic rights; the main target is domestic societies; the violence perpetrators are angry native citizens and foreign migrants; and the usual policy reaction is state defensive restriction of external border access. Both types of violence operate without limits on tactics or innocence of victims.

	DISCRIMINATORY VIOLENCE TOWARD LONG-STANDING DOMESTIC MINORITIES	XENOPHOBIC VIOLENCE TOWARD RECENT FOREIGN IMMIGRANTS
Principal Cause	Majority population angry about prospect of cherished lifestyle eroding	Majority population angry about entrance into domestic society of people and values seen as alien
Immediate Trigger	Growing culturally distinct minorities seen as not assimilating and as potentially being criminals	Growing culturally distinct immigrants seen as not assimilating and as being potential terrorists
Acceptance Impediment	Racial or religious differences	Foreign-domestic differences
Mutual Understanding	Perceived as reasonably high	Recognized as abysmally low
Violence Perpetrators	Long-standing domestic bigots and nativists	Recently displaced domestic xenophobes
Cross-State Tensions	Low probability	High probability
Policy Reaction	State political legislation promoting internal discrimination and tribalism	State political legislation promoting external border crossing restrictions

FIGURE 3.1: Identity-Based Hate Violence Against Locals Versus Outsiders

	TRANSNATIONAL TERRORIST VIOLENCE	DOMESTIC INTOLERANCE-BASED VIOLENCE
Principal Cause	Alienation with the values and structure of the dominant system	Entrance of people and values seen as alien into Local society
Immediate Objective	Radical political change in state ideology and leadership	Radical cultural shift restoring societal integrity
Long-Term Goal	Overturning the existing status quo	Protection of natives' imagined benevolent status quo or protection of foreigners' imagined basic rights
Main Target	National governments	Domestic societies
Violence Perpetrators	Disaffected foreign political or religious ideologues	Angry domestic native citizens and foreign immigrants
Policy Reaction	National government offensive initiation of external punitive military action	National government defensive initiation of external border access restrictions

FIGURE 3.2: Transnational Terrorist Violence Versus Domestic Intolerance-Based Violence

Typical Interdependence, Intolerance, and Violence Progression

Figure 3.3 shows the typical progression from global interdependence to native citizen–foreign migrant intolerance to violence. First, interdependence's and globalization's failure to achieve their lofty goals can result in widespread disappointment, with powerful societies becoming aware of eroding national identity and control and poor societies becoming aware of rising global inequality and their increasingly miserable plight. Next, socioeconomic protection initiatives proliferate, as native citizens rush to protect the status quo from increasingly visible foreign migrants' cultural and economic disruption and foreign migrants rush to protect their rights and identities from natives' discrimination and oppression. Then intolerant mutual blame occurs, given growing nationalism, xenophobia, tribalism, and deep cultural and economic grievances, where native citizens and foreign migrants each scapegoat the other for local problems rather than taking responsibility for fixing them. Afterward, extremist elements escalate native citizens' desires to fortify borders and foreign migrants' desires to open borders. Next, states vainly attempt to manage the turmoil, impeded by poor monitoring and reporting and perpetrator impunity, amplifying public dissatisfaction. Finally, barbaric domestic violence may ensue, aided by the availability of weapons and the spread of private vigilantes, private contractors, or transnational criminal smugglers, occasionally in the form of action-reaction cycles of mutually escalating brutality.

This sequence of steps is more suggestive than definitive. Interdependence and globalization are not the only roots of intrasocietal intolerance, for other elements such as age-old antagonisms or terrorism may play a role. A massive influx of immigrants is not necessary for intolerance, as it can easily escalate without it, shown back in 1973–1974, when the anti–United States Arab oil embargo alone increased American intolerance of Arab citizens from the Middle East. Intolerance does not always lead to any form of coercive action and instead can simmer for a long time without exploding. Lastly, even when violence does occur, it may not lead to action-reaction cycles because sometimes victimized groups lack either the will or the capacity to respond to alleged slights with force.

Nature of Intolerance-Based Violence Threat

The current global threat of intolerance-based violence is summarized in Figure 3.4. The dangers identified suggest a truly precarious native-foreigner

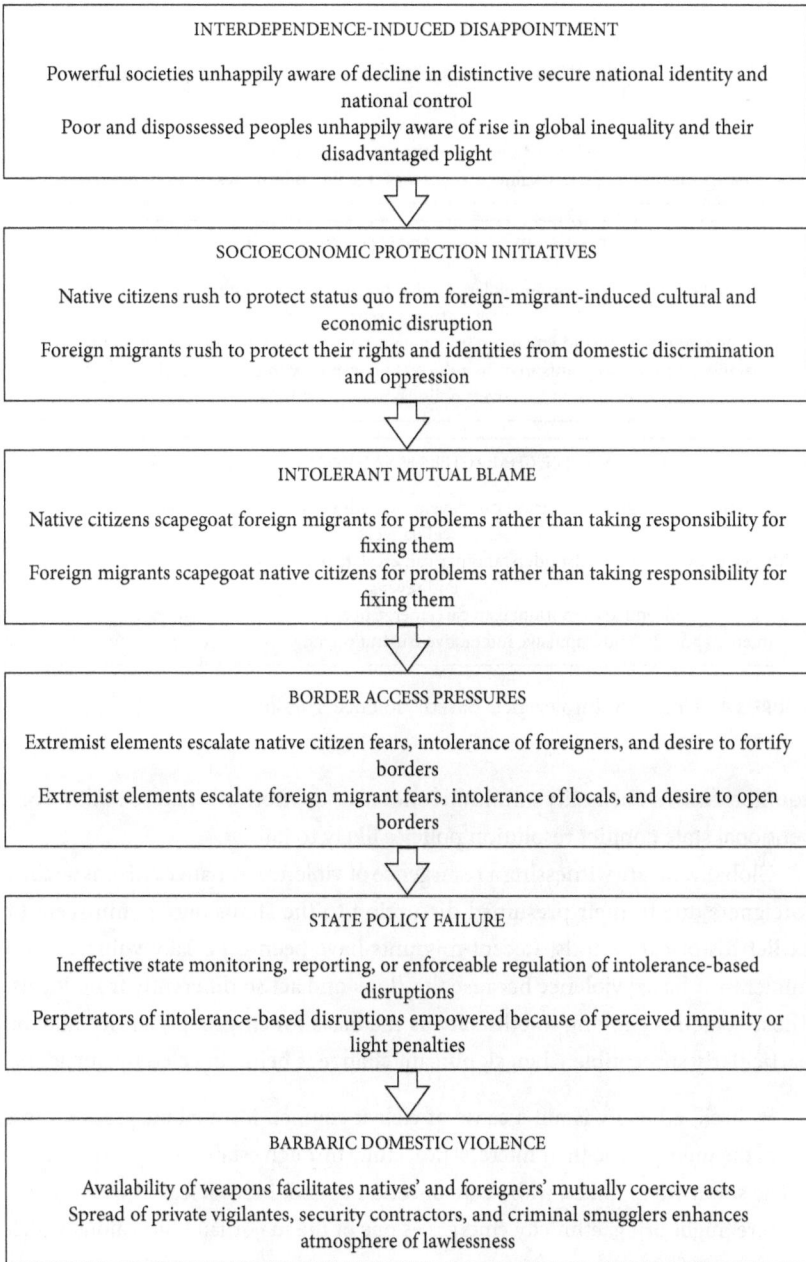

```
┌──────────────────────────────────────────────────────────────────────┐
│                  INTERDEPENDENCE-INDUCED DISAPPOINTMENT                 │
│                                                                        │
│  Powerful societies unhappily aware of decline in distinctive secure   │
│                 national identity and national control                 │
│  Poor and dispossessed peoples unhappily aware of rise in global       │
│            inequality and their disadvantaged plight                   │
└──────────────────────────────────────────────────────────────────────┘
                                  ⇩
┌──────────────────────────────────────────────────────────────────────┐
│                   SOCIOECONOMIC PROTECTION INITIATIVES                  │
│                                                                        │
│  Native citizens rush to protect status quo from foreign-migrant-      │
│         induced cultural and economic disruption                       │
│  Foreign migrants rush to protect their rights and identities from     │
│         domestic discrimination and oppression                         │
└──────────────────────────────────────────────────────────────────────┘
                                  ⇩
┌──────────────────────────────────────────────────────────────────────┐
│                         INTOLERANT MUTUAL BLAME                        │
│                                                                        │
│  Native citizens scapegoat foreign migrants for problems rather than   │
│         taking responsibility for fixing them                          │
│  Foreign migrants scapegoat native citizens for problems rather than   │
│         taking responsibility for fixing them                          │
└──────────────────────────────────────────────────────────────────────┘
                                  ⇩
┌──────────────────────────────────────────────────────────────────────┐
│                        BORDER ACCESS PRESSURES                         │
│                                                                        │
│  Extremist elements escalate native citizen fears, intolerance of      │
│         foreigners, and desire to fortify borders                      │
│  Extremist elements escalate foreign migrant fears, intolerance of     │
│         locals, and desire to open borders                             │
└──────────────────────────────────────────────────────────────────────┘
                                  ⇩
┌──────────────────────────────────────────────────────────────────────┐
│                         STATE POLICY FAILURE                           │
│                                                                        │
│  Ineffective state monitoring, reporting, or enforceable regulation of │
│         intolerance-based disruptions                                  │
│  Perpetrators of intolerance-based disruptions empowered because of    │
│         perceived impunity or light penalties                          │
└──────────────────────────────────────────────────────────────────────┘
                                  ⇩
┌──────────────────────────────────────────────────────────────────────┐
│                       BARBARIC DOMESTIC VIOLENCE                       │
│                                                                        │
│  Availability of weapons facilitates natives' and foreigners' mutually │
│         coercive acts                                                  │
│  Spread of private vigilantes, security contractors, and criminal      │
│         smugglers enhances atmosphere of lawlessness                   │
└──────────────────────────────────────────────────────────────────────┘
```

FIGURE 3.3: Typical Interdependence-Intolerance-Violence Progression

PRIMARY THREAT FROM NATIVE CITIZENS
Resurgence in native citizen violence against foreign migrants due to presumed status quo disruption Targets are those not in dominant group with visible differences Uncertainty and fear of the future stimulate anxieties Barbarity maximizing shock value through mass media undermines societal complacency

SECONDARY THREAT FROM FOREIGN MIGRANTS
Less publicized foreign migrant violence—due to frustration about mistreatment—against native citizens Migrants may be indoctrinated into violent acts by extremists in refugee camps Vulnerable desperate migrants may be induced to conspire with criminal and terrorist groups Migrants may be used for covert political infiltration by intrusive outside states

PROVOCATIVE CHARACTER OF NATIVE-MIGRANT TENSIONS
Mutual native-migrant confusion can develop, clouding distinction between perceived and real dangers Mutual native-migrant misunderstandings can escalate because of tribal impulse for survival and revenge Incendiary emotionalism can emerge over perceived mistreatment Intense sporadic and impulsive interactive frustration, anger, and resentment can surface

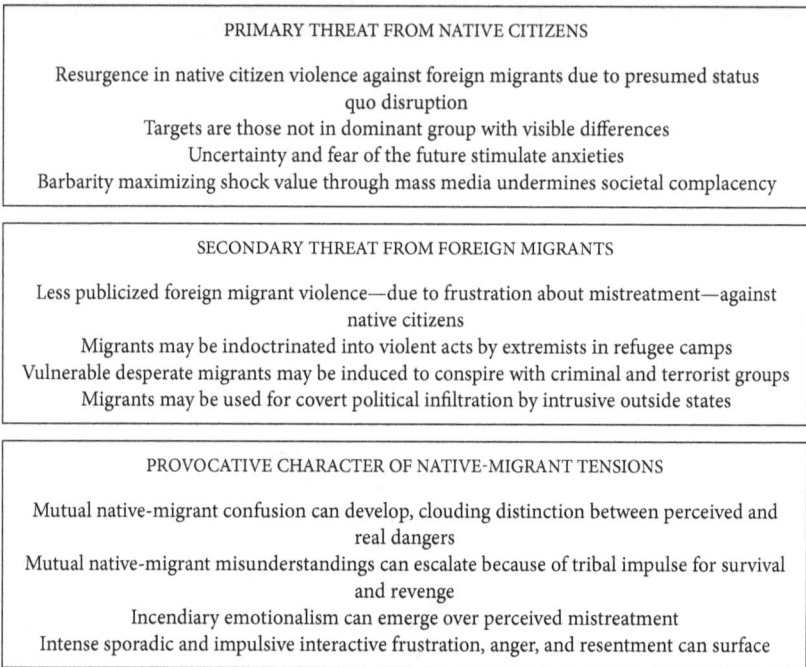

FIGURE 3.4: Nature of Intolerance-Based Violence Threat

equilibrium. The brutality's multidirectional and emotional nature makes conventional state conflict resolution policies likely to fail.

Globally, we are witnessing a resurgence of violence by native citizens against foreigners due to their presumed disruption to the status quo, reminiscent of earlier historical periods. Recent migrants have been especially vulnerable to intolerance-based violence because they look and act so differently from locals. Those societies clinging to ethnicity as the basis for in-group identity may be particularly susceptible when significant change is being injected by outsiders:

> By itself, ethnicity is not a cause of violent conflict. Most ethnic groups, most of the time, pursue their interests peacefully through established political channels. But when linked with acute uncertainty and, indeed, fear of what the future might bring, ethnicity emerges as one of the major fault lines along which societies fracture.[8]

Human Rights First noted back in 2011 that "around the world, refugees, asylum seekers, migrants, and others viewed as 'foreign' have been the targets of violent attacks," producing "a devastating and crippling effect on the targeted communities."[9] UN secretary-general António Guterres confirmed in 2017 that "discrimination and violence were on the rise, borders were closing and vulnerable communities were being cast as scapegoats."[10] This barbarity, often designed to maximize its mass media shock effect,[11] undermines any societal complacency about the existing status quo's stability.

Although the fact is far less widely publicized, foreign migrants also initiate violence against native citizens. The UN International Organization for Migration acknowledges that "on occasion, asylum seekers and migrants have indeed perpetrated attacks against host societies."[12] If foreign migrants' frustration escalates about mistreatment and nonacceptance by native citizens, sometimes it can boil over into intolerance-based violence. When acting on their own, the distorted underlying premise of foreign migrants initiating violence is that because they feel that they are being denied the basic right to survive and thrive in their new societies, with no effective channels available for voicing their concerns, they have every right to use force to signal their frustration, even though many host refugees are themselves fleeing from violent extremism. In such cases, native citizens within migrant host states can feel the same insecurity and fear that foreign migrants typically do about becoming "victimized"[13] by violent strangers.

However, sometimes foreign migrant violence perpetrators do not act independently. Three sources using migrants to further their own violent ends are (1) extremists infiltrating refugee camps, (2) transnational criminal and terrorist groups, and (3) intrusive outside states. In such cases, vulnerable foreign migrants become innocent pawns manipulated by forces whose ends they may not understand.

Considering first migrant manipulation by extremists in refugee camps, such camps designed for other purposes can inadvertently breed violent extremism. This outcome can be due to the presence of poor education, extremist religious or ideological indoctrination, high unemployment, or forced confinement. These camps may be places where violent extremist fighters rest and recuperate, where violent extremist groups recruit, or where peaceful refugees become radicalized to engage in societal violence.[14] Weak states with porous borders seem especially vulnerable to outside political mobilization efforts creating "refugee-warrior communities,"[15] which may illicitly smuggle arms or drugs across borders or ally with antigovernment domestic groups.[16]

Turning to migrant manipulation by transnational criminal and terrorist groups, foreign migrants' combination of vulnerability and desperation makes

them perfect targets. Groups that may use migrant flows to their advantage include unruly nonstate groups, including violent transnational criminal smugglers seeking economic profits, transnational terrorists seeking domestic political change, and even warring factions within weak states engaged in civil
wars.[17] In 2004, the Nixon Center hyperbolically reported that "immigration
and terrorism are linked—not because all immigrants are terrorists but because all, or nearly all, terrorists in the West have been immigrants."[18] In 2018,
the U.S. Justice Department reported that three out of every four people convicted of terrorism between September 11, 2001, and December 31, 2016, were
foreign-born.[19]

Concluding with migrant manipulation by intrusive outside states, other
countries can use foreign migrants to promote domestic host state turmoil.
Such sinister and covert foreign-state-initiated political infiltration is designed
to weaken, destabilize, and even overthrow target national governments. For
example, General Philip Breedlove, NATO's Supreme Allied Commander Europe, stated in 2016 that Russia and Syria have been using migration as a desta-
bilization tool in Europe, "deliberately weaponizing migration in an attempt to
overwhelm European structures and break European resolve," as the migrant
influx "masks the movement of criminals, terrorists, and foreign fighters" sympathetic to ISIS into Europe.[20] The flood of Syrian refugees trying to enter Europe has been described as "infiltrated with Muslim extremists," as a potential
"ISIS Trojan horse,"[21] and as "spreading like a cancer" throughout Europe.[22]
The presumed motive of such informal penetration is for native citizens to vent
their anger against local Muslims, raising ISIS to recruitment, and to create a
"crisis of confidence" in European governments fostering "a new era of intolerance and nationalism."[23]

This multidirectional nature of intolerance-based violence can arouse and
be aroused by negative emotions emanating from a wide variety of differing
sources, triggering mass public confusion about the differences between perceived cultural disparity or economic displacement and real security dangers.
Afterward, mutual misunderstandings can easily escalate; *New York Times* columnist Thomas Friedman points out that "the tribal impulse for survival and
revenge is like a political blowtorch," as "no amount of rational argument can
tone it down."[24] Exemplifying this level of incendiary emotionalism, on May 19,
2019, hundreds of illegal immigrants stormed the Charles de Gaulle airport in
France, shouting "France does not belong to the French! Everyone has a right to
be here!" and demanding to meet with Prime Minister Édouard Philippe about

the country's asylum policy.[25] Thus the intolerance-based violence threat is typically not based on purely dispassionate analysis of costs and benefits about native-foreigner interaction, but rather on more-difficult-to-predict intense sporadic and impulsive interactive frustration, anger, and resentment.

Paradoxes Surrounding Intolerance-Based Violence

Key paradoxes—displayed in Figure 3.5—surround intolerance-based violence. Considering native perpetrators, (1) although brutality can promote changes in national immigration policies, it does not usually induce foreigners to leave the country or to fully assimilate dominant values; and (2) the societal status quo many natives seek to restore through violence usually can be more illusory than real because it cannot be reconstructed. Considering foreign perpetrators, (1) violence does not usually improve their treatment by natives and can often make it worse; and (2) the rights, freedoms, and opportunities sought may be somewhat illusory because even marginalized native citizens may lack them. For both groups, critical mutual domestic and global interdependencies usually make such violence counterproductive. Violence perpetrators rarely

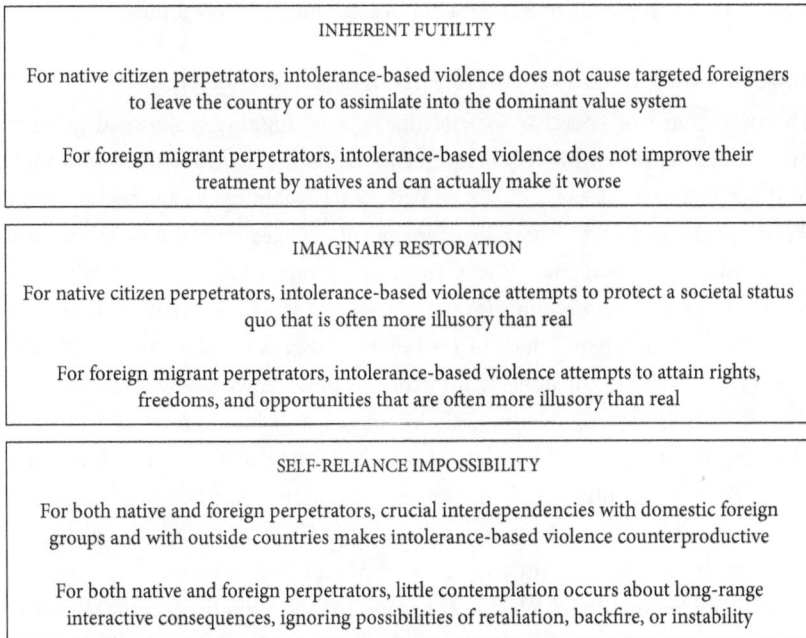

INHERENT FUTILITY

For native citizen perpetrators, intolerance-based violence does not cause targeted foreigners to leave the country or to assimilate into the dominant value system

For foreign migrant perpetrators, intolerance-based violence does not improve their treatment by natives and can actually make it worse

---

IMAGINARY RESTORATION

For native citizen perpetrators, intolerance-based violence attempts to protect a societal status quo that is often more illusory than real

For foreign migrant perpetrators, intolerance-based violence attempts to attain rights, freedoms, and opportunities that are often more illusory than real

---

SELF-RELIANCE IMPOSSIBILITY

For both native and foreign perpetrators, crucial interdependencies with domestic foreign groups and with outside countries makes intolerance-based violence counterproductive

For both native and foreign perpetrators, little contemplation occurs about long-range interactive consequences, ignoring possibilities of retaliation, backfire, or instability

---

FIGURE 3.5: Paradoxes Surrounding Intolerance-Based Violence

contemplate the long-range interactive consequences of their attacks, ignoring the possibilities of retaliation, backfire, or instability. So intolerance-based violence has little chance of actually achieving the desired societal transformation, making it more of a symbolic frustration release than a strategic instrument calculated to achieve meaningful societal change.

After trying to use established channels and seeing little movement, and after concluding that negotiation, compromise, and working through the system to make improvements is decidedly off the table, then exasperation and intolerance sets in when natives or foreigners see their way of life at stake. Violent outcomes can result from perpetrators being convinced that force is justified to safeguard cherished traditions, representing the only signal that those with differing languages, values, and traditions would truly understand. Native citizen violence perpetrators develop feelings of resentment since they see their society as so superior that everyone would naturally be attracted to it and therefore can be baffled when migrants' gratitude, assimilation, and compliance with national norms do not immediately follow. Foreign migrant violence perpetrators develop feelings of resentment because, given the miserable circumstances they flee from and the societal contributions they can make, they can be baffled when native acceptance of differences does not immediately follow.

State Inability to Manage Intolerance-Based Violence Threat

The occurrence of coercive societal disruptions highlights national governments' security policy inadequacies in two distinct areas: inability to find ways to deter native intolerance-based violence, and inability to anticipate pernicious unintended insecurity consequences of policies undertaken to manage intolerance-based violence. Aside from situations where governments lack resources to address ongoing intolerance-based violence, often such failings result from state officials' lack of (1) focus on this particular kind of disruption, (2) creativity in considering unorthodox policy alternatives, (3) consistent rigorous application of existing policies, or (4) sufficient appropriate forward planning including consideration of a wide variety of future contingencies. When the UN recently asked states to assume more responsibility for refugee protection, the request was met with "stiff opposition."[26] Such state inadequacies have broad security consequences, especially when linked to migration, because the manner in which states respond to migration flows can itself cause international conflict.[27] Together these top-down shortcomings highlight how bamboozled national governments have been in managing intolerance-based violence, with the outcome being growing bottom-up feelings of vulnerability.

State Inability to Deter Intolerance-Based Violence

Societal insecurity is enhanced by a continuing cycle of state inability to deter native intolerance-based violence, as shown in Figure 3.6. This cycle is due to both (1) the presence of few enforceable state regulations and (2) little effective state monitoring preventing violence perpetrators from entering the country, committing acts of violence, and continuing to do so over time. People vary considerably in terms of the kinds of intolerance they generate or encounter, and state government policies are often too sweeping to be sensitive to the full spectrum. Within affected societies, egregious offenders frequently behave with relative impunity, because worldwide effective hate crime prosecutions remain rare: the paucity of meaningful prosecution can be due to victims' fear of perpetrator retaliation, deportation, and victimization by law enforcement officers sympathizing with perpetrators; loss of faith in state protection; uncertainty about how or where to report incidents and about the value of doing so; or interfering language barriers.[28] Sometimes national governments do not recognize any obligation to protect "nonnationals."[29] Intolerance-based violence perpetrators remain confident that they can escape without negative consequences or with minimum "slap on the wrist" penalties. State law enforcement officials often contend that they are overwhelmed with other matters. Moreover, defining what constitutes a "hate crime" is complicated and subjective: within many countries, ambiguity or disagreement exists about the meaning of intolerance-based violence, and so the law enforcement system works slowly and weakly. If a brutality victim is an undocumented foreign migrant, then the chances for a meaningful punitive outcome plummet even further. As long as angry bigoted xenophobes feel that they can get away with violence, native citizens seem relatively unconcerned about its occurrence and its toll on foreigners, and law enforcement authorities remain hamstrung, intolerance-based violence seems likely to continue.

In contrast, national governments appear to be slightly better in responding to foreign migrant violence against native citizens, at least partly because of greater societal consensus that this kind of intolerance-based violence deserves to be a security priority. Many ways exist to deter this violence, including trying to stop certain kinds of foreigners from getting into the country[30] and hiring

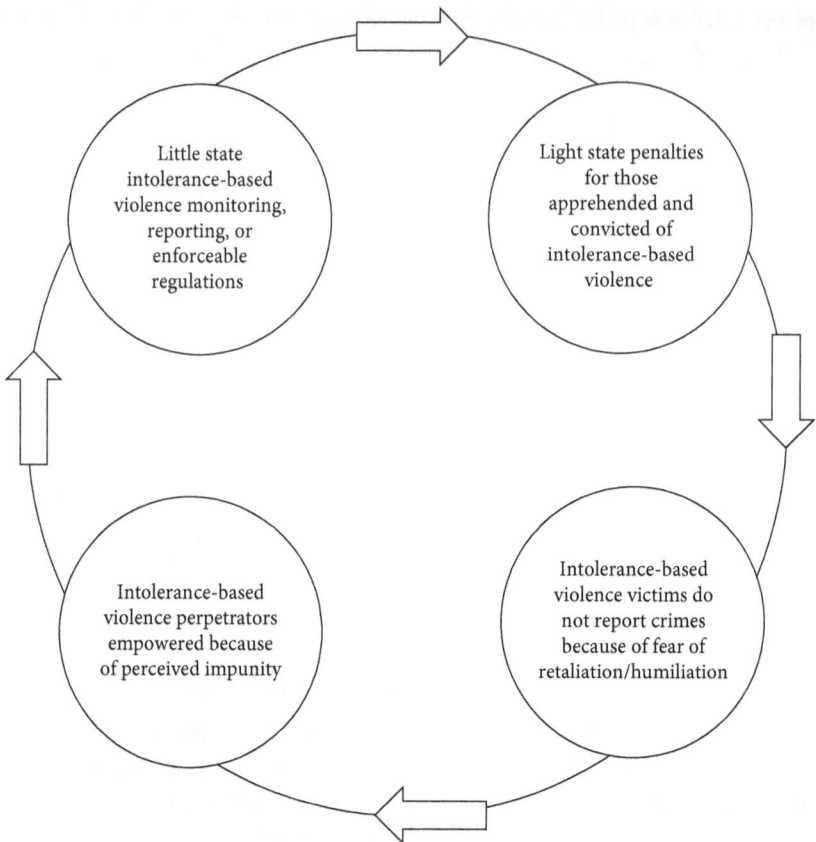

FIGURE 3.6: Cycle of State Inability to Deter Intolerance-Based Violence

more police to try to reduce migrants' crimes once they cross the border.[31] Once migrants come in, they are often confined and monitored, at least initially. Such confinement and monitoring gives governments at least a brief opportunity to manage any emerging violence, although this physical separation can reduce mutual understanding between natives and migrants and thus could indirectly increase the chances of future violence after tight migrant confinement and monitoring end. In addition, state management of migrant violence could be hampered if the ongoing violence threat primarily consists of migrant assaults against other migrants rather than against native citizens; in such situations, local police may avoid the area of carnage altogether, figuring that it is too dangerous for them to be effective and that, since native citizen lives and property are not at stake, the insecurity consequences seem relatively unimportant.

Unintended Negative Consequences of State Anti-Violence Policies

Unintended negative consequences of state efforts to curb intolerance-based violence, shown in Figure 3.7, can heighten societal insecurity. National governments are certainly not blind to the possibility of intrasocietal tensions resulting from immigration; state reluctance to open up national borders is partially due to acknowledged worries that the influx of foreigners may produce xenophobia among native citizens and trigger intrasocietal conflict.[32] However, states often miss key unintended negative consequences of their policy responses,

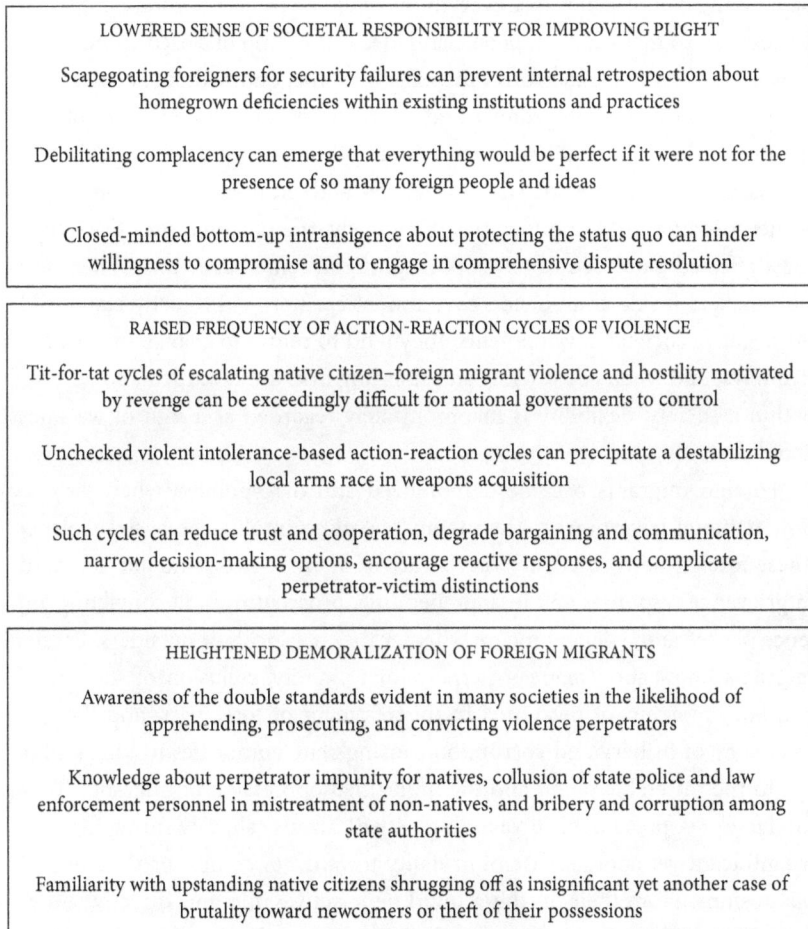

LOWERED SENSE OF SOCIETAL RESPONSIBILITY FOR IMPROVING PLIGHT

Scapegoating foreigners for security failures can prevent internal retrospection about homegrown deficiencies within existing institutions and practices

Debilitating complacency can emerge that everything would be perfect if it were not for the presence of so many foreign people and ideas

Closed-minded bottom-up intransigence about protecting the status quo can hinder willingness to compromise and to engage in comprehensive dispute resolution

RAISED FREQUENCY OF ACTION-REACTION CYCLES OF VIOLENCE

Tit-for-tat cycles of escalating native citizen–foreign migrant violence and hostility motivated by revenge can be exceedingly difficult for national governments to control

Unchecked violent intolerance-based action-reaction cycles can precipitate a destabilizing local arms race in weapons acquisition

Such cycles can reduce trust and cooperation, degrade bargaining and communication, narrow decision-making options, encourage reactive responses, and complicate perpetrator-victim distinctions

HEIGHTENED DEMORALIZATION OF FOREIGN MIGRANTS

Awareness of the double standards evident in many societies in the likelihood of apprehending, prosecuting, and convicting violence perpetrators

Knowledge about perpetrator impunity for natives, collusion of state police and law enforcement personnel in mistreatment of non-natives, and bribery and corruption among state authorities

Familiarity with upstanding native citizens shrugging off as insignificant yet another case of brutality toward newcomers or theft of their possessions

FIGURE 3.7: Unintended Negative Consequences of State Anti-Violence Policies

including the lower sense of societal safety responsibility, heightened demoralization of foreign migrants, and greater chances of action-reaction cycles of violence. Together these ripple effects can impede native-foreigner cooperation within and across societies.

Perhaps the most devastating unintended consequence from state responses to intolerance-based violence is unwillingness among native citizens to take responsibility for improving their plight. Scapegoating of foreigners for all of one's security failings means that internal retrospection about what is going wrong within institutions created by political leaders and private citizens will never occur. Dysfunctional attitudes and behaviors then continue, along with a debilitating complacency that everything would be perfect if it were not for the presence of so many foreign people and ideas. This kind of closed-minded bottom-up intransigence to protect the existing status quo within societies could reduce incentive for compromise and retard conflict resolution[33] for both domestic and international issues, impeding both meaningful attention directed at existing homegrown societal deficiencies and enduring cross-group agreements to manage these difficulties. Ultimately, the outcome may leave those most affected paralyzed in terms of meaningful remedial action. When decision makers inside and outside government are not held directly responsible for negative societal developments, they tend to refuse to change in constructive ways, and when consistency and standing firm are rewarded and admired within a society, flexibility is inappropriately regarded as a sign of weakness and defeat.

Foreign migrants become demoralized and disappointed when they see how national governments treat them regarding intolerance-based violence. These foreign newcomers are very aware of many societies' double standards in grievance responses and in apprehending, prosecuting, and convicting violence perpetrators, depending on whether they are locals or outsiders. Foreign migrants know about natives' perpetrator impunity, collusion of state police and law enforcement personnel in mistreatment of foreigners, and the high frequency of bribery and corruption causing state authorities to turn a blind eye to the miserable plight and the unjustified oppression of migrants. These foreigners see presumably upstanding native citizens callously shrugging off as insignificant yet another case of brutality toward newcomers or theft of their possessions. From their on-the-ground perspective, migrants directly witness how spotty the monitoring can be of crimes against them compared to crimes against the native population.

Regarding action-reaction cycles of violence, national governments often fail to anticipate how sluggishness or inattentiveness in responses to intolerance-based violence between native citizens and foreign migrants can easily lead in the long run to an endless escalating cycle of brutality between the two groups. This emergence of tit-for-tat cycles of violence and hostility can prove exceedingly difficult for national police to control because of high emotionalism and desires for vengeance on both sides. The likelihood of native citizen attacks against foreign migrants rises with reports of repeated violent crimes attributed to allegedly illegal aliens, and the reverse pattern applies as well. Unchecked violent action-reaction cycles can sometimes precipitate a destabilizing local arms race in weapons acquisition. Considering future native citizen–foreign migrant encounters, such cycles can easily reduce hope for mutual trust and cooperation to emerge,[34] causing those affected to close their minds to any possibility of better contact, communication, or reconciliation the longer the cycle of mutually hurtful violence persists. Such a dire predicament can degenerate further when confusion emerges about who is the perpetrator and who is the victim of violence.

Mass Public Cynicism About State Management of Threat

Many private citizens have lost confidence in their national governments' ability to thwart globalization-induced migration pressures, to control their borders, and to protect their way of life from identified outside dangers.[35] This pattern can occur both within strong states where native citizens are proud of their traditions and worry about their maintenance in the face of an influx of outsiders, and within weak states that may not be able to maintain their citizens' loyalty and allegiance.[36] National governments vary considerably in their capacity to control migrant entry; such control is especially challenging for countries with lengthy coastlines or land borders, and notably "states that are capable of defending themselves against missile, tank, and infantry attacks are often unable to defend themselves against the intrusion of thousands of illegals infiltrating across a border in search of employment or safety."[37] In recent decades, few countries experiencing extreme foreign immigration pressure have manifested effective ways to restrict their entrance.

Illustrating native citizens' loss of confidence in states' abilities to protect them from foreigners was the 2015–2016 European refugee crisis. During that period, "the remorseless and often pitiless struggle" by European governments to secure their state borders[38] satisfied nobody. Many national governments verbally promised native citizens that they need not worry about the dangers of foreign migrants threatening the societal status quo because there would be exceptionally careful screening of those allowed entrance,[39] preventing criminals and terrorists from gaining entry. However, during the peak of the European refugee crisis, the volume of desperate foreigners pressing for entrance was so large that there was no systematic way to thwart those most determined to find their way across borders. Many clever migrants crossing borders found ways to disguise their nationality (pretending to be Syrian so as to be viewed as a conflict refugee) or their religion (pretending to be Christian rather than Muslim), or to conceal drugs, arms, violent intent, or diseases:

> Moving among the tens of thousands of Syrian war refugees passing through the train stations of Europe are many who are neither Syrian nor refugees, but hoping to blend into the mass migration and find a back door to the West. There are well-dressed Iranians speaking Farsi who insist they are members of the persecuted Yazidis of Iraq. There are Indians who don't speak Arabic but say they are from Damascus. There are Pakistanis, Albanians, Egyptians, Kosovars, Somalis and Tunisians from countries with plenty of poverty and violence, but no war. It should come as no surprise that many migrants seem to be pretending they are someone else. The prize, after all, is the possibility of benefits, residency and work in Europe.[40]

During this peak period, as long as they bunched up with asylum seekers, economically motivated foreign migrants did not have to show passports to officials; although authorities asked for names and countries of origin, they did not carefully scrutinize accompanying migration documents.[41] This inability to screen effectively was especially acute because those EU states "most devastated by the 2008 global economic crisis happened at the time to be the primary entry points for migrants seeking access to Europe."[42] When facing such overwhelming pressures, proper migrant screening is difficult:

> At the migratory hubs in these countries, the EU [European Union] is trying to allow for a more orderly processing of refugees and migrants by providing coordinated and reinforced support by EU [European Union] agencies like Frontex [the European Union's border control agency] and EASO [European Asylum Support Office] and member states' experts. . . . This could also include intensified security screenings by, for example, systematically checking refugees against police data bases and anti-terror lists. But such measures will take time

to be implemented. At the moment Italy, Greece or Croatia still do not even (manage to) fingerprint and register refugees in a systematic manner.[43]

Although Frontex agents deployed interpreters to judge migrants' accents and used locational questions to try to determine country of origin, their effectiveness was spotty at best.[44] As a result, the credibility of European national government security officials' empty rhetoric in managing the identified migrant threat plummeted in the eyes of many European citizens.

In parallel fashion, many migrants have lost faith in the capability and willingness of national governments to protect them from citizen-initiated intolerance-based violence threats. As discussed earlier, this loss of faith stems from the low priority that foreign migrants feel their safety is given compared to that of native citizens. Persistent doubts about state security intentions and capabilities are naturally highest among foreign groups explicitly denied state protection.[45] Besieged foreign migrants do not have high hopes that this vulnerability will decrease in the future.

Human, State, and Global Insecurity Due to Intolerance-Based Violence

Given state management deficiencies and popular cynicism about state protection, ongoing intolerance-based violence has multifaceted effects on human, state and global insecurity, shown in Figure 3.8. This pattern reflects a growing sense of profound unease. Native citizens fear that traditional enduring values, essential to enhance their sense of security, are vanishing; foreign migrants feel exclusion, with no easily identifiable path toward economic success in their new location or cultural acceptance by the dominant society; and national governments worry that they are losing control in a world where what transpires is increasingly influenced by outside forces. A paranoid antagonistic atmosphere can begin to pervade domestic society, impeding cooperative management of common security challenges. Ultimately, in the worst-case global security scenario, if the intolerance associated with ethnic nationalism and xenophobia continues, the resulting civil unrest potentially could fuel massive intra-state and interstate violence.[46]

A society characterized by multiple layers of insecurity—among individuals, groups, and national government officials—cannot function properly. These three levels of security are deeply intertwined—for example, individual human security really cannot be maintained when there is severe and sustained

---

HUMAN INSECURITY

Confusion, despair, resentment, scapegoating, and friction increase
Trauma affects both those directly hurt and those indirectly suffering psychological harm
Difficulties grow in distinguishing malevolent initiators from innocent victims
Turmoil spreads, facilitated by global spread of instruments of violence

---

STATE INSECURITY

State finds its monopoly on the legitimate use of force violated
Fearful citizens defend themselves and property through hiring private security contractors
Angry citizens form anti-migrant vigilante groups to reduce perceived foreign migrant threat
Foreign migrants try to bypass state access restrictions through criminal smuggling groups

---

GLOBAL INSECURITY

Intolerance-based violence becomes highly contagious across societies
Obstacles mount to isolating or containing local disruptions or discrimination incidents
Foreign sympathizers with links to disgruntled societal groups are quickly alerted
Specter of outside intervention becomes destabilizing

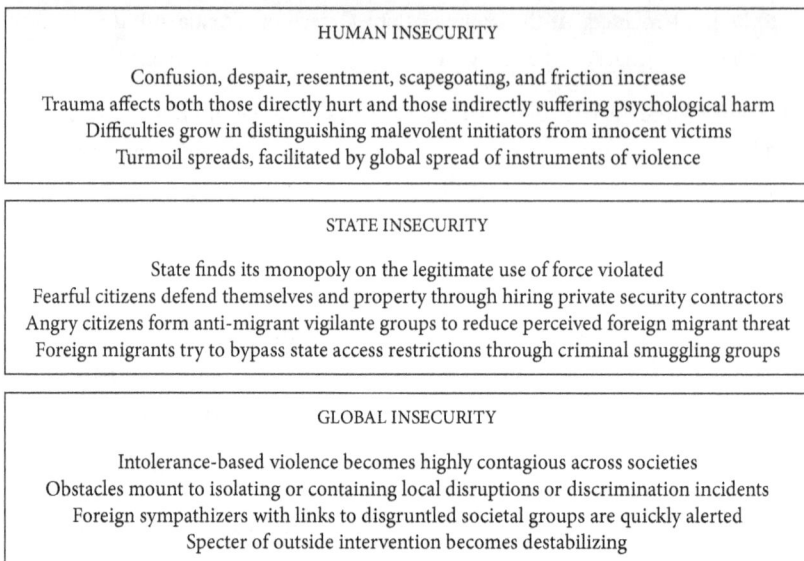

FIGURE 3.8: Human, State, and Global Insecurity Due to Intolerance-Based Violence

state insecurity.[47] Frequently, because such insecurities may seem intractable especially when accompanied by rapid unpredictable change, members of the society can feel hamstrung in terms of their ability to do anything with a high chance of substantially ameliorating the situation. Particularly if people see no available channels through which to vent frustrations or if people feel that their miserable plight is being systematically ignored, this situation can become so stressful that resorting to violence may appear to be the only way out. Moreover, even if such channels exist and relevant authorities are attentive, this may mean little if the dominant perception is that misery is increasing, protection is inadequate, and violence is proliferating. Thus public awareness of strategies being undertaken to enhance security may actually backfire and foster insecurity if such strategies are seen as failing.

Human Insecurity Impact

Intolerance-based violence can increase the insecurity of both native citizens and foreign immigrants within affected societies. Confusion, despair, resentment, scapegoating, and friction may be evident. Natives feeling displaced or vulnerable can get upset that a home environment previously perceived as safe has badly degenerated, and may be angry at their own government for not adequately protecting their way of life. Similarly, foreign migrants despairing about their miserable predicament in a host society can get upset about the shattering of dreams of a secure life with economic opportunity.

Human insecurity impacts are wide-ranging. Insecurity can be experienced not only by those directly experiencing loss of life and property damage but also by those indirectly suffering psychological harm because of their constant uneasiness and fear of attack; for example, when intolerance-based violence occurs against a member of a foreign immigrant group, the other members of that group then live in fear, impeding efforts to integrate them successfully into mainstream society.[48] Perpetrators of intolerant brutality often frame fellow fighters as "underdogs," and this defensive frame may encourage and legitimize others to engage in violence,[49] by making it harder to distinguish malevolent initiators from innocent victims and to isolate and contain threat sources. When intolerance-based violence perpetrators realize that state apprehension, prosecution, and conviction of them for their crimes is challenging, because of scarce law enforcement resources, inadequate monitoring, or lack of concern by law enforcement officials with this type of brutality, they feel less constrained in launching future attacks; when intolerance-based violence victims realize that these perpetrators may escape punishment, injured parties are less likely to report such hate crimes and are more likely to live their lives dejectedly in constant fear of further violent assaults.

Facilitating intolerance-based violence's broad human insecurity impacts is the global spread of instruments of violence among the mass population. In the twenty-first century, for the first time since the emergence of the nation-state, private citizens have more military weapons than do national governments,[50] and this arms diffusion has amplified the potential for increased frequency and lethality of bottom-up violence. The spread of weapons across national boundaries has constituted a major security threat; given that globalized porous national borders prevent any weapons technology from remaining proprietary for very long, arms sold by states and nonstate groups have ominously spread far beyond national government armies and police forces to angry intolerant societal groups of all stripes.[51] Overall the combination of growing populations, intensifying interdependence, and advancing weapons and communications technology can be a "deadly mix," reducing the likelihood that existing conflicts can be kept nonviolent;[52] thanks to globalization-induced technological advances, now "we have to fear ever more remote and ever more lethal attacks from an ever wider array of ever less accountable people."[53]

Intolerance-based violence hurts most the security of foreign refugees fleeing from oppression. For those under duress just seeking a safe haven, things may go from bad to worse—the UN High Commissioner for Refugees stresses that "refugees who flee intolerance at home are increasingly finding more intolerance in the countries where they seek protection."[54] Those who have suffered in getting to their foreign destination may then be abused and mistreated once they arrive. Physically, many migrants have died traveling to or arriving at their destination because of exposure to harsh conditions, poor health, and little access to basic survival needs; psychologically, evidence has mounted about devastating mental health consequences from war and migration.[55] Only the hardiest persevere and make it through, and once they do, they start at the bottom, with few rights or privileges, high risk of natives' violence, and with the only jobs available being ones nobody wants. If migrants are undocumented, even the best state-promoted safety nets do not work well. Thus Human Rights Watch notes that intolerance-based violence can not only "result in deaths, serious injuries, mass displacement, and a range of other protection challenges" but also "prevent vulnerable individuals from seeking available services and protection—including education, medical care, food aid, and, for some, access to formal asylum procedures—for fear of being attacked at places where these services are offered."[56]

State Insecurity Impact

In September 2017, the U.S. Federal Bureau of Investigation (FBI) surprisingly assessed the societal threat of nationalist identity-based hate violence as being comparable to that posed by ISIS.[57] Some analysts have even suggested that the "new nationalism," nurtured by insecurity, fear, and hatred and emphasizing exclusion of outsiders, "will contribute to a wild, anarchic form of globalisation, characterised by violence and inequality."[58]

The spread of intolerance-based violence can reduce the state monopoly on the legitimate use of force by causing fearful citizens to turn to nonstate protection alternatives. Those who can afford it may turn to private security initiatives to promote their sense of safety, reducing reliance on the state to fulfill its most important obligation—protecting its citizenry—in the social contract between the rulers and the ruled. Such privatized security, including gated communities, may have arbitrary security limits and disregard for overarching national government rules and norms of engagement. Private security usually results in very uneven levels of community protection, translating economic inequality in the ability to purchase protection into social inequality.[59] Moreover, privatizing security can enhance tribalism and weaken individuals' feeling of mutual responsibility and of broader obligation to the greater community—reducing loyalty to the state and a sense of "nationhood"—because it causes people to focus more microcosmically on their own protection;[60] privately protected enclaves concern themselves only with the welfare of those in their in-group, and this narrowed security focus can increase suspicion about out-groups, lack of caring about their plight, and a breakdown of respect for governmental authority.[61] Besides hiring private security forces to protect themselves and their property, native citizens terrified of the immigrant threat may also form independent private vigilante groups to ensure that unsanctioned foreigners are cordoned off and do not interfere with natives' lives. When native citizens turn in the direction of either defensive private security contractors or offensive private vigilante groups, the security power of the state to control what goes on within its national borders is substantially diminished.

State insecurity about intolerance-based violence often leads to government attempts to restrict the entrance of foreign immigrants, inflaming divides among societal groups and irritating would-be migrants' countries of origin. For example, in the prelude to the 2015–2016 European refugee crisis, a 2012 public opinion poll showed that most French (64%), Belgian (62%), Italian (62%), Swedish (59%), Spanish (54%), and German (51%) citizens supported reintroducing of border controls;[62] Denmark enacted a law allowing the government to seize possessions from foreign migrants to compensate for the costs of them being in the country.[63] In many countries, awareness of border control difficulties can lead to more restrictive pressure—"scenes of rioting at borders, at train stations and at ports lead to more barbed wire, more attacks on refugees and more fodder for populist politicians."[64] Barriers to entry have been accelerating in both the Global North and the Global South; in the Global North, some wealthy states have built fortified boundaries to prevent the entrance of unwanted foreign migrants, often from Muslim states, and in the Global South, since early 2015 several countries have constructed or reinforced fortified boundaries, exemplified by Kenya on its border with Somalia and India on its border with Jammu and Kashmir.[65] However, while on the surface the most direct way to restore calm to a fearful society may seem to be reducing the influx of outsiders, states that do so face a "regulation-expectation paradox"—the more they attempt to regulate migrants' entrance, the more native citizens controversially believe that, with the right commitment, borders can be effectively controlled.[66]

State anti-immigration restrictions usually stimulate transnational criminal activity. Obstructing the flow of immigrants amplifies the monetary gains from smuggling and thus may "encourage rather than deter cross-border illicit ac-tivities."[67] So constraining undocumented migrant transfers presents a "terrible paradox": the more strictly states enforce national laws against this illicit activ-ity, the more criminals engaged in illicit human transfers choose to use extreme tactics to overcome existing barriers so as to make a profit.[68] Because of their high vulnerability, illegal migrants often become dependent on the services provided by criminal networks facilitating their cross-border transport, and then can coercively be induced to become part of these networks, engaging in protection rackets, money laundering, and turf wars as they occur.[69] Thanks to globalization, "migration mafia" can operate globally with no territorial limits whatsoever, unconfined by both political borders and geographical distance[70] as their smuggling operations reap payments from potential migrants for their transport to destination countries and sometimes for their jobs once they get there.[71] Cross-border migrant smuggling is becoming increasingly sophis-ticated and expensive.[72] This illicit activity flourishes because of low risks, as penalties tend to be minimal and enforcement tends to be lax:[73] porous global borders and high-volume international human traffic impedes its detection, as criminal smuggling operations are cleverer in avoiding border patrols than most migrants, and globally the punishment for human smuggling has been relatively lenient compared to that for smuggling narcotics.[74] For example, within Western Europe, greedy criminals have routinely promised desperate people forged papers and illegal transport to desired destinations and have caused "chaos and death on and within Europe's borders," a pattern avoidable if at least for a limited number of migrants more "open, safe, legal channels for people to move through" had been available.[75] Since the outset of the Syrian civil war, criminal black markets for Syrian passports have thrived in Croatia, Serbia, Hungary, and Austria.[76] Because most European countries do not allow many African migrants to enter, the only option for many of them has been to cross borders undercover with criminal help.[77] When Libya was the main departure point for African migrants going to Italy,[78] and Italy was the largest entry point for them to Europe,[79] criminal Libyan mafias were eager to provide transit to all who could pay to enter Europe illegally, reportedly upward of one hundred thousand Africans a year in 2018.[80] Back in April 2015, the EU adopted a plan calling for comprehensive efforts to capture and demolish smugglers' oceangoing vessels, but the scheme did not sufficiently take into account the desperation of those migrating, as poverty, oppression, and war have left many migrants "with no recourse but to flee."[81] So for most countries, government efforts to end criminal cross-border migrant smuggling have largely failed, highlighting the broader futility of state attempts at border closure.

Global Insecurity Impact

Perhaps the most globally dangerous insecurity outcome of intrasocietal intolerance-based violence is its contagion across countries. When violent incidents occur, fears of instability emerge among both native citizens and foreign migrants not only within the affected country but also indirectly in neighboring countries concerned about such coercive brutality's uncontrolled spread. Even if a society has no current or recent experience with intolerance-based violence, the presence of such violence in nearby states, highly publicized by sensationalist media, can easily trigger not only domestic insecurity fears but also citizen pressure on governments to take steps to prevent such forceful disruption from occurring at home. A 2019 *New York Times* study found that at least a third of the xenophobic and racist violence occurring since 2011 "was inspired by others who perpetuated similar attacks" in other locales.[82]

Violence linked to interdependence-induced migration thus can readily increase international insecurity. Globalist pressures make it harder to isolate or contain local disruptions or discriminatory incidents. In recent decades, internal conflict has usually involved neighboring states and undermined regional stability[83] because improvements in communication and transportation quickly alert foreign sympathizers with religious, ethnic, or national links to disgruntled societal groups. Afterward, such advances can help outside sympathizers find ways to try to respond and intervene. While national governments differ in their willingness to intervene when their citizens are mistreated in other countries,[84] oppressed migrant groups often have private ties with external supporters who may provide economic and sometimes even military aid to them. Today growing globalization and interdependence pressures, combined with rapid technological progress, "mean that instability, insecurity and terror are now more easily exported than ever before."[85] Because societies are more tightly interconnected but possess decidedly differing migration norms, each state finds it more difficult than in the past both to prevent its internal frictions from seeping across borders and to insulate itself from potentially destabilizing external turmoil.

4   Intolerance-Based Violence Cases

COMPARATIVE CASE STUDY ANALYSIS, detailing global intolerance-based violence between native citizens and foreign migrants in host states, illustrates the management challenges. Twelve cases are discussed in alphabetical order by the site of violence:

- Haitian Migrants in the Dominican Republic
- Sudanese Migrants in Egypt
- North African and Middle Eastern Migrants in Germany
- African and South Asian Migrants in Greece
- Muslim Migrants in Hungary
- African Migrants in Italy
- Burmese Migrants in Malaysia
- Sub-Saharan African Migrants in Morocco
- Central Asian Migrants in Russia
- Malawi, Mozambican, and Zimbabwean Migrants in South Africa
- Afghan, Sub-Saharan African, and Syrian Migrants in Turkey
- Hispanic and Muslim Migrants in the United States

These cases are geographically diverse, encompassing one in Central America, two in North Africa, one in northern Europe, two in southern Europe, one in Eastern Europe, one in Southeast Asia, one in central Asia, one in sub-Saharan Africa, one in the Middle East, and one in North America. The cases do not claim to comprehensively cover all twenty-first century global intolerance-based violence occurrences, and instead constitute a representative sample of incidents reflecting a continuing pattern of significant damage to persons and property. However, in choosing which cases to cover, great care has been taken not to include simply those displaying the most extreme carnage or those receiving the greatest global publicity, for "though the most visible and brutal of these attacks may make the news headlines, the large majority of cases of violent attacks and day-to-day physical and verbal harassment remain under the radar."[1]

Given the subjectivity of domestic intolerance-based violence between native citizens and foreign migrants, and the incompleteness of valid and reliable data available, the methodology used is comparative case study analysis rather than aggregate quantitative data analysis. The implications of this choice are that general conclusions reached are inescapably tentative. To maximize the potential for systematic comparative insights, each case discussion is structured in an identical way, encompassing five key components:

- Role of interdependence and roots of intolerance
- Nature of intolerance-based violence
- Security impact of intolerance-based violence
- Response to intolerance-based violence
- Lessons for managing intolerance-based violence

As long established by comparative case study methodology,[2] this parallel case treatment helps to highlight overarching patterns, consistent with this investigation's emphasis on unearthing broad trends rather than focusing on interesting but idiosyncratic details of each incident.

A key explanation of why each case analysis inevitably rests on somewhat sparse and fragmentary evidence is that national governments experiencing domestic intolerance-based violence are not eager to publicize or be transparent about what has occurred, even in some cases blocking access by those attempting to find out details about what transpired. Nonetheless, every effort is made to unearth multiple sources of information about key insights in order to increase the validity and reliability of findings and to draw more balanced and dispassionate conclusions about societal insecurity implications. Within each case, there is explicitly no attempt to make moral judgments about what is transpiring—to isolate whose behavior deserves the most criticism or the most praise—but rather simply to understand the causes, consequences, responses, and lessons associated with attitudes expressed and behaviors undertaken. Because determining ultimate culpability for violent native citizen–foreign migrant encounters can be complex, the focus here is less on whom to blame and more on how to minimize the likelihood of intolerance-based violence continuing in the future. As it turns out, many different completely disconnected societal sources, encompassing a wide variety of private citizen groups and national government agencies, have contributed directly or indirectly to the occurrence of intolerance-based violence.

Haitian Migrants in the Dominican Republic

An enduring pattern exists of Dominican exploitation of Haitian migrants, with the intolerance-based violence perpetrated by Dominicans against Haitians being both unrelenting and vicious. Transnational human rights groups have repeatedly accused the Dominican Republic of systematic abuse of Haitians, given the long legacy of Haitian migrants, refugees, and asylum seekers being victims of racist xenophobic attacks.[3] In addition, humanitarian organizations report that in recent years "tens of thousands of Haitians have been summarily expelled from the country by individuals and the government, forcing them to abandon loved ones, work and whatever money or possessions they might have."[4] Given the huge cultural and economic disparities between the two neighboring states, tolerant resolution of tensions face significant challenges.

Role of Interdependence and Roots of Intolerance

Interdependence plays an important role in intensifying the Dominican Republic's discriminatory policies and practices toward Haitian immigrants by facilitating Haitians' awareness of opportunities in the Dominican Republic and their ability to migrate there. Haitians constitute about 12 percent of the Dominican Republic's population, not counting the large number of undocumented illegal migrants,[5] and thus are a highly visible presence within Dominican society.

The two countries share the Caribbean island of Hispaniola, and Dominican-Haitian animosity has deep historical roots. In 1937, Rafael Trujillo, then the Dominican dictator, had around thirty-seven thousand Haitians executed in what historians have called "a ruthless campaign of ethnic cleansing"—because of the carnage, the river separating Haiti from the Dominican Republic is now called the "Massacre River."[6] This event caused the sharp division between the two countries to be "drawn in blood"; for Dominicans, this massacre confirmed that Haitians constituted "a long-term subversive outsider incompatible with what it means to be Dominicans."[7] So today many Dominicans label Haitian migrants as a national sovereignty threat,[8] and these natives even deny citizenship to most migrant children born in the Dominican Republic.

Intolerance by Dominicans against Haitian migrants has had multifaceted amplifiers. Regarding economic roots of tension, although both Haiti and the Dominican Republic are poor, Haiti's degree of destitution is far more severe, and so Haitian workers go to the Dominican Republic for jobs many locals reject, such as harvesting sugarcane.[9] The sugarcane industry has had a long tradition of relying on inexpensive Haitian migrant labor,[10] with Haitian workers subject to "quasi-slavery working conditions on sugar plantations."[11] In 2005, Mayor José Francisco Pérez of the Dominican town of Guatapanal—containing two thousand Haitians and only five hundred Dominicans—irritably called Haitians migrants there "an invasion":

> Area landowners stopped hiring Dominican workers for $10 a day because Haitians accepted less than half that, he said. "Now instead of hiring 40 Dominican workers for a field, they hire 400 Haitians, and the Dominicans are left with nothing," Mr. Pérez said. "There's too many Haitians. If the government is not going to help us get rid of them, then we will do it ourselves."[12]

Regarding cultural roots of tension, the intolerant remarks of Polivio Pérez Colon, one of the Dominican overseers who helped lead mobs attacking Haitians, shows the depth of the native resentment:

> "They are people who do not use bathrooms," he said, referring to Haitians, many of whom live in shacks without running water and electricity. "They walk around drinking and making a lot of noise at night. Sometimes the men dance with each other. It's not that they are all bad. But they have to submit to our way of life. If not, these problems will keep happening."[13]

Regarding racial roots of tension, exacerbating the intolerant reactions by Dominicans to the foreign migrants are the difference in physical appearance between Haitians and Dominicans: "Racism helps fuel the anti-immigrant sentiment, human rights groups say, since Haitians tend to have darker skin than Dominicans and are therefore often assumed to hold a lower social status."[14] Regarding religious roots of tension, in the Dominican Republic there is significant fear of voodoo-practicing Haitians.[15] Overall, the Dominicans "created a national identity that defined Dominicans as white, Catholic, and culturally Hispanic, in stark contrast to Haitians whom they characterized as being black, voodoo practitioners, and culturally African."[16] Finally, Dominican politicians' biased mass media coverage and nationalist speeches[17] have amplified existing cross-group tensions, where both leaders and the press characterize Haitians simply as a drain on limited Dominican resources.[18]

Nature of Intolerance-Based Violence

Within the Dominican Republic, Haitian refugees, migrants and stateless persons of Haitian descent have been brutalized and murdered, including "street attacks, arsons, and a beheading."[19] The perpetrators include private citizen groups who have undertaken "vigilante-style" revenge against Haitians in retaliation for alleged assaults[20] and state soldiers who have "rounded up thousands of people *en masse* on the basis of their 'Haitian' appearance and forcibly transported them over the border into Haiti, regardless of whether they had Dominican citizenship or were legal residents of the country."[21]

The twenty-first-century legacy of Dominican brutality against Haitians is extensive. In May 2005, after a Dominican woman was stabbed to death, Dominican mobs wreaked havoc beating Haitian migrants and setting their dwellings on fire, after which state police forced around two thousand Haitians to board buses headed for the border.[22] In August 2005, close to the Dominican capital Santo Domingo, four Haitians were covered with flammable liquid and set on fire, causing three to die.[23] In September 2005, in response to the killing of a Dominican worker allegedly by two black men, Dominican mobs systematically beat numerous Haitian migrant tobacco field workers in Guatapanal, causing over half of the town's Haitian workers to flee back across the border to Haiti.[24] In November 2008, in Neiba and Guayubín, a Dominican mob targeting Haitians killed at least two people and left many others severely injured.[25] In May 2009, a Haitian man was beheaded by an angry mob in Santo Domingo.[26] In October 2009, a group of armed assailants attacked and killed three Haitians, including two minors, who were preparing charcoal from illegally harvested trees near Jimani.[27] In January 2011, a three-year-old Haitian boy was killed in an arson attack on his family's house by a group of Dominicans.[28] In February 2015, Dominican police retrieved a dead Haitian man found hanging from a tree in a park in the city of Santiago.[29] In March 2018, in the border town of Pedernales, responding to a Dominican couple's murder allegedly committed by two Haitian brothers, some Dominican residents broadcast over loudspeakers mounted on a pickup truck that Haitians in the town should leave peacefully or face forced removal and return to Haiti.[30]

Security Impact of Intolerance-Based Violence

Mistreated Haitian immigrants have been utterly demoralized. Despite their contribution to the Dominican economy, their communities are culturally and economically marginalized:[31]

> "We do all the work, but we have no rights," said Victor Beltran, one of about 150 Haitian immigrants, most of them barefoot and dressed in rags, who had taken refuge in a rickety old barn. "We do all the work, but our children cannot go to school. We do all the work, but our women cannot go to the hospital. We do all the work," he said, "but we have to stay hidden in the shadows."[32]

Making these discriminatory practices worse is the reality that Haitian immigrants and their families are forced to live in a condition of "permanent illegality" because they find it impossible to acquire documents proving that they are employed or attend school or even in some cases that they were born in the Dominican Republic.[33] For decades, the Dominican national government has formally refused to give birth certificates to people of Haitian descent,[34] a severe human rights violation. Because of their vulnerability, sexual exploitation of Haitian migrant women is commonplace—"many young Haitian emigrants are sold into the sex slave trade within the Dominican Republic and are transported either somewhere on the island of Hispaniola, or are sold into sexual slavery as an export."[35]

Haitian migrants in the Dominican Republic serve as scapegoats for Dominican natives' troubles and as means of preserving a rigid status quo within the dominant society.[36] Although many Dominicans are not bigoted when it comes to foreign migrants, fervent nationalists have consistently pushed discriminatory treatment of Haitians.[37] Nonetheless, Haitians desperate to escape the abject poverty within their country say that they "have little choice but to accept Dominican exploitation."[38] Those impacted by the Dominican government's anti-Haitian measures often are "left in a state of statelessness" with "no home on either side of the island"[39] and "no legal access to work, education, basic services, or even minimal legal protections."[40]

Native Dominicans perceive that the massive Haitian immigration hurts them economically. Many Dominican workers "have been slowly pushed out of work by Haitian immigrants who will work for less, and so they are leaving their homeland in droves on rickety boats headed toward Puerto Rico, even though the Dominican Republic is one of the fastest growing economies in the

Caribbean."[41] These native workers see the employment situation as zero-sum, where employed migrants take jobs away from them and where compromise beneficial to both sides is impossible.

Response to Intolerance-Based Violence

The Dominican government has little incentive to do anything about the poor treatment of foreign Haitians within their borders, for the status quo predicament provides them with both flexibility and profits:

> "By keeping Haitians in a limbo of illegality, the government can do whatever they want with them," said the Rev. Regino Martínez Bretón of the Jesuit-run agency Solidaridad Fronteriza, in Dajabón, a city on the Dominican border. "The government can bring as many Haitians here as they want and then throw them away when they don't want them anymore."[42]

Although numerous Dominican political leaders have hypocritically promised progressive change, given that within the Dominican government "police and the military have made fortunes trafficking Haitians into the country to supply labor for agriculture and construction," independent human rights groups have confirmed that the plight of Haitian immigrants and their families has not improved over time,[43] even after the Inter-American Court of Human Rights ruled that the Dominican government's treatment of Haitian migrants and their descendants violated international human rights law.[44] If Dominican political leaders ever decided to earnestly try to address the Haitian migrant mistreatment problem, they would face key obstacles: the Dominican Republic possesses substandard political, economic, and social infrastructure that might otherwise be capable of managing the mass deportation and abuse of Haitian migrants,[45] and Dominican state officials defensively claim that their government struggles with inadequate resources to secure its porous borders and control the Haitian immigrant flow, which these officials "blame for rising crime rates and overburdened schools, hospitals and housing."[46] The Dominican government rarely investigates native attacks on Haitians thoroughly and impartially or holds accountable violence perpetrators.[47]

To protest Dominicans' violence committed against Haitian citizens, the Haitian government has tried temporarily recalling the leader of its diplomatic mission in the Dominican Republic,[48] but this move had little impact. Although the countries are next-door neighbors, it appears that Haiti has not been able to have much influence on Dominican Republic migration policies.

Lessons for Managing Intolerance-Based Violence

As with many foreign-migrant-dependent economies, the Dominican Republic has faced a "you cannot have your cake and eat it too" lesson. Long-term stability within a country seems incompatible with it having many foreign migrant agricultural workers with no rights or protection. The Dominican sugarcane industry's need for inexpensive Haitian workers does not mix well with widespread Dominican cultural condescension, hatred, and fear toward Haitians. Given that the Dominican Republic's economy is growing, it seems odd that the country cannot find a way to structure better employment opportunities for both native workers and Haitian migrants. Both the Dominican government and native citizens need to recognize better key trade-offs and to promote efforts to explore middle-ground economic solutions.

Moving from economics to culture, questions surround the feasibility and desirability of the Dominican society's implicit expectation that for Haitians to be accepted, they need to fit quickly and totally into the Dominican way of life. For this expectation to be realistic, the Dominican government needs to launch more extensive education and training programs for Haitian migrants to help them with acculturation. Moreover, given vast differences between Haitian and Dominican cultural norms, accepting some level of multiculturalism might be wiser than demanding immediate assimilation into native values and practices.

Lastly, the case shows that long-term contact, familiarity, interaction, and interdependence are not sufficient to foster meaningful mutual tolerance and cooperation. Indeed, "in the case of the Dominican Republic and Haiti, it is precisely their racial closeness [along with geographical proximity and high interaction] that exacerbates conflict."[49] Mutual respect and sensitivity have yet to emerge between the two countries' citizens.

Sudanese Migrants in Egypt

Mistreatment of Sudanese migrants is rampant in Egypt, as human rights organizations confirm that xenophobia, racism, and violence against refugees, asylum seekers, and migrants are widespread there.[50] Newcomers from Sudan, Somalia, Ethiopia, and Eritrea—where most Egyptian migrants originate aside from Iraq[51]—have been the main targets of native discrimination.[52] Moreover, illegitimate deportations from Egypt have been quite common; for example, between January and April 2017, Egyptian government officials deported at least fifty asylum seekers—including young children—from Eritrea, Ethiopia, and Sudan back to their home countries without any opportunity for legal representation or assistance from the UN High Commissioner for Refugees.[53]

Role of Interdependence and Roots of Intolerance

Interdependence and globalization have stimulated transportation and communication channels facilitating the large movement of people into Egypt, as either a final destination or a transit point to Europe. For decades sub-Saharan migrants fleeing from war or poverty have sought refuge in Egypt, and as a result in 2020 Egypt hosted more than six million migrants, over half of whom came from Sudan and South Sudan.[54] Only a small proportion of them registered as refugees with Office of the UN High Commissioner for Refugees.[55] Since 1956, when Egypt relinquished control over Sudan and the country become independent, the Sudanese people have been continuously engaged in civil wars that have caused "total economic and infrastructural collapse," causing millions to flee Sudan either as refugees seeking asylum from regime persecution or as economic migrants seeking a better life.[56] Meanwhile, Egyptian political, economic, and social instability hurts the plight of incoming Sudanese migrants[57] because "nationalism has the tendency to turn more xenophobic in moments of hardship."[58] As a poor country with few available jobs, Egypt has little capacity to absorb a large number of immigrants. As a result, relationships between native citizens and foreign migrants within Egypt have become quite strained.

Nature of Intolerance-Based Violence

Intolerance-based violence against foreign migrants within Egypt has been quite frequent. The forms of discrimination range from "harassment on the streets to extortion from landlords to poor treatment at hospitals" and include many violent attacks.[59] On December 30–31, 2005, Egyptian riot police in Cairo attacked a Sudanese migrant squatter camp of about two thousand people set up as a protest to press the UN High Commissioner for Refugees's Cairo office to approve better living allowances and relocation of migrants to another country, killing in what later became known as "the Mustapha Mahmoud Park Massacre" at least twenty-seven Sudanese (including seven small children) and wounding many others; then three days later the police released from detention camps the hundreds who survived onto the streets without any money or places to live.[60] Human Rights Watch reported in 2008 that Sudanese refugees and asylum seekers were often being subjected to abuse by Egyptians, with the mistreatment including violent physical assaults.[61] In June 2013, Egyptian violence against asylum seekers and refugees dramatically escalated. In one case, Ethiopian migrants were targeted after the Ethiopian government announced that it planned to divert the course of the Blue Nile and to start construction of the Great Renaissance Dam; the Egyptian media helped ignite this violence by framing Egypt's chronic water shortage as if it then faced "a severe water scarcity crisis."[62] Within Egypt, female migrants are particularly prone to be victims of violence, for "they suffer violence in their country of origin, on their journey through Egypt, and while residing in Egypt," with some refugees reporting incredibly that within Egypt "every Sudanese woman has witnessed rape or sexual ill-treatment."[63] In the Sinai Peninsula, there has been a substantial increase in the number of refugees who have been coerced into human trafficking or who have been victims of violent abuse.[64] In 2008, a year after Egypt and Israel signed an agreement to try to limit migrant flows, Egyptian forces killed at least thirty-three African migrants near the border during a seventeen-month span;[65] in November 2015, Egyptian forces murdered five illegal Sudanese migrants as they attempted to cross the borders between Egypt's Sinai and Israel;[66] and as of mid-2017, Egyptian coast guards had shot more than fifty migrants attempting to cross from Egypt into Israel."[67] Back in Cairo, on February 9, 2017, after an Egyptian man set a dog loose to attack Sudanese migrant children at a community-run refugee center, a South Sudanese teacher who protested was beaten to death by the xenophobe who released the dog, yet despite being apprehended and sentenced in 2018 to seven years the perpetrator never served any prison time.[68]

Security Impact of Intolerance-Based Violence

Within Egypt, foreign migrants continuously experience significant insecurity due to palpable native intolerance. Racism and xenophobia within the country are directed on a daily basis at foreigners, especially those from non-Arab countries.[69] The aggregate impact on Sudanese migrants has been devastating:

> Since 1997, only about 20,700 out of 67,000 migrants were granted refugee status in Egypt. Those awarded refugee-status were guaranteed immunity from the risk of arrest and deportation, but still faced a two-to-four year wait for resettlement, as well as a lack of access to basic rights and services. Only 14,300 of the 67,000 have been resettled so far. The rest of the Sudanese migrants, forced and voluntary alike, face ill-treatment, deportation and repeated threats against their safety.[70]

Sudanese refugees feel extremely marginalized and vulnerable in Egypt,[71] and they are often reluctant to report abuse to the police because of incomplete documentation or fear of reprisal.[72] These migrants have truly gone from the frying pan into the fire: "having escaped the 'most successful genocide in a century,' Sudanese refugees seek shelter in Egypt, only to find themselves the agonised victims of a modern-day, silenced apartheid"; they are "forced to endure the daily humiliation of street harassment, psychological abuse, and institutional neglect." They constantly hear racist epithets (Egyptians shun Sudanese with their darker skin color) because "racial discrimination and colorism are paradoxically ingrained in the collective consciousness" and are "a scapegoat for Egypt's economic downturns, as people often blame immigrants and refugees for the lack of jobs and inflation."[73] Because of widespread extreme discrimination and poverty, the suicide rate is extremely high among Sudanese migrants in Egypt, with two or three cases occurring each week.[74]

Response to Intolerance-Based Violence

The Egyptian government has been quite insensitive and uncaring in response to foreign migrants' plight. Human Rights Watch notes that foreign migrants in Egypt complain that "often police officials failed to protect them or were themselves the agents of violence."[75] Numerous reports indicate that refugees living in Cairo have faced more discrimination and less help from the authorities since President Hosni Mubarak's removal from power in 2011.[76] Egyptian authorities have also been criticized for failing to prosecute criminal traffickers who kidnapped, detained, and tortured African refugees and migrants, demanding ransom for them and in some instances harvesting their organs.[77] Private Egyptian citizens exhibit racism and xenophobia toward Sudanese migrants, and they say that Egyptian police are reluctant to provide them protection.[78] Government officials' unconcern is compounded by the reluctance of Sudanese and Somali victims, particularly women, to make complaints to the police after being brutalized, a pattern that is not surprising given that there have been many incidents of female migrants being sexually abused in Egyptian police stations and prisons.[79] Vividly demonstrating the lack of Egyptian government concern (or international community concern) about migrant safety in the country, in April 2016, a boat full of migrants capsized right off Egypt's Mediterranean coast, and over five hundred mostly East African men, women, and children died; following this tragic incident, nobody—not the Egyptian government, the

UN, the EU, NATO, or any maritime or police agencies—initiated any kind of official investigation to figure out how it happened.[80]

Although, in response to foreign migrant pressures, Egypt and Sudan signed an accord in 2004 permitting Sudanese migrants to enter Egypt without a visa or the need to seek refugee status, this accord failed to provide these migrants with access to education, employment, or health care, and in any case the Egyptian government never fully ratified it.[81] In 2004, the situation deteriorated after the UN High Commissioner for Refugees decided to cease granting refugee status to Sudanese migrants following a cease-fire between the Sudanese government and the Sudan People's Liberation Army; after the December 2005 park massacre, the predicament deteriorated further, as Sudanese migrants experienced increasing Egyptian government discrimination, deprived of social justice and subject to relatively random arrest and detention.[82] In May 2006, an obvious corrupt internal police investigation concluded that there had been "no wrongdoing on the part of the police" participating in the massacre.[83] Female migrants, despite stated legal and institutional Egyptian government guarantees purporting to protect them against violence, remain completely vulnerable and unprotected.[84]

In Sinai, despite visible mistreatment of foreign migrants, state neglect has persisted over time. The Egyptian government has consistently refused to intervene to enforce the law to deter future foreign migrant harassment, as no arrests or prosecutions have occurred so far regarding perpetrators of violence against migrants, and more broadly the Egyptian government has failed miserably in providing basic safety services to protect migrants and their property or in promoting any form of constructive communal conflict resolution.[85] However, one positive development is that, in response to the April 2016 migrant boat disaster, the Egyptian government finally decided to enact legislation to crack down on human smugglers responsible for the growing number of attempts by desperate migrants to cross the Mediterranean Sea.[86]

The Sudanese government has tried on its own to ameliorate the situation. In November 2015, the Sudanese embassy in Cairo submitted a memo to Egypt's Ministry of Foreign Affairs complaining about the mistreatment of Sudanese nationals in Egypt, specifically mentioning "a noticeable increase in abuses, including arbitrary arrests and stop-searches, against Sudanese nationals by Egyptian police and other security forces."[87] However, much like futile Haitian government efforts to try to change Dominican Republic migrant policies, despite this pointed Sudanese complaint, no change in Egyptian behavior followed. In both cases, the pleas of weaker countries with no tangible leverage are systematically ignored.

Lessons for Managing Intolerance-Based Violence

A key lesson from the Egyptian case is that if law enforcement authorities share the prejudicial sentiments of intolerance-based violence perpetrators, there is little hope for improving foreign migrants' plight. When regardless of established law, the police fail to protect foreign migrants or engage in their own harassment of migrants with impunity, then refugees, migrants, and asylum seekers become totally defenseless in their miserable experience of endless barbaric treatment by native citizens. It is abundantly clear that the Egyptian government considers discrimination and mistreatment of foreign migrants an extremely low-priority issue.

Another lesson is that combining racial hate-based bigotry with fear-based xenophobia is toxic, impeding restraint of violence against foreign migrants. Even though Egypt and Sudan share cultural and religious heritage and common Nile River basin management, racial and cultural differences between the two countries' populations have caused a deep and enduring split. The typical pattern of those with lighter skin oppressing those with darker skin is vividly evident in this case and directly increases intolerance-based violence.

A third lesson is that if a migrant-receiving country is beset by its own political, economic, and social problems obstructing the emergence of stability and prosperity, then it is less likely to be sympathetic or compassionate toward those fleeing from violence and instability in a neighboring country. Egypt has been unable to manage its own severe socioeconomic problems, so it is in no position to civilly integrate foreign refuges from neighboring states. Moreover, as with Haiti, if the government of a weaker state like Sudan protests mistreatment of its migrants abroad, then—even with existing international interdependencies among states in close geographical proximity—little meaningful change is likely to result. Thus despite hopes for mutual solidarity or compassion, migration from one poor Global South country to another may manifest the same indifference as migration from the Global South to the Global North.

North African and Middle Eastern Migrants in Germany

Because Germany took the lead in Western Europe, thanks to the efforts of Chancellor Angela Merkel, to initiate a policy of tolerance and inclusion toward foreigners by opening its doors in 2015 to asylum seekers and refugees, the world has watched closely to see the implications. Up to this point, the verdict has to be a negative one, with domestic intolerance-based tensions on the rise since that time. In many ways, for the rest of the world Germany has become a model of how not to deal with foreign migrant pressures.

Within Western European states more generally, since 2015 native-foreigner turmoil has increased, with growing incidents having racial or religious overtones.[88] Exemplifying this brutality, "boats of refugees are turned back to sea, refugee centers are set on fire, [and] politicians are violently attacked for supporting refugees."[89] Specifically, European assaults against foreign immigrants have been steadily rising. Yet despite such activity, a substantial number of members of the Organization for Security and Co-operation in Europe still lack explicit policy provisions defining bias as an "aggravating circumstance" with respect to intolerance-based attacks.[90]

Role of Interdependence and Roots of Intolerance

Interdependence played a key role in stimulating the European refugee crisis of 2015 to 2016 and in indirectly stimulating the nationalist and xenophobic backlash against foreigners in Germany. EU vice commissioner Frans Timmermans confirmed that "most of the approximately 2 million people who entered Europe in the great wave of 2015–2016 were not refugees but economic migrants seeking jobs,"[91] and this movement was directly stimulated by globalization-induced awareness of better opportunities elsewhere and by anticipated global mobility of labor. Since 2015, responding to Merkel's open-door policy, over a million migrants and refugees—many fleeing from war and persecution in Afghanistan, Iraq, and Syria—entered Germany.[92] Notably, most newcomers originated in Muslim-majority countries.[93]

Nature of Intolerance-Based Violence

Significant intolerance-based violence occurred on December 31, 2015, in Cologne[94]—one of Germany's most ethnically diverse cities, with over ten thousand refugees arriving in 2015—in the main train station and the nearby public square. There simmering tensions exploded after "scores of young women in Cologne had been groped and robbed on New Year's Eve by gangs of men described by the authorities as having 'a North African or Arabic' appearance."[95] The Cologne police said that they believed several hundred men, ages fifteen to thirty-five and visibly drunk, instigated the violence, about which the police received ninety complaints from victims, one of whom said she had been raped.[96]

In June 2016, a police report on the incident confirmed that most of the perpetrators were from North Africa and had just arrived in Germany during the European refugee crisis.[97] Having the perpetrators described "as young foreign men who spoke neither German nor English immediately stoked the debate over how to integrate such large numbers of migrants and focused new attention on how to deal with the influx of young, mostly Muslim men from more socially conservative cultures where women do not share the same freedoms and protections as men."[98] Having already been heavily criticized for failing to prepare for the social and economic costs of her migrant open-door policy, Merkel called the assaults "disgusting" and demanded a full investigation.[99]

The emotional reaction to the Cologne attack was growing intolerance by native Germans toward Arab Muslim immigrants from the Middle East and North Africa. Both German political authorities and German news media were accused of having tried to downplay or cover up the brutal attacks to prevent a violent backlash by native Germans against refugees.[100] Extremist German anti-immigrant groups were quick to condemn the assaults as proving the significant dangers of a large foreign migrant influx in Germany:

> "It is time to send a signal," said Christopher Freiherr von Mengersen, head of the nationalist Pro-NRW movement, based in the state of North Rhine-Westphalia. "We locals can no longer put up with everything that is being routinely swept under the rug based on a false sense of tolerance."[101]

Even more moderate Germans became concerned because of this incident that their government's openness to migrants came "at too high a price to social stability."[102]

The Cologne migrant attack on German citizens was not isolated. On the very same night, in Hamburg, Germany, the police said ten women reported that they were sexually assaulted and robbed in a similar fashion.[103] In October 2016, a seventeen-year-old Afghan migrant, who had arrived in Germany in November 2015, raped and murdered a nineteen-year-old female German university student in the southwestern German city of Freiburg.[104] On December 19, 2016, a Tunisian asylum seeker drove a truck through a bustling Christmas market in Berlin, killing twelve people and injuring forty-eight people.[105] In December 2017, a Sudanese migrant raped a German woman in the southwestern German town of Speyer.[106] On December 27, 2017, in Kandel—a quiet provincial town of about ten thousand in southwestern Germany—a teenage boy stabbed his ex-girlfriend in the heart with an eight-inch knife in a drugstore; the girl was a fifteen-year-old native German and the boy was an Afghan migrant.[107] In late May 2018, a twenty-year-old Iraqi asylum seeker, who had arrived in the country in October 2015, raped and strangled a fourteen-year-old German girl near Wiesbaden in southwestern Germany,[108] and on July 10, 2019, he was sentenced to life in prison for the crime with minimal chances for parole.[109]

In January 2018, the BBC reported that between 2015 and 2016, when Germany had welcomed foreign migrants during the European refugee crisis, police reported an increase of 10.4 percent in violent crimes in Germany; a German government study found that over 90 percent of this rise in violent crime was attributable to young male migrants, with migrants two times as likely to be reported for these crimes to the German police as were native citizens.[110] The data also revealed that foreign refugees with little chance of gaining asylum in Germany were far more likely to commit crimes than those from war zones certain of being granted asylum, with 17 percent of the crimes committed by North Africans, "who find out as soon as they arrive that they are totally undesirable" from the perspective of German citizens and the German government and have little chance of gaining legal status in Germany.[111]

German citizens have not remained passive in the face of foreign-migrant-initiated violence, and indeed both the far right and the far left there have retaliated, producing a decidedly insecurity-enhancing atmosphere within Germany:

> The country has faced a wave of xenophobic and anti-Muslim hate crimes, mostly by the far-right. There has also been a surge in violence by the far-left, most often directed at the police, security forces, and perceived rightwing extremists. Violence is increasingly accepted at the margins of German society.[112]

Over time, anti-immigrant assaults have been rising in Germany—in 2016 alone, over 3,500 were recorded, including 595 beatings and 116 arson attacks.[113]

A few examples of native German citizen coercion against foreign migrants illustrate this destabilizing clash. In mid-2015, eight native Germans believing in what was characterized as "xenophobic, extremist, and Nazi ideology" violently attacked asylum seekers and migrants in the town of Freital in eastern Germany.[114] On January 10, 2016, violent retaliation by German citizens to the Cologne attacks ensued quickly, as native citizens beat eleven foreigners—six

Pakistanis, three Guineans, and two Syrians—right near the area where the sexual assaults had occurred, with the beatings so severe that the victims needed to be hospitalized.[115] In July of that same year, in nearby Düsseldorf, a coercive citizen vigilante group was formed in reaction to the threat from foreigners, attracting over three thousand members within two days.[116] In the first half of 2017, German authorities reported 143 native attacks on asylum shelters and 642 attacks on refugees and asylum seekers outside their homes.[117] In early January 2019, in response to an alleged attack by four drunken Afghan and Iranian asylum seekers injuring twelve passersby in the Bavarian town of Amberg, a German far-right group launched a similar vigilante-style street patrol, accusing town authorities of failing to protect citizens living there; around the same time on New Year's Eve, a fifty-year-old unemployed German citizen launched a xenophobic attack by steering his car directly into a group of immigrants in Bottrop, Germany, killing four people and inciting panic among all those in his path.[118] In February 2020, an angry native German killed eleven immigrants in the western town of Hanau (near Frankfurt) after posting an extremist video on the Internet.[119]

Security Impact of Intolerance-Based Violence

The net social disruption of intolerance-based violence in Germany has been high. Moreover, the tensions initiated by the influx of foreigners have caused the country to be "deeply divided";[120] in 2019, "two decades after the country stopped defining citizenship exclusively by ancestral bloodline, the far right and others have started distinguishing between 'passport Germans' and 'bio-Germans'" as ethnic hatred and violence were rising.[121] As with elsewhere in Western Europe, even Merkel conceded that Germany has "high-crime, largely Muslim immigrant neighborhoods" where "state authorities fear to tread,"[122] and she simultaneously contended that multiculturalism is a "sham" and that refugees should quickly "assimilate to German values and culture."[123]

German citizens have responded to this disruption with shock and outrage. Myriam Kern, a former councilor for the right-wing Alternative for Germany party (AfD), voiced these concerns:

> Since Germany has been pursuing the policy of open borders that is illegal, against our constitution, against our law and order, we have massive problems, as we do not know who comes into this country. We are not in control. We have lost control. We do not know what identity, what people are coming here.[124]

In a similar vein, Rainer Wendt, head of the German police officers' union, expressed grave worries:

> "People feel that the state has lost control," Mr. Wendt said. "There are thousands of people in the country and we don't know who they are. That is an enormous security risk."[125]

As a result, intolerant populist influence—taking isolated violent acts and magnifying them—is rising.[126]

The growing psychological alarm among the German mass public has been quite heartfelt and has promoted insecurity. Resulting fears have induced many Germans to criticize their country's open-door policy toward migrants.[127] Indeed, "every transgression by a migrant gets disproportionate attention" and dramatically magnifies the uneasiness of native Germans having culturally dissimilar foreigners permanently reside in their country.[128] In the end, the noble 2015 experiment of a wealthy advanced industrial society enacting an open-door policy to a flood of quite dissimilar foreign migrants has dramatically decreased native citizens' sense of protection and well-being.

Response to Intolerance-Based Violence

Extremist voices have dominated the German state response to intolerance-based violence. Horst Seehofer, head of the Bavarian sister party to the chancellor's Christian Democratic Union, called for a cap of two hundred thousand refugees allowed into the country per year; the right-wing Christian Social Union in Bavaria demanded deportation of any asylum seekers found to be among the perpetrators in Cologne; and the left-leaning *Süddeutsche-Zeitung* echoed that sentiment, arguing that German law justifies such action.[129] Rainer Wendt, head of the German police officers' union, proposed improved border protection, illegal immigration prevention, and "a national offensive to deport more people who simply have no right to be here"—"the delinquents need to be the first ones that are sent home."[130] So on June 7, 2019, Germany passed a law facilitating the deportation of failed asylum seekers and expanding related police and immigration authority powers.[131] Although moderate voices have suggested more temperate options, national support for these has been tepid: for example, a 2018 German state-commissioned research report concluded that "the best chance of reducing violent crime among migrants was to offer more help with integration through language courses, sport and apprenticeships."[132]

Some German cities have taken matters into their own hands regarding anti-immigrant action. In 2017, the German cities Salzgitter, Delmenhorst, and Wilhelmshaven in the northern state of Lower Saxony issued immigrant bans, claiming that otherwise there would be insufficient resources to handle the number of migrants arriving; in January 2018, the German city of Cottbus, located 120 kilometers southeast of Berlin and host to three thousand migrants since 2015, issued a temporary ban on the entrance of refugees into the city after police arrested two male Syrian teenagers on suspicion of stabbing a German teenager in the face with a knife.[133] These independent urban initiatives, while accurately reflecting native citizen resentment and fear toward foreigners and growing countrywide dissatisfaction with Chancellor Merkel, can decrease overall societal stability, because one German city closing its doors to foreign migrants can simply put more pressure on other neighboring cities to accept them.

Lessons for Managing Intolerance-Based Violence

First, if a political leader implements open and receptive foreign migrant policies without first preparing the native population to receive and smoothly integrate them, then natives tend to vent their anger at both that leader and the foreign migrants. The German people have severely criticized Merkel following her open-door policy toward foreign migrants, and her political party has severely suffered as well. The perception of a foreigner-sympathetic government can also stimulate the formation of citizen vigilante groups, such as in Düsseldorf.

Second, the image of foreigners' threat may be far more important than its reality in triggering intolerance-based violence. Although within Germany overall violent crimes—including murder and rape—have been declining for a decade, every time a foreign migrant commits a crime it becomes "a fresh occasion for national hand-wringing"; according to Christian Pfeiffer, author of the 2018 German-government-sponsored violence report, "the paradox is that Germany is still a very safe country, much safer than even a few years ago," "but the perception is the opposite—people feel less safe."[134] So it becomes crucial to address native citizens' xenophobia and perceived loss of domestic control.

Third, a domestic violent action-reaction cycle reinforces scapegoating and negative stereotypes among both natives and foreigners. It is easier to fear and hate when the other group has just undertaken violence. In this pernicious tit-for-tat predicament, neither side asks itself if it did something that could legitimately provoke retaliation, ignoring past violent or intolerant acts it has committed. The result is "a worrying breakdown of civility and political discourse in an increasingly polarized Germany," where people "have lost the ability to respect one another."[135]

Finally, the relationship between a low probability for a migrant of receiving asylum and the high probability of that migrant engaging in violence toward natives needs greater recognition. If foreign migrants believed they could obtain asylum in a country with good behavior, then perhaps they would be more compliant and docile while waiting for the decision and pose less of a threat.

African and South Asian Migrants in Greece

In Greece, largely as a result of growing domestic economic frustrations, intolerance-based violence has recently escalated against foreign refugees, asylum seekers, and migrants, directed especially at nationals from Afghanistan, Iraq, Iran, Pakistan, Sudan, and Somalia.[136] As a country proud of its hospitality to foreign tourists, with the longest tradition of democracy and with visitors from all over the world coming to see its classical treasures, Greece has become decidedly inhospitable to foreigners seeking a permanent home; Human Rights Watch points out that "migrants and asylum seekers face a hostile environment, where they may be subject to detention in inhumane and degrading conditions, risk destitution, and xenophobic violence."[137]

Leading this intolerant charge in Greece has been the anti-immigrant group Golden Dawn (Chrysi Avgi). This notorious organization has engaged in physical attacks on migrants, destruction of their property, and verbal assaults mainly directed at "Muslim, non-white migrants of Asian, Middle Eastern, and African origin."[138] In June 2012, the Golden Dawn Party claimed eighteen of the Greek parliament's three hundred seats, and a week later fifty of its members riding motorcycles roared through Nikaia (a suburb of Athens) delivering an ultimatum to immigrant businesses:

> "They said: 'You're the cause of Greece's problems. You have seven days to close or we'll burn your shop—and we'll burn you,'" said Mohammed Irfan, a legal Pakistani immigrant who owns a hair salon and two other stores. When he called the police for help, he said, the officer who answered said they did not have time to come to the aid of immigrants like him.[139]

Since that time, Golden Dawn and its supporters have increasingly intimidated and undertaken violent acts toward foreign migrants, with "threats, beatings

and vows by Golden Dawn followers to 'rid the land of filth,'" becoming commonplace.[140] In 2018, Golden Dawn declared that "Islam is incapable of co-
existing with western culture."[141] Up until now, Greece's national government
has not engaged in effective interdiction or deterrence of this kind of private
vigilante violence, as the state appears to be content with just letting such brutality flourish because Golden Dawn's actions implicitly further unstated state
objectives.

Role of Interdependence and Roots of Intolerance

In 2010, Greece's national government announced a plan, approved by the
Greek parliament on June 29–30, 2011, to implement austerity measures to cut
public spending and raise taxes in exchange for an interdependence-induced
EU bailout addressing the severe Greek debt crisis. In early 2013, as a result
of such measures, the devastating impact was 27 percent unemployment and
a third of Greek citizens living below the poverty line, with more wage and
pension cuts yet to be implemented.[142] Indeed, "in Greece the homeless line up
at soup kitchens, pensioners commit suicide, the sick cannot get prescription
medicines, shops are shuttered, and scavengers pick through dustbins—conditions almost reminiscent of the 1940s."[143] In response to their misery, in January
of that year public outrage erupted in a series of bomb attacks targeting the
country's largest shopping mall, and government offices, banks, and journalists
defended state efforts to cope with the financial crisis.[144]

The root of Greek citizens' frustration has been largely economic, and globalization seems to have made matters worse. The Greek government ran up a
huge debt when the economy was strong at the start of the twenty-first century,
and then, when the 2008 recession hit, Greece suffered tremendously because
its two main industries—shipping and tourism—were highly sensitive to economic downturn. In the words of one protester, "those who govern are the ones
who brought this country into the crisis, and made people poor; we are from
two directly opposite worlds that will never stop clashing."[145] The combination
of poverty, social exclusion, and rising police brutality has made popular dissatisfaction inevitable.[146]

Meanwhile, in the midst of economic crisis, Greece was a major migrant
gateway to Europe, with tens of thousands of foreigners from Asia and Africa
moving into poor neighborhoods in the center of Athens and causing an emotional backlash from local residents.[147] In 2011, human rights groups estimated
that about five hundred thousand illegal immigrants were living in Greece.[148]

Given that Greek citizens feel overburdened by the government-imposed austerity program, many have chosen to vent their frustration on destitute foreign migrants from poor countries.[149]

Nature of Intolerance-Based Violence

Xenophobic Greeks have found an ideal scapegoat in foreigners for rising joblessness and crime:[150] Greece has recently experienced escalating native citizen violence against foreign migrants, amplified by the ruthless vigilante group Golden Dawn. Over time, popular support among Greek citizens for these brutal attacks on foreigners has been rising.[151] During 2018, for example, out of 117 incidents of racist violence in Greece with more than 130 victims, 74 involved migrant or refugee victims,[152] including "attacks on houses where foreigners resided, attacks on refugees' shops, and beatings and stabbings of refugees, asylum seekers, and migrants in the streets."[153]

The freedom felt by Greek natives to engage in such anti-migrant brutality appears to be increasing. In May 2009, after a march by Golden Dawn where supporters waved flags stating "foreigners mean crime" and "we have become foreigners in our own country,"[154] anti-immigrant demonstrators hurled stones and fireworks at a vacant eight-story Athens courthouse building, where mostly illegal migrants were living (five African migrants were injured) in terrible conditions surrounded by garbage and human waste with no power or water.[155] On May 10, 2011, after two Afghan migrants allegedly stabbed, robbed (stealing a camera), and killed Manolis Kantaris, a forty-four-year-old Greek man preparing to take his wife to a hospital in central Athens to have a baby, in direct retaliation gangs of Greeks converged on the area where it occurred, shouting "foreigners out" and "Greece is for Greeks," and they "indiscriminately attacked migrants and asylum seekers, chasing them through the streets, dragging them off buses, beating and stabbing them."[156] In the days following this violent action-reaction cycle, "ultranationalist mobs took to the streets in neighborhoods with large migrant populations and attacked more than 100 Asians and Africans; hundreds of youth wielding baseball bats reportedly chased, punched, and kicked foreigners; dozens of immigrant-owned shops were attacked or looted," injuring many people and killing a twenty-one-year-old Bangladeshi migrant.[157] On August 13, 2013, a mob of around twenty Greek men initiated a brutal knife attack on two Pakistani migrants on the island of Crete.[158] Beginning on Christmas 2017, in Piraeus (a port city near Athens), violence took place targeting over thirty homes over forty days where migrant workers—mostly from Pakistan—resided: native attackers broke glass windows, spray-painted anti-Muslim slogans on entrances and walls, and shouted nasty comments such as "you're dirty, leave our country" as they went about their destructive business.[159] The violence increasingly targeted Pakistani workers in areas around Athens, particularly in industrial Aspropyrgos—from August 2016 to August 2017, between seventy and eighty violent attacks targeting migrant workers occurred in that area.[160] In August 2018, Greek police inflicted a series of vicious beatings on migrants and asylum seekers—visibly evidenced afterward by prominent scars on their backs—illicitly attempting to enter the country from Turkey.[161]

Outside urban areas on the Greek mainland, the Greek islands appear to be a special vortex for intolerance-based violence. On April 22–23, 2018, on the Greek island of Lesbos, in response to about 200 Afghans camping for several days in a central square of the principal port city of Mytilenein order to protest both wretched living conditions in government-run camps and asylum application processing delays, anti-migrant Greek residents "pelted the migrants in the square with flares, firecrackers and stones broken off sidewalks, and some chanted 'burn them alive,' according to local news media."[162] Lesbos has for years been heavily overburdened by the refugee influx, being home to about 8,700 of the 60,000 largely African and Asian migrants living in Greek refugee camps; around 500 desperate new people arrived every week in 2018, dramatically exceeding the capacity of healthcare services and fostering considerable violence.[163] Given this exasperating volatile predicament, native tolerance reached a breaking point, and anti-immigrant groups exploited citizen resentment.[164] Roughly fifteen thousand migrants had to wait on the Greek islands, including Lesbos, Chios, Samos, Leros, and Kos, while their asylum claims were processed, and most of these newcomers ended up being trapped in overcrowded refugee camps with deteriorating living conditions, a predicament making both refugees and local residents increasingly frustrated.[165]

Security Impact of Intolerance-Based Violence

Intolerance-based violence in Greece directly promotes state insecurity. The combination of pervasive poverty among middle-class citizens, lower credibility among national government officials, and escalating intrasocietal violence jeopardizes the country's fragile political stability.[166] As of mid-2018, both Greek state officials and human rights groups agreed that tensions and the conflict potential are rising, especially on the eastern Aegean islands housing tens of thousands of refugees arriving via Turkey.[167]

Intolerance-based violence also increases the human insecurity of Greek citizens. Many members of the mass public feel unsafe because of the arrival of so many unexpected culturally different foreigners within a relatively short period of time:

> Gun shop owner John Poulakis is among those Greeks who blame rising job-lessness and crime on illegal immigrants. As a result, he says, everybody wants to have a gun. "Now you cannot walk in the night—people, they're scared," he says.[168]

Angry Greek citizens have demanded that the Greek government should "take the people [foreign migrants] somewhere else."[169] In parallel fashion, the presence of violent vigilante groups, especially Golden Dawn, roaming the streets can heighten both foreign migrants' and native citizens' apprehensions and insecurities.

Response to Intolerance-Based Violence

Despite repeated instances of Golden Dawn violence against foreigners, Greek government investigations and prosecutions of assaults against migrants have been rare.[170] After the May 2009 anti-migrant attack in Athens, a victimized Moroccan immigrant commented that in response "the police did nothing—here in Greece, human rights don't exist."[171] After the May 2011 anti-migrant attack in Athens, nobody was arrested, and some citizens blamed the foreign migrants themselves.[172] After the 2013 anti-migrant attack on Crete, often the police were found to be just standing around as the violence took place.[173] After the April 2018 anti-migrant attack on Lesbos, riot police waited several hours before intervening, then returning the migrants to their refugee camps and not charging anyone with a crime.[174] Human Rights Watch has accused the Greek state police of increasingly looking the other way when confronted with evidence of violence, and even just standing by during migrant beatings.[175] In March 2020, the *New York Times* revealed that the Greek government detained migrants incommunicado at a secret location before expelling them to Turkey without due process.[176] Three strategies have legitimized intolerance-based violence in the eyes of many Greek government officials: "denying the social or systemic nature of anti-migrant violence, based mainly on a narrative of

'isolated events' and doubting the truthfulness of claims of mistreatment; dis-
engaging violence against migrants from racism; and rationalizing violence as
a response to perceived threats posed by migration."[177]

Lessons for Managing Intolerance-Based Violence

A key lesson from the Greek case is that the combination of economic downturn and growing foreign migrant influx is toxic for intolerance-based violence. Regardless of the causes of the economic slump, having disgruntled native workers witness a flood of foreigners arriving right when locals are in dire
straits in terms of their finances and employment can be truly disheartening
and can serve as the last straw even for some moderate citizens. Thus the recent
emergence of mutual action-reaction cycles of violence is not surprising.

Second, the existence of an independent aggressive nationalist anti-immigrant
vigilante group, especially one politically legitimized by significant national
government representation, can make it much harder for any national political
leader to promote tolerance and compromise in native citizen–foreign migrant
relations. Golden Dawn has had a huge impact in Greece, with its efforts so
pervasive and well-organized that it can easily thwart any national government
effort at native-foreigner reconciliation. In a setting where citizens are already
angry at migrants, the state has every incentive to remain passive—as the Greek
government is—when migrant violence occurs, for the focus on vulnerable foreign migrants as a scapegoat for problems deflects attention away from citizens
realizing that the national government is a key culprit.

Muslim Migrants in Hungary

In response to the 2015–2016 European refugee crisis, Viktor Orbán, the prime
minister of Hungary, took the most hard-line stance on the continent. To divert foreign migrant flows, he had a barbed-wire fence built initially along
the 175-kilometer Serbian-Hungarian border, then later along the Croatian-
Hungarian border.[178] With his strong anti-immigrant sentiments, the erection
of this fence was just the most visible of many strategies to keep foreigners
away.[179] As a result, a "deep political divide" emerged between Hungary and
some of its EU allies, perhaps most notably Germany, due to fear that his extremist rhetoric and policies could sow such intense xenophobic hatred among
Europe's mass public that violence between native citizens and foreign migrants
could escalate.[180] This Hungarian antipathy has been most venomous regarding

foreign Muslim migrants; one native Hungarian shouted in support of excluding foreigners, "they are Muslims—they have no honour."[181]

Hungary's religious intolerance toward non-Christian foreigners reflects a broader European pattern. In September 2015, European political leaders in Hungary, Poland, Bulgaria, and Slovakia said "Christian refugees are more welcome than their Muslim counterparts."[182] In March 2018, Iceland announced it planned to ban circumcision of young boys, angering both Jews and Muslims.[183] Because of growing nationalism, banning the wearing of the burqa, a garment worn by Muslim women that covers the face and body, has become common. In April 2011, France banned its wearing in any public place, a ban upheld by the European Court of Human Rights in July 2014; in July 2011, Belgium followed suit; in May 2015, Holland approved a partial ban on face-covering Islamic veils on public transport and in public areas; in December 2016, Germany imposed a similar partial ban; in January 2017, Austria banned wearing of full-face veils in courts and in schools; and in May 2018, Denmark banned garments covering the face, including burqas.[184] Of course, discrimination against Muslims occurs outside Europe and the West—in July 2019, the Chinese government ordered Muslim restaurants and food stalls in Beijing to remove from their signs Arabic script and Islamic symbols as "part of an expanding national effort to 'Sinicize' its Muslim population."[185]

Role of Interdependence and Roots of Intolerance

Interdependence and globalization heighten for people not only awareness of opportunities abroad but also expectations about the possibilities of moving across boundaries, and this certainly has been true of foreign migrants seeking to traverse through Hungary to get to desired destinations in Western Europe. In early September 2015, thousands of angry migrants launched a protest against their detention in Budapest because they were thwarted in their earnest desire to continue their journey to Western Europe.[186] The underlying motive for most of the hundreds of thousands of foreign migrants risking their lives to travel to Hungary was finding a better future in Europe, pushed out of their own countries by the Arab Spring revolts and Middle Eastern civil wars.[187] Most of these migrants come from Afghanistan, and the rest come from Pakistan, Syria, Iraq, Iran, Egypt, and Lebanon.[188] Hungary is situated in a strategic corridor between Serbia and Austria, providing a convenient and popular entry point into Europe.[189] In his restrictive response to this foreign migrant pressure to enter his country, Prime Minister Orbán blatantly and intentionally thwarted the globalization-induced pressures of the EU. Currently around forty thousand Muslim migrants live in Hungary, many from Arab countries.[190]

Nature of Intolerance-Based Violence

Foreign migrants in Hungary have been regularly subject to considerable brutality, particularly within border areas. Over time, this violence against foreigners has intensified and become more humiliating.[191] This migrant insecurity predicament has been decidedly deteriorating, affecting even innocent children: what is officially termed "deep border control" has resulted in Hungarian border police often using barbaric forms of physical violence on refugees attempting to cross the border into Hungary, with the types of increasingly terrifying abuses reported ever more frequently by refugees including "the use of dog attacks, beatings, the use of pepper spray, and various other forms of humiliation and assault."[192]

Numerous recent anti-migrant violent incidents illustrate this pattern of degrading violence. In July 2016, Human Rights Watch reported that "people who cross into Hungary without permission, including women and children, have been viciously beaten and forced back across the border"; while callously "taking selfies and laughing" as they engaged in this brutality against foreign migrants, Hungarian border soldiers "often used spray that caused burning sensations to their eyes, set dogs on them, kicked and beat them with batons and fists, put plastic handcuffs on them and forced them through small openings in the razor wire fence, causing further injuries."[193] In September 2016, Amnesty International reported numerous cases of Hungarian authorities severely beating foreign migrants while these outsiders waited in Hungarian detention camps in the hope of gaining asylum,[194] with the outcome of this long and painful wait usually being "expulsion from Hungary without any individual investigation."[195] In spring 2017, Oxfam reported that Hungarian government officials were "alleged to have forced migrants to strip and sit in the snow as they poured water over them."[196] From January 2016 to February 2017, Médecins Sans Frontières confirmed the reported violence when its doctors treated 106 patients whom Hungarian border patrols had intentionally injured, including many with bruises from beatings, abrasions from dog bites, and skin irritation from tear gas and pepper spray.[197] In March 2017, the Hungarian newspaper *Magyar Nemzet* revealed that "contrary to the government's statements refuting allegations of abuse, more than 40 investigations had been launched into instances of excessive use of force by police at the border over period of 18 months," and "most of the investigations were closed without further action."[198] In 2018, Muslims praying at Hungary's largest mosque in Budapest were severely abused, with local citizens setting the Muslims' automobiles on fire in the midst of rowdy anti-migrant protests.[199] In May 2019, the UN highlighted the savage mistreatment of many migrants and asylum seekers in detention in transit zones, where for up to five days at a time they were "deliberately deprived of food, which can lead to malnutrition and is both detrimental to their health and inherently inhumane."[200]

Security Impact of Intolerance-Based Violence

Hungarian citizen fear and hatred of foreign migrants is now incredibly high. In the past decade, there has been a marked increase in anti-immigrant extreme-right political movements and xenophobic rhetoric in Hungary.[201] Compared to other European countries, Hungarians have extraordinarily deep and pervasive apprehensions about refugees—a 2016 Pew Research Center survey reported that 76 percent of Hungarians believe that hosting refugees raises the chances of terrorism, the highest rate among the ten states sampled.[202] When in 2017 a hotelier in Ocseny—a village of 2,300 people in southwest Hungary—offered a free holiday at his guesthouse to a group of refugees to show Hungarian hospitality and to demonstrate that refugees pose no danger, "a vicious public backlash" ensued, in which locals confronted him, "threatened to cut off his head," and actually slashed his car tires.[203]

For migrants themselves, humiliating brutality from Hungarian government officials and citizens is not the only indignity they suffer. An Oxfam representative notes that stories of violence against migrants have encouraged "desperate people to turn to people smugglers instead of attempting to use legal channels to claim asylum"; "the brutal illegal actions of law enforcement officials create a climate of fear among refugees and other migrants," and this extreme trepidation "pushes many to rely on smugglers to continue their journey to other places in Europe, which is very dangerous as it leaves already vulnerable people exposed to the criminal underbelly of trafficking and violence."[204] Ironically, migrants fleeing from horrific violence in their countries of origin often find themselves in Hungary unjustly experiencing even more brutality.[205] Muslim migrants currently living in Hungary feel absolutely terrified about their security plight, and in the future they fully expect their predicament to deteriorate even further; Sultan Sulok, the president of the Organization of Muslims in

Hungary, stated that some of the five hundred people who regularly gather for prayers on Fridays at Hungary's largest mosque in a suburb of Budapest "expect 'pogroms and killings' before the country's leadership reacts to increasing anti-Muslim sentiment."[206]

Response to Intolerance-Based Violence

No national government appears to care less about the plight of foreign migrants than that of Hungary. On multiple counts, the Hungarian government is flagrantly violating international human rights and refugee law and European Union–mandated asylum procedures; state officials persist in intentionally undermining such agreements and in failing to respect the dignity of migrants who should otherwise have a fair opportunity to make a case for asylum.[207] Although human rights groups have lodged many complaints about state police brutality against migrants, so far the effect has been negligible, with hardly any of the perpetrators of violence against migrants being apprehended and sentenced.[208]

Private vigilante groups have assisted government personnel in barbaric anti-migrant coercion. In 2016, Human Rights Watch reported that in the town of Asotthalom, local authorities established a Hungarian civil militia, "so-called field guards," to patrol sections of the Hungarian-Serbian border; these militia, equipped with camouflage uniforms, weapons, batons, torches, and gas spray, move about in vehicles with color and markings similar to those used by the Hungarian government police.[209] In May 2019, a far-right party in Hungary formed a uniformed "self-defense" force called the National Legion, with the anti-immigrant vigilantes focused on "guarding of traditions" of the country.[210]

The Hungarian government has recently doubled down on its anti-immigrant stance. The regime is clearly responsible for citizens' xenophobic upsurge, having initiated lavish anti-migrant advertising campaigns" claiming that "migrants rape, kill and multiply," with the prime minister describing them as "a 'poison' and the 'Trojan horse of terrorism.'"[211] In early September 2017, responding to an adverse ruling by the Court of Justice of the EU, Hungary's foreign minister, Péter Szijjártó, "angrily declared that 'politics has raped European law and values,' vowing that no one would be relocated to Hungary against its wishes."[212] In April 2018, after a strident anti-migrant campaign full of "intimidating and xenophobic rhetoric" fixating on his role as "the defender of Europe's traditional Christian identity" against "the phantom menace of Muslim migrants and refugees overwhelming Hungary," Viktor Orbán won a resounding reelection victory.[213] During the campaign, the local public television station focused on negative stories linking migrants to crime and terrorism, with a participating journalist noting the climate of fear created when "tolerance is regularly criticised, while anti-immigration sentiment is presented as the only valid opinion."[214] On July 18, 2018, Szijjártó announced Hungary's withdrawal from a new UN global agreement on migration designed to preserve migrants' human rights, joining the United States in refusing to comply.[215] Hungary's extreme anti-migrant stance runs the risk of alienating key allies, because to some European observers it "shames Europe and represents an attack on basic international asylum standards and human decency."[216]

Lessons for Managing Intolerance-Based Violence

One lesson from this case is that groups who earlier fought for their own freedom quickly forget and begin to oppress others. In retrospect, "it is particularly sad to see countries that so poignantly celebrated the lifting of the Iron Curtain now argue, as Hungary does, that being asked to take in a small number of Muslim immigrants is somehow a violation of European laws and values."[217] Moreover, Hungary's exclusionist approach to foreign migrants—in defiance of the EU—has been gaining greater traction among other Eastern European and central European leaders: for example, in January 2018, Austrian chancellor Sebastian Kurz said the EU's migrant distribution plan "isn't working" and jointly with Viktor Orbán called for "opposition to illegal migration to Europe."[218]

A second lesson is that closing one's borders to migrants may inadvertently increase the presence of unsavory criminal elements on one's border. As with elsewhere in the world, the ironic impact of enforced legislation barring immigration has been to increase the lucrative role that transnational criminal smugglers play in getting people into a country. Because such criminals may stimulate both corruption and violence within areas of operation, the threat they pose is not just to the human security of the foreigners who pay them to cross borders but also to the host state's security—especially to the integrity of key national government border guards—in attempting to keep migrants out.

African Migrants in Italy

In recent years, intolerance-based violence has emerged as a major problem for Italy. Having been (along with Greece) a major entrance point for migrants from Africa, and facing (as does Greece) major domestic economic challenges, during the European refugee crisis Italy felt overwhelmed by foreigners, causing tremendous native resentment. Within Italy, prejudice against foreign migrants has been steadily rising since the 2008 financial crisis, at least in part because Italy has only recently been emerging from a debilitating decade-long period of economic stagnation.[219]

Role of Interdependence and Roots of Intolerance

Italy's foreign migrants come from a wide range of countries, including Albania, China, Ghana, Egypt, Eritrea, Libya, Morocco, Nigeria, Romania, Senegal, and Somalia.[220] Since 2014, over six hundred thousand African migrants have migrated by boat to Italy.[221] Overall, nearly five million immigrants live legally in Italy (around 8 percent of the overall population); about one million irregular immigrants live and work in Italy; one out of eight newborns in Italy is the child of immigrants; and one out of fourteen students in Italian schools is of immigrant origin.[222] Many foreign migrants are miserable—at least ten thousand live in inhumane conditions, lacking adequate food, shelter, and medical care, with many of those employed able to find only seasonal agricultural work.[223]

Because of interdependence-induced migration, racism and xenophobia have mushroomed in Italy:

> "In Italy, xenophobia is growing exponentially," the director of the national anti-discrimination office at the ministry of equal opportunities, Luigi Manconi, told the *Guardian*.
>
> "In the background, there is an economic and social crisis where foreigners are perceived as the cause and, as a consequence, migrants become real scapegoats. It is a worrying phenomenon also because the institutions tend to feed it with knee-jerk reactions and irresponsible gestures."[224]

With a wave of anti-migrant fervor sweeping the country, many Italian natives now actually believe rather irrationally that a sharp reduction in foreign immigrants alone would dramatically improve their plight and that of their country. That xenophobic fear has lately translated into "spiraling hostility" toward outsiders.[225]

Nature of Intolerance-Based Violence

Between January 2007 and July 2009, there were 186 assaults in Italy, including 18 murders, allegedly motivated by racism or xenophobia, with immigrants and refugees the most frequent victims.[226] After the far-right Northern League formed a coalition with the anti-establishment Five Star Movement, the frequency of racially motivated attacks largely targeting foreign migrants tripled between 2017 and 2018.[227] Notably, Italian xenophobia against migrants—and tacit acceptance of anti-migrant violence—also comes from the center-left Partito Democratico (Democratic Party).[228]

Intolerance-based violence has become commonplace in Italy. Considering first attacks between 2008 and 2010,[229] in September 2008, a recent Burkina Faso migrant was bludgeoned to death on the street in Milan after a petty theft from a café; on January 25, 2009,a Moroccan migrant was killed by three Italians, with his body thrown into Lake Garda; in February 2009, a Senegalese migrant was verbally abused with racist epithets and beaten at a street market while he was in Rome buying a pair of jeans; in July 2009, a refugee from the Democratic Republic of Congo was attacked by two men armed with a bat and a knife while in Rome distributing flyers, with his attackers threatening to kill him saying "we're doing the will of the government . . . helping to chase out the Africans"; on January 7, 2010, a group of Italian men shot at two African seasonal migrant workers on their way back from work in the town of Rosarno, a small town in the southern region of Calabria, and eleven African migrant workers were injured in the mob attacks that followed; and in March 2010, Bengali migrants were assaulted by a group of 15 to 20 Italians in a bar in Rome, resulting in four people being injured and significant property damage. Since that time, this pattern of anti-migrant violence has continued unabated. In October 2013, a ship full of refugees capsized and sank in the central Mediterranean, killing 260 people—mostly Syrian refugees, among whom were 60 children; even though an Italian warship was close to the ship and had received numerous distress calls, it refused to help.[230] On February 3, 2018, an avowed neo-Nazi Italian injured five men and one woman of African origin in a shooting spree in Macerata, a small town in central Italy; when police arrested him, the perpetrator—motivated to undertake the violence because he heard that a Nigerian drug dealer was a suspect and had been arrested regarding the death of a native teenage girl—was "wrapped in an Italian flag, performing the Roman salute, and screaming 'Viva l'Italia.'"[231] On March 5, 2018, an Italian citizen fired six pistol shots at close range and killed a Senegalese street vendor while he was selling leather bags, umbrellas, and trinkets in Florence, one of Italy's most popular tourist destinations.[232] On February 24, 2019, in Naples, two Italian boys aged 10 and 13 pepper-sprayed a 51-year-old man from Benin; and in February 26, 2019, in Bari in southern Italy, Italian men and women kicked and punched a woman from Ivory Coast while shouting racist insults.[233] Among the sparks igniting vengeful potentially violent native anger against migrants are situations where foreigners are accused of committing dishonorable acts toward natives; for example, in October 2018, the Italian police arrested three migrants from Senegal and Nigeria—two of whom were in the country illegally, with the third having an expired residency permit—for drugging, gang-raping, and killing a 16-year-old Italian girl in Rome.[234]

Security Impact of Intolerance-Based Violence

Italian citizens have consistently feared the disruption to their lives emanating from foreign migrants. Despite evidence that immigration had not caused a rise in crime, a 2008 survey indicated that 60 percent of native Italians believed that immigrants posed a major security threat.[235] In 2012, 26 percent of Italians saw foreign immigrants as endangering personal safety and public order; and in September 2017, 46 percent of the public saw foreign migrants as a threat—66 percent among those with less education.[236] In early March 2018, the openly anti-immigration Northern League political party made huge gains in popular support, up a whopping 17 percentage points from the 2013 national election.[237]

Private vigilante groups have sprung up in recent years in response to foreign migrant fears. Back in 2008, private vigilante groups had been quite active in some Italian cities, endangering anyone who even looked like a foreigner.[238] In fall 2016, civilian vigilante patrols flourished in around twenty northern Italian towns whose frightened residents thought that state police were providing inadequate protection from allegedly dangerous foreign migrants.[239]

As one would expect, in Italy feelings of insecurity among foreign migrants in Italy—especially Africans—have escalated at the same time. Foreigners who had resided in Italy for decades now are scared that they will be lumped in with the new migrants, and they particularly worry that the reputation they worked hard to establish will be tarnished by unruly newcomers; for example, a migrant from Mauritius—who had worked in Milan as a concierge for eleven years—was anxious because now "people who have a different skin tone are all treated like we are all wretched and poor."[240] Reinforcing Italian natives' paranoid xenophobia and migrant fears has been the Italian mass media, tending to embellish the image of migrants as criminals and threats to society.[241]

Response to Intolerance-Based Violence

Human rights groups contend that the Italian government has not been doing enough to address intolerance-based violence.[242] When confronted with extreme anti-migrant xenophobia, most mainstream political parties have failed to condemn it as unacceptable.[243] In March 2011, Human Rights Watch accused the Italian government of "failure to identify racist and xenophobic violence as a serious issue," with prosecutions for such violence being quite rare.[244] Overall, national government law enforcement authorities have been prone to minimize the scope of intolerance-based violence in Italy, calling such incidents episodic and unusual.[245]

Although much violence against migrants in Italy is attributed to isolated deranged individuals, inhibiting a concerted government response, the February 3, 2018, attack suggests otherwise:

> While lone-actor terror is carried out by single individuals, it does not occur in a vacuum. The attack took place in a political landscape of heightened public anxiety, following widespread anti-immigration campaigns. The tepid political reactions to the attacks over the past week pushed immigration further to the forefront of the electoral debate, increasing the visibility of extreme-right propaganda, as well as the real danger of further violence.[246]

In Italy, most perpetrators who seem to act alone actually have ties to an array of disruptive groups.[247]

Compounding rampant Italian immigrant-protecting law enforcement problems has been a systematic pattern of incomplete data collection on intolerance-based violence and inadequate specialized training of law enforcement and judiciary personnel in investigating and prosecuting violence perpetrators.[248] The director of the Italian National Police Training Institute and the head of a major Italian police officers' union stated confidently that "racist and xenophobic violence is not a statistically significant problem within the country" because of the low volume of complaints received; however, that statement fails to consider common victim underreporting of intolerance crimes.[249]

Italy's government has been complicit in migrant mistreatment. In May 2009, the state unilaterally began to interdict boats full of migrants on the open ocean and return them to Libya, violating human rights and refugee law because of the lack of screening to determine who might be a valid refugee, or who might be sick or injured, pregnant, underage, or hapless victims of criminal smuggling operations.[250] In early 2017, Northern League party head Matteo Salvini, who was the de facto political leader in Italy, stated that irregular migrants should be rounded up and sent home "in 15 minutes"[251]—Italy requires "a mass cleansing, street by street, neighborhood by neighborhood, doing this the hard way if needed."[252] In mid-2018, Salvini—after becoming Italy's deputy prime minister and minister of the interior—asked the EU to "defend its border" against African migrants, not only blocking the arrival of humanitarian ship *Aquarius* full of 630 foreign migrants but also threatening to deny entry into Italian ports of private organizations saving migrants, violating humanitarian laws.[253]

These restrictive anti-migrant state actions promote human insecurity. Thousands more migrants, already facing truly treacherous travel conditions, could lose their lives attempting to make the perilous voyage across the Mediterranean; in 2017 Italy began training Libyans to stop migrants and return them to Libya, where they then suffer in detention "inhumane living conditions, including rape and torture."[254] Even foreigners who successfully enter Italy often end up living in miserable conditions equivalent to slavery.[255]

Lessons for Managing Intolerance-Based Violence

A first lesson from the Italy case is that if a national government is in a state of denial about the pervasiveness and severity of intolerance-based violence within its country's borders, then hope for effective management of the problem seems remote. Recognition of the true scope of a grave security disruption—particularly one like intolerance-based violence, which is often kept hidden by embarrassed national governments—seems an absolute prerequisite for finding effective and legitimate ways to minimize its occurrence.

Second, if a political leader like Salvini (and like Trump in the United States or Orbán in Hungary) rises to power in a migrant-receiving country with the top agenda item—emphasized both before and after political ascendancy—being undertaking anti-foreign-migrant national policies, then the likelihood of compromise or moderation seems remote. In other words, if populist anti-foreigner sentiment within a country is strong enough to support such political leaders' election, then extreme anti-migrant policies after assuming office unquestionably play to a highly sympathetic audience. Unsurprisingly, since Salvini's rise to power, xenophobia has been "growing more bold, widespread, and violent in Italy";[256] in the 2018 national elections, most of the parties campaigning, including the center left, have persisted in focusing on anti-immigrant sentiment as a means of attracting voters.[257]

Third, the absence of systematic, valid, and reliable data collection on intolerance-based violence incidents, along with a lack of special training for police in how to deal with such coercive situations, constitutes a key roadblock to managing successfully this important security threat. According to a Médecins Sans Frontières report, refugees and migrants in Italy are "living on the margins of society because of an inadequate reception system and harmful border policies,"[258] and thus they have little audible voice and few effective communication channels when it comes to pleading for progressive change in Italy's policies toward foreigners living in the country. With their current severe economic plight, native Italians would generally lack sympathetic ears for such foreign migrant pleas.

Burmese Migrants in Malaysia

In Malaysia, native citizens have become increasingly intolerant of foreign migrants, particularly those emanating from Burma/Myanmar. This intolerance has been so severe that it has led to anti-migrant violence initiated by both a government-hired private security contractor and native citizens operating independently.[259] Over time, foreign migrants have been targets for a growing campaign of "harassment, arrest, whippings, imprisonment and deportation."[260]

Role of Interdependence and Roots of Intolerance

Interdependence and globalization has helped to flood Malaysia with foreign migrants, because in addition to domestic employers many multinational corporations have found Malaysia to be an attractive manufacturing site because of the availability of cheap labor and a stable business climate. Over the past quarter century, the number of foreign migrant workers in Malaysia has grown by an astounding 340 percent.[261] Today Malaysia's foreign migrants constitute about half of construction workers and 60 percent of manufacturing workers, and nearly 40 percent lack any formal education.[262] The "pull" element of job availability for foreign workers has been readily apparent. Most of these foreign migrants come from Burma and Indonesia, with others coming from Bangladesh, Nepal, Cambodia, Sri Lanka, Somalia, Iraq, and Afghanistan.[263] Over four million undocumented foreign migrants work in Malaysia—most newcomers arrive legally but then later become undocumented, at least in part because many employers staunchly refuse to renew their work permits.[264] While in 2017 the Myanmar embassy estimated that four hundred thousand Myanmar migrant workers were in Malaysia, more reliable estimates suggest that number is closer to between five hundred thousand and seven hundred thousand, and many lack legal documentation.[265] The large proportion of undocumented Myanmar migrants has increased their vulnerability to native citizen abuse. Outside of exploitation due to global economic competitiveness, having Myanmar be primarily a Buddhist country and Malaysia being primarily Muslim makes matters worse, inflaming native-migrant religious antagonisms.

Nature of Intolerance-Based Violence

Native citizen violence against Burmese migrants in Malaysia is well-documented. Between June 2013 and September 2014, twenty-five Myanmar migrant workers were killed, reflecting nonstop brutality against the newcomers.[266] By early 2017, facing a growing cycle of brutality in Malaysia were hundreds of thousands of Buddhist migrant workers.[267]

In 2005, the Malaysian government converted an anti-communist civilian self-defense force begun in the 1960s into the private security contractor Ikatan Relawan Rakyat Malaysia (RELA), empowered to catch illegal immigrants.[268] Since then, RELA committed many migrant atrocities:

> RELA's approach is particularly problematic, consisting of crude profiling based on apparent race or ethnicity, and a general attitude of "arrest now, investigate later." These largely untrained RELA agents frequently subject the people they arrest to humiliation, physical abuse, theft and extortion. Amnesty International heard many accounts that reinforced the conclusion that RELA agents are often more interested in illicit personal gain, through any means available to them, than in carrying out a legitimate immigration enforcement role.[269]

RELA members as young as sixteen engaged in illegitimate extortion, detention, beatings, canings, rape, and theft.[270] In one such case, an assault on a Burmese national with a club left the victim blinded.[271] Although in August 2010 Amnesty International stated that "RELA agents are responsible for the most rampant human rights abuses against migrants and refugees in Malaysia," in that same month RELA's director-general announced a plan to expand its membership from 1.6 million to 2.6 million by the end of the year.[272] However, in April 2012, the Malaysian state curtailed RELA's powers because of alleged crimes and excessive use of force.[273]

Ordinary native citizens have also committed violence against Burmese migrants. In April 2008, native assailants stabbed, set on fire, and killed a Burmese refugee.[274] On September 14, 2014, natives killed two Burmese migrant workers in Penang.[275] In June 2016, masked Malaysian men riding motorcycles stabbed three Myanmar migrants in Penang; on October 25, 2016, Malaysians kidnapped, killed, and dismembered four migrants in Kota Bahru; and in early January 2017, a Malaysian mob in the Serdang district near Kuala Lumpur killed five and critically injured two Myanmar migrant workers.[276]

Security Impact of Intolerance-Based Violence

Foreign migrants' security plight in Malaysia has been truly miserable, as they find it extremely difficult to find safe refuge. Undocumented foreign migrants especially face truly untenable employment conditions. Migrants work hard for extended hours with little pay, often have no access to schooling or health care, and are constantly subject to locals' intimidation; in Kuala Lumpur, the capital city, where many migrant workers put in fourteen-to-fifteen-hour work shifts and live in unsanitary conditions in worker hostels, natives regularly beat and rob them as they walk home at night.[277] In 2015, the Nepali government reported that 461 Nepali workers in Malaysia died because of substandard working conditions, occupational stress, and inadequate health care.[278] Migrant women have been especially harassed, with rampant gender-based violence particularly occurring against vulnerable refugee women;[279] often they have to surrender their passports to employers, impeding their ability to leave if they are mistreated, sometimes they are forcibly trapped in their workplaces without adequate food, and employers verbally and physically molest—including sexually abuse—them.[280] Among Burmese migrants suffering are the Rohingya, an ethnic Muslim minority fleeing genocide in Buddhist-majority Myanmar only to face mistreatment—often committed by transnational smugglers—in their newfound home.[281]

Malaysian citizens' discrimination toward migrants perpetuates this abuse. The International Labour Organization notes that "scapegoating of migrants, regardless of the realities, has contributed to an environment where exploitation and abuse are sometimes viewed as acceptable"; Malaysian natives often think each foreign migrant comes just to take their food, money, and position and thus treat each foreigner "like a second-class person."[282] Human Rights First says "racial and ethnic prejudices, along with other issues such as an increase in competition for jobs, have given rise in recent years to distinct xenophobic attitudes among certain segments of the society toward refugees and migrants."[283]

For native Malaysians, the basis for this prejudice against foreign migrants is both economic and cultural. The Malaysian economy's heavy reliance on undocumented foreign migrants hurts native workers. Even this dependence remains high for menial jobs because locals tend to shun this kind of work,[284] and native workers still resent displacement by undocumented foreigners. The exploitation of migrant workers directly affects the job market for native Malaysians:

> If employers can easily hire migrant workers with no-to-low labour protection, thus saving them various costs, migrant workers will always be the preferred choice when it comes to hiring. This scenario creates a situation of competition to the bottom in our local job market, with Malaysians having to either lower our own demands or risk unemployment especially for those at the bottom of the employment ladder. Ultimately, this competition to the bottom will affect everyone.[285]

For many Malaysian employers, costs associated with recruiting documented workers are unaffordable[286] because of fierce global competition for their products and services. As in Haiti, this economic predicament leaves both foreign and native workers poorer and mutually resentful. Yet the stark reality is that having so many migrant workers from Myanmar in Malaysia benefits both countries—the Malaysian economy can flourish as a key center for global production, and the Myanmar economy is buoyed by remittances that Myanmar migrants send back to family members living in their home country.[287]

Response to Intolerance-Based Violence

In reaction to the huge influx of foreign migrants, the Malaysian government has done little to enhance their security after they arrive. Because the Malaysian government refuses to protect or provide education for foreign migrants, their only work option is often "finding odd jobs in the informal sectors as cleaners, waiters or construction workers."[288] Malaysian labor laws exclude migrant domestic workers from humane benefits such as a weekly day of rest, annual leave, and working-hours limits.[289] The pervasiveness of migrant workers' physical and psychological abuse in Malaysia clearly reflects an officially sanctioned work environment norm denying basic human rights.[290] Amnesty International points out that "Malaysia effectively maintains that refugees and asylum-seekers do not exist in the country—there is currently no legislative or administrative framework for dealing with refugees, and Malaysian law makes no distinction between refugees, asylum-seekers and irregular migrants."[291] Moreover, because Malaysia is not a signatory to the 1951 UN Refugee Convention, technically the country views all refugees as illegal migrants awaiting resettlement elsewhere.[292] The absence of any state protection amplifies migrant workers' vulnerability to exploitation.[293]

In terms of shielding foreign migrants from intolerance-based violence, the Malaysian government record is abysmal. Malaysia consistently fails to protect Burmese migrant workers from violent attacks, reflecting a basic inability or unwillingness to hold citizens accountable for this unjustified brutality.[294] Even when blatant attacks occur on foreign migrants, such as the June and October 2016 incidents, the state police have not arrested anyone responsible for the violence.[295] Government police, whom some migrant workers describe as "robbers in uniform," do not do much to ensure the safety of foreign migrants, and especially undocumented migrants are terrified of state police because law enforcement officers may beat them up for bribes.[296] Having even government immigration agents exhibit routine corruption and readily take such bribes[297] contributes to the perpetuation of discrimination, xenophobia, and harassment in Malaysia. Moreover, Human Rights First notes that the high frequency of government crackdowns against migrants has discouraged migrant victims of violence from reporting abuse "for fear of deportation or other reprisals."[298] In 2015 to 2016, 118 foreign migrants—of whom 63 were from Myanmar—died in Malaysian government detention camps due to abuse and poor conditions.[299]

In December 2016, Myanmar took concrete steps to attempt to ban its workers from going to Malaysia. Myanmar's deputy director general of the Ministry of Labour, Immigration and Population said that "there are several reasons for the ban on Myanmar migrant workers going to Malaysia, including security concerns and the fact that they are trying to stir up political troubles against Myanmar," but with few employment opportunities in Myanmar, these warnings were unlikely to deter migrants from crossing into Malaysia.[300] Notably, in April 2019, it was reported that "while Myanmar used to send 3,000 to 4,000 workers to Malaysia each month, it is now sending 5,000," and the abuse of these migrants continues.[301]

Lessons for Managing Intolerance-Based Violence

If a national government does not care about refugee or migrant rights and allows a private security contractor with little restriction on its freedom of action to deal with illegal migrants, the situation becomes very dire for foreign newcomers. Violence and brutality will almost certainly ensue, with the state's hiring of a private contractor symptomatic of government willingness to turn a blind eye to any abuses committed against vulnerable refugees and migrants.

When much of the discrimination, mistreatment, and violence against foreign refugees and migrants takes place within private corporate workplace environments, as happens in Malaysia, it appears even more difficult for successful public abuse exposure or sound remedial policies to emerge. Effective regular monitoring by even a concerned government would thus be difficult, and huge disincentives—with both their job and their ability to stay in the country in jeopardy—would exist for migrant workers to report this abuse. Further inhibiting such reporting and subsequent corrective action is migrants' knowledge that government officials and corporate executives tend to be corrupt and respond more to monetary bribes than to any sense of justice.

When a country is a massive exporter of finished products to the rest of the world, as is the case with Malaysia, having the cheapest labor and the fewest workers' rights protections can be a boon within a highly competitive global business environment in attracting more foreign firms to invest in one's society. So strong interdependence-related economic incentives would generally keep the Malaysian government unwilling to intervene and improve the predicament for foreign migrant workers, as cracking down on foreign migrant abuse and guaranteeing migrant workers' basic rights could generate massive global economic costs for the country. Malaysia is not alone in having economic profits decisively outweigh humanitarian concerns regardless of domestic or global outcry. Nonetheless, some observers feel that "if the country wants to continue to attract foreign migrants" for its workforce, "it needs to stop the violence."[302]

Sub-Saharan African Migrants In Morocco

Thanks to a formal series of twenty-first-century agreements with the EU, Morocco's status for migrants has been altered. Over the last decade and a half, with the EU tightening its border controls and externalizing the responsibility for keeping migrants away, Médecins Sans Frontières notes that Morocco has transformed "from being just a transit country for migrants en route to Europe to being both a transit and destination country by default."[303] Once migrants enter Morocco, they find themselves trapped, unable to go to Europe or to return to their countries of origin,[304] as they begin to see entering Europe as nearly impossible and returning home as shameful and dangerous.[305] The EU-Morocco agreements to strengthen border security have proven to be quite lucrative; in 2006 alone, the Moroccan regime received $80 million from the EU for this task, with France, Italy, and Spain especially eager to seal the border.[306] In 2015, with EU funding, Morocco built a nine-meter-high razor-wire fence and deep trench at the border to Melilla, a minuscule Spanish enclave on

Morocco's North African coast.[307] While migrants used to see Morocco as a gateway to Europe, now the country has transformed into one of Europe's gate-keepers; most outsiders now view the country as an "'outsourced' gendarme for southern Europe,"[308] with EU-Morocco collusion representing the latest version of "the neocolonialist outsourcing of border and migration controls from Europe to countries in Africa."[309]

Role of Interdependence and Roots of Intolerance

Morocco requires cordial relations with Europe because of interdependence; many Moroccans live within Europe, and Morocco relies heavily on European tourism and trade, especially in agricultural exports.[310] Although the presumed general thrust of interdependence is to facilitate cross-border interaction, Morocco's arrangement with the EU was explicitly designed to block migrants' free movement across national boundaries. However, regardless of the strength of the fortified barriers erected between Morocco and Western Europe, foreign migrants' struggle to escape from poverty and oppression at home seems likely to continue unabated, and thus the most immediate effect of the concerted attempt to prevent their border crossing seems likely to be more frequent and severe migrant injuries and fatalities, "deaths that lie in the hands of the EU and its member states."[311] Notably, in reaching the Moroccan agreements, the EU did not show the slightest interest in addressing root causes of the problem—the abysmal conditions in home states causing inhabitants to become desperate to leave.

Migrants to Morocco come from many countries, including Cameroon, the Central African Republic, the Democratic Republic of Congo, Guinea, the Ivory Coast, Mali, Nigeria, Senegal, and Sierra Leone, with growing numbers from Iraq.[312] About seventy thousand sub-Saharans live in Morocco, a country of around thirty-five million people; twelve thousand to fifteen thousand illegal sub-Saharan migrants reside there, with around 30 percent of all young people in the country unemployed.[313] Closure of other migration transit zones has intensified migration pressures in Morocco to get to nearby Spain; Greece and Italy had been the major entry points for migrants to get to Europe, but when these were shut down, foreigners began to focus on Spain as the entry point, and by October 2018, the number of undocumented African migrants arriving in Spain surged to 40,623, making it the top entry point that year.[314]

Nature of Intolerance-Based Violence

The legacy of violence against migrants in Morocco is quite extensive. In 2005, the Moroccan police shot dead at least five migrants in a mass attempt by them to scale barriers and enter Melilla.[315] In March 2009, three Moroccan natives insulted and attacked a registered refugee on the street, with no following prosecutorial action.[316] In June 2009, a female Congolese refugee participating in a protest about miserable living conditions in Morocco had stones thrown at her as she walked down the street.[317] In March 2010, a UN High Commissioner for Refugees report noted that many refugees in Morocco "had been subject to racist and xenophobic attitudes and in some cases had been victims of theft and physical aggression by local delinquent groups."[318] In summer 2012, for the first time since the 2005 attempt, a large number of African migrants attempted simultaneously to cross the border fences into Melilla, and Moroccan security forces and the Spanish Guardia Civil responded with brutality and excessive violence.[319] In 2014, rising tensions between native citizens and foreign migrants led to the killing of a Senegalese student in Tangier.[320] In early February 2015, Moroccan police raided a migrants' camp near the border with Melilla, "destroying and burning their camp and belongings, and detaining over 1200 people including children," who were later summarily dumped outside the cities of Rabat, Fes, and Casablanca.[321] In July 2015, Moroccan police evicted foreign migrants from the Boukhalef district of the port city of Tangier, killing one and seriously injuring another while forcibly rounding them up regardless of their refugee or asylum status and placing them on buses headed south to Rabat and Taroudant.[322] In June and July 2018, a widespread brutal Moroccan government crackdown against sub-Saharan migrants intensified after at least six hundred migrants successfully crossed to the Spanish enclave of Ceuta in northern Morocco; migrants affected were forcibly loaded onto buses with just the clothes they were wearing, and then faced arrest, relocation to remote areas in Morocco hundreds of miles to the south, or expulsion from Morocco.[323] These raids, publicly acknowledged by Moroccan government officials, were explicitly coordinated with Spain and the EU to prevent migrants from coming to Europe.[324]

Sub-Saharan migrants are the special target of Moroccan violence. These beleaguered asylum seekers encounter verbal threats and physical attacks[325] daily, leading them to live in a continual state of terror.[326] Several human rights organizations have identified Morocco as a notorious site for violence against refugees, asylum seekers, and migrants,[327] noting the focused targeting of sub-Saharan African refugees and migrants with racist harassment and random physical assaults.[328] Since the beginning of this Moroccan crackdown, about 6,500 migrants have been arrested and displaced, and over 91 expelled; many sub-Saharans are now terrified about possible arrest and displacement, living in fear even when they stay at home.[329]

For these sub-Saharan migrants, the mistreatment experienced seems to have no bounds. Since December 2011, Médecins Sans Frontières observed that Moroccan and Spanish security forces have dramatically increased their abuse and violence toward Moroccan migrants; egged on by European states, especially the Spanish government, the barbaric raids on sub-Saharan migrant communities in Morocco have escalated, heightening these migrants' profound insecurity.[330] Even before arriving in Morocco, most migrants experience severe physical and psychological trauma during their journeys; in a 2013 Médecins Sans Frontières survey of sub-Saharan migrants in Morocco, 63 percent of those interviewed said they had experienced violence, and three-quarters of those had experienced multiple episodes of violence.[331] Once in Morocco, violence against women—rape and other forms of sexual violence—is a huge problem, with about one-third of migrant women living in Morocco reporting severe abuse on their way to North Africa.[332] Migrants and refugees to Morocco have to contend with the anxiety of endless waiting while living in abject poverty,[333] and meanwhile they are exposed not only to state-initiated violence but also to criminal gang violence.[334] Moreover, the police often rob the migrants of whatever they have.[335] In spring 2018, when twenty-five-year-old Guinean Mamadou Sidy Diallo failed in his attempt with a friend to escape from Morocco by scaling a fence and entering Melilla, he was left "in the clutches of traffickers who tortured him and left him for dead on a trash pile—'four days of sexual, physical, mental violence—they tortured us to the point of death,' said Diallo, 'it's a miracle that I'm still breathing'" (his friend died).[336]

Native Moroccan citizens' anti-foreigner hostility has ballooned over time. Many migrants report that they appear in public only in groups to prevent attacks:

> "Even when you're at work, your heart isn't at peace," said a 39-year-old woman from the Ivory Coast, who gave only her first name, Pelagie. "Our kids are terrorized. We can't even go out to food shop without the fear of getting mugged."[337]

Thus harassed migrants in Morocco cannot find any kind of safe haven, and many feel forced to hide in the bush, "living like animals" without any rights or protection whatsoever.[338]

Security Impact of Intolerance-Based Violence
Having so many foreign migrants is in Morocco highly tension-inducing. Native Moroccans tend to scapegoat foreign migrants for any problems, especially crime and unemployment.[339] This resentment exists in an enduring hostile

context where "sub-Saharan Africans have never been welcomed by native Moroccans, who see them as soaking up state benefits in a country that struggles to provide jobs and health care for its citizens."[340] The hostility persists in part because native Moroccans have limited social interaction with foreign migrants, causing the natives to lump all sub-Saharan migrants together using simple stereotypes, seeing men as diseased criminals and women as sex workers.[341]

The vulnerability of sub-Saharan migrants in Morocco seems to grow the longer they stay in the country.[342] As a result, Médecins Sans Frontières notes that the "disparity between the expectations of a better life and the reality of their situation in Morocco can cause psychological shock and trauma for many migrants"; when sub-Saharan migrants realize that they are stuck in Morocco without basic survival needs, they experience "intense feelings of helplessness, guilt, anguish, failure and frustration," and being constantly subjected to discrimination and integration barriers "due to their race, gender, legal status, appearance or cultural and social practices can severely undermine their mental health."[343] Moreover, with all sub-Saharan migrants technically classified as illegal, most live in constant fear of arrest, expulsion, exploitation, abuse, and violence committed by Moroccan security forces, human smuggling networks, and native xenophobes.[344]

Foreign migrants are appalled at their inhumane treatment. For example, a female migrant in a makeshift Moroccan refugee camp stated that "the Moroccans see us like sheep—they do not accept foreigners" and "there is no work or security for us in this country";[345] a Nigerian migrant remarked that the Moroccans think "they can do whatever they want to us"—"the police rip off our identity cards and arrest us and people hold their noses when they see us."[346] Despite widespread rumors of extreme mistreatment in Morocco, most incoming migrants are unprepared for the horrors they encounter.

Response to Intolerance-Based Violence

The Moroccan government has turned a blind eye to foreign migrants' miserable plight. In an August 2010 report by the Moroccan human rights organization Groupe Antiraciste de Defense et d'Accompagnement des Etrangers et Migrants (GADEM), victims of intolerance-based violence reported being met with little or no assistance when they told police about their abuse, or being threatened with *refoulement*(forcible return of individuals back to a country where they risk serious human rights violations). GADEM noted that since 2006, it had "registered testimonies of numerous persons who have been attacked without the possibility of being protected by the law being offered, because of their legal status or because of the simple fact that the competent authorities (police or military police) do not register their complaints."[347] As Médecins Sans Frontières points out, perpetrators of violence against foreign migrants feel safe on two counts:(1) the "vast majority of sub-Saharan migrants who are beaten, abused, raped and attacked will not seek medical help, protection or justice due to fear of arrest or other repercussions," and (2) most violence initiators, especially human smugglers, "are able to act with impunity knowing that their victims are viewed as 'illegal' or 'criminals' by the Moroccan state and will receive no protection."[348] Even among the Moroccan state authorities themselves, high levels of impunity exist for migrant abuses they commit.[349]

The Moroccan government exhibits hypocrisy in response to the foreign migrant dilemma. King Mohammed VI of Morocco has made public pronouncements consistently welcoming sub-Saharan Africans,[350] and he endeavors to project to the rest of the world an image of being a moderate, tolerant, and progressive leader. However, the on-the-ground situation differs; a thirty-six-year-old Ivory Coast migrant notes "there is a big difference between the official discourse and the reality—we see that the king wants us to have our rights, but it's not always easy with the authorities here."[351] Despite publicly proclaimed support, the king may simply intend migration in Morocco to serve as "a lever to pry concessions out of Europe."[352]

Lessons for Managing Intolerance-Based Violence

With the sub-Saharan migrants' Moroccan predicament dismal, and the EU countries ignoring the abuse as long as Morocco prevents these migrants from crossing their borders, little hope exists to address the widespread intolerance-based violence. Although the EU has praised Morocco for its efforts to prevent sub-Saharan migrants from entering the continent, migrant advocates contend that Morocco is intentionally hiding serious persistent problems.[353] Over time, EU officials tend to "avert their eyes from the human rights violations committed by state authorities," especially against sub-Saharan communities in Morocco, to the extent that many observers doubt that EU states care at all about civil society and sub-Saharan integration in Morocco.[354] Despite lofty rhetoric, the EU clearly prioritizes keeping refugees and migrants away over protecting their lives and well-being, and Moroccan government brutality clearly occurs "with the support and sponsorship of the European Union."[355] So the broader

lesson here is that just because countries espousing enlightened liberal internationalist values enter into an agreement with an authoritarian regime about
foreign migrant treatment, this does not mean in any way that migrant lives are
likely to improve in the slightest.

Neither Morocco's government nor its citizens have made the adjustments
necessary for a stable sustainable societal outcome to accommodate having foreign migrants stay long-term rather than just using the country as a transit
point. In 2012, an Oxford migration expert remarked, "Morocco has to deal
with the reality that there are more migrants who are not just transiting but who
are settling in the country."[356] Repeated government raids on foreign migrant
camps are certainly unlikely to provide any kind of durable solution. What is
most needed—and what appears to be least likely to occur—is a long-term Moroccan plan for coping in a humane way with a potentially permanent rather
than temporary presence within their society of a large number of foreigners—
most of whom are racially and culturally quite different from native citizens.

The highly restrictive and oppressive Moroccan policy toward foreign
migrants has opened the door to the pervasive operations of both local and
transnational criminal smugglers. Tighter border controls seem to have had
"the paradoxical effect of increasing the market for smugglers and traffickers
who the European Union has tried to eradicate but who are ever more involved
in the migration process; the difficulties in reaching Europe from Africa now
mean that it is almost impossible to undertake the journey without the assistance of a smuggler or trafficker, and the demands of these traffickers are thus
more onerous for the migrants, creating further sources of insecurity."[357] Criminal smuggling operations care neither about the foreign migrants transported
nor the national government preferences of the country to which they bring the
migrants, being concerned only about profiting from human misery. So today
smuggling and human trafficking networks increasingly endanger the lives of
foreign migrants already in great peril.[358] So from an EU perspective, while
the Moroccan pacts have succeeded in keeping out foreign migrants, they have
abysmally failed in attracting in transnational criminal smugglers.

Lastly, the migrant predicament in Morocco is dramatically worsened because racial discrimination against sub-Saharan Africans in Morocco—common in North Africa, as the Egypt case indicates—compounds native Moroccan resentment of foreign migrants due to high unemployment rates. Indeed,
Moroccan and Spanish media have extensively reported on the "Peril Noir"
(Black Danger) associated with thousands of sub-Saharan Africans flooding

into Europe.[359] The combination of pressures from the EU to keep migrants from crossing over to that continent and severe racial discrimination toward migrants from native Moroccans makes many sub-Saharan Africans feel totally worthless. In addition to the dominant racial component, a religious divide exacerbates the problem, because the Islamic Moroccan government falsely believes that all foreign migrants are Christian and thus fears their influence.[360] Unless the Moroccan economy gets back on its feet, the condescension, discrimination, mistreatment, and violence seem likely to continue.

Central Asian Migrants in Russia

Russia is in a peculiar position when it comes to foreign migrants. Officially, unlike many countries in the covered cases, it welcomes them with open arms because it desperately needs their labor. Unofficially, however, both the Russian government and the Russian people exhibit huge discrimination and mistreatment regarding foreign migrants. This rhetoric-reality contradiction—quite parallel to that in the Moroccan case—makes monitoring major policy change and undertaking significant constructive policy reform quite difficult, and it leaves the foreign migrants themselves somewhat befuddled.

Role of Interdependence and Roots of Intolerance

Russia is home to almost 12 million foreign migrants (the world's third-largest foreign-born population), many lacking visas, constituting roughly 15 percent of the Russian workforce.[361] Within Moscow, Muslims are the fastest-growing group—overall, Russia's Muslim population is now over 20 million, and it is expected to be almost 20 percent of Russia's population by 2030.[362] Refugees and asylum seekers in Russia mostly emanate from largely Muslim central Asian countries;[363] over three million migrants—mostly illegal—from Uzbekistan, Tajikistan, and Kyrgyzstan work in the Moscow metropolitan area."[364] Other migrants come from Georgia, Afghanistan, Iraq, and various African states.[365] Most central Asian migrants come into Russia with the hope that they will "make money and solve the financial problems of their families, relatives, and friends."[366] Because the native Russian population is decreasing—by 2050 it is estimated to decrease by 30 million, to 112 million—the Russian national government acknowledges the need to attract foreign workers,[367] especially those willing to do municipal services such as street cleaning that are shunned by natives, and that "the immigrant economy is very much part of its recovery from a prolonged recession."[368] However, state recognition of the benefits of interdependence on foreign countries for migrant workers to assist in resuscitating the Russian economy is not widely shared within the native Russian workforce.

Nature of Intolerance-Based Violence

The frequency of intolerance-based violence in Russia has changed over time. Earlier in the twenty-first century, neo-Nazi skinhead groups within the country had regularly undertaken violent attacks on migrants "with an alarming frequency";[369] in 2007, the number of violent attacks on nonwhite foreigners in Russia had skyrocketed up to about five killed each month,[370] and between 2004 and 2012, native intolerance-based attacks killed 556 people, with 3,507 people beaten or wounded—220 of those murdered and 568 of those injured were central Asian migrants."[371] However, in recent years, the intolerance-based violence numbers have appeared to decline: in 2016 there were just forty-eight attacks within Russia on "ethnic outsiders," in 2017 just twenty-eight such attacks, and in 2018 just twenty such attacks.[372] The recent violence targets are largely migrants from central Asian countries, even though some unruly perpetrators target indiscriminately anyone they encounter looking non-Slavic.[373]

This violence tends to be committed by a small subsection of society—mostly young males—even though underlying xenophobic attitudes are much more widespread.[374] A major brutality case occurred late 2010 on the always busy Moscow subway, where in broad daylight local Russians assaulted several central Asian migrant workers:

> In mid-December 2010, ultranationalist groups were able to quickly mobilize thousands of supporters to spread xenophobic rhetoric and rally in downtown areas. The police were late in responding to the riots, characterized by numerous racist attacks on innocent by-passers on the subway and elsewhere in the city. President Medvedev and Prime Minister Putin reacted with strong condemnation of both the attacks and the unrest, yet their calls did not lead to arrests or concrete improvements, thereby further reinforcing impunity.[375]

The rhetoric-reality gap evident here seems all too common when dealing with state responses to intolerance-based violence. On January 13, 2011, six young natives assaulted a Congolese migrant near a metro exit in Moscow, with police patrolling the area choosing not to interfere with the attack, which the victim claimed was racially motivated.[376] On March 2, 2011, in St. Petersburg, a native Russian killed a twenty-eight-year-old Tajikistan migrant, who was stabbed repeatedly in the head, neck, and stomach.[377] In mid-October 2013, in the worst ethnic disturbance in Moscow in three years, Russian police rounded up more than 1,600 migrants in Moscow after natives in a southern neighborhood rioted because of a fatal stabbing of a Russian blamed by many residents on a migrant man from the Caucasus region.[378] Afterward, migrants from Russia's mainly Muslim Caucasus region and from central Asia were placed on alert because of the increased risk of attacks.[379] In December 2017, a group of young Russians carrying nunchaku and a knife entered a train at the Technological Institute station in St. Petersburg and beat up two passengers whose appearance was non-Slavic, pushing one of them out onto the platform while shouting, "The car for Russians!"[380] In June 2018, three Internet videos appeared as part of the "white car" campaign (attacks in commuter train cars against migrants from central Asia or the Caucasus), and the videos graphically depicted groups of young Russians beating up commuter train passengers who did not look Slavic.[381] In many cases, central Asian migrants appear to be "soft targets" for violence, for they may fatalistically "see being covered in bruises as an inescapable side-effect of living in Russia."[382]

Central Asian migrants themselves sometimes undertake violence in Russia, occasionally fostering violent action-reaction cycles. Jihadists have recruited central Asians after they leave their home countries, part of a general pattern in which violent politically motivated extremist groups target and recruit foreign migrants in Russia.[383] Violent migrant political disruptions include the June 2016 Ataturk airport bombing, the January 2017 Istanbul nightclub attack, and the April 2017 St. Petersburg metro bombing.[384] As to nonpolitical migrant-initiated violence, on March 17, 2019, after a female resident of Yakutsk in Siberia was kidnapped and raped, three migrants allegedly from Kyrgyzstan became suspects, and one of them was detained.[385] The causes of migrant-initiated violence include social isolation, poor working conditions, economic hardships, and discriminatory abuse.[386] However, there may be exaggeration of the level of violent extremism among central Asian migrants in Russia—radicalization of central Asian migrants there may be occurring only on a relatively small scale,[387] suggested by the relatively low frequency of recent violent terrorist attacks involving central Asian labor migrants in Russia.[388]

Security Impact of Intolerance-Based Violence

Despite Russia's avowed need for foreign migrants, populist anti-immigrant sentiments are commonplace among native citizens, who believe foreigners steal their jobs, and so state police raids at work sites occur with great regularity.[389] Many Russians fear that eventually migrants will take over not only their employment but also their towns and their country as a whole.[390] The most xenophobic native Russians tend to be from the traditionally dominant ethnic groups—Russians, Ukrainians, and Belarusians—and counterintuitively also tend to be higher-income Russians.[391] Russian media commentators have been known to "let rip about the threat migrants [pose] to the health, security and cultural identity of the nation"; on November 4, 2011, when Russia officially celebrated National Unity Day, at least seven thousand Muscovites including skinheads in masks chanted racist slogans and blamed the weakest social group—the foreign migrants—for their problems.[392]

Recent public opinion polls in Russia confirm this native intolerance of outsiders. In 2011, almost half of Moscow's citizens were anti-immigration, and many said that they "would like to see all migrants forcibly deported," with a particular focus on Muslim migrants as a threat.[393] About half of Russian citizens polled before the 2014 war with Ukraine said they wanted to restrict immigrants from the Caucasus and central Asia, and in 2017 an even higher proportion—66 percent—supported tighter immigration controls.[394] A 2018 Pew Charitable Trust survey revealed that Russians have become "increasingly intolerant of the newcomers," with nearly 70 percent of Russian natives feeling that their country in the future should allow in fewer or no migrants.[395]

Of all foreigners in Russia, central Asians are by far the greatest targets of discrimination, mistreatment, and violence. Because most of Russia's lowest-paid workers come from poor central Asian countries (with Uzbeks being the largest group), and because both Russian government officials and private citizens associate central Asian migrants with criminal activity, these newcomers become "the most visible targets of anti-immigrant vitriol."[396] Amplifying natives' resentment of central Asian migrants is the reality that these newcomers tend to work outdoors and thus are highly visible.[397] Central Asian laborers in Russia struggle daily to survive given their exceedingly low pay and the discrimination and harassment they face from natives; many migrants hear false promises about prospects for legal Russian residency, with those lacking Russian language skills or formal education most likely to be violence victims.[398] Central Asian migrants suffer continuing threats, and they fear for their lives and their health and well-being from not only extremist private Russian citizens but also state law enforcement officials:[399]

> These largely poor and uneducated Central Asians will accept menial, low-paid jobs that Muscovites don't want to do—slaving on construction sites, sweeping

streets and hauling heavy loads at city superstores and markets. Once citizens of the same country bonded by a shared language and communist ideology, Central Asian migrants now live on the fringes of Russian society, hounded by police, exploited by employers and increasingly disliked by much of the population.[400]

During frequent construction site raids by migration and counterterrorism police units, central Asian migrants are often subject to police abuse.[401] These migrants face special challenges with legal registration, making it more likely that they will be classified as illegal, economically exploited, socially marginalized, and framed as terrorists by the press.[402]

Response to Intolerance-Based Violence

As is typical of authoritarian regimes, the Russian government does not acknowledge its domestic intolerance of foreigners, instead sweeping the issue under the rug. Instead, the Russian regime promotes xenophobic nationalism to deflect citizen attention away from domestic problems such as economic stagnation or inequality.[403] Compounding this responsibility deflection is violence victims' reluctance to report incidents; unless native citizens' attacks on central Asian migrants lead to death or serious injury, these newcomers rarely report such incidents to the police,[404] and violence perpetrators thus feel empowered by this hesitancy.

Since the St. Petersburg Metro attack on April 3, 2017, where a twenty-two-year-old Kyrgyzstan migrant killed fourteen people and injured fifty-one others,[405] law enforcement agencies have become more wary about migrants[406] and more concerned with monitoring and controlling their behavior than with respecting their rights. Moreover, while Moscow courts are overwhelmed with migrant abuse cases, few end with migrant-favorable settlements.[407] On February 13, 2013, in response to native xenophobia, Russian government officials announced the creation of a private anti-migrant network serving as a "volunteer brigade" to catch illegal migrants.[408]

Lessons for Managing Intolerance-Based Violence

As in the case of Malaysia, state recognition of dependence on foreign workers does not necessarily lead to better migrant treatment. Although Russia does have an unambiguous need for foreign migrant workers, central Asian workers also depend on Russia for stable employment, and so the Russian government does not feel constrained by its economic needs to change its behavior. Further-more, the refusal of the Russian regime to acknowledge mistreatment of foreign migrants, combined with their reluctance to report crimes against them, makes feasible remedial solutions really unlikely.

Having the highly nationalistic leader Vladimir Putin has tacitly given li-cense for ultranationalist nativist and xenophobic groups in Russia to be more vocal. The Russian regime is notorious for being skeptical of any international agreement unfairly tying its hands, and certainly under Putin it has pursued Russian power above all else. If challenges to Russian authority come from for-eign migrants, the Russian government implicitly counts on Russian national-ists' support to assert hegemonic control.

The combination of socioeconomic insufficiencies, racial differences, edu-cational deficits, and language variances place central Asian migrants in Russia in a distinctly vulnerable and disadvantageous position. The action-reaction cycle of central Asian migrant violence with the Russian government serves only to increase native support for legitimate Russian government discrimina-tion against them. However, by downplaying societal oppression of migrants, the Russian government risks the possibility of extremist Islamist indoctri-nation inducing religious radicalization and anti-regime political sentiments among Muslim central Asian migrants.[409]

Malawi, Mozambican, and Zimbabwean Migrants in South Africa

In the twenty-first century, native South African citizens have displayed signifi-cant violence toward foreign migrants. In a country best known for rejecting apartheid through the inspired leadership of Nelson Mandela, this intolerance is particularly troubling.[410]

Role of Interdependence and Roots of Intolerance

Interdependence-induced immigration into South Africa is a key root of con-tinuing intolerance there. In 2015, South Africa had about two million docu-mented and undocumented immigrants—largely from Zimbabwe, Mozam-bique, Lesotho, Nigeria, and Somalia[411]—representing about 4 percent of the total population of the country.[412] By far the largest proportion of refugees, asy-lum seekers, and migrants in South Africa comes from neighboring Zimbabwe, with one to three million Zimbabweans living in South Africa.[413] After Man-dela became president in 1994, refugees from other countries in Africa fleeing from oppression and conflict saw South Africa as a beacon of hope.[414]

Nonetheless, foreign migrants entering South Africa encounter a society-wide backlash:

> The health minister claims they crowd hospitals. The largest opposition party promises to secure the borders against them. Police stop them at random, demanding to see their IDs. And sometimes their own neighbors violently turn against them, looting their shops, stabbing them in the street, and even burning them alive.[415]

The South African government's xenophobic strategy of "demonizing and excluding foreigners in the interest of political stability and unity" instead has backfired and "created pockets of insecurity and alienation that threaten its efforts at national consolidation."[416] In 2006, a Southern African Migration Programme (SAMP) xenophobia survey confirmed that, compared to people in other parts of the world, "South Africans are the least open to outsiders and advocate the greatest restrictions on immigration."[417] Given that South Africa is a leading travel spot for wealthy Africans because of its developed infrastructure[418] and extensive global ties, the severe foreigner intolerance becomes considerably more visible and irritating. Because of globalization-induced awareness about rising nationalism within the United States and the United Kingdom, native intolerance of foreign migrants in South Africa has recently worsened.[419]

Nature of Intolerance-Based Violence

Having many foreign migrants enter an already violent society can be truly toxic. South Africa's troubled historical legacy involves a "culture of violence," where brutality is viewed as an acceptable means of resolving conflicts.[420] Economic insecurity causes mostly black South Africans to assault black African migrants, with "the vulnerable attacking the most vulnerable."[421]

In 2008, South African xenophobic violence hit a boiling point. On May 11, 2008, native South Africans beat, stabbed, and set on fire a Mozambican national, Ernesto Alfabeto Nhamuave, and this barbaric killing triggered a series of violent assaults against foreign migrants in South Africa.[422] Between May 11 and May 25, 2008, sixty-two people—mostly foreign nationals—died in Johannesburg, Cape Town, Durban, and the Free State and Eastern Cape, with over one hundred thousand people displaced with violence occurring in 135 different locations in the country.[423] Most victims were Zimbabweans fleeing from oppression and poverty.[424] Native violence perpetrators burned down many shacks and small businesses, looting and dispossessing foreign migrants' belongings and properties "worth millions of rands."[425] Through these devastating attacks, violence perpetrators manifested extreme brutality and "a flagrant disregard for both the law and the basic humanity of the victims."[426]

After 2008, South African violence continued to erupt unabated. On January 4, 2009, an angry native mob attacked a building inhabited by refugees, asylum seekers, and migrants in KwaZulu-Natal province:

> Two people fell to their deaths from the high-rise building and one was seriously injured as they tried to escape the 150-person mob armed with knives. Reports indicated that despite the fact that the armed crowd marched past a police station moments before the attack, police did not intervene until the attackers left. The attack was reportedly part of a community crime-fighting initiative led by the local municipal ward councilor. Following a public outcry, four men, including the councilor, were brought to trial on charges of public violence. One was also charged with attempted murder.[427]

On November 17, 2009, local residents, angry over access to jobs on local wine farms, attacked and demolished the shacks of Zimbabwean workers in De Doorns, Western Cape.[428] On February 7, 2010, local South Africans looted stores owned by Ethiopian nationals in the town of Siyathemba, fifty miles east of Johannesburg, while not touching South African–owned businesses, in the process displacing over a hundred foreigners.[429] In July 2010, local residents attacked and injured four foreigners in the township of Kya Sands.[430] In the midst of the 2010 World Cup in South Africa, within several cities reports of the possibility of such violent incidents circulated, terrifying foreign migrants within the country.[431] Beginning on June 7, 2014, residents initiated a six-day attack on Somali shop owners in and around the township of Mamelodi, northeast of Pretoria; although the impact cost "lives and livelihoods," there was no response from the police at the time.[432] In January 2015, local thugs set ablaze foreign-owned businesses in a violent outburst.[433] In mid-April 2015, violence broke out in the port city of Durban, South Africa:

> Shops looted and set ablaze. Terrified foreigners hiding in police stations and stadiums. Machete-wielding attackers hacking immigrants to death in major cities in South Africa.
>
> As attacks against foreigners and their businesses rage on, killing at least six people this week, other nations in the continent are scrambling to evacuate their citizens from South Africa.[434]

On February 24, 2017, natives in Pretoria launched a street protest against extreme poverty, unemployment, and inequality, blaming foreign migrants for
these economic problems; these residents burned down twelve dwellings that
they claimed Nigerians were using as "drug dens and brothels" and looted more
than thirty foreign-owned shops in Pretoria, with the ensuing violence becoming so intense that police had to respond using tear gas, water cannons, and
rubber bullets.[435] On May 27, 2017, the "Red Ants," a state-police-hired private
security contractor executing evictions, beat and killed a Mozambican migrant
in Ivory Park, Johannesburg.[436] In early September 2018, angry protesters killed
four people in the Soweto area of Johannesburg, with mobs once again looting and demolishing the property of foreigners, many of whom were Somalis,
this time accused of selling fake or expired food products.[437] From March 25
through April 2, 2019, native xenophobic attacks displaced hundreds of foreign
nationals (many of whom were Malawi) in Durban, South Africa, killing some
foreign nationals and injuring several others.[438]

Security Impact of Intolerance-Based Violence

The response of South African native citizens to foreign migrants has been unrelenting rejection and hostility. This native resentment has been over rising
crime rates, corruption, poverty, and porous borders.[439] Given the 27 percent
unemployment rate and huge income inequality within the country—"South
Africa is one of the most unequal societies in the world, with the gap between
the rich and the poor growing"[440]—native South Africans regularly blame foreign newcomers for committing crimes, stealing their jobs, or exploiting natives by running businesses in impoverished areas.[441] With South African government officials refusing to take responsibility for shoddy public services and
growing populism among the mass public, it is no wonder that "the target for
all the country's ills" is the African immigrant community.[442]

As a result, foreign migrants in South Africa remain in a state of constant
anxiety. In retrospect, despite earlier violent incidents targeting foreign migrants, such as violence lasting several months in 2006 in Cape Town,[443] the
massive scale and scope of intolerance-based violence in May 2008 perpetrated
against foreigners across South Africa was unprecedented and should have led
to major changes in combating intolerance; called by Bishop Paul Verryn an
"unexpected thunderstorm,"[444] it managed to jolt even South Africans highly
desensitized to continuing violence because it constituted the first instance of
widespread enduring civilian post-apartheid violence in South Africa.[445] However, in the wake of this cataclysmic disruption, the vulnerability of foreigners

within the society has persisted, as foreign migrants living within South Africa continue to struggle for full societal inclusion[446] and refugees constantly have to renew their asylum visas. In May 2018, Amnesty International reported that "ten years after an outbreak of horrific intolerance-based violence claimed 60 lives in South Africa, refugees and migrants are still facing daily discrimination and living in constant fear of physical attacks."[447] So it appears that scope and barbarity of the 2008 carnage was decidedly insufficient to stimulate necessary tolerance-enhancing adjustments by either the national government or the society as a whole.

Response to Intolerance-Based Violence

The South African government response to the massive May 2008 anti-migrant violence was way too sluggish. When the regime finally declared a state of national emergency and deployed the South African National Defence Force (SANDF), it was much too late to prevent the bulk of the damage.[448] Although South African police arrested over two hundred people on a variety of charges including rape, robbery, and murder,[449] and the government vehemently condemned the violence, "there appeared to be little or no accountability for the perpetrators of the attacks"[450] because the police typically release suspects because of community pressure or witnesses' reluctance to identify guilty parties.[451] In March 2010, the South African Human Rights Commission (SAHRC) published a comprehensive report about the May 2008 tragedy: the report concluded that after the brutal attacks there were severe deficiencies in accessing justice for xenophobic violence victims as well as considerable impunity for the violence perpetrators.[452]

This South African government's poor response record regarding anti-migrant violence persists:

"The violence that spread across South Africa in 2008 should have been a wake-up call for the government, underscoring the catastrophic consequences of its failure to root out hatred against refugees and migrants. But 10 years on, refugees and migrants still feel the echoes of that terrifying period," said Shenilla Mohamed, Executive Director of Amnesty International South Africa. "Ongoing xenophobia in South Africa is compounded by the failed criminal justice system, with many cases remaining unresolved, which allows perpetrators to attack refugees and migrants with impunity. There has been a marked failure to bring those responsible for the 2008 attacks to justice, emboldening future attackers and leaving refuges and migrants in a constant state of fear."[453]

Indeed, there has been little modification of state policy toward migrants over time.

Amnesty International notes that often South African political leaders' "hate-filled rhetoric" helped spark native citizen xenophobia. The April 2015 violence in Durban resulted from Zulu king Goodwill Zwelithini kaBhekuzulu's decidedly xenophobic comments that foreign migrants "should pack their bags and go" because they are taking jobs from citizens.[454] In December 2016, the executive mayor of Johannesburg, Herman Mashaba, called foreigners residing there "'criminals' who had hijacked the city," blaming them for the high crime rates.[455] In July 2017, the South African deputy police minister hyperbolically announced that most foreign nationals in Johannesburg were engaged in criminal activity.[456] In January 2019, South African president Cyril Ramaphosa, speaking in Durban, discussed the centrality of "effective border management" for public protection, vowing to focus more on illegal trading and vending counterfeit products, which natives perceive as closely tied to undocumented migrants.[457]

Domestic critics have lambasted the South African government's inept violence response record. In September 2018, Thifulifeli Sinthumule, director of South Africa's Consortium for Refugees and Migrants, accused the government of downplaying xenophobia as a national problem, and political leaders of taking advantage of the popularity benefits derived from scapegoating foreigners:

> They have learned from the streets that they can advance themselves by making claims against foreigners and distract people from what they have not done. It's an easy excuse for things which are very difficult to deal with. So the more politicians say it, the more people are likely to believe it, but what we all need to understand is that this is a strategy of distraction.[458]

Reacting to the 2019 xenophobic violence in Durban, Vusumuzi Sibanda, chairperson at the South Africa–based African Diaspora Forum, complained that "apart from its call for an end to attacks on foreign nationals, the South African government has done little to ensure the arrest and prosecution of those responsible," and indeed no arrests followed the assaults; in April 2019, Dewa Mavhinga, Southern Africa Director at Human Rights Watch, argued that "reintegration of foreign nationals into communities without justice and accountability for past xenophobic attacks is a recipe for disaster—to deter those who attack foreign nationals, there is an urgent need for effective policing, arrests, and prosecutions."[459]

The South African government has clearly been more interested in harassing foreign migrants than in apprehending and prosecuting native citizens committing intolerance-based violent acts, with political gains taking precedence over social justice. Although on March 5, 2019, the South African government launched a five-year plan to combat xenophobia, racism, and discrimination, it did not address the fact that virtually nobody has been convicted for crimes against foreigners.[460]

Internationally, the intolerance-based violence in South Africa has angered nearby African states. Aside from condemning the attacks, Kenya, Malawi, and Zimbabwe have evacuated their citizens from South Africa; a Zambian radio station said it will not play South African music in a show of solidarity with the victims of intolerance-based violence; and in Mozambique, the South African energy and chemical company Sasol sent around 340 South African nationals back to their country because of Mozambican employees' violence-inspired protests about the presence of South Africans there.[461] However, this outrage from its neighbors has been insufficient to prod meaningful change in the South African government's response to violence by locals against foreigners.

Lessons for Managing Intolerance-Based Violence

One key lesson from the South Africa case is that states experiencing intolerance-based violence have to be honest about what is transpiring within their borders. In South Africa, xenophobic violence has been rampant within a country still trying to portray itself to the world as a diverse "rainbow" nation.[462] Despite continuing carnage, government officials persist in denying any official support for populist intolerant sentiments, and national government willingness to confront the true scope of the problem is inadequate. The long-standing South African culture of violence has decidedly made matters worse, as has the malfunctioning South African criminal justice system, which has allowed intolerance-based violence perpetrators to escape unpunished.

Another important lesson is that even without any major racial or religious differences between native citizens and foreign migrants, intolerance-based violence can flourish within societies. For analysts who inappropriately confound white nationalist violence against racial minorities with native citizen violence against foreign migrants, this case constitutes a wake-up call that the two differ markedly. Within some countries, political nationality differences can create just as many gaps in understanding and acceptance as any differences in culture, ethnicity, or skin color—if not more. Moreover, both native citizens and foreign migrants can be just as sluggish in managing to understand the dysfunctionality of allowing intolerance-based violence to persist when dealing with nationality differences.

Afghan, Sub-Saharan African, and Syrian Migrants in Turkey

As with Morocco, native citizen–foreign migrant frictions intensified in Turkey after it signed a migrant-receiving agreement with the EU. Afterward, human rights groups reported that Turkey quickly turned into a truly unsafe place for foreign migrants seeking to go to Europe.[463]

Role of Interdependence and Roots of Intolerance

Turkey became a vortex of migration challenges after March 18, 2016, when it signed the interdependence-reinforcing EU pact. Turkey agreed to take back any refugees who traveled to Greece and did not receive asylum: for each Syrian refugee Turkey took back from Greece, one would be resettled from Turkey into the EU; Turkey would receive a grant of six billion euros to help pay for refugees' food, shelter, education, and health care; and Turkish citizens would benefit from early visa-free travel and faster progress in EU membership talks.[464] However, this pact's long-term practical viability is in jeopardy because in March 2020, the Turkish president announced that millions of migrants would soon be released and heading toward Europe because Turkey could no longer cope with a new wave of refugees after the Syrian conflict escalated.[465]

Besides 450,000 non-Syrian refugees (mostly from Iraq, Afghanistan, and Iran),[466] Turkey is home to more displaced Syrians—3.7 million in 2020—than any other country in the world.[467] From 2012 to 2018, at first Turkey was resilient in taking in Syrians, granting special protection to those fleeing from the civil war,[468] but as time progressed Turkish citizens' anti-Syrian bigotry has mushroomed;[469] while Turkish natives were initially supportive of Syrian refugees, their "compassion is waning" because "host communities—particularly those who feel marginalised by ethnic, sectarian or ideological cleavages—perceive Syrians as a threat to their political and economic interests."[470] Overall, native-foreigner relations are now quite strained because of the high volume of newcomers; for example, within Istanbul, Turkey's capital and largest city, between 2016 and 2018 the number of Syrians officially almost doubled to 565,000, with the real figure possibly exceeding 700,000.[471]

Nature of Intolerance-Based Violence

In Turkey, intolerance-based violence against refugees and asylum seekers has many forms, including severe beatings and sexual assaults.[472] Between mid-2016 and mid-2017, the level of violence between native Turks and Syrian migrants tripled, with at least thirty-five people killed—including twenty-four

Syrians—in these incidents.[473] Geographically, the potential for anti-migrant violence is highest in the metropolitan areas of Istanbul, Ankara, and Izmir—hosting around 23 percent of the Syrians in the country—where residents view Syrians as culturally different and resent their competition for customers and low-paying jobs, particularly affecting the informal economy.[474]

Numerous incidents of bias-motivated violence against refugees, asylum seekers, and migrants have occurred in Turkey in recent years. Aside from Syrians and Afghans, these attacks have primarily targeted minorities of African origin from countries such as Sudan, Democratic Republic of Congo, and Guinea.[475] In 2014 natives in Ankara stoned and set ablaze a building inhabited by Syrian refugees and then proceeded to go on a protest march against these newcomers.[476] In early 2015, a "wave of xenophobia" surfaced in Turkey, amplified by the media, increasing the misery of Syrian refugees who were already characterized as criminals stealing natives' jobs and who were held "responsible for anything that goes wrong."[477] In mid-May 2017, in Sultanciftligi—a lower-class neighborhood in Istanbul normally full of young Afghan and Pakistani migrants toiling for up to twelve hours a day in basement garment factories and residing in dilapidated and overcrowded employer-controlled apartments—violence commenced as the Turkish police raided homes and rounded up hundreds of migrants who were beaten and stabbed, with six Pakistanis rumored to have been killed in the skirmishes.[478] In that same month, in Istanbul's Vefa district, five Turkish men assaulted an Afghan migrant who was pulling a cart weighing hundreds of pounds through the city's streets to collect plastic, glass, and cardboard to sell to Turkish recyclers, and he became so scared after the vicious beating that he decided to return to his home country.[479]

Amid this legacy of Turkish brutality, an action-reaction cycle of violence has been evident between native citizens and foreign migrants, highlighting the pent-up feelings of hostility between the two groups. In July 2017, in the Demetevler neighborhood of Ankara's Yenimahalle district, after a social media rumor that a Syrian refugee had raped a five-year-old Turkish girl, clashes occurred between "dozens of Syrian and Turkish men who fought each other with sticks, stones and knives," with the fighting so intense that it took all night for government police—three of whom were stabbed—to end the skirmish.[480] On September 27, 2018, in Sanliurfa (located in southeastern Turkey), Syrian migrants killed two Turkish youths following an argument between neighboring families, and then for days afterward an angry local mob assaulted Syrian migrants and their businesses, forcing many foreigners to remain within their homes for most of the following week; this violence site is notable because the Sanliurfa province has more Syrian refugees than any other in the country, with almost a quarter of its residents being Syrian.[481] These two examples of inter-active violence are by no means isolated incidents; in the second half of 2018 the number of violent incidents between Turks and Syrians tripled, as verbal arguments "descended into pitch battles involving dozens of people armed with knives and guns."[482]

Security Impact of Intolerance-Based Violence

The foreign migrant population within Turkey feels constantly under duress. Women migrants entering Turkey are especially in peril, as Turkish soldiers, border guards, and migration officials have inflicted many forms of violence on Syrian female migrants, including rape, sexual harassment, forced and early marriage, polygamy, and human trafficking.[483] Sometimes steps foreign migrants take to increase their security can inadvertently increase their vulnerability to violence from natives who misunderstand their motivations; for example, foreign refugees often choose to move about in clusters with fellow nationals, and this can sometimes inadvertently become a violence trigger because when young Syrian men walk together in large groups for self-protection, they can "appear hostile and dangerous to locals."[484]

Turkish natives have become increasingly upset at the growing number of foreign migrants, particularly from Syria, whom they see as societally disruptive. Locals label refugees fleeing the Syrian civil war "as criminals, beggars, burglars and prostitutes, unable to adapt to Turkish culture"; the principal grievances are economic and cultural, as typical native accusations include that Syrians are "taking our jobs and our homes," "Syrians do not adapt to our culture," and "crime in Turkey increases because of Syrians."[485] Integrating so many immigrants amplifies preexisting tensions within Turkey stemming from unemployment and underemployment.[486] Public opinion polls confirm the hardening of Turkish citizens' attitudes toward Syrian refugees. Surveys conducted in Istanbul and Ankara in 2009 and 2015 found a significant increase in negative perceptions of foreigners; a December 2016 survey revealed that 72 percent of Turkish citizens living in Istanbul experienced discomfort when encountering Syrians, with 76 percent having "no sympathy" for Syrian refugees; an October 2017 survey showed that 78 percent of citizens believed that Syrians made their society unsafe; and a December 2017 survey found that 75 percent of Turkish citizens did not feel that they could coexist peacefully with Syrians.[487]

Despite religious commonality, cultural and language differences have contributed to feelings of insecurity, particularly in urban areas, on the part of both
native Turks and foreign migrants.

> In major cities, the refugees' inability to speak Turkish limits opportunities to
> find and build on shared values and interests. "The differences in subculture are
> more distinct in cities farther from the border," said an international agency of-
> ficial. The lack of interaction between refugees and hosts reinforces the latter's
> conviction that Syrians do not conform to Turkish societal norms. "Eighty per
> cent of Syrians think they can integrate, while around 80 per cent of Turkish
> citizens say they can't," an EU official said. A recent study confirms this trend:
> 63 per cent of Turkish citizens either feel "far" or "very far" to Syrians, while 72
> per cent of Syrians feel "close" or "very close" to Turkish society.[488]

This major tolerance-reducing native-foreigner perceptual gap in Turkey is amplified because (1) native citizens and foreign refugees do not typically interact
much within Turkish society, and this separateness can readily lead to profound
misunderstandings which end up turning violent; and (2) unlike many other
countries such as Germany and the United States, Turkey does not give refugees the option of taking cultural orientation courses.[489]

Response to Intolerance-Based Violence

The Turkish government's official policy supports foreign refugees, at least from
Muslim countries. The Turkish president has proclaimed that "Turkey is a sanctuary for the refugees":[490]

> The ruling party promotes the notion that Turkish citizens should "help Muslim
> brothers and sisters in need." This concept of faith-based solidarity has been
> at the centre of its efforts to contain and counter negative sentiments toward
> refugees. "It is thanks to religion that we do not see much violence," said an
> official working with an Islamist charity in Istanbul. "The concept of 'honour'
> (*namus*) is restraining people." Turkish citizens in pious neighbourhoods con-
> firm this view, but also say that over time real-life challenges overwhelm faith-
> based solidarity.[491]

However, the influx of foreigners has been so massive and rapid, with little
advance preparation or acclimation by either natives or migrants, that socioeconomic tension may eclipse hopes that religious affinity would produce native compassion for foreign migrants. Making matters worse is that Turkey

officially accepts Syrian refugees as "guests," not as "refugees," because of the unorthodox nature of Turkish government asylum policies.[492]

Any hope that the Turkish government would become more responsive to the plight of foreign migrants is dampened by its poor violence monitoring. State authorities rarely receive reports of intolerance-based violent incidents victimizing foreign migrants, and little reliable data on racist or xenophobic violence is available in Turkey.[493] In February 2011, the European Commission Against Racism and Intolerance (ECRI), a Council of Europe body, urged the Turkish government to intensify its efforts to document, monitor, and combat racist violence by thoroughly investigating all allegations of racist violence and taking racist motivations of these offenses into account in prosecutions.[494]

Since the March 2016 agreement between Turkey and the EU, the Turkish government has decidedly not increased its concern with the welfare of foreign migrants within its borders. Since that time, the state has implemented numerous crackdowns against both foreign migrants and criminal smugglers and reduced the number of migrants leaving for Europe.[495] The EU pact apparently did not foresee, or have provisions to deal with, the resulting native-foreigner tensions within Turkish society.

Lessons for Managing Intolerance-Based Violence

Assimilating a huge foreign migrant influx usually is highly difficult even if a key cultural similarity—in this case religion—exists between newcomers' home and host states. Generous motives of compassion and brotherhood across societies are strained when dealing with especially high foreign migrant volumes, economic competition and stagnation, and major cultural disruption. More broadly, idealistic motives reflecting desires to help the displaced and dispossessed may easily end up being undercut and overshadowed by pragmatic expediency concerns such as overwhelmed social services, economic pressures, irritating cultural differences, and rising citizen resentment about the inability or unwillingness of foreigners to assimilate properly.

Turkey's willingness to reach an agreement with the EU to receive compensation in return for becoming a depository for refugees seeking entrance to Western Europe does not reflect a desire to promote reasonable treatment of the newcomers. As is the case with Morocco, the EU appears to be less concerned with the treatment of foreign refugees and migrants in Turkey than it is with assurances that they will not make their way into Western European countries, and Turkey has interpreted the arrangement with the EU as a mandate to do whatever it wishes with the outsiders. As long as this agreement is honored, Turkish society will continue to face major challenges in terms of fairly and peacefully integrating the burgeoning diverse migrant population.

Lastly, the action-reaction cycles of violence between native Turks and Syrian migrants illustrate the dangers of what ensues when neither party receives appropriate orientation beforehand or afterward about how to reach compromises or adjust peacefully to the new challenges faced. As in Russia, when such interactive cycles occur, the legitimacy of a national government crackdown on foreigners within national borders can rise in the eyes of native citizens. In the long run, such cycles can also obfuscate the true nature of the oppression and abuses experienced by foreign migrants within the society and reduce the chances it will ever be addressed.

Hispanic and Muslim Migrants in the United States

Globally, since 1970 the United States has been by far the favorite destination of global migrants, now receiving a whopping 20 percent of them.[496] Moreover, the number of foreign residents in the country has almost quadrupled—from under 12 million in 1970 to 46.6 million in 2015[497]—representing 13.4 percent of the American population.[498] Over the past two decades, "the United States has experienced the largest wave of immigration—in both absolute and relative terms—in its history."[499] This attractiveness to foreign immigrants has created special security challenges, which up to this point the United States has been unable to manage smoothly.

Role of Interdependence and Roots of Intolerance

Within the United States, the September 11, 2001, al-Qaeda terrorist attacks were a key trigger for a massive upsurge of native nationalism and xenophobia: American citizens responded to these surprise attacks with uncertainty and fear[500] and a mix of shock, pride, and anger; they hung American flags everywhere, attended large prayer vigils, and listened approvingly to Toby Keith's country song "Courtesy of the Red, White and Blue (Angry American)," promising swift and decisive violent retaliation.[501] Reinforcing this inward focus were rising anti-globalization sentiments, linked to the declining American ability to control global commerce associated with a desire to retreat from the world economy.[502]

Recent intolerant anti-foreigner sentiments have two primary focal points— fears of Hispanic immigrants coming in from south of the border and fears of Muslim immigrants coming in from the Middle East. Regarding Hispanic immigrant intolerance, the economic and cultural interdependence between Mexico and the United States exacerbates the problem, with over $300 billion in annual cross-border trade, tens of millions of American and Mexican citizens in binational families, and over fourteen million people residing near the almost two-thousand-mile shared border.[503] Regarding Muslim immigrant intolerance, heavy American dependence on oil imports from Muslim Middle Eastern countries also complicates the predicament.

Nature of Intolerance-Based Violence

Long gone is the humanitarian sentiment engraved on the Statue of Liberty (from Emma Lazarus's famous poem), inviting in the "tired," "poor," "tempest-tost," "huddled masses yearning to breathe free." American historian John Higham remarks that "with the passing of faith in the melting pot, there perished the ideal of American nationality as an unfinished, steadily improving, cosmopolitan blend."[504] Long before the xenophobic fears accelerated by the 9/11 terrorist attacks and Donald Trump's presidential candidacy, in September 1994 President Bill Clinton tentatively announced the American intention to invade Haiti unless its military regime relinquished power, directly in response to the overwhelming domestic mass public outrage about the flood of refugees from Haiti to the United States fleeing from both poverty and political oppression. Indeed, "in almost every generation, nativists portray new immigrants as not fit to become real Americans: they were too infected by Catholicism, monarchism, anarchism, Islam, criminal tendencies, defective genes, mongrel bloodlines, or some other alien virus to become free men and women in our democratic society."[505] When foreign groups arriving in the United States finally manage to secure a position of comfort and security, knowing what they went through to get it, they often become wary of a new wave of migrants shoving them aside and taking the opportunities that they have worked so hard to attain.

Perpetrating native citizen violence against foreign migrants are those who are losing ground targeting those who are most vulnerable. Broadly, coercive xenophobic action within the United States targets especially poor foreigner communities where a non-native language is spoken and where lots of undocumented migrants live.[506] Both economic displacement and cultural and political security fears explain the recent uptick in intolerance-based violence.[507] Members of a diminishing majority who see their influence waning are afraid that their country will become so overwhelmed by foreign influences that it would be totally unrecognizable and alien to them, escalating the urge to defend and protect it even through violence.

Regarding intolerance-based violence targeting Hispanics, the motives for native frustration are multifaceted. Eleven million undocumented migrants are in the United States, mostly from Mexico and Central America, along with many million more Latinos "who are not far removed from a border-crossing story."[508] Many are migrant agricultural workers. Driving this migration are not only by poverty, unemployment, income disparities, and Mexican American economic links, but also the web of social and family connections and the cultural experience Mexicans have in the United States.[509] The recent polarizing national debate within the United States about immigration has helped to inflame fears and to incite natives' xenophobic attacks against Hispanic migrants, particularly when they reside in areas with otherwise homogeneous populations.[510] Pat Buchanan, a leading American nativist, has staunchly contended that Mexico is slowly but surely reclaiming the American Southwest.[511] In a speech announcing his presidential candidacy in June 2015, Donald Trump fanned the flames of domestic intolerance by describing Mexican migrants as criminals:

> "When Mexico sends its people, they're not sending their best. . . . They're sending people that have lots of problems, and they're bringing those problems with us. They're bringing drugs. They're bringing crime. They're rapists. And some, I assume, are good people."[512]

Among intolerance-based attacks, those targeting people of Hispanic origin rose nearly 40 percent between 2003 and 2007 and began increasing again in 2010.[513] The Southern Poverty Law Center reported a 54 percent rise in the growth of hate groups operating in the United States since 2000, attributed mainly "to the anti-immigrant fervor sweeping the country."[514] On January 25, 2017, President Donald Trump signed an executive order calling for a wall to be built along the United States–Mexico border; prioritized deportation of migrants, especially ones suspected of committing crimes; and canceled federal funding for "sanctuary cities" that violate national government law about apprehending irregular migrants.[515] In that same year, thanks to widespread American anti-immigrant sentiments, hate incidents increasingly targeted Latinos in both urban and rural areas, with Hispanic migrants and their families being "the victims of racist slurs and harassment, intimidation, vandalism and even assault."[516] Given a pervasive native citizen sense of socioeconomic displacement, an "us versus them" mentality increasingly characterized domestic relations. For example, in November 2017, a Denver man shot and killed three Latinos at a Walmart, explicitly motivated by hatred of immigrants;[517] in August 2019, a Texas native killed twenty people at a Walmart in El Paso after posting an online document bemoaning "the Hispanic invasion of Texas."[518] The dangers of native assaults on foreigners escalate when the migrants themselves are accused of instigating violence, such as in January 2019, when an illegal nineteen-year-old El Salvadoran migrant was charged with killing four people in Nevada.[519]

Regarding intolerance-based violence targeting Muslims, the native backlash is striking. Many Americans increasingly fear a Muslim terrorist threat within the United States.[520] The association of Muslims with terrorist violence stems back to the 9/11 terrorist attacks, and more recent ISIS-inspired violence against the West confirmed existing apprehensions.[521] Notably, the 9/11 attacks generated a significant anti-Muslim backlash in both Europe and the United States.[522] Since that time, many natives have considered Muslims in the United States to be "presumptive terrorists, not citizens" and "unassimilable aliens, not Americans,"[523] and Muslims have been victims of greater discrimination, harassment, and mistreatment from both the American government[524] and the American people.[525] According to the FBI, police reports of intolerance-based violence against Muslims surged after the 9/11 terrorist attacks; the 481 anti-Muslim crimes in 2001 were a substantial increase from the preceding year.[526] This pattern of suspicion and distrust has been remarkably persistent, even though the Migration Policy Institute reported that of the 745,000 refugees who came to the United States between September 11, 2001, and the end of 2015, only three were arrested on charges of terrorism.[527] Nonetheless, from 2002 to 2014, Pew Research surveys found that the proportion of Americans believing that Islam was more likely to encourage violence doubled from 25 to 50 percent; in 2015 FBI data showed that there were 257 hate crimes against Muslims, a surge of 67 percent over the previous year.[528] Pew Research findings also indicate that anti-Muslim violent acts within the United States rose significantly between 2015 and 2016, substantially surpassing the 2001 peak after the 9/11 attacks.[529] Consistent with Donald Trump's continuing characterization of Muslims as a "problem" needing to be addressed,[530] many Americans appear to be unable to make a meaningful distinction between devout Muslim believers committed to peaceful pursuit of their beliefs and extremist Islamic fundamentalists committed to the use of violence to promote change; Americans lump them all together as uniformly posing severe threats to the American way of life. Nationalist and xenophobic fears have stimulated both threatening rhetoric and violent acts against those suspected of being illegal aliens,[531] including hate crimes against Muslims perceived as foreigners. Given that the Muslim population in the United States is composed mostly of immigrants and children of immigrants from all over the world,[532] aside from religious prejudice an intense anti-foreigner sentiment is clearly a major component of this native intolerance.

Even considering only recent identity-based hate crimes, American intolerance-based violence has not targeted exclusively foreign Hispanics and Muslims. Illustrating nationality oriented intolerance-based violence in the United States, violent attacks against South Asian, Sikh, Middle Eastern, and Arab communities in 2017 surpassed that in 2016 by "a staggering 64%."[533] Illustrating religious-oriented intolerance-based violence within the United States, anti-Semitic incidents within the United States surged nearly 60 percent in 2017;[534] on October 27, 2018, an avowedly bigoted shooter who stated that he wanted all Jews to die killed eleven worshippers at the Tree of Life synagogue in Pittsburgh, Pennsylvania; and on April 27, 2019 a shooting occurred at the Chabad of Poway synagogue in Escondido, California.[535] Outside of foreign national and religious identity, racism toward domestic African Americans has of course long been a key part of intolerance-based violence within the United States, with a recent notable manifestation occurring on August 11, 2017, when a violent nativist and xenophobic rally occurred in Charlottesville, Virginia, favoring a racialized national identity as the condition for political belonging to this country.[536]

Security Impact of Intolerance-Based Violence

Given the huge number of foreigners wishing to migrate to the United States, the resurgence in natives' anti-immigrant sentiments is easy to understand, if not accept:

> Over the past decade, millions of Hispanic immigrants have bypassed traditional urban destinations and put down roots in the American heartland. With large groups of newcomers moving to some of the most homogeneous, tradition-steeped places in the country, a backlash was predictable. But no one could have foreseen the breadth and fury of the new nativism that has risen up from Middle America with an ominous roar.[537]

In July 2016, presidential candidate Donald Trump announced at the Republican National Convention that "Americanism, not globalism, shall be our creed."[538] Despite their political differences, it is notable that "Trump's rhetoric taps into some of the same populist anti-elite anger articulated by Bernie Sanders when attacking big corporations, big donors, and big banks."[539] Recent American presidential candidates have quickly capitalized on people's fears and blamed foreigners for domestic woes, contending that "foreigners and their flood of goods are the economic problem, foreigners and their conflicts are the political problem."[540] Across time, "nativism is old wine in new bottles that perennially quenches the thirst of America's fearful and suspicious"; "native-born Americans, some only a generation or two themselves from arrival or even less, sought to slam shut the door in fear of job competition, the distortion of their cultural values, challenges to their religious beliefs, or even the dilution of their gene pool by amalgamation."[541]

Within the United States, foreigner intolerance can emerge from both the left and the right. Both the Democratic and Republican parties contain significant elements that are both pro-immigration and anti-immigration.[542] Indeed, American intolerance can go in all directions; during the 2016 American presidential campaign, as Donald Trump was unfairly maligning Mexican and Muslim migrants as undesirables, his opponent Hillary Clinton was unfairly maligning American citizens supporting Trump as "a basket of deplorables."[543] American intolerant anti-foreigner sentiments parallel those in Western Europe, with recurring cultural, religious, and economic themes: Cas Mudde, a populism expert, argues that "much of the racial nativism in the United States is very similar to the cultural nativism in Europe," and—despite the massive justified publicity gained by racial discrimination within the United States—"most of the recent nativist debates are about ethnic outsiders, notably Hispanics and Muslims, rather than the traditional racial outsider, African Americans."[544]

Anti-immigrant groups and politicians regularly inflame American citizens' antagonisms toward illegal immigrants. Powerful organizations such as the Federation for American Immigration Reform (FAIR) and nationalist lobbies such as Team America PAC (founded by former Colorado congressman Tom Tancredo) launch venomous attacks on political candidates seen as soft on immigration. Over the last decade, the ties among xenophobic political rhetoric, anti-immigrant policies, and violent acts have tightened,[545] with politicians' provocative speeches becoming more overtly incendiary, and, as Human Rights

First notes, with politicians "coming to power by teasing out these fears and prejudices."[546]

Many Americans doubt that their national government can adequately monitor and safeguard its long southern border from the influx of illegal Mexican and Central American immigrants or protect the country against the entrance of would-be terrorist Muslims. In the minds of many fearful citizens, a significant challenge to American national identity comes from the huge volume of immigrants from Latin America, especially Mexico, with a much higher fertility rate than among the native population.[547] In a 2015 poll, 46 percent of Americans favored a temporary ban on Muslims entering the United States, with 59 percent feeling that it was too easy for foreigners to legally enter the United States.[548] The spike in anti-Hispanic and anti-Muslim sentiment linked to Donald Trump's presidential election reflects deep societal insecurity. American fears routinely link foreign immigrants to both terrorism and crime; extremist publications "are full of short news articles about criminal offenses, such as murder and rape, committed by 'aliens,'" arguing that "immigrants are much more likely to commit criminal acts than the host population, but that the real level of crime is being kept from the public by politically correct politicians."[549]

A key outcome of American citizen xenophobic fears has been the rise of private vigilante groups, with which the United States has had a long history, to help maintain law and order. Such armed groups have operated for years along the southern border attempting to curb the flow of migrants into the United States. Between 2004 and 2009, the Minutemen were a powerful anti-immigrant vigilante movement, believing that the national government was inept in maintaining border security and that they needed to "take enforcement into their own hands."[550] Patrolling the southern Arizona border, they normally simply detain illegal migrants attempting to cross the border and turn them over to state border patrol agents, but in May 2009, a renegade member was charged with killing a Latino man and his young daughter in Arizona.[551] 2006 marked the founding of the vigilante group Texas Border Volunteers, which now "has some 300 recruits who dress in fatigues and patrol private ranches in South Texas."[552] Founded in 2011 was the anti-immigrant vigilante group Arizona Border Recon, with its stated mission being "protecting America's 'back door.'"[553] In April 2019, the vigilante group the United Constitutional Patriots—wearing military-style uniforms and police-style star badges and holding combat weapons—began major operations in southern New Mexico, detaining migrant families seeking asylum and then handing them over to Border Patrol agents; a spokesman for the group said, "we're just here to support the Border Patrol and show the public the reality of the border."[554]

Foreign migrants in the United States feel great insecurity because of their increasing realization of deep native citizen xenophobia. In response to these citizen fears, some stereotyped foreign migrants attempt to gain local respect by showing natives that they are hardworking people who would make productive citizens able to contribute to society in order to differentiate themselves from predominant native images.[555] Other foreign refugees and migrants respond to the atmosphere of hatred simply by simmering with resentment about discrimination during their attempts to prove themselves; "there are small but very profound layers of humiliation attached to a nationality that's assumed to be criminal and inferior."[556]

Response to Intolerance-Based Violence

The common nativist image linking disruptive violence to illegal migrants has led to a strong American push to restrict border access. Within the United States, the suspicion, prejudice, and xenophobia toward foreigners common among the mass public often has generated increased support for restrictive immigration policies.[557] Currently the American government amazingly "spends more on immigration enforcement agencies (U.S. Customs and Border Protection and U.S. Immigration and Customs Enforcement) than it does on all other principal criminal law enforcement agencies combined."[558]

In 2016, preparing for the American presidential election, candidate Donald Trump consistently pushed two tangible proposals reflecting foreign intolerance—building a Mexican border wall and implementing a Muslim immigration ban.[559] In his presidential campaign, Trump repeatedly vowed that if elected he would build a wall keeping out illegal migrants from the south, and in early April 2019 he threatened to totally shut down any immigration from Mexico.[560] Similarly, on December 7, 2015, Trump promised if elected to indefinitely ban all Muslims from entering the United States;[561] after being elected, on January 27, 2017, he introduced a ban on immigration from seven predominantly Muslim states—Iran, Iraq, Libya, Somalia, Sudan, Syria, and Yemen—which went into effect on June 29, 2017, despite court challenges.[562] Sensing rising widespread citizen insecurity about foreigners, Trump approved U.S. Immigration and Customs Enforcement's (ICE) Secure Communities program, designed "to identify and deport criminal aliens through state and local collaboration with federal immigration authorities";[563] established Victims of Immigration Crime Engagement (VOICE), designed to help victims of crimes committed by "removable aliens";[564] and in April 2017 began assembling a "nationwide deportation force" to safeguard against illegal immigration dangers.[565] Fears surrounding deportation[566] have dramatically reduced the willingness of migrants to report abuse.

By mid-2019, the American attempt to restrict Central American migrants from entering the United States had truly reached a breaking point. The flow of migrants—"seeking to escape from gang violence, sexual abuse, death threats and persistent poverty"—had mushroomed to record levels; for example, the February 2019 total was 560 percent above that of the previous year, completely overwhelming the American border security system.[567] Complaints by border officials escalated about their inability to handle the volume of migrants encountered. In response, aside from beefing up border security expenditures, on March 29, 2019, Trump directed the State Department to stop giving $500 million in aid to El Salvador, Guatemala, and Honduras as punishment for their failure to prevent their citizens from attempting to migrate into the United States.[568]

The Trump administration's consistent anti-immigration stance has indirectly interfered with effective monitoring of intolerance-based violence incidents targeting foreign migrants within the United States. Because of this forceful anti-immigrant American government response to the pressures of unsanctioned foreigners crossing its national boundaries, foreign immigrants' realization that they are feared and hated by natives has increased their suspicions about government law enforcement officials and thus decreased their willingness to report hate crimes against them to these officials.[569] So even in the United States, "many immigrants don't report hate crimes because of language barriers and mistrust of police."[570]

Moreover, Trump's anti-migrant rhetoric and threats to close the southern border have had a key backfire effect. They have indirectly "helped supercharge the pipeline of migrants from Honduras, Guatemala and El Salvador" by increasing migrants' perceived need to rely on transnational criminals covertly smuggling them into the United States; "smugglers lately have been buying radio ads in Central America, warning that Mr. Trump is about to shut down all immigration—if you ever want to go to the United States, they say, go now!"[571] While the United States has long received the highest number of smuggled migrant laborers of any country in the world,[572] this latest development makes matters a lot worse.

Lessons for Managing Intolerance-Based Violence

Even within a country founded by immigrants, rigid exclusionary policies toward newcomers can quickly ensue within a heated atmosphere of fear and resentment. Within the United States, perhaps the ultimate irony is that refugees and asylum seekers fleeing from extreme insecurity abroad frequently end up being identified as a primary security threat within their supposed refuge. A *Washington Post* reporter astutely notes that while "it's tempting to blame Trump for igniting the fires of xenophobia, betraying the great tradition of embracing immigrant strivers," in reality "the embarrassing truth is that the United States has always been hostile to immigrants, or at least, a strong and vocal faction has been—this nativist streak dates back even to the earliest days of the republic."[573] Because in recent decades American interventionism has not always worked well, many Americans support movement in the direction of isolationist retrenchment rather than expanded international ties and responsibilities, and this set of attitudes has contributed to uncaring or antagonism toward the plight of foreign migrants.

Many Americans today neither understand nor trust foreign influences within their society. In contrast to citizens of many other countries, most Americans do not receive as much education about the histories, languages, customs, and values of other societies, and because the United States is the most powerful country in the world, many American citizens feel confident about "American exceptionalism," combining the superiority of their beliefs with the lack of necessity for foreigners' contribution to an already successful society. Many intolerant Americans take it for granted that most other societies would be far better off if they adopted American values and practices.

The targeting of Hispanics and Muslims demonstrates how a single society can have very different strains of intolerance-based violence toward differing groups. Muslims are hated and feared primarily because of their religion, while Hispanics are hated and feared primarily for cultural and demographic reasons. At different times and in different parts of the United States, the antagonism is greater toward one than the other. Although the persistence within the United States of native citizen intolerance toward foreign migrants over the centuries seems to indicate that it fulfills some sort of basic societal need, the particular focal points—which national, ethnic, racial, or religious groups are most feared and hated—transform over time.

5

Intolerance-Based Violence Findings

THE CASE FINDINGS HIGHLIGHT the truly broad scope of intolerance-based violence. It appears to be as at home in the Global North as it is in the Global South, in well-educated societies as in poorly educated societies, and in urban areas as in rural areas. It can occur when a host society is doing well or doing poorly, when outsiders come from nearby or faraway home states, or when outsiders are seeking economic opportunity or fleeing from persecution and conflict. Globally, intolerance-based native-foreigner violence seems highly improbable only if a country is totally isolated and cocooned from any international interaction, a situation that is increasingly rare within today's globalized interdependent world.

Despite ubiquitous prospects of intolerance-based violence, it is important to determine the circumstances most linked to its occurrence. After general state and society findings, identified are (1) the background elements most conducive to intolerance, (2) the situational triggers of escalating intolerance, and (3) the conditions most likely to facilitate intolerance-based violence. To provide as complete a picture as possible, this comprehensive discussion combines case insights with findings from other relevant research.

Because the precursors to intolerance-based violence are complex, it is vital to isolate the circumstances when it is most likely to erupt. Countries inescapably have limited security resources, and no society can be vigilant at all times in all areas for the possibility of intolerance turning really ugly. Because of the need to be relevant to practitioners and policy makers tasked with finding stabilizing remedies to minimize this security disruption, and because preemptive prevention of contagious intolerance-based violence from emerging within societies is always preferable to postdisruption reactive remediation, it seems vital to provide clues about when to be most prepared for its outbreak.

General State and Society Intolerance Patterns

The cases highlight a few noteworthy general state and society intolerance patterns, summarized in Figure 5.1. These patterns are (1) volatile societal prejudices, (2) unproductive government responses, and (3) interfering private groups. Together they hint at what many observers see as nearly insuperable obstacles surrounding breaking the cycle of deeply felt intrasocietal cross-group hatred and fear.

Looking first at volatile societal prejudices, the case findings reveal globally pervasive racial bigotry, religious antagonism, and sexual exploitation associated with intolerance-based violence. Regarding racial prejudice, in all the cases—the Dominican Republic, Egypt, Germany, Greece, Hungary, Italy, Malaysia, Morocco, Russia, Turkey, and the United States—except for South Africa, intrasocietal resentment and hostility patterns are reinforced by racist prejudice, with lighter-skinned native citizens mistreating darker-skinned foreign migrants. Regarding religious antagonism, in over half the cases—the Dominican Republic, Germany, Greece, Hungary, Italy, Malaysia, and the United States—religious differences between native citizens and foreign migrants played a prominent role in deepening existing antagonisms, with hostility

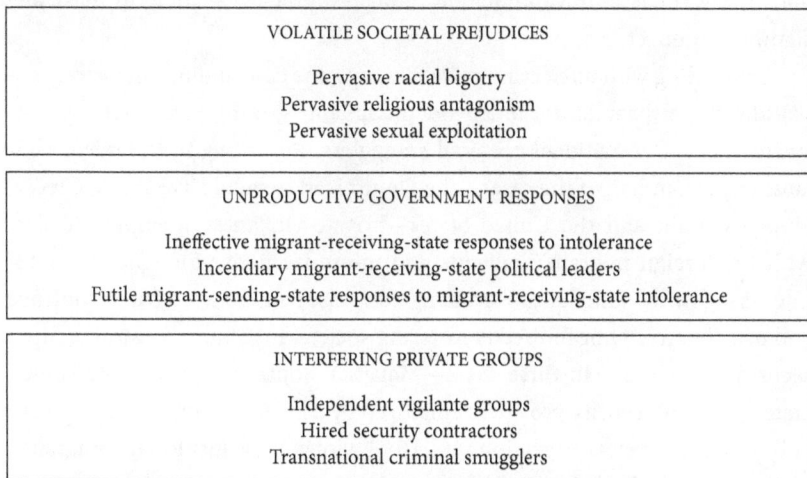

VOLATILE SOCIETAL PREJUDICES

Pervasive racial bigotry
Pervasive religious antagonism
Pervasive sexual exploitation

UNPRODUCTIVE GOVERNMENT RESPONSES

Ineffective migrant-receiving-state responses to intolerance
Incendiary migrant-receiving-state political leaders
Futile migrant-sending-state responses to migrant-receiving-state intolerance

---

INTERFERING PRIVATE GROUPS

Independent vigilante groups
Hired security contractors
Transnational criminal smugglers

FIGURE 5.1: General State and Society Intolerance Patterns

toward Muslims particularly salient. Regarding sexual exploitation, in two-thirds of the cases—the Dominican Republic, Egypt, Germany, Italy, Malaysia, Morocco, Russia, and Turkey—sexual exploitation of women (often underage girls) resulted from discriminatory interactions between native citizens and foreign migrants, where in some cases native citizen women were victims and other cases foreign migrant women were victims.

Turning to unproductive government responses, the case findings highlight globally popular yet ineffective migrant-receiving-state reactions to intolerance; incendiary migrant-receiving-state political leaders; and futile migrant-sending-state reactions to migrant-receiving-state intolerance. Regarding ineffective migrant-receiving-state reactions to intolerance, in all of the cases the national host state governments managed to do little in terms of effective response to domestic intolerance and violence, with many state regimes not even putting in a significant effort to do so. Regarding incendiary migrant-receiving-state political leaders, in one-third of the cases—Hungary, Italy, Russia, and the United States—the presence of highly nationalistic xenophobic heads of state impeded the emergence of tolerance-reducing policies, with all explicitly pushing foreigner entry restrictions. Regarding futile migrant-sending-state responses to migrant-receiving-state intolerance, two-thirds of the home countries of mistreated emigrants undertook no significant action when their citizens were harassed in host states, with those home states that did protest or try to prevent their natives from going to such host states—including Haiti, Sudan, Myanmar, and Mozambique/Zimbabwe/Malawi—failing to make any significant impact.

Concluding with interfering private groups, the case findings show frequent worldwide participation of independent vigilante groups, hired security contractors, and transnational criminal smugglers. Regarding independent vigilante groups, in half of the cases—the Dominican Republic, Germany, Greece, Hungary, Italy, and the United States—private vigilantes attempted to deal with the foreign migrant challenge and minimize native-foreigner tensions, interfering with national government control of intolerance-based violence and usually directly or indirectly fostering societal instability. Regarding hired security contractors, in three cases—Malaysia, South Africa, and the United States—private security providers employed by a host government or by native citizens for their own protection undertook violence against foreign migrants, and the net result again seemed not to be improved stabilization of native-migrant relations. Regarding transnational criminal smugglers, in almost half of the cases—Egypt, Hungary, Morocco, Turkey, and the United States—private transnational criminal smugglers played a major role in facilitating migrant transfers across borders, and in most of the other cases such smugglers likely played at least a minor role in this illicit activity: given the resulting reduction of moderated government control over who gets into countries, corruption and violence appear highly likely to increase.

Background Elements Conducive to Intolerance

Figure 5.2 summarizes the case findings' five important clusters about societal background elements conducive to intolerance. For migrant-receiving societies, these are (1) bogus beliefs, (2) curious composition, (3) debilitating dependencies, (4) petrifying paranoia, and (5) uninformed unfairness. Together these

BOGUS BELIEFS

Belief that heritage foundation for citizenship ensures solidarity
Belief that cross-cultural contact automatically induces harmony
Belief that sharply curtailing or banning immigration eliminates native-foreigner frictions

---

CURIOUS COMPOSITION

Problematic mono-ethnic societies with low experience integrating foreigners
Problematic heterogeneous societies lacking mutual trust because of cross-group inequalities
Problematic delicate domestic balances upset by entrance of newcomers

---

DEBILITATING DEPENDENCIES

High dependence on domestic undocumented foreigners
High dependence on extremely competitive foreign exports
High dependence on migrant-related foreign payoffs

PETRIFYING PARANOIA

Fear and distrust tied to private coercion reliance
Fear and distrust tied to multilevel intolerance foundations
Fear and distrust tied to rapid total assimilation expectations

---

UNINFORMED UNFAIRNESS

Lack of relevant intolerance-based violence data
Lack of advance planning for integrating incoming foreigners
Lack of national government impartiality regarding migration

FIGURE 5.2: Background Elements Conducive to Intolerance

constitute early-warning signs of the security dangers associated with explod-ing societal intolerance. Some background elements are the intended product of formal policies, while others are the unintended by-product of emerging historical patterns, societal customs, or long-standing traditions. Regardless of their origins, managing global intolerance-based violence requires special con-sideration of these important initial precursors.

Bogus Beliefs

Addressing first bogus beliefs, the cases suggest that some common controver-sial assumptions about cross-group relations within host societies increase the chances of intolerance emerging. Three critical premises are the belief that (1) a heritage foundation for citizenship ensures societal solidarity, (2) cross-cultural contact automatically induces societal harmony, and (3) sharply curtailing or banning immigration eliminates native-foreigner frictions. Together these dis-tortions can potentially propel even a state with a sincere desire to manage intolerance down a decidedly unproductive path.

Looking first at the belief that a heritage foundation for citizenship ensures societal solidarity, basing nationality and national identity more on racial, ethnic, or religious heritage rather than on civic loyalty to the state is highly problematic in today's fluid interconnected world. While a few studies report little correlation between ethnic loyalty and out-group hostility, providing hope for peaceful multi-ethnic societies,[1] most analyses conclude that the existence within a state of groups with strongly held distinctive ethnic identities increases the risk of xenophobia toward foreigners living within the country.[2] Within the United Kingdom, for example, natives who emphasize the role of ancestry in citizenship tend to be more likely to report that they are racially prejudiced and more likely to be intent on reducing the number of immigrants and removing undocumented immigrants.[3] Notably, Europe has traditionally had more eth-nic than civic concepts of nationhood, helping to explain the persistence there of foreign intolerance and the difficulties there in socially integrating ethnically distinct minorities, particularly those from Muslim countries.[4] In Hungary, where political leadership identifies the national identity as a Christian state excluding Muslims, the potential for cross-cultural religious tolerance appears to be nonexistent. Such ethnicity-based national identity policy contaminates relations not only with excluded migrant groups but also with the home coun-tries from which the excluded foreign groups emanate.

Frequently this heritage-based approach to nationality entails direct or indi-rect out-group disparagement. Clarifying distinctive national identity through demeaning others is problematic for advancing tolerance-promoting efforts, which generally require shunning nationalist movements emphasizing inferiority of outsiders, discarding negative stereotyping of other cultures based on the behavior of extremists, or characterizing foreign groups as intrinsically evil or the root of all troubles. Given record levels of foreign penetration into most states, and increasing numbers of people within every society coming from multi-ethnic backgrounds, it seems foolhardy in today's globalized world to attempt to base national identity or citizenship on racial, ethnic, or religious heritage or on where people's ancestors lived.

Turning to the belief that cross-cultural contact automatically induces societal harmony, a dangerous premise among some migrant-receiving societies is that maximizing contact between natives and foreign migrants, without attention to context, is sufficient to promote peaceful coexistence. Contrary to the long-standing and widespread belief that the more interaction one has with members of other groups, the less prejudice one will have against those groups,[5] long-term contact, familiarity, interaction, and interdependence may not alone foster deep understanding and tolerance of foreign migrants; while globalization increases contact among people from all over the world, at the same time it can produce greater misunderstanding among them—often leading to hostility—because of the lack of meaningful context for interpreting others' words and actions.[6] Substantial evidence exists that, without the proper facilitation, internationally increased intergroup contact can often increase intergroup misunderstanding and conflict.[7] Many analysts believe that a key precursor to cross-group tensions is antagonism among groups of people coming into contact with each other while espousing opposing cultural practices and belief systems,[8] as deep value divides may cause groups to find each others' communication styles somewhat opaque and unintelligible. This pernicious pattern seems especially likely—illustrated by Germany—when foreign migrants and refugees think that there is little chance no matter what they do of remaining in the country to which they have migrated. As American discrimination toward Hispanics and Muslims suggests, even within a country basically founded by immigrants, closed-mindedness toward outsiders can flourish despite high native-migrant contact if mutual understanding is low. Furthermore, sometimes political regimes may use deeper knowledge of other ways of thinking for "mass manipulation and exploitation" rather than "facilitating the effort towards a more peaceful and harmonious living."[9] Regardless, today many people around the world seem to form their impressions about foreigners and their beliefs based on mass media rather than on personal experience or contacts.[10]

In some countries such as Morocco and Turkey, there has been little meaningful contact and interaction between natives and foreign migrants, due either to foreign migrants being segregated away from natives or to natives' loathing of foreign migrants. This reluctance to interact can be reinforced by the emergence of native-foreigner mutual hostility, which causes both parties to close their minds to any possibility of future contact, communication, tolerance, or reconciliation the longer the ignorance-based antagonism persists. However, sometimes even in situations where there is a high level of cross-cultural contact and interaction—such as between native Dominicans and Haitians—the longer foreign migrants stay in the country, the more they experience suffering.

Concluding with the belief that sharply curtailing or banning immigration eliminates native-foreigner frictions, attempting to address the foreign migrant problem simply by passing regulations to dramatically reduce or eliminate the entrance of foreigners into one's society may create as many problems as it solves. Every state has the sovereign right to control who legally crosses its boundaries and becomes permanent residents, and certainly sometimes restrictive immigration policies can be constructive in regulating cross-border traffic in goods, services, people, and capital; protecting jobs threatened by foreigners via trade, outsourcing, or immigration; and enhancing national security.[11] Nonetheless, the European refugee crisis of 2015–2016 demonstrated this approach's frequent futility; instead of trying to address some of the underlying tensions behind native-foreigner hostility, most European states engaged in "pandering to anti-immigration sentiment"[12] by implementing restrictive policies that did markedly improve native citizen–foreign migrant relations within their societies. The ironic impact of enforced legislation barring immigration has been to increase the lucrative role of criminal smugglers getting people in and out of countries, benefiting neither the national government nor the migrants.

Exclusionist approaches among states within the same region can easily become contagious, as one country closing its borders to migrants automatically puts more pressure on its neighbors to accept them, thus causing proximate states to reconsider any existing foreign migrant openness. For example, some of Hungary's neighbors, especially Austria, have been contemplating further foreign migrant restrictions because of Hungary's closure. In today's globalized world, if people really want to get into a country, they will often find a way or die trying; the Morocco case shows that despite significant fortification of borders, foreign migrants' struggle for freedom of movement seems likely to continue, with increased barriers often just leading to increased fatalities and injuries. Barring the entrance of foreigners, however effective for other purposes, decidedly does not contribute to any form of meaningful cross-cultural tolerance.

Curious Composition

Moving to curious composition, a key background characteristic associated with intolerance is the level of preexisting diversity within a foreign-migrant-receiving society. The three principal problem areas are (1) mono-ethnic societies with low experience integrating foreigners; (2) heterogeneous societies lacking mutual trust because of inequalities among groups; and (3) entrance of newcomers upsetting delicate domestic balances. The tolerance any host society has toward incoming foreign immigrants depends somewhat on the nature and intensity of past interaction with outsiders.

Considering first culturally mono-ethnic host states (such as Japan or Iceland), the high value placed on ethnic homogeneity makes perceived threat, nationalism, and intolerance particularly likely when culturally dissimilar migrants enter their societies.[13] Within such societies, immigrants may be seen as complete strangers, posing a security challenge because there is "a low tolerance for difference" and people "strive to attain homogeneity."[14] If foreigners entering a homogenous society display sharply visible ethnic, racial, or religious differences, then rejection and mistreatment may be even more severe, especially if they are poor (internationally, Haitian, Somali, and Sudanese migrants seem particularly likely to suffer), because ethnically homogeneous states seem least adept at smoothly integrating visibly different foreigners into mainstream society. Because of lack of prior exposure, local natives may be ignorant of foreigners' values and customs and misinterpret them, conflating nationality and ethnicity in pejorative ways. The influx of foreign Muslim migrants from Arab states into Hungary exemplifies this kind of intolerance toward religious beliefs alien to most natives.

Turning to extremely diverse heterogeneous host states, absent key civil society prerequisites, high diversity can potentially increase the frequency and severity of intrasocietal conflict—due to adverse effects on mutual trust and cooperation and on ethnic, linguistic, and religious fractionalization—by cultivating resentments rooted in economic or social inequality.[15] Moreover, political instability caused by potential cross-group frictions within ethnically diverse societies may impede investment and growth, corruption minimization,

and societal diffusion of technological innovations.[16] Within diverse multicultural societies, it is unlikely that each of the distinct racial, religious, or national
groups has similar social status and economic well-being, and so comparative
assessments by various groups seem virtually inevitable, with perceived inequalities generating cross-group resentments. If, within such diverse societies,
one or more groups possess special opportunity advantages over other groups
in terms of social acceptance or political links to the ruling regime, then intrasocietal antagonisms fester further. The entrance of foreign Hispanic and Muslim migrants into the United States illustrates such problems even in a wealthy
heterogeneous country with a long history of substantial foreign immigration.
Nonetheless, although multiculturalist values do not guarantee open native
attitudes toward migrants, a few ethnically diverse states—such as Canada—
with strong internal cross-group differences but also with decent intergroup
communication, multiculturalism-promoting infrastructure, and civil society
norms, have had little cross-group intolerance or interethnic violence.[17]

Concluding with the entrance of newcomers upsetting delicate domestic
balances, sometimes the composition of a country is such that its economic or
cultural stability is fragile rather than robust, and thus can be easily upset by
strangers. Within such societies, "prolonged stays by migrants, especially those
of low class standing, are seen as a threat" to a society's social cohesion, and
"the acceptance of newcomers is provisional upon their compliance with a set
of norms and behaviours dispelling impressions of their perceived dangerous
character."[18] When foreign migrants enter this kind of society, peaceful integration into the existing mix is challenging. Delicate power balances could easily be upset or inflamed by a large foreign migrant influx if—in the economic
sphere—opportunities for economic advancement become rarer because of intensifying competition among existing domestic groups, and if—in the cultural
sphere—cultural insecurity escalates because of the perceived association of
crime and instability with the outsiders. The destabilizing influence of Haitians
pouring into the Dominican Republic exemplifies this pattern.

Debilitating Dependencies

Addressing next debilitating dependencies, the cases suggest that some long-
standing internal and external dependencies—linked to global interdependence—constrain response flexibility and generate intolerance of foreigners.
The three main problematic dependencies are high reliance on (1) domestic undocumented foreigners, (2) competitive foreign exports, and (3) migrant-related

foreign payoffs. Together these can prevent societies from making prudent fluid adjustments to cope with a large influx of foreign migrants.

Looking first at high dependence on domestic undocumented foreign migrants, such heavy reliance by a country for economic success is extremely dangerous, with intolerance and mistreatment toward illegal aliens highly likely because of their vulnerability and lack of legal protection within host societies. Many native citizens perceive illegal foreign migrants as a drain on society not deserving rights similar to citizens. Exemplifying countries that depend heavily on undocumented migrant agricultural workers are the Dominican Republic, Malaysia, and the United States—Dominicans on Haitian workers, Malaysians on Burmese workers, and Americans on Central American workers—to maintain their economy. Moreover, the Greece, Morocco, Russia, and South Africa cases illuminate other problems associated with undocumented foreign migrants. When foreign migrant mistreatment occurs within private corporate agricultural or industrial workplace environments, the chances are lower that wide public exposure of the abuses or sound remedial policies will occur. It is highly paradoxical and tension-inducing that, when a country relying on undocumented foreigners recognizes at least tacitly that its economic success depends on them, it still tries to restrict their entrance and mistreat them when they cross the border. Hypocrisy is blatant here, with direct contradictions evident between national governments' anti-foreign-immigrant public statements and pro-foreign-immigrant private corporate policies. As a result, intolerance victims frequently lack any sort of societal protection, and effective incident reporting by abuse victims is rare. Often elusive transnational criminals with "everything goes" mind-sets engage in smuggling or human trafficking operations to get such beleaguered foreigners into the host countries, and then lawless private groups harass these vulnerable migrants once they cross the border.

Even if economic growth occurs, intolerance can still persist with high dependence on foreigners, as revealed in the Dominican Republic. At the same time, Egypt shows that a country beset by economic problems seems especially unlikely to be sympathetic or compassionate toward those fleeing from instability in a neighboring country. When severe domestic economic downturn is combined with a massive influx of foreigners, as in Greece, intolerance tends to escalate.

Moving to high dependence on competitive foreign exports, intensifying "dog-eat-dog" global economic competition among states and corporations to make money from sales of domestic goods and services in foreign countries stimulates a drive to keep production costs low. For example, in situations where a country is a huge exporter of finished products to the rest of the world, such as Malaysia, often having the cheapest labor with the lowest workers' rights protection—readily leading to foreign migrant abuse—can be beneficial within a highly competitive global business environment both in maintaining attractive foreign retail prices and in attracting more foreign firms to invest in one's country. In this classic "race to the bottom," globalization of production and interdependence among states for goods and services can directly worsen the plight of foreign migrant workers. The quest to maximize competitive advantage and profit margins by keeping productivity high and wages low drives this pattern of exploitation. If foreign workers enter countries illegally, their mistreatment intensifies, for companies can easily ignore minimum wage guidelines (if they exist) with undocumented migrants.

The result of this competitive drive for global markets is often that internal pressures for domestic reform in foreign migrant worker rights become outweighed by incentives to maximize international profits. In the end, an unambiguous inverse relationship emerges between domestic migrant worker protection and global revenues, with both states and companies legitimately able to argue that if they treated these workers better there would have to be significant layoffs because the resulting products and services would become more expensive and therefore would much experience lower international sales.

Concluding with high dependence on migrant-related foreign payoffs, international political pressures even from states avowing liberal enlightened values can sometimes worsen foreign migrants' plight. For example, since 2016 the EU has made large regular payments to Libya, Morocco, and Turkey to keep foreign migrants away from the continent, and in 2018 and 2019 the EU set up centers in Niger and Rwanda to process foreign asylum seekers, because Western European states feel "so overwhelmed" by migrant pressures that they have felt the need to buttress exclusionary policies.[19]

Despite these policies' success in stemming the flood of migrants into Western Europe, and despite the EU's positive global image, countries' willingness to reach agreements with the EU as compensated depositories for those fleeing poverty and violence does not promote improved treatment of refugees, migrants, and asylum seekers. To the contrary, the result can be disastrous for migrants seeking sanctuary, because the states that are being paid off—which over time may become increasingly reliant on the payoff money for their economic viability—often interpret these political pacts as giving them informal license to do whatever they wish to the foreigners quarantined within their borders. While making these payments, EU countries maintain a "not in my backyard" mentality and thus turn a blind eye to abuses within the states doing their bidding as long as would-be migrants are kept out. Although the EU has defended remote migrant detention centers as thwarting smuggler networks and providing "a fair chance at a new life," transnational humanitarian groups such as Human Rights Watch have sharply criticized this "morally perilous" EU policy as instead promoting vulnerability to severe human rights violations, condemning foreign detention centers with "deplorable conditions" and without any real chance of detainees gaining foreign asylum.[20] Most outside observers interpret such exclusionary international agreements as a clear sign that countries initiating them are unwilling to take any responsibility to manage on their own the unwanted foreigner problem.

Petrifying Paranoia

Addressing next petrifying paranoia, the cases suggest that profound domestic terror can enhance native-foreigner intolerance. The three principal native-foreigner fear issues are (1) private coercion reliance, (2) multilevel intolerance foundations, and (3) rapid total assimilation expectations. Together these elements can leave both government officials and private citizens so scared and paralyzed that they become unable to respond effectively and legitimately to the presence of foreigners.

Looking first at fear and distrust tied to private coercion reliance, these can raise tensions between native citizens and foreign migrants within host states. Two kind of reliance are evident, with the common aim of smoothly managing the migrant border-crossing problem but with starkly contrasting methods: (1) reliance by fearful native citizens on independent private vigilante groups or hired private security contractors to maintain domestic order, and (2) reliance by fearful foreign migrants on coercive transnational criminal smugglers for transport. Either way, over the long run nationalism-motivated security contractors and vigilante groups and profit-seeking private smuggling groups may increase societal insecurity within host states, at least partially because of the perceived unpredictability and unconstrained lawlessness of these groups' behavior.

In response to fears surrounding immigrants, either (1) native citizens may form vigilante groups on their own or (2) governments or citizens may hire established security groups. If a national government is cavalier enough to explicitly delegate foreign migrant management to private security contractors or to allow independent vigilante groups to try to maintain order with little restraint, foreigners usually suffer as local anarchy increases. For example, in April 2020, the government of Malta felt so overwhelmed with foreign migrant pressures that it hired a small fleet of private merchant vessels to intercept migrants at sea and return them by force to Libya;[21] elsewhere, anti-immigrant vigilante groups, such as Greece's Golden Dawn, assume that citizens must do "what the federal government refuses to do."[22] Both actions thwart any state impulses toward moderation in migrant policies.

In response to tighter host state entry restrictions, foreign migrants often feel that relying on transnational smuggling operations is the only viable avenue for getting them to their desired destinations. For a fee, transnational smugglers (called "coyotes") promise safe and secure passage across otherwise impassable national borders. Frequently such unscrupulous criminals choose to bribe host state border guards and government officials in order to secure this allegedly "safe" passage for foreign migrants, and thus as with private security contractors host governments can sometimes be complicit in making resorting to coercive private groups a viable option. The net security impact often amplifies both corruption and violence.

Moving next to fear and distrust tied to multilevel intolerance foundations, intolerance and insecurity are heightened if multiple reasons exist for native citizens' resentment of foreign migrants. In particular, if in addition to economic grievances racial or religious bigotry exists, then native-foreigner antagonisms become difficult to manage successfully. Egypt illustrates this multilevel resentment problem in combining racist condescension-based bigotry and fear-based intolerance toward Sudanese migrants; Morocco exemplifies the dangers when economic displacement fears combine with racial discrimination against sub-Saharan Africans; and Russia seems representative in showing how the combination of socioeconomic challenges, racial differences, educational deficits, and language variances place central Asian migrants to Russia in a distinctly vulnerable and disadvantageous position relative to natives.

Racial and religious prejudices play an especially important role in exacerbating multilevel intolerance. Regarding racial bigotry, most cases reveal the existence of some sort of racial discrimination—usually toward foreigners with darker skin color—viewing target groups as inherently inferior and therefore dangerous to the native society. Regarding religious bigotry, most cases combine religious discrimination with racial discrimination, making harassment even more intractable. While often native religious discrimination targets Muslims, in the Dominican Republic the primary natives' fear is of voodoo-practicing Haitians, and in Morocco a primary natives' fear is of Christian sub-Saharan Africans. A pernicious commonality between racial and religious discrimination is that natives' fear and hatred toward foreigners is incredibly deep and intractable, not easily changeable by the migrants themselves, leading to native citizen pessimism that any form of intervention or socialization could normalize relations with targeted foreigners.

Concluding with fear and distrust linked to rapid total assimilation expectations, host societies' insistence on foreign migrants' speedy and complete assimilation can be toxic. The governments of the Dominican Republic and Germany, for example, both explicitly expect that in order for foreigners to be accepted and integrated into domestic society, they must be willing to conform precisely and speedily to native traditions. In such situations, native citizens may view any level of multiculturalism—even just in language—as tantamount to totally destroying their sense of national identity, and foreign migrants may view any traditional form of "melting pot" assimilation as tantamount to totally destroying their indigenous culture.

Insisting on narrow rigid citizenship requirements rejects recognition that broad-minded flexibility or patience about adaptation can be a key to domestic stability. Pushing hard for internal homogeneity is highly troubling because of the need to respect differing civil values, accept that some differences in cultural practices pose little national threat, understand how deep and wide foreigners' cultural barriers to complete assimilation really are, show that national strength does not rest on complete uniformity, and clarify that tolerance does not depend on total agreement. As Turkey illustrates, successful assimilation of a huge number of foreign migrants is highly difficult and tension-creating even if a key cultural similarity—here, religion—is shared between home and host states. Moreover, requiring immediate complete foreigner assimilation can raise the specter of "cultural imperialism"—attempting to impose one's values on others. In the end, demanding speedy forced assimilation by incoming migrants usually turns out to be infeasible.

Uninformed Unfairness

Addressing finally uninformed unfairness, the cases suggest that intolerance toward foreigners can be linked to ignorance, impulsiveness, and prejudice. The three main troublesome gaps are lack of (1) relevant intolerance-based violence data, (2) advance planning for integrating incoming foreigners, and (3) national government objectivity regarding migration. Together these deficiencies can prevent both government officials and private citizens from making appropriate balanced and informed judgments about how to reduce their insecurity associated with growing tensions between interdependence and intolerance.

Looking first at the lack of relevant intolerance-based violence data, if a migrant-receiving state possesses little systematic comprehensive valid and reliable information on past domestic intolerance-based violence incidents, or on national government and private citizen responses to such incidents, then intolerance and societal insecurity can readily escalate. This data gap can be intentional because of (1) national government complicity in the occurrence of intolerance-based violence; (2) a misplaced government desire to maintain societal stability by preventing mass awareness of the scope of the problem and the failure of its management efforts; or (3) a misguided state desire to prevent migrants' home countries from knowing the scope of their mistreatment. This gap's impact is to reduce the ability to learn from the past or from others inside and outside one's society about how to deal with intolerance abuses. Human Rights First reports that "most governments have yet to develop monitoring systems that provide data on the bias motivations (e.g., racism, xenophobia, antisemitism, anti-Muslim intolerance, and homophobia)" behind intolerance-based violence, and that "underreporting of crimes remains one of the principal impediments to improved government responses, especially among irregular migrants, refugees, asylum seekers, and displaced persons, and other vulnerable minorities."[23] Italy particularly exemplifies this pattern, as its combined lack of intolerance-based violence data and lack of special training for Italian police in how to react to and minimize such violence facilitate intolerance.

Given the emotional nature of native-foreign intolerance-based violence, sometimes intolerance initiators and targets tend to ignore actual evidence, and sometimes—as in Germany—the image of foreign migrant threat may be far more important than its reality. Nonetheless, having considerably wider access to better information about both the scope of the problem and the effectiveness of responses seems to be an essential foundation for not only sound development of remedial policies but also effective reduction of mass public fears. For migrant-receiving societies like Russia and Turkey, where native citizen–foreign migrant interaction is minimal, the absence of widespread intolerance-related violence data availability, transparency, and dissemination would seem especially debilitating.

Turning to the lack of advance planning for integrating foreign immigrants, if neither national governments nor concerned citizen groups engage in forward thinking about the implications of long-term foreign migrant presence, then turmoil seems likely. Within Europe as a whole, during the 2015–2016 refugee crisis "nobody had foreseen what was going to happen,"[24] and the difficulties coping with immigration were so dire that some observers said "Europe is committing suicide."[25] For example, before Germany opened up in 2015 to the migrant influx largely from the Middle East and North Africa, Human Rights First contends that the German national government "did not do enough to prepare communities to integrate refugees, to consider regional differences or how prevailing social attitudes would impact a community's readiness to receive refugees," to "provide law enforcement with sufficient resources to protect refugees from hate crimes," or to "communicate to its citizens not just the moral imperative to accept refugees but also the benefits of diversity."[26] Similarly, Morocco vividly demonstrates that if neither a national government nor its native citizenry has planned ahead and made proper adjustments to accommodate foreign migrants remaining in the country, then domestic instability is highly likely. Similarly, the Dominican Republic's government failed to prepare Haitian migrants in a way that would facilitate their smooth assimilation into Dominican society. Often top-down government failure to prepare in advance for a migrant influx is compounded by bottom-up civil society failure to hold state officials accountable for addressing the societal insecurity impacts,[27] which is admittedly difficult when governments are de facto nonresponsive to native citizen pressures, let alone to foreign migrants' concerns.

Concluding with the lack of national government objectivity regarding migration, a preexisting blinding state bias against foreign immigration can significantly contaminate policy. The consequence is that foreigners become highly vulnerable to intolerant behavior with no recourse when harassment occurs. If a political leader rises to power in a migrant-receiving country with anti-foreign-migrant policies as the top agenda item—emphasized both before and after political ascendancy—then the likelihood of compromise, moderation, or societal tolerance seems remote. This pattern has been especially evident with Viktor Orbán in Hungary, Matteo Salvini in Italy, Boris Johnson in the United Kingdom (who assumed power in July 2019), and Donald Trump in the United States. Similarly, Russia's highly nationalistic leader Vladimir Putin certainly has tacitly given license for ultranationalist nativist and xenophobic groups in Russia to become more vocal. If, as in Egypt, law enforcement authorities share the bigotry of those committing intolerance abuses, there is little hope for internally generated improvement in foreign migrants' plight. If, as in Italy, national government officials are in a state of denial about the pervasiveness and severity of intolerance abuses within their country, then hope for effective management of the problem seems remote. A key lesson from South Africa is that states exhibiting intolerance abuses have to be honest about what is transpiring within their borders, because otherwise nobody will be accountable for discriminatory behavior and nothing will be done to remedy underlying tensions. Nonetheless, within democratic societies, because elected political leaders with strong anti-immigration biases are likely to reflect the presence of the same prejudice among the native citizenry, it would be inappropriate to consider the solution to this tolerance impediment to be simply a change in national political leadership.

Situational Triggers of Escalating Intolerance

Scrutinizing next case findings about the specific triggers of escalating intolerance, Figure 5.3 displays four tangible sparks fanning the flames of existing native-foreigner hostility within host states. These are (1) recent foreign-terrorist-induced tragedies or past outside disruption or exploitation; (2) sharply intensifying economic stagnation, decline, or displacement; (3) an unregulated, rapid, massive, and unexpected foreign migrant influx; and (4) the creation of a domestic crisis atmosphere. Together these triggers signal serious intrasocietal tensions, only some of which are controllable through changes in state policy. Of all these triggers, the massive, unexpected, rapid influx of foreign migrants, increasing native citizen-foreign migrant tensions because of unanticipated major lifestyle disruptions, appears to have the most powerful impact on escalating mutual intolerance. The specific triggers identified here highlight an even more urgent need than that identified by the previously discussed intolerance background elements to take preemptive remedial action.

Looking first at a legacy of recent foreign terrorist attacks or outside disruption or exploitation, if a country has memorable political insecurity experience with foreign attacks, oppression, disruption, or domination emanating from other countries—particularly foreign-terrorist-induced tragedies—then intolerance seems likely to escalate. This hostile pattern is substantiated within the United States and Europe by the sharp increase in xenophobia against Arabs in 2001 following the 9/11 terrorist attacks, and in 2015 against foreign Muslims following the November 13 Paris terrorist attack and later following the

---

RECENT PERNICIOUS OUTSIDE ENCOUNTERS

Foreign-terrorist-induced carnage or foreign military attacks
Ongoing suffering, disruption, or exploitation at the hands of outsiders

---

ESCALATING ECONOMIC DISPLACEMENT FEARS

Rapidly worsening domestic economic stagnation and decline, scapegoating others
Skyrocketing local unemployment creating a zero-sum image of native-foreigner
opportunities

UNREGULATED, RAPID, MASSIVE, AND UNEXPECTED FOREIGN MIGRANT INFLUX

Flood of foreign migrants into societies where natives are unprepared to handle them
Social service and law enforcement institutions totally overwhelmed

---

PRESENCE OF A DOMESTIC CRISIS ATMOSPHERE

High-stakes, unexpected, time-pressured, out-of-control dangers seen as public safety threats
Native citizens' and foreign migrants' feelings that their lifestyle is endangered and collapsing

---

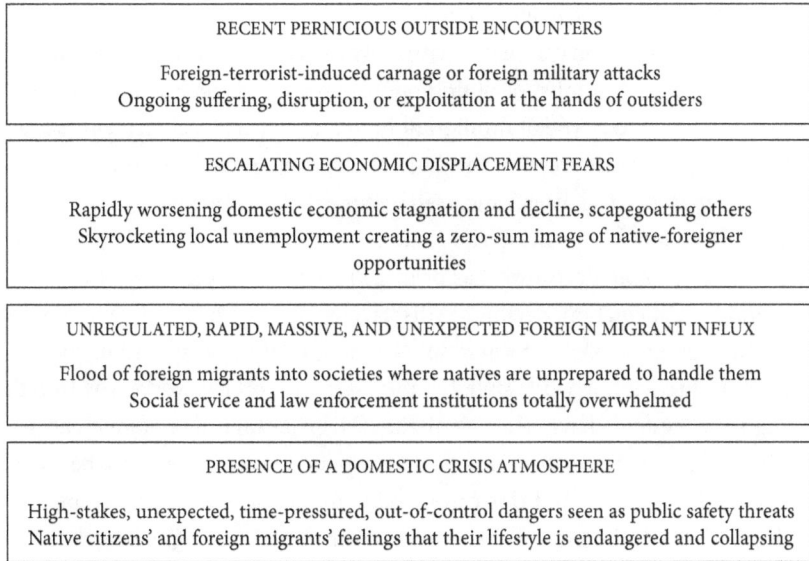

FIGURE 5.3: Situational Triggers of Escalating Intolerance

December 2 San Bernardino terrorist attack.[28] After such foreigner attacks, the
pressure to close borders expands to include migrants from other states beyond
the disruptors' home countries. Alternatively, if there is a perceived past history
of suffering at the hands of another country, even if no recent violent attacks by
foreigners have occurred and local foreign migrants had nothing whatsoever
to do with these past incidents, these newcomers who simply remind local citizens of past traumas may undeservedly bear the brunt of the pent-up anger and
resentment. One example of this past history of externally induced suffering is
that because of Buddhist Myanmar's past repressive policies toward Muslims in
their country, when Burmese migrants enter Muslim Malaysia they automatically have a strike against them because of this past external oppression. The
more recent, devastating, and seemingly unprovoked the past foreign-induced
disruptions are, the more likely they are to trigger greater intolerance toward
foreigners.

Turning to sharply intensifying economic stagnation, decline, or displacement, in such circumstances bottom-up native-foreigner intolerance seems
likely to intensify, especially if a widening rich-poor gap exists.[29] When severe
economic downturns make life unbearable for native citizens, feelings of "resentment and hatred" can emerge,[30] and then "nativism, xenophobia, and the

pressure for protectionism almost inevitably increase."[31] Economic interdependence and globalization can make matters worse, as in many parts of the world they have led to "lost jobs, declining or stagnant wages, and marked income inequality,"[32] and to a type of immigrant influx that many local residents see as "a drain on public resources."[33] This kind of disgruntlement is common among native citizens who feel disenfranchised because it allows them to find someone else to blame for their misery. The chances of frustration-induced aggression rise if the economic downturn has been going on for a long time with growing economic stagnation, decline, or displacement; if the national government seems unwilling or unable to find any solution; or if key distinctions in economic productivity or work style by domestic and foreign workers with differing value systems have been highlighted. During high-unemployment periods, a debilitating zero-sum image of job opportunities can emerge between natives and foreigners, and this can increase intolerance because members of each group think the other is preventing them from working; particularly in societies where there is a high number of unemployed young men with nothing but time on their hands, the potential seems huge for cross-group frictions to escalate. Economic hard times within a society affect not only native citizens but also foreign migrants, who feel exploited and oppressed and may scapegoat native citizens for their misery. These newcomers often feel disillusioned, finding that the streets in their new communities are not really "paved with gold," that local intolerance is much higher than expected, and that advancement opportunities are truly scarce.

Moving to an unregulated, rapid, massive, and unexpected pattern of foreign migrant influx, if this jolting pattern (contrasted to a slow gradual anticipated arrival of a few foreigners) occurs, then the receiving society has little time or capacity to make the many necessary adjustments to cope with the flood of outsiders and increasing domestic intolerance. Numerous studies confirm that a large and rapid influx of foreign immigrants is likely to stimulate threat perceptions among native citizens, usually followed by the rather speedy introduction and passage of highly restrictive anti-immigrant laws.[34] The result is severe unease on the part of foreign migrants, who are unprepared for the suffering, discrimination, or exploitation they receive at the hands of native citizens who themselves are unprepared and in many cases unwilling to integrate them into society. Indeed, "most societies react with alarm when there is an unregulated large-scale illegal migration of people who do not share their culture and national identity."[35] Such escalated intolerance seems particularly likely

if the rapid, massive and unexpected migrant influx is seen as largely composed of illegal aliens rather than with legally sanctioned and vetted migrants,
with illegal migration constituting "the main thorn in the nativist's flesh"[36] and
with most host state citizens likely to demand stronger sanctions against that
identified threat.[37] The magnitude of the dramatic undesired and unexpected
change and resulting identity and control challenges can be especially disruptive to societies with low adaptive capacities. Amnesty International asserts that
some reluctant host state governments complicate this distinction by engaging
in "intentional blurring of the lines between seeking asylum and other forms
of migration," indiscriminately "labeling refugees and migrants as 'illegal' and
as threats to national security."[38] In addition, significant changes in a society's
ethnic mix due to this kind of foreign migrant influx tend to amplify native
citizens' intolerant anti-immigrant perspectives.[39] In many countries, social
services infrastructure and economic employment opportunities cannot readily cope with this level of increased demand, and education and health care fa-
cilities can be drastically overburdened. For example, because of the Syrian civil
war, the Lebanese government felt overwhelmed after taking in over one million Syrian refugees to constitute almost a third of Lebanon's total population,[40]
and the German, Greek, Hungarian, and Italian governments felt overwhelmed
in 2015–2016 by the flood of Middle Eastern and North African refugees trying
to gain entrance into these countries.

Finally, regardless of the size and pace of the foreign migrant presence or
influence, sometimes (as discussed in Chapter 2) government leaders or media
outlets portray it as a national crisis, identifying high-stakes, surprise, time-
pressure, and relatively out-of-control dangers to public safety, causing private citizens to panic.[41] For example, in early April 2019 U.S. president Donald
Trump declared to the country that the flood of immigrants attempting to cross
the southern border of the United States had created a "national emergency,"[42]
which increased native citizen intolerance of outsiders. Similarly, as discussed
earlier, in spring 2020 the coronavirus pandemic emanating from China created a crisis atmosphere, causing a rise in American native citizen intolerance
of Asians. Given the high probability that because of the high stakes some relevant information is classified, private citizens often cannot gauge whether the
sense of crisis urgency is being purposely overblown as a diversionary tactic,
given the previously discussed tendencies of political leaders to use outsider
scapegoating for self-serving purposes. When native citizens believe that they
are experiencing a major crisis, they feel that their basic lifestyle is immediately

endangered and on the verge of collapse, and the emotions surrounding the threat can rise to a fever pitch because of a sense of absolute desperation. Similarly, when foreign migrants believe that their host country is in crisis and that they are being identified as a culprit, they will most likely react by feeling on edge and insecure about their societal status, raising their sense of emotional desperation. Thus during crises, demeaning distortions and rigid opinions emerge between natives and foreigners, far more ominous than in routine situations.[43] Indeed, while some observers naïvely anticipate that global crises will bring people together across national boundaries because of a shared common experience of peril, instead insular divisive nationalist and xenophobic sentiments are often reinforced. Because of high stress, the danger may be framed as so pressing, preparation so small, and time pressure so great that chaos can ensue, with national government officials' assessment of identified societal threats not well-formulated, and state policies reacting to these threats not well-executed in terms of fully taking into account their short-term and long-term consequences. It is ironic that precisely when the need is greatest to think clearly to protect both native citizens and foreign migrants, crisis-induced stress can create paralysis or critical breakdown in national government decision making, often through groupthink or "satisficing,"[44] leading to choices that inadvertently make matters worse for native-foreigner tensions.

Furthermore, the crisis atmosphere usually leads to the creation of narrow, exclusionary, and sometimes arbitrary dividing lines. Choosing to delineate boundaries about who is included and who is excluded within societies is "particularly powerful in times of crisis, whether political, economic, or social";[45] in crises "the 'chosen people' must be clearly defined so as to provide a shelter behind which the losers or battle weary in the competitive environment might find comfort."[46] During national identity crises, there are always government and media worst-case alarmists who are prone to be extremely vocal about having found hard evidence supporting their dire security predictions of unexpected massive calamities, often causing preexisting fears to spiral out of control.[47] Frequently such native citizen fears may focus on the alleged foreign sources of the domestic migrant threat, tending to generate tremendous native anger within a migrant-receiving state that the national governments of foreign migrants' countries of origin have not done more to stop the flood of those seeking to leave. Exemplifying the endpoint of such fear was the decision announced by Trump on March 29, 2019, to cease giving foreign aid to El

Salvador, Guatemala, and Honduras as punishment for failing to prevent their citizens from continually attempting to migrate into the United States.

Conditions Facilitating Intolerance-Based Violence

Finally, examining case findings about the particular circumstances when intolerance seems most likely to become violent, Figure 5.4 summarizes exactly when ongoing prejudice turns really ugly. The four clusters of circumstances conducive to this type of violence are (1) access barriers, (2) coercion facilitation, (3) perpetrator impunity, and (4) violent dishonor. In some of the cases, several preconditions were present at the same time in the same place, making it a tinder box for exploding intolerance-based violence. Sadly, the identified circumstances seem all too commonplace within the current volatile global security environment. Together the presence of these inflammatory conditions may indicate that an affected society has passed the point where it could effectively try to forestall the occurrence of intolerance-based violence, leaving it in a highly vulnerable situation where attempting to minimize the resulting carnage is the only viable option. In other words, compared to the previously discussed background elements conducive to intolerance and situational triggers

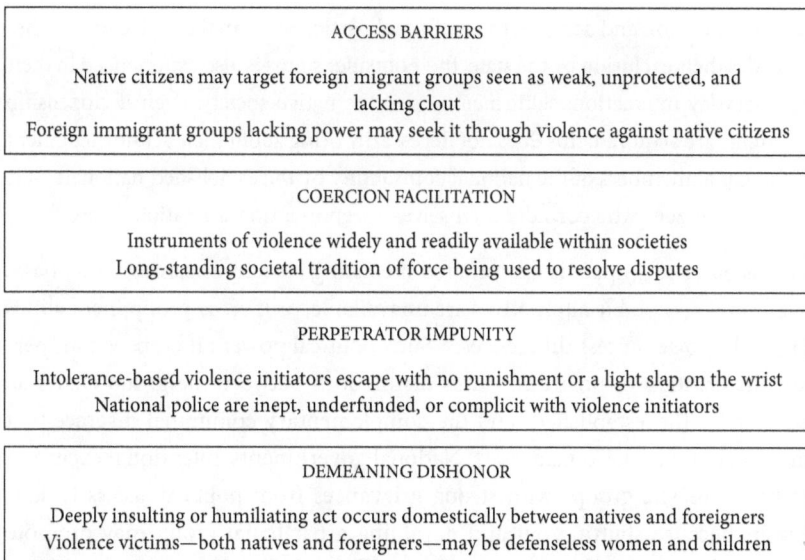

ACCESS BARRIERS

Native citizens may target foreign migrant groups seen as weak, unprotected, and lacking clout
Foreign immigrant groups lacking power may seek it through violence against native citizens

---

COERCION FACILITATION

Instruments of violence widely and readily available within societies
Long-standing societal tradition of force being used to resolve disputes

---

PERPETRATOR IMPUNITY

Intolerance-based violence initiators escape with no punishment or a light slap on the wrist
National police are inept, underfunded, or complicit with violence initiators

---

DEMEANING DISHONOR

Deeply insulting or humiliating act occurs domestically between natives and foreigners
Violence victims—both natives and foreigners—may be defenseless women and children

---

FIGURE 5.4: Conditions Facilitating Intolerance-Based Violence

of escalating intolerance, the ominous conditions identified here suggest that any past preventive policies have failed to promote societal civility.

Looking first at access barriers, denial of access to influence—especially when such denial is a dramatic change from previous policies or when affected groups possess high expectations of political access—can trigger intolerance-based violence. This can work in two directions. When foreign immigrants lack this political access, "they are especially likely to seek it through violence"[48] because they feel there is no other option to get their grievances heard; when nationalistic or xenophobic native citizens lack this political access (because their national government is not listening to their security concerns), they seem more likely to initiate intolerance-based violence, with targets being the most hated or feared foreign immigrant groups perceived as weak, unprotected, and lacking political access, because more vulnerable migrant groups are less in a position to challenge their public image[49] or poor treatment received in host societies. Unlike legal immigrants, undocumented migrants usually lack political access because they cannot form strong economic and social ties because of their lack of legal standing.[50] However, even legal immigrants can sometimes perplexingly find their political access blocked within certain societies:

> In most cases immigrants lack citizenship, which formally attests to their outsider position and deprives them of equal participation in the native society. Besides their exclusion by the state, their outsider status is also experienced in their everyday interactions with members of the native society. Even if citizenship rights are acquired, this does not necessarily bring about their acknowledgment as equal members of the national community by the established nationals—i.e. those citizens who consider themselves as representing the national core.[51]

Access barriers' impact is exacerbated if existing structures cannot fulfill basic needs and acceptable alternatives are unavailable, or if cross-group inequalities highlight power access differences.[52] Such political power differences can "permit the creation of polarized status distinctions between the group charisma claimed by the 'established,' and the complementary communal disgrace that they attribute to the 'outsiders.'"[53] National governments' intentional exclusion of key domestic groups with strong grievances from political access is dangerous because shutting out and devaluing a particular group may promote violence because of its simmering unaddressed frustrations. Exemplifying marginalized foreign migrants' violence against native citizens are the December 31, 2015, sexual attack in Cologne by Middle Eastern and North African migrants on scores of young German women; the May 10, 2011, killing by two Afghan migrants of a forty-four-year-old Greek man; the April 2017 St. Petersburg Metro attack by a Kyrgyzstan migrant; the September 2018 Syrian migrant attack in Sanliurfa on two Turkish citizens; and the November 13, 2015, Paris shootings by a recent migrant posing as a refugee.[54] Exemplifying marginalized native citizens' violence against foreign migrants is brutality targeting African and South Asian migrants in Greece, Muslim migrants in Hungary, African migrants in Italy, and Burmese migrants in Malaysia. Thus for societal stability, readily available political access channels need to be in place to allow frustrated societal groups' voices to be heard—the International Organization for Migration notes that "there is wide acknowledgment that radicalization to violent extremism among settled migrants and refugees and their descendants is a symptom of social exclusion."[55]

Turning to coercion facilitation, if instruments of violence become widely available within a society, then the likelihood of intolerance-based violence tends to increase, especially where there are long-standing societal traditions of using force for dispute resolution. The South Africa case illustrates the dangers of a violent culture, and the cases in Morocco and the United States show the ominous impact of widespread weapons availability. It is not that weapons cause violence, but rather that intolerance-based violence seems more likely—and certainly more destructive—in areas where arms are plentiful and easily obtained by angry frustrated groups. Indeed, "information that refugees may have weapons and ties with militant groups has a particularly strong effect on attitudes and threat perception among the locals."[56] In some cases, native-foreigner violence occurred without formally manufactured weapons, using batons, torches, baseball bats, rocks, and even fists, but the ready availability of guns—due to perceived greater likelihood of successful violence outcomes—can facilitate native citizen attacks on foreign migrants and foreign migrant attacks on native citizens. Arms availability can make these attacks more likely to lead to target resentment and anger, and thus more likely to lead to violent action-reaction cycles. If such violent acts have occurred domestically in the past, then they seem likely to continue in the present and future because of a deepening desire for revenge based on perceived intensification of long-standing intrasocietal disputes. Instruments of violence can also make it easier for destabilizing migrant-harassing independent vigilante groups, hired security contractors, or transnational criminal smugglers to operate. The continuing visibility of violence and instruments of violence makes resorting to physical coercion seem to be a more natural and immediately accessible option. Human Rights First notes that "violence against one vulnerable group increases the possibility of violence towards others—as well as social anxiety about it—and interferes with the peace and stability of the nation as a whole."[57] Often governments wish to avoid having violence facilitation seen as a continuous disruptive pattern and prefer instead to label violent acts as rare idiosyncratic occurrences, a dismissive response that can worsen long-run insecurity. Given the pervasive recidivism, postviolence resentment tends to persist, impeding durable political stability.

Considering perpetrator impunity, if there is an upsurge in violence perpetrators escaping severe punishment or increased public awareness of this pattern, then violence escalates. Such violence-promoting perpetrator impunity usually occurs where a fervent anti-immigrant climate exists.[58] When violence initiators escape with no punishment or a light slap on the wrist, the reason is usually that government police are inept, underfunded, or complicit with these perpetrators—"when the perpetrator of violence against refugees and asylum seekers is the host government, or the host government is complicit in the abuse, the credibility of the refugee protection mandate is obviously in doubt."[59] The Egypt, Morocco, Russia, and South Africa cases highlight such perpetrator impunity. Within areas with deep long-standing cross-cultural intolerance, potential perpetrators' fear of punishment may be the only tool available for maintaining social order. Although intolerance-based violence is often highly emotional and often impulsive, perpetrators do not totally avoid calculating the potential for apprehension and punishment, and if the penalties are light and the changes of apprehension are low, this deterrent may disappear.

Concluding with demeaning dishonor, if a country's citizenry believes that foreign migrants committed a deeply insulting or humiliating violent act against a native, or if a foreign migrant group believes that native citizens committed such an act against one of their members, then violent retaliation seems likely.[60] This pattern particularly applies when victims, such as women and children, are seen as defenseless. Recently, the number of migrants who are women and children has dramatically increased, with women now constituting about half of the global migrant population,[61] and there has been a concomitant increase in sexual violence toward female refugees, asylum seekers, and migrants both by host society natives and transnational criminal smugglers. For women, "the insecurities of migration are a reality which is likely to continue and even worsen in the future".[62]

> Migrant and refugee women are subject to the same types of violence as non-migrant women. . . . However, the specificity of their positions as migrants and refugees may in some cases increase their vulnerability to certain forms of violence, and may limit the forms of protection and redress to which they have access. Moreover, migrant and refugee women may be more vulnerable than migrant and refugee men to violence because of gendered inequalities within the migratory process and in both their countries of origin and new host countries. Migrant and refugee women may thus be seen to be in a situation where they are "doubly" vulnerable to violence—as migrants/refugees and as women.[63]

Interestingly, the direction of the sexual violence seems to differ depending on the type of host country for foreign migrants. Within wealthier or more powerful host countries such as Germany, Italy, and Russia, the dominant pattern of sexual violence seems to be foreign migrant men harassing native women, with indignant angry native retaliation quickly ensuing, whereas in weaker, poorer host countries, the dominant pattern of sexual violence appears to be native society men harassing foreign migrant women, with notable cases of migrant women being sexually harassed by native citizens in countries including the Dominican Republic, Egypt, India (against female Chin refugees from Burma), Malaysia, Morocco, and Turkey.[64] Young female migrants traveling alone are particularly vulnerable to intolerance-based violence. Because illegal female migrants lack international legitimacy, they have no rights, so they are often most abused and mistreated without fear of notice or retribution.

The bidirectional pattern of intolerance-based violence over violent dishonor, with humiliating native-foreigner interactions initiated by either party, harks back to ancient primordial intrasocietal and cross-societal violence. In the end, this type of brutality appears to be difficult to minimize because the humiliation so often ignites emotional "honor-shame"-type fury, where the offended party develops—especially if the victim is a vulnerable native citizen—a hot-blooded feeling that they must exact revenge against the alien culprits so as to deter any future violation of norms and laws. Given the impact of preexisting stereotypes, this violence-inducing sense of dishonor seems particularly likely within societies where attribution is perceived by violence perpetrators as murky. Sometimes preexisting prejudices against foreigners, particularly against women, dominate state decision making about who is apprehended, prosecuted, and convicted of a humiliating violent crime.

6 Managing Intolerance-Based Violence

THE PRIMARY VALUE OF UNDERSTANDING intolerance-based violence between native citizens and foreign migrants within host states is to discover how to minimize its frequency and the severity of ensuing security disruptions. No tried-and-true formula has yet been developed to cope with this security challenge. With intolerance-based violence having such multifaceted origins, surmounting the many obstacles to brutality minimization is a monumental task.

Critical questions inescapably arise about how host societies should formulate and evaluate their management of intolerance-based violence. They need to weigh any costs, including diverting efforts away from other sources of societal instability or increasing societal divides and intractable conflicts, against any benefits, including reaping gains from a more vibrant and diverse domestic population and receiving approval from source countries and the rest of the international community for such compassionate behavior. Both pragmatic expediency and moral principles should be part of this cost-benefit analysis, with explicit recognition of underlying value clashes and different senses of fair play among those experiencing frustrating circumstances. Globally, the answers to these questions need to exhibit overarching coherence while being attentive to differing norms within and across countries; perhaps the ideal form of intolerance-based violence management would integrate "both a comprehensive and a tailor-made approach."[1] Any solutions proposed need to be both flexible and adaptive, incorporate input from both native citizens and foreign migrants to overcome existing communication barriers, and provide durable remedies to existing mutual prejudices and fears. More broadly, "in an interdependent world, a security strategy must of course address short-term hard security threats, but must also be able to motivate the long-term investment in cooperative institutions, relationships and governance needed to tackle underlying drivers of insecurity and conflict and the negative side of globalisation."[2]

General Intolerance Management Concerns

Prior to presenting recommended remedies, three general intolerance management policy concerns, shown in Figure 6.1, deserve attention: (1) management responsibility limits; (2) management speed, timing, and uniformity; and (3) management probing depth. Together these three emphasize less which management initiatives are selected and more how initiatives are undertaken. Given existing fragile sensibilities, the implementation modes are just as important as the strategies chosen in determining public acceptance and policy effectiveness.

Management Responsibility Limits

Debates rage about the responsibility limits for preaching and practicing social tolerance, and this divisive discussion often impedes violence minimization. Such controversies frequently center on the question "Should liberal societies tolerate the intolerant?"[3] Many analysts have a quick definitive answer—one observer quips, "ultimately, there is no place for the tolerance

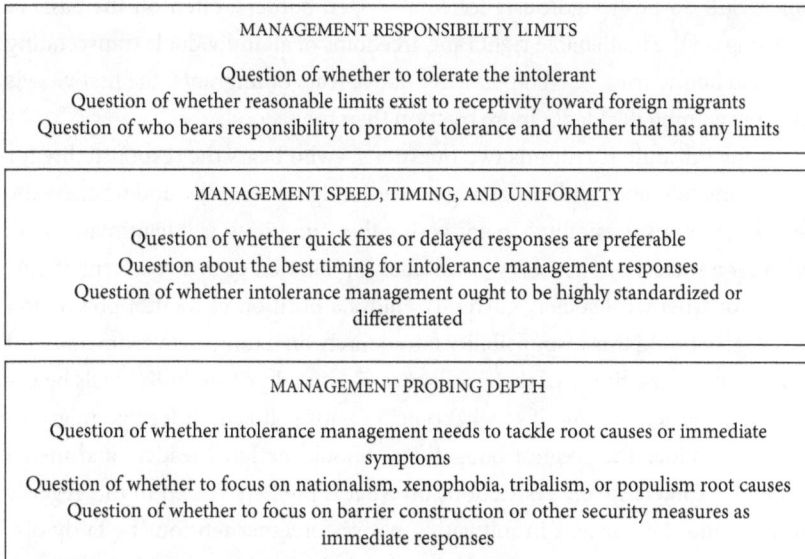

MANAGEMENT RESPONSIBILITY LIMITS

Question of whether to tolerate the intolerant
Question of whether reasonable limits exist to receptivity toward foreign migrants
Question of who bears responsibility to promote tolerance and whether that has any limits

---

MANAGEMENT SPEED, TIMING, AND UNIFORMITY

Question of whether quick fixes or delayed responses are preferable
Question about the best timing for intolerance management responses
Question of whether intolerance management ought to be highly standardized or differentiated

---

MANAGEMENT PROBING DEPTH

Question of whether intolerance management needs to tackle root causes or immediate symptoms
Question of whether to focus on nationalism, xenophobia, tribalism, or populism root causes
Question of whether to focus on barrier construction or other security measures as immediate responses

---

FIGURE 6.1: General Intolerance Management Concerns

of intolerance"[4]—but within many socially progressive societies the response is not so black-and-white. For example, another commentator argues that if "people value a sense of place and wish to be surrounded by others who speak a familiar language and who follow customs they think of as their own," and if "they want to sustain these comforts by keeping away people unlike themselves or cultural imports from elsewhere," then "(assuming certain moral basics of nondiscrimination are observed) that is their right."[5] Ultimately, this second position seems to be more widely accepted, because the perception of which groups merit tolerance is subjective.

A parallel disagreement concerns the question "Does each society bear unlimited responsibility for accepting foreign immigrants, and if so, are there proper limits to this receptiveness?" For example, regarding Europe, one observer restrictively contends that "any sensible policy on immigration and integration would have taken into account that although this ship of Europe may occasionally save people in distress from the seas around us, there is a point—where we take too many people on board, take them on too quickly, or take on those with bad intent—at which we will capsize the only vessel that we, the peoples of Europe, have."[6] In contrast, other analysts assert that no migrant-receiving limits are ever justifiable; although admittedly "no politician of any consequence anywhere wants to open all borders,"[7] many pro-immigration voices still do push vigorously for totally open borders, often on the basis of focusing on the inalienable rights and freedoms of all individuals transcending national boundaries.[8] Given pervasive native fears of migrants, the first view is globally gaining decidedly more traction than the second.

A final dispute surrounds two questions—who bears the responsibility for promoting tolerance and mitigating native-foreigner tensions, and what are the limits of that responsibility? In answering these inquiries, is it legitimate to ask whether a society has a history of colonial exploitation or mistreatment of outsiders, or whether a society currently enjoys a position of wealth, power, and privilege? Should this responsibility fall squarely on national governments, and if so what are the limits of their obligations? Should private individuals be expected to participate, and if so what types of native citizens or foreign migrants should shoulder the greatest obligations? Should national leaders and media outlets be subject to any restrictions on what is publicly voiced in this regard? How should the burdens in mitigating native-foreigner tensions be fairly distributed within and across societies? An underlying controversy behind many such questions revolves around whether potential intolerance-based violence victims should bear any obligation to try to improve their future safety. Attempting to deflect such potentially divisive questions by announcing tritely that there is collective responsibility for remedies among all members of society is not helpful. Given that a key dynamic surrounding the current inability to successfully manage intolerance-based violence involves deflecting accountability for problems encountered away from oneself and one's society by scapegoating outsiders, answering these questions emphasizing the appropriate vortex of responsibility in a much more differentiated way seems particularly vital.

Management Speed, Timing, and Uniformity

Key debates surrounding intolerance management involve optimizing its (1) speed—quick or gradual; (2) timing—preemptive or reactive; and (3) uniformity—standardized or differentiated. Most societies today lean toward quick, reactive, and standardized responses, although such choices may not always work best.

Regarding response speed, the choice is between quick fixes that address emerging tensions right away and delayed, more enduring responses. The dangers of quick fixes include that they could be ill-thought-out in terms of consequences or products of impulsive emotionalism, resulting from bottom-up pressure by angry groups on governments to respond—as "policy based on fear may be expedient for politicians and profitable for the media and the security sector, but it is generally bad policy."[9] Both native citizens and foreign migrants tend to be impatient after perceived slights from the other for a speedy state response, regardless of long-run consequences, and so states seem much more prone to undertake quick "Band-Aid" stopgap measures than thoughtfully considered durable ones. In contrast, durable long-term solutions may incorporate all affected parties' interests, but they usually are implemented so slowly that circumstances deteriorate, escalate out of control, and produce major societal disruption.

Regarding response timing, the choice is among doing so prior to the entrance of foreign migrants into a society, prior to the emergence of widespread societal intolerance toward foreigners, or only after intolerance-based violence breaks out. Should the focus be preventing intolerance from emerging, preventing intolerance from translating into violence, or preventing intolerance-based violence from producing widespread societal insecurity? Considering responses prior to foreign migrants' entrance into a society, two common receiving-state economic means to discourage immigration are to restrict remittances—the transfer of money by foreign migrants to their families and communities in their home countries—and to increase foreign aid to countries from which migrants come to improve conditions there so as to reduce people's desire to emigrate. However, neither approach has had much success in producing stability. The handicap of remittance restrictions is their "little effect on sending states' compliance" and on reducing the migrant influx because even when severe remittance restrictions are in place migrants "devised ways to send remittances home via third countries";[10] the handicap of foreign aid is that "no amount of foreign aid is going to stop the exodus of undocumented migrants" as long as their home states "remain impoverished, dangerous and unstable."[11] Considering responses after intolerance-based violence actually erupts, the obvious problem is that it is usually too late to address underlying causes, and the societal costs of remediation become much higher. More broadly, it is difficult to know where and how to intervene early without engaging in some kind of demeaning, morally objectionable, and perceptually illegitimate profiling. Although waiting to intervene until after tangible harm occurs may garner greater international community and private citizen legitimacy, such delays could lead to decidedly less effective responses in providing security protection than if preemptive action—earlier in the sequence of steps leading to violence—had been taken beforehand.

Regarding response uniformity, the choice is between highly standardized or highly differentiated intrasocietal policies. Standardized approaches, often resulting from globalization's homogenizing pressures for "one-size-fits-all" solutions, have the advantage of being seen as legitimate and consistent within and across countries, but intolerance-based violence precursors vary not only from country to country[12] but also even from area to area within a country; "although international institutions such as the EU should play a role in coordinating immigration policy, democratic states must be allowed to tailor their own policies to the preferences of their voters."[13] In contrast, more differentiated policies, though tuned to each setting's special needs and able to address circumstantial differences, could easily lead to accusations of irregularity and unfairness across areas by both native citizens and foreign migrants affected.

Management Probing Depth

Significant controversy surrounds whether solutions to intolerance-based violence need to tackle root causes or just immediate symptoms. On the surface, it may seem that addressing root causes will always be vital to get at the heart of the problem and prevent its recurrence—"by fixating on the symptoms, we remain blind to the root causes."[14] Yet most policy makers reject this logic because they see many root causes as structural, so deeply embedded in societal traditions, values, and institutions that they would be quite difficult to change. Focusing just on immediate symptoms seems much easier, but then key tensions are left unresolved.

Exemplifying this symptoms focus is the 2015–2016 European refugee crisis response. To "stem the tide of migrants," European political leaders needed to "address the root causes of migration, helping to broker an end to Syria's civil war, restoring stability to Libya, and upping aid to sub-Saharan Africa,"[15] yet European states preferred "to erect more barriers" and to "pay for more security measures"[16]—dealing with just the immediate symptom of the migrant influx rather than any of its root causes.

Addressing the root causes of intolerance-based violence still leaves open whether it is most vital to focus on roots of intolerance,[17] migration,[18] nationalism,[19] xenophobia,[20] tribalism,[21] populism,[22] corruption and government management failures,[23] or all of these. Should the emphasis be why native-foreigner hate and fear exists, why so many foreigners are leaving their home countries, or why frustrated people resort to the use of force? Highly relevant here is the extensive research by charitable foundations, local community groups, migrant associations, nongovernmental humanitarian organizations, religious bodies, transnational watchdog outfits, and university institutes on the roots of intolerance-based violence.[24] However, sometimes the causal direction among the intertwined elements can be confusing, such as whether "the refugee problem is to be regarded simply as a consequence and manifestation of the lack of peace and security," or alternatively as "one of the root causes of insecurity."[25] Moreover, frankly exploring root causes can be both costly and painful to societies.

Recommendations for Managing Intolerance-Based Violence

Figure 6.2 summarizes constructive recommendations for managing global intolerance-based violence. The five clusters of public and private security-enhancing ideas are increasing (1) awareness, (2) inclusiveness, (3) liability, (4) recovery, and (5) sensitivity. As discussed earlier, just keeping migrants away is neither feasible nor tolerance-promoting. Frequently advocated here are increased promotion of visionary leadership and involvement of transnational watchdog, civil society, and humanitarian groups, because of bureaucratic state

INCREASING AWARENESS

Improving state and international organization monitoring and reporting of intolerance-based violence, responses to such violence, and the ease of prosecuting offenses

Using social media and education better to raise awareness and appreciation of the vital domestic role and contribution of natives and foreigners

Encouraging sincere tolerance-promoting speeches by political leaders within tension-laden societies to set civil national expectations

INCREASING INCLUSIVENESS

Working to broaden the notion of national citizenship so that it is more fluid and less linked to fixed elements such as race, religion, or ethnicity

Amplifying noncoercive bottom-up citizen initiatives in cooperation with government aimed at increasing cross-cultural civility, providing channels for the voices of all affected parties

Minimizing security gaps between those people most and least protected within a given society so as to expand equal opportunity

INCREASING LIABILITY

Promoting improvement in commitment to advance-planning and early-warning systems, incorporating creative contingency options

Enlarging political and social accountability for comparable legal, attitudinal, and behavioral treatment of natives and foreigners

Discovering better means to rehabilitate violence perpetrators to prevent recidivism in the form of continued harassment of others

INCREASING RECOVERY

Boosting resiliency of victims of intolerance-based violence within a society so that they may quickly resume their normal lives

Helping foreigners smoothly integrate into society by making language training and technical skills available, allowing them access to secure employment

Forming societal support groups whose role is to assist with emerging challenges experienced by intolerance-based violence victims

INCREASING SENSITIVITY

Avoiding demanding that either natives or foreigners within a society make overly rapid or radical adjustments to cope with security challenges

Respecting existing desires by foreign migrant groups for reasonable levels of cultural autonomy while avoiding associated divisive societal passions

Fostering the emergence of civil society norms committed to resolve disagreements through discourse and to leverage complementary cross-cultural assets for mutual gain

FIGURE 6.2: Recommendations for Managing Intolerance-Based Violence

and international organization limitations in addressing such issues. To enhance compliance, each suggestion explicitly considers perceptions of native citizens, foreign migrants, and national governments, however misguided they may be. Since the prescriptions may initially seem idealistic, each addresses how to overcome feasibility obstacles in today's world. Each idea is designed to be undertaken not alone but as one component of a broader long-run remedy package.

Increasing Awareness

Addressing first increasing awareness, greater attentiveness is important both for government officials and private citizens because affected societies often ignore, minimize, or purposely redirect their attention away from the pervasiveness of intolerance-based violence. Three principal avenues for increasing awareness are (1) improving state and international organization monitoring and reporting of intolerance-based violence incidents, responses to such violence, and the record of punishing perpetrators; (2) using social media and education better to raise appreciation of the vital contributions of both natives and foreigners; and (3) encouraging sincere tolerance-promoting speeches by political leaders within xenophobic societies. Together these strategies could potentially alter societal perceptions surrounding some of the background elements conducive to intolerance, specifically reducing the bogus beliefs, petrifying paranoia, and uninformed unfairness concerns, and through these changes, these strategies could create sufficient understanding of intolerance-based violence that appropriate remedial action could be undertaken.

Of the five clusters of recommendations for managing global intolerance-based violence, it seems easiest to increase widespread awareness of the problem. The rationale is that dramatic international technological improvements in communications and monitoring systems have made it much less costly and time-consuming to collect and disseminate relevant information through a wide variety of outlets. However, two key challenges need to be overcome: having information collected and disseminated (1) be noticed, interpreted correctly, and sincerely cared about by state and society recipients; and (2) not be contaminated by "fake news" or other intentionally distorted messages designed to muddy common understandings. To address these obstacles, data collected and disseminated would need to be transparent in identifying reliance on multiple sources widely perceived as credible, as well as creative and clever in finding ways to capture the audience's attention in the midst of a sea of alluring distractions.

To ensure that these awareness-enhancing mechanisms are feasible, what needs to be avoided at all costs is the assumption that presenting to intolerance-based violence perpetrators and their supporters objective empirical data about foreign migrants' positive societal contributions, challenging negative preconceived notions, would alone be sufficient to change perpetrators' attitudes and behavior. Nationalism expert Andreas Wimmer notes that "information campaigns portraying immigrants as cultural enrichments instead of demonising them as dangerous competitors certainly do not change xenophobic attitudes,"[26] because xenophobes can easily discredit or ignore such contrary information, given their idiosyncratic cultural, economic, or political lenses and their closed-minded misperceptions unreceptive to reasonable restraint. Moreover, the International Organization for Migration admits that "amid the often polarized political, public and media discussions and debates on migration, evidence, knowledge and balanced analyses that encompass historical insights as well as strategic implications appear to have little space or traction."[27] Promoting positive refugee images not only "does not necessarily make the locals more supportive of refugees" but also "can actually backfire."[28] So for effective enhancement of natives' appreciation of foreigners, evidence presented about migrants' societal contributions needs to be augmented by other means—such as direct testimonies by native group members about how without these migrants their lifestyle could not be maintained.

Looking initially at improving state and international organization monitoring and reporting of intolerance-based violence, responses to such violence, and the record of punishing perpetrators, dramatic improvement is vital. Human Rights First recommends that state governments expand their acknowledgment and condemnation of this brutality, strengthen relevant law enforcement and prosecution of violence perpetrators, and improve monitoring and public reporting of violent acts.[29] Given notoriously poor intolerance-based violence reporting (due to state fears about growing mass public anxiety), understandable victim reluctance to report abuses, and unconcerned, ineffective, or collusive state law enforcement authorities, both private citizens and transnational watchdog groups need to assist with this monitoring and reporting, which need to equally scrutinize native and foreign violence perpetrators. More reliable and comprehensive data about perpetrator punishment—gathered by watchdog groups if state governments do not do so—may help spotlight and ultimately reduce the tendency toward perpetrators' impunity through increasing onlooker outrage about the extent to which they are not penalized for their actions.

Moving to using social media and traditional classroom education better to raise awareness and appreciation of the vital contributions of both natives and foreigners, a two-pronged approach seems most effective in increasing mutual tolerance. While the public is exposed to lots of conflicting messages, if communication is done properly, closed-minded exclusionary attitudes could be changed. Although social media often promote intolerance, it seems advisable for national governments and transnational humanitarian organizations to expend more effort countering this negative message—given the increasing global attention paid to this type of news outlet—using the same kind of platform. This effort entails injection of more frequent and attention-grabbing stories about the societal interdependence of native citizens and foreign migrants and the value of both for community welfare. Up to this point, most national governments have lacked comprehensive strategies for responding to the spread of nationalistic and xenophobic hatred online.[30]

Considering traditional education, teaching is a powerful means to promote mutual tolerance and appreciation of other groups. Cross-cultural educational programs[31] could at least begin by emphasizing positive contributions of both natives and migrants to foster respect for diversity, framed as a challenging blessing rather than as a curse. For example, the composition and background of the French soccer team that won the World Cup in 2018 could be promoted especially within France to reduce intolerance; the team included twelve players of African ancestry deriving from nine different African states; 78.3 percent of the French squad came from some kind of migrant background; and "France's newest superstar, forward Kylian Mbappe, was born to an Algerian mother and a Cameroonian father, yet is a hero for millions of French youngsters of all ethnicities."[32] The educational goal would be "a recognition and celebration of the fact that our fellow world citizens, in their different places, with their different languages, cultures, and traditions, merit not just our moral concern but also our interest and curiosity."[33] The educational focus should be on youth, including "helping children develop open-mindedness, empathy, resilience, and the values of tolerance and inclusion,"[34] through not one-sided indoctrination but rather inculcating balanced receptivity in reacting to perceived differences. Basic orientations about fear and trust of outsiders are formed in childhood, and the current classroom emphasis in many countries on "stranger danger" sets the stage for later adult xenophobia. Native citizens need to receive education to "counter public misperceptions and misinformation about refugees and asylum seekers."[35] Government law enforcement officials need to receive enhanced special education in how to deal with the distinctive challenges associated with a large societal influx of foreign immigrants, after which—as advocated by Human Rights First—these officials can conduct outreach and education efforts in affected communities.[36]

Concluding with encouraging sincere tolerance-promoting speeches by political leaders within xenophobic societies, instead of crisis-escalating fear-mongering speeches identifying either nativists or migrants as scapegoats, national leaders need to become societal role models to establish civil national expectations. The emphasis in such political speeches, even if they need to include comments about border control restrictions or apprehension of undocumented migrants, should be on how cooperation between natives and foreigners with differing skills and backgrounds can produce optimal societal outcomes. Human Rights First specifically reinforces the need for political leaders publicly speaking out against intolerance.[37] Contrary to presumed citizen disregard of political leaders' remarks, a strong speech by a head of state condemning intolerance of foreigners can promote restraint; for example, after increased intolerance-based violence against foreigners following the 9/11 terrorist attacks on the United States, a significant drop ensued when on September 17, 2001, President George W. Bush delivered a speech urging greater tolerance.[38]

National leaders need pragmatic incentives to give such tolerance-promoting speeches. Although if addressed incorrectly this approach could limit free speech opposing open borders because of legitimate security concerns, within democratic societies there needs to be demonstration of palpably strong mass public aversion to intentionally polarizing political speeches. One way to develop this kind of aversion would be if transnational watchdog groups could circulate more tangible convincing evidence and arguments about the connection between such divisive speeches and increases in intolerance-based violence negatively affecting everyone in society. If the mass public demonstrates this aversion, then perhaps media outlets dependent on readership for revenues might at least temporarily abandon their insatiable lust for sensationalist inflammatory reporting and instead expand positive coverage of politicians' tolerance-promoting speeches. Within authoritarian societies, perhaps the only realistic way to promote tolerance-enhancing head-of-state speeches might be if the direct reward was increased economic, military, or political support from approving outside states.

Increasing Inclusiveness

Addressing next increasing inclusiveness, both government officials and private citizens should take steps to level the playing field so that all those living within their societies have equal opportunity to contribute productively to overall societal welfare. The three principal avenues for increasing inclusiveness are (1) working to broaden the notion of national citizenship so that it is more fluid and less linked to fixed elements such as race, religion, or ethnicity; (2) amplifying noncoercive bottom-up citizen initiatives in cooperation with government aimed at increasing cross-cultural civility, providing channels for the voices of all affected parties; and (3) minimizing security gaps between those people most and least protected within a given society so as to expand equal opportunity to be productive without having to worry about safety concerns. Together these strategies could induce both homogeneous and heterogeneous societies to be more open to diversity, making all in society feel that they have value.

Of the five clusters of recommendations for managing global intolerance-based violence, it appears hardest to find ways to improve inclusiveness within societies not just in rhetoric but also in reality. The rationale for this difficulty is that the manner in which citizenship is defined is often deeply and firmly embedded in each country's distinctive histories and traditions, so citizens may think that changes incorporating outsiders challenge their core national identity. However, in this case the high within-society interdependence between native citizens and foreign migrants can help to overcome this challenge; after native citizens finally and fully acknowledge that foreign migrants are going to be residents of their countries for the long run, and that foreign migrants have become integral in national production and consumption in ways that are directly nationally beneficial, the door could be opened to constructive mutual dialogue and compromise.

To ensure that this cluster of inclusiveness-enhancing mechanisms is feasible, what needs to be avoided here at all costs is the tendency to create systems that provide—or are widely perceived as providing—just token input and influence by foreign migrants in societal decision-making processes. To pacify nationalistic or xenophobic native citizens, many countries use this kind of tokenization deceptively to create the illusion of inclusion, but in the end nobody from underrepresented groups is fooled. For example, regarding opportunities to be a journalist in Germany working for print and broadcast media, having a foreign migrant background can help with getting a job, but at the same time "it can lead to either 'tokenism,' when staff may feel they are hired solely for their perceived advantages, or outright exclusion, with them being treated as less competent"; in both cases, "deeper, more institutional biases in migration coverage" may remain unaddressed.[39] The best way to avoid this roadblock is for watchdog groups to scrutinize closely the meaningfulness of new institutional diversity-promoting initiatives and to have the foreign migrants who success-fully use new meaningful societal channels for political, cultural, and economic input and influence publicly attest to their value.

Looking initially at working to broaden the notion of national citizenship so that it is more fluid and less linked to fixed elements such as race, religion, or ethnicity, countries need to realize that their national identities have already evolutionarily changed in the past, and that attempting to insulate cultures from change and keep them static is both infeasible given globalization pressures and undesirable given rapid external changes. What is needed instead of rigid de-fensive protection of the cultural and economic status quo is for every country to figure out better ways to integrate the kinds of changes that both natives and foreign migrants feel will not interfere with established core values and cul-tural traditions. Inspired political leadership can play a key role in stimulating this change. Conversations with both native citizen and foreign migrant groups need to determine what dimensions of their interaction each considers to be most disruptive and most useful. To make such conversations most construc-tive, "what such divided countries now need most is a break-up of stereotypes and group identities—concepts such as 'people,' 'elite,' Establishment, populism and Islam must be refuted and invalidated as false entities."[40] Requirements for citizenship ought not to be watered down so far as to become meaningless but rather should focus on elements that reflect civic loyalty rather than ethnic identity, and acceptance of national government laws rather than relying on ancestry or native language. This thrust reverses the insistence in today's world of certain countries on granting preferred immigration status to foreigners able to prove genetic ancestry/bloodline connection to native citizens, based on the underlying yet unstated controversial premise that this genetic link makes as-similation easier.

Moving to amplify noncoercive bottom-up citizen initiatives in cooperation with government aimed at increasing cross-cultural civility while providing channels for the voices of all affected parties, tighter government-citizen col-laboration is essential. Political leaders should find fresh avenues to harness the dynamics of nationalist pride in constructive directions; "instead of promoting jingoism and xenophobia, leaders should appeal to people's innate in-group tendencies in ways that incentivize cooperation, accountability, and care for one's fellow humans."[41] Because tensions between native citizens and foreign migrants have both top-down and bottom-up roots, a joint effort—forging co-alitions for cross-cultural and citizen-government understanding—is essential for success. This inclusive understanding should stress that what is often seen as a "debilitating dependency" on foreign migrant labor may in many ways be an asset benefiting the society as a whole. Concerned citizen groups—including civil society, human rights, and humanitarian organizations—should not wait for governments to take the first step in promoting cross-cultural civility. Having readily available formal and informal channels for input by underrepresented migrant groups—and even by fringe nativist groups—could help reduce frustration-inducing access barriers. In addition, mediation channels for reconciling native-foreigner differences within societies may sometimes help foster more harmonious societal outcomes from cross-cultural contact. Given the importance of cooperative interaction between natives and foreigners, a hopeful sign for increasing civility is that local communities experiencing a large influx of foreign migrants have found ways to engage in constructive inclusionary activities—with foreigners slowly recognized as being there for the long run—rather than in initiation of anti-migrant policies.[42]

Concluding with minimizing security gaps between people who are most and least protected within societies so as to expand equal opportunity, mutual acceptance within societies is impossible without a base level of human security and protection for everyone who resides within a country's borders. A situation where everyone is competing with each other to survive, in the face of insufficient available resources or unprotected marginalized groups, is sure to promote an atmosphere of hatred, suspicion, resentment, and fear. Downplaying protection of a vulnerable area because it is a traditional hotbed of violence and crime or because it is largely inhabited by illegal foreign migrants or nativist extremists ends up hurting not only residents of the unprotected area but also the integrity of the broader society. Moreover, perceived intrastate inequalities in protection—quite common within societies with large foreign migrant populations[43]—can amplify mutual resentment between natives and foreigners. So to reduce perceived as well as real security differences among contending societal groups, efforts should be launched to replace skewed, asymmetrical, and exploitative relationships with more reciprocal, even-handed, and mutually beneficial exchanges regarding safety. For example, "governments should develop public goods projects that benefit people of all colors, regions, and class backgrounds, thereby avoiding the toxic perception of ethnic or political favoritism"; indeed, "reassuring working-class, economically marginalized populations that they, too, can count on the solidarity of their more affluent and competitive fellow citizens might go a long way toward reducing the appeal of resentment-driven, anti-immigrant populism."[44] Transnational or local watch-dog groups could provide significant help in monitoring the quality and coverage of protective police and law enforcement services in different areas for different groups to ensure the reduction of gaps that are obvious both to those protected and those seeking to exploit vulnerabilities for selfish purposes. Receptivity to foreign or native residents' concerns about how security measures are working is essential for success, because attempting to judge the effectiveness or legitimacy of legislated changes through just the top-down national government lenses is grossly inadequate.

Increasing Liability

Within a society experiencing intolerance-based violence, everyone—natives and foreigners, and government officials and private citizens—needs to begin by recognizing a shared responsibility to manage intolerance-based violence and to prevent its future occurrence. The three principal avenues for increasing liability are (1) promoting improvement in commitment to advance-planning and early-warning systems, incorporating contingency options; (2) enlarging societal accountability for similar legal, attitudinal, and behavioral treatment of natives and foreigners; and (3) discovering better means to rehabilitate intolerance-based violence perpetrators to prevent recidivism in the form of continued mistreatment of others. Together these strategies could minimize even during perceived crises scapegoating others for a society's own problems and arguing that finding intolerance-based violence solutions should be burdens shouldered exclusively by others.

Of the five clusters of recommendations for managing global intolerance-based violence, increasing liability among all affected parties seems to require the greatest shift from what is currently transpiring. The rationale here is that without every relevant party being willing to lend a hand to help to address the complex set of precursors to intolerance-based violence, the brutality will continue. Admittedly, the feasibility issues here are quite daunting, second only to achieving genuine inclusiveness: "me first" and "I deserve" self-obsession attitudes permeate many parts of global society, impeding willingness to sacrifice or even devote time to fulfill obligations to care for others or to address broader problems than those currently directly affecting a given individual or group. However, the best way to improve shared societal responsibility for dealing with intolerance-based violence is for civil society organizations to confront members of the society with tangible examples of native-foreigner tensions that have had wide-ranging direct and indirect effects on everyone and that cannot be effectively managed without multiple responsible parties cooperating. That is exactly how neighborhood-watch and block-home initiatives began in addressing a different type of societal violence.

To ensure that this cluster of liability-enhancing mechanisms is feasible, what needs to be avoided here at all costs is to attempt to do so by focusing exclusively on attribution, placing all of one's efforts on simply trying to identify and blame which natives or foreigners initiated acts of intolerance-based violence. In today's world, particularly when dealing with interactive native-citizen violence, the direct and indirect responsibility may be diffuse: for example, when explaining the origins of South African xenophobic violence in 2017, a local reporter notes that "very few of the people who call themselves leaders in our society can escape blame here; and if any of them think that they can blame someone else, it's time they took a look in the mirror."[45] Yet the dominant tendency is to engage in finger-pointing, emphasizing blaming outsiders for ongoing woes and avoiding any form of self-examination to determine culpability for violence-inducing tendencies. Amnesty International directly warns against an exclusive focus on blaming others when dealing with intra-societal violence; "we must refuse to accept narratives of demonization and build instead a culture of solidarity" and "we must seek constructive answers— rooted in human rights—to the frustrations, anger and alienation that provide a ready context for toxic political narratives of blame."[46] Although identifying and punishing violence perpetrators is vital for deterrence, focusing on that as the only concern can deflect attention away from more general systemic tensions facilitating the brutal incidents. In other words, if perpetrators are always considered unrepresentative and deranged, completely isolated from ongoing escalating native citizen–foreign migrant frictions, then chances are that even with effective perpetrator prosecution, intolerance-based violence will persist.

Looking first at promoting improvement in commitment to advance-planning and early-warning systems and incorporating contingency options, national governments need better forward thinking about how to minimize future societal instability. It is important to develop sensitive and accurate early-warning systems alerting relevant parties to imminent intolerance-based violence dangers while minimizing ensuing panic, including both well-thought-out directives about what parties receiving the warning should do and continuous monitoring of changing threats. The focus should be on "contingency planning and preventive measures on behalf of potential host states and the international community coupled with capacity building of the law-enforcement services of the country of asylum."[47] Preparing native citizens for outsider exposure at an early stage—long before foreigners step foot on native soil—seems prudent to minimize tensions after migrants arrive, and preparing migrants before or immediately after entrance to a host state for challenges with native citizens seems crucial for smooth relations with locals.

Turning to enlarging political and social accountability for comparable legal, attitudinal, and behavioral treatment of natives and foreigners, political leaders should ensure that societal residents' rights and obligations are not a function of their skin color, religious or ideological beliefs, gender or sexual preference, or country of origin. Historical evidence suggests that in confronting populist nationalism, "democratic accountability is necessary for both political stability and economic welfare."[48] Transnational watchdog groups should help establish a mutual accountability system—encouraging national government officials to be more vigilant about private citizen intolerance-based violence, and private citizens to be more vigilant about state officials sanctioning such violence. Such watchdog groups also need to promote more widely accepted and enforced codes of conduct[49] for both Internet news providers and conventional media news outlets, preventing baseless public statements inflaming mutual native-foreigner intolerance. To encourage governments to find accountability-enhancing ways to leverage the complementary assets for natives and foreigners for mutual gain, these watchdog organizations need greater support, with their expanded role including monitoring societal safeguards against (1) violations of the rights of natives and foreign migrants, (2) any form of retaliation against those reporting abuses, and (3) corruption in law enforcement systems' evenhanded apprehension, prosecution, and conviction of those committing acts of intolerance-based violence. If national government officials are complicit in migrant mistreatment, then international organizations need to more "effectively investigate, report, and promote the prosecution of those who perpetrate violence against refugees."[50] Members of society need to be incentivized—through product labeling, advertising, and even pricing changes(such initiatives might include informing consumers when potentially abused illegal migrant labor is used or lifting certain surcharges or taxes when illegal migrant labor is not used)—to embrace this mutual accountability not only through laws but more importantly through everyday norms. With this approach, countries with rigid hierarchical traditions would need to find more fluid means to ensure equal accountability regardless of social stratification.

To increase host governments' responsibility for refugees, they should exhibit greater transparency and predictability about the chances of obtaining asylum, as "speeding up refugee-status determination for asylum seekers living in limbo" could through increased state responsibility "discourage the perpetration—or allowance—of attacks on refugee communities."[51] If "migration interdependence" exists between sending and receiving states, the opportunity exists for "cross-border population mobility" to generate "opportunities for leverage" through which a migrant-receiving state can noncoercively increase the cooperative accountability of a migrant-sending state for managing native-citizen frictions by inducing it to make mutual stability-enhancing policy shifts.[52]

Concluding with discovering better means to rehabilitate intolerance-based violence perpetrators to prevent recidivist continued harassment of others, long-term simmering native-foreigner resentment and hostility will not vanish simply because violence perpetrators receive fines or prison sentences. Because xenophobia runs deep in many societies, enough social reinforcement exists that others could gleefully encourage past offenders to strike again despite their past incarceration. Assuming that genuine rehabilitation is realistically possible, just as illegal migrants should not be discarded as unworthy of attention because in the past they broke the law by entering a country or by committing crimes after entrance, so native violence perpetrators ought not to be discarded as hopeless just because in the past they initiated barbaric acts against innocent foreigners. For rehabilitating past violence perpetrators, along with more careful state monitoring and regulation of weapons availability to them, it seems vital to have private humanitarian groups promote "the rehabilitation and reintegration of violent extremist offenders" to address "the full lifecycle of violent extremist radicalization and recruitment."[53]

Increasing Recovery

Turning to increasing recovery, since intolerance-based violence cannot be totally eliminated, both government officials and private citizens need to help native or foreign victims smoothly rebound from abuse, while at the same time allowing these victims to assume some level of responsibility for their own safety. The three principal avenues for increasing recovery are (1) boosting resiliency of victims of intolerance-based violence within societies so that they may quickly resume their normal lives; (2) helping foreigners quickly integrate into society by making employment-related language training and technical skills available; and (3) forming societal support groups whose role is to assist with emerging challenges experienced by intolerance-based violence victims. Together such strategies could help mitigate the soaring physical and psychological stress experienced by many foreign migrants who feel humiliated and unwanted within societies and promote greater understanding and assistance by native citizens.

Of the five clusters of recommendations for managing global intolerance-based violence, achieving improvements in helping abuse victims rebound quickly and smoothly seems to require the greatest "outside the box" thinking. The rationale here is that many of the most immediately obvious means for improving violence victim recovery and reintegration into society, such as throwing money at the problem by creating standard victim recovery programs, do not always work well. Given that victims are often afraid to report crimes committed and believe that state authorities are either collusive with or uncaring about the perpetrators, even if funds received are well-spent they would not successfully reach all those who need it. Instead, the needed creativity here should focus on creating an image among victim groups of the receptivity, privacy, and respect embedded in those authorities facilitating violence recovery. To maximize the feasibility of success in this regard, those establishing the recovery processes need to be highly aware of cross-cultural differences in willingness to express pain and to receive help, with restitution programs extremely flexible in meeting a wide variety of differing needs and communication styles.

To ensure that this cluster of recovery-enhancing mechanisms is feasible, what needs to be avoided here at all costs is to engage in just short-term relief at the expense of long-term development ensuring that violence victims can resume their normal lives. Too often, in the immediate aftermath of violence, governments provide immediate restitution for injuries, deaths, or property damage, but afterward leave victims on their own to fend for themselves. During refugee crises, as the International Organization for Migration notes, domestic and international help may be "available at the start of a crisis, but dwindle over the long term."[54] Given that intolerance-based violence incurs both psychological and physical damage, the caring for victims needs to be much more sustained for long-run effectiveness.

Looking first at boosting resiliency of intolerance-based violence victims so that they may quickly resume their normal lives, deciding to leave a victimized group destitute and ignored—as is common in many places—tends only to make it more likely that they will be harassed again in the future. Better ways need to be found to enhance the future ability of both native citizens and foreign migrants "to resist and contradict discriminatory patterns that devalue their background and ultimately exclude them from social resources in the receiving society";[55] self-help tools should include means to improve vigilance about imminent dangers, to improve constructive responses when dangers are actualized, and to accelerate abilities to quickly resume normal lifestyles. A sign of hope here is that even for vulnerable female migrants, "there is evidence of their resilience and ingenuity in developing means not only of surviving but of creating new lives for themselves."[56] Although resiliency-aiding mechanisms can come top-down from national governments, whose own resiliency can make a mass migrant influx less of a threat,[57] for mutual appreciation it would be better if they were bottom-up, with greater private humanitarian organization help to those who have suffered from violent traumas linked to permanent relocation.

Moving to helping foreigners smoothly integrate into society by making employment-related language and technical skills training available, even highly educated foreign migrants can be stymied if they encounter language barriers, mismatch of skills possessed and skills needed, or unfamiliarity with local cultural norms. This training effort, entailing the need for receiving states to "retool immigration policies so as to be able to better integrate newcomers"[58] and for native employers to refine hiring practices, can improve migrants' ability to fill employment voids left vacant by native workers. Cross-cultural tolerance would benefit if migrant employment contributions did not demonstrably undercut those of natives. A modest input of state-sponsored or citizen-sponsored language or vocational training—showing how existing migrant skills carried over from the country of origin can be constructively transformed in the host country—often generates massive societal payoffs. Overall, such economic strategies generating employment "make much more sense" for societies experiencing native-foreigner tensions, "even though they are not the strategies that are currently being emphasized."[59]

Concluding with forming societal support groups whose role is to assist with emerging challenges experienced by intolerance-based violence victims, often after immediate traumas have been handled new problems emerge where affected parties need significant additional outside help. A key component of this approach is improving the provision of a variety of victim support services—possibly funded through private donations—including medical and mental health care for those who need it and financial loans for those who have experienced property loss. Native citizens and foreign migrants may not be aware of the full range of societal support options, may be hesitant to take advantage of those they know about, and may need an opportunity to talk challenges over with others who have experienced or are experiencing similar issues. This support group help should come either from civil society and humanitarian organizations or less formal local community initiatives, with extensive participation needed by both current or former native violence victims and foreign migrant violence victims. One example of this kind of constructive societal support initiative began in 2016 in Portland, Oregon, where a coalition of nonprofit organizations created Portland United Against Hate, through which intolerance-based violence victims can get professional advocates serving as liaisons between them and the police in pursuing just restitution.[60]

Increasing Sensitivity

Lastly, concluding with increasing sensitivity, inducing both government officials and private citizens to deepen their understanding of the limits of people's adaptability while at the same time demanding basic cross-cultural civility appears to be a winning formula for reducing intolerance-based violence. The three principal avenues for increasing sensitivity are (1) avoiding demands that either natives or foreigners make overly rapid or radical adjustments to cope with domestic security challenges; (2) enhancing respect for cultural autonomy desires while avoiding divisive passions; and (3) fostering the emergence of civil society norms handling disputes through discourse and leveraging complementary cross-cultural assets for mutual gain. Together such strategies could maximize the chances for peaceful resolution of disputes within and across societies among groups possessing strong disagreements about pressing issues but still expecting respect for their basic human dignity.

Of the five clusters of recommendations for managing global intolerance-based violence, increasing sensitivity through heightening understanding of the limits of people's adaptability while at the same time demanding basic cross-cultural civility seems to be the most intangible and to have the greatest start-up costs. The rationale here is that in order to understand the nature of each societal group's particular predicament, identifying both where room for forward movement exists and how to improve interaction with other dissimilar groups, considerable background research needs to be undertaken beforehand and the modes of expression by those trying to instill the improved cross-cultural sensitivity need careful forethought and prescreening. There is no shortcut for being culturally sensitive or for being perceived as culturally sensitive. The best way to increase the feasibility of increasing cross-cultural sensitivity is to get members of all opposing groups with grievances about their societal treatment and status—including both native citizens and foreign migrant groups—to engage in unconstrained impactful face-to-face discussions and decisions about how to improve mutual understanding, sensitivity, and cooperation.

To ensure that this cluster of sensitivity-enhancing mechanisms is feasible, what needs to be avoided here at all costs is dysfunctional and debilitating projection of one's own group's values and thought processes onto others. Often political leaders' insensitivity to their own cultural biases impedes tolerance of foreigners, reflecting "constraints on one's thinking, acquired during maturation from widely-held beliefs, practices or cognitive styles that characterise one's specific social environment."[61] When one group judges others according to its own values, morals, and customs, cross-cultural tolerance is blocked,[62] as society falls victim to "what Admiral David Jeremiah called the 'everybody-thinks-like-us mindset' when making significant judgments that depend upon knowledge of a foreign culture"; "people in other cultures *do not* think the way we do," and "failure to understand that others perceive their national interests differently from the way we perceive those interests is a constant source of problems."[63] When natives and foreigners interact, many observers tend to project their own rational receptor system onto both groups in attempting to promote peaceful coexistence, seeing what such observers want to see or expect to see rather than what is actually occurring.

Looking first at avoiding demanding that either natives or foreigners within a society make overly rapid or radical adjustments to cope with security challenges, both groups face adaptation challenges and each needs time to find ways to compromise and coexist without losing their sense of who they are. Such flexibility can occur because "the homogenization brought about by globalization is superficial and is limited to the material level of the consumer goods used by people and a certain consumer culture that is artificially promoted by the media; it does not affect how people relate to each other and how they find meaning and purpose in life."[64] Often national governments and native citizens seem too impatient in expecting foreigners from different backgrounds to totally assimilate quickly to local values and traditions, and often foreigners seem too impatient in expecting natives to understand and accept their unconventional communication and behavior. In a parallel fashion, in addressing intolerance-based violence, political leaders need to avoid resorting to the most extreme solutions—"completely sealing off . . . borders is neither sensible nor humane, but nor is it sensible or humane to admit unlimited numbers of people whose cultures and value systems are so fundamentally different from those of the native population."[65] Because asking for patience is difficult when native-foreigner relations are tense, private humanitarian groups need to play a more important monitoring role, ensuring that the pace of expected change and the compromise solutions proposed are reasonable. Moreover, for smooth transitions, it seems useful to incentivize the entrance of "secondary migrants"— those who first migrate to another country as a stepping-stone before entering their target state and thus generally tend to be better educated and more prepared to enter the skilled workforce than one-time migrants.[66]

Moving to enhancing respect for cultural autonomy desires while avoiding divisive passions, a push for cultural autonomy does not automatically equate to disruptive subnational separatism or pressure for complete self-rule. Yet "because states usually view such demands as anathema to their sovereignty," political leaders typically are "disinclined" to grant to frustrated subnational groups any form of regional autonomy, and such stubbornness "tends to radicalize the aggrieved minority, causing them to aim instead for full-fledged independence, often through violence."[67] Foreign migrants' desire to maintain their own form of dress, holidays, religious beliefs, and social customs does not threaten the broader national society until or unless natives suffer significant tangible negative spillover effects. However, the viability of granting increased autonomy to a societal group as a means to lessen potential cross-group intolerance-based violence requires mutual trust, as "no assurances of cultural protection, power-sharing, and autonomy seem to be sufficient for ending the confrontation . . . once the trust in their peaceful coexistence is broken."[68] More involved transnational humanitarian groups and more flexible political leaders could play a much more central role in sensitively brokering this kind of trust.

Concluding with fostering the emergence of civil society norms handling disputes through discourse and leveraging complementary cross-cultural assets for mutual gain, discovering new means to promote civility seems essential. Promoting discourse as the means to resolve disputes, which is remarkably rare—"only a small proportion of the world's population has thus far become actively involved in global civil society"[69]—can reduce residents' motivations "to embrace political violence"[70] through providing alternative outlets for existing grievances. Highly divided multi-ethnic societies, without ways to address common problems amicably and breeding exclusionary tendencies and intergroup hostility, cannot constitute a sound basis for a durable state. When not banned by a national government, engaging locally tuned civil society organizations, such as the People's Coalition Against Xenophobia[71] in South Africa, appears to be particularly useful in promoting this constructive discourse.

Spreading civil society norms seems to be especially important in societies with readily available instruments of violence and long traditions of force use, enhanced by pressing economic displacement fears, rapid and massive inflows of foreign migrants, or coercive encounters with outsiders. In many parts of the world, "civil society is profoundly fractured along kinship, ethnic or other sectarian lines," stimulating the emergence of nonstate groups that "are prepared to use violence in the pursuit of their political or ideological agendas."[72] Given the common pattern of disrespect both between local communities and law enforcement authorities and between native citizens and foreign migrants within a community, in order to advance civil society, mutual respect needs to be restored, facilitated by better sensitivity training for police, natives, and foreigners concerning their mutual interactions.[73] To flexibly manage value differences within civil society, it seems vital (1) to foster extensive dialogue among differing groups on a wide variety of concerns; (2) to decry the stifling dominance of exclusionist national identities; and (3) to overcome the persistent obstacle that "the foundations of our morals are articulated mostly in negative ways, based on fear and closure, rather than on open discussions of difficult issues and a willingness to ground political positions in a positive affirmation of basic values and principles."[74] A cornerstone for mutual respect is promoting belief in the "basic human decency"[75] of all residents of a country accompanied by the realization that possessing significant disagreements on societal issues should not interfere with mutual recognition of the basic dignity of all people.

Conclusion

LINKING INTOLERANCE-BASED violence to liberal international order norms through interdependence and globalization eliminates the possibility of dismissing such brutality as highly aberrant behavior undertaken by small and unrepresentative fringe elements composed of deranged irrational impulsive extremists, completely disconnected from the structures, processes, and incentives embedded in the current global system. The findings here sharply diminish the viability of national political leaders arguing that their ongoing attitudes and actions are perfectly fine—that they do not need to alter their behavior because they are the civilized members of the international community, and that the obligation to change lies strictly with the uncivilized barbarians who perpetrate intolerance-based violence. Given the liberal international order's significant role in stimulating through induced cross-state migration the backlash that has contributed to this disruptive behavior, there needs to be a lot broader acknowledgment of responsibility by parties—particularly heads of state—who have directly or indirectly contributed to the unraveling of enlightened global dreams, and each of these parties needs to listen more carefully to the heartfelt grievances of natives and foreigners so as to figure out better how to address them.

The advent of the liberal international order, along with intensifying interdependence and globalization, created high hopes for accelerated maturation among the world's political heads of state and private citizens, and for receptivity to and acceptance between natives and outsiders becoming a universal norm. Unfortunately, in many places, this lofty expectation failed to materialize, and what emerged instead has been a reversion to older primitive patterns of in-group/out-group resentment and rejection. Native-foreigner frictions appear to be getting worse, not better; outsiders seen as looking and acting very differently from domestic citizens, along with natives seen as overprotective of their society, have felt overtly and covertly ostracized, marginalized, and excluded, and sometimes the result is societal violence.

To promote greater tolerance it seems crucial to find stabilizing balances for competing concerns among natives, foreigners, and national governments; this entails responding more effectively and legitimately (1) to native concerns, given adherents' resistance to change and opponents' anger at patriotic beliefs; (2) to migrant concerns, given the diversity of their special needs for stable long-term resettlement; and (3) to state concerns, given burgeoning social service costs, uneven benefits and ability to pay within a diverse population, and citizen fears about foreigners receiving preferential treatment. Attaining such balances requires learning how to interpret (1) dependence on and cooperation with foreigners as a sign of strength rather than as a sign of weakness; (2) foreigners' impact through long-term rather than short-term lenses; (3) foreign shocks as involving cross-national spillovers requiring joint action rather than as opportunities to insulate one's society from their impact; and (4) domestic security challenges as opportunities to take responsibility for fixing societal woes rather than to blame others.

Achieving these balances is extremely difficult within a world where avenues for frank and open discussion about cross-cultural equity, foreign stereotypes, national identity, and interdependence and globalization are either nonexistent or strongly discouraged because of their emotional volatility. Just as with discussing politics and religion in many social settings, so initiating discussions about the complexities surrounding interdependence, diversity, and intolerance—where fundamental questions of every kind are on the table—is usually considered taboo because of the high probability of some participant being overly sensitive and taking offense at what was stated or implied. We simply do not know how to approach these issues with frankness and civility without ruffling feathers. Somehow there needs to be a breakthrough in the capability and willingness of the various stakeholders to directly confront these issues, while at the same time recognizing ethical dilemmas due to longstanding cultural chasms, so as to be able to jointly formulate mutually acceptable solutions. Otherwise, misunderstandings and tensions seem likely to continue to simmer or escalate about what is most troubling to natives and foreigners living together and about what remedies would work best.

One of the key lessons here is the need to look more holistically at questions related to intolerance-based violence, avoiding the dangers of constrained binary "either-or" "black-and-white" thinking. Regarding who is undertaking the brutality and why, it seems all too easy for investigative analysts—through inappropriate tendencies that the violence perpetrator myths will reveal—to fall prey to the same kind of mindless oversimplification that occurs if nativists blame all their problems on foreigners or if migrants blame all their problems on nativists. Regarding what scope of issues deserves attention, it seems all too likely for observers to undertake overly segmented piecemeal approaches—such as ones addressing exclusively overwhelming migration, economic stagnation, or societal pride—in attempts to manage intolerance-based violence. Regarding how to fix intolerance-based violence, it seems all too probable for commentators to assign all obligations simply to national governments,[1] whose mandate is eroding from both above and below; to assume that state-initiated legal or institutional changes would suffice to resolve underlying tensions; and then to blame government officials when their efforts fail to produce societal tranquility. Although the inclination is to approach complex intolerance-based violence in a reductionist manner, addressing only one facet of the problem or placing "all the eggs in one basket" consistently proves to be woefully inadequate.

What is required instead—and what seems most difficult to achieve given cross-national tendencies to compartmentalize both responsibilities and remedies for societal ills—is full integration by both political leaders and the mass public of all relevant tools—political, social, economic, military, and psychological—to address the full spectrum of issues surrounding intolerance-based violence. Genuine durable tolerance under interdependence between native citizens and foreign migrants rests on mutual openness, respect, trust, participation, flexibility, and accountability, incorporating efforts both to help newcomers adjust to life in their new setting and to help locals adjust to the presence of outsiders. This outcome necessitates considerable coordinated work by multiple societal elements to have a decent chance of creating and sustaining meaningful societal cohesion.

Debunking Violence Perpetrator Myths

The case findings provide an important corrective to some widely held but distorted myths about intolerance-based violence perpetrators. The three pernicious myths, summarized in Figure C.1, are that these perpetrators always

---

PERPETRATORS ALWAYS ARE NATIVE CITIZENS TARGETING FOREIGN IMMIGRANTS

Common belief reflects monodirectional focus artificially restricting the identity of initiators and victims of global intolerance-based violence

Actual reality is intolerance-based violence can also be initiated by recent foreign migrants—because of their own frustrations—against native citizens of the receiving society

The net security implication is that there needs to be much broader wariness about interactive violent action-reaction cycles involving both native citizens and foreign migrants

---

PERPETRATORS ALWAYS ARE PROPONENTS OF FAR-RIGHT IDEOLOGIES

Common belief reflects mono-ideological contention artificially constraining the convictions of initiators of global intolerance-based violence

Actual reality is today's rising populist anti-establishment sentiment attracts a wide swath of support within and across societies and can also involve far-left groups

The net security implication is that there needs to be much wider monitoring of violence precursors from both left and right extremist sectors of society

---

PERPETRATORS ALWAYS ARE LARGELY DRIVEN JUST BY ONE KIND OF GRIEVANCE

Common belief reflects monocausal explanations artificially limiting the roots of initiators' choice to undertake global intolerance-based violence

Actual reality is both economic and cultural elements can play critical roles in explaining global intolerance-based violence

The net security implication is that there needs to be much more comprehensive scrutiny about when all sources of violence-inducing tensions escalate among the mass public

---

FIGURE C.1: Debunking Violence Perpetrator Myths

are (1) native citizens targeting foreign immigrants, (2) proponents of far-right ideologies, and (3) consequences of just one kind of grievance. Such myths have often led to profound misunderstandings about how to think about such violence, inappropriately narrowing and oversimplifying its complex multifaceted manifestations and excluding or downplaying key elements from consideration. Ultimately, these myths increase the chances that intolerance-based violence management policies will be ineffective by jeopardizing treatment of the full range of underlying intertwined tensions and long-term security ramifications associated with the outbreak of this brutality.

Looking first at the myth that intolerance-based violence perpetrators are always native citizens targeting foreign immigrants, the dominant mode is to characterize the issue as monodirectional, artificially restricting the identity of initiators and victims of this kind of disruption. Indeed, most analyses of ethnic nationalism and intolerance-based violence focus almost exclusively on "the uptick in hate crimes against immigrants."[2] However, although it is more common to hear about native citizen violence against foreign migrants, in reality the cases confirm Chapter 3's contention that intolerance-based violence can also be initiated by frustrated foreign migrants against native citizens. This pattern is vividly shown by the 2005 and 2018 allegations that Haitian migrants killed native Dominicans; the December 31, 2015, sexual attacks in Cologne on scores of young German women by at least twenty-one asylum seekers from the Middle East and North Africa; the May 10, 2011, killing by two Afghan migrants of a forty-four-year-old Greek man; the April 2017 St. Petersburg Metro attack in Russia by a Kyrgyzstan migrant; and the September 2018 Syrian migrant attack in Sanliurfa on two Turkish citizens. Considering intolerance-based violence to be a product of interactive tensions between natives and foreigners allows a more inclusive scope within a broader context through which to uncover more enduring remedies, in comparison to seeing this brutality as simply being one-way and being insistent on assigning all the blame to one side. Violent action-reaction cycles between native citizens and foreign migrants, evident in the same Dominican Republic, German, Greek, Russian, and Turkish cases, constitute a common violence pattern[3] that can sometimes be accompanied by conflicting reports about who initiated them. Thus this myth corrective suggests that for societal stability there needs to be broader attentiveness to circumstances where the type of intolerance-based violence initiator cannot be definitively determined; where violent action-reaction cycles seem most likely to emerge; and where because of degraded communication and reactive policies these cycles can become most dangerous, prone to escalate in scope and to spread to other areas.

Moving to the myth that intolerance-based violence perpetrators are always proponents of far-right ideologies, such mono-ideological claims common both in the media and in scholarly literature artificially constrain identifying and responding to intolerance-based violence initiators' convictions. For example, many analyses squarely label xenophobic populism as exclusively right-wing: "the new right-wing populism that emerged in the last decade of the last century can be called populist because they claim to represent 'the people' and to be mobilising them against a domineering establishment; and they can be classified as right-wing populist because they claim to be defending and shielding national, cultural or ethnic identity against 'outsiders' or external influences."[4] Even the respected British magazine *The Economist* has fallen into this trap, leading readers to believe that only right-wing groups focus on opposing the influx of foreign immigrants: "it is understandable if mass immigration causes concerns," but "it is unforgivable if far-right parties exploit them in a racist way."[5] However, although it is more common to hear about right-wing intolerance-based violence, in reality intolerance attracts a wider swath of support within societies: "it comes from the far left and the far right, attracting the young and educated from urban areas as well as the older and underemployed from the heartland."[6] Indeed, nationalism expert Andreas Wimmer argues that "identifying nationalism exclusively with the political right means misunderstanding the nature of nationalism and ignoring how deeply it has shaped almost all modern political ideologies, including liberal and progressive ones."[7] Moreover, in recent years, "progressive and left-wing leaders and voters are becoming more openly comfortable with policies that have a distinctly nationalist flavor."[8] The German and Italian cases show this pattern of left-wing xenophobia, and a growing wave of intolerant anti-migrant left-wing politicians has been spreading across Europe.[9] Thus this myth corrective suggests that societal stability requires wider monitoring of circumstances where violence precursors emerge among the full range of extremist groups within societies, with a greater focus on when and how each type of volatile group is likely to initiate violence.

Concluding with the myth that intolerance-based violence perpetrators are always largely driven by just one kind of grievance, much of the existing literature is surprisingly myopic and intent on identifying a single monocausal explanation, artificially limiting understanding of the full scope of violence perpetrators' decision-making calculus. Usually this dominant explanation focuses on economics or culture, although a few analysts misguidedly even more narrowly focus exclusively within the cultural dimension on racial or religious differences. On the economic grievances side, many analysts issue pronouncements such as "the real debate between nationalists and globalists is less about identity than about economics."[10] Such commentators argue that native citizen–foreign migrant "conflicts are really all about material interests and not about culture"—"what is routinely presented as a cultural conflict between supposedly authentic rural heartlands and cosmopolitan cities usually involves a much less dramatic fight over how opportunities are distributed through regulatory and infrastructure decisions, from the price of airline tickets for flights to more remote areas, to the status of community banks, to policies that determine the cost of housing in big cities."[11] On the cultural grievances side, many analysts are equally dismissive of alternative explanations. Typical claims include a *Washington Post* reporter stating, "I don't think the immigration debate is about economics anyway—it's about culture and it's about fear";[12] a contention by a senior fellow at the Brookings Institution that "peoples across Europe perceived a risk to their livelihoods, to some extent to their security, but most of all to their culture" in response to a flood of Middle East and North African immigrants;[13] a Migration Policy Institute study concluding after assessing the relationship between foreign immigration and domestic nativism that "the key theme is cultural, in which immigrants are considered a threat to the cultural homogeneity of the nation because of an inability or unwillingness to assimilate";[14] and a Harvard Kennedy School analysis that "the rise of populist parties reflects, above all, a reaction against a wide range of rapid cultural changes that seem to be eroding the basic values and customs of Western societies," as "those who were once the privileged majority culture" have "now come to feel that they are being marginalized within their own countries."[15]

However, in reality both cultural and economic elements can play critical roles in explaining intolerance-based violence. Nationalism expert Jack Snyder notes that while scholars debate whether populist nationalism and xenophobia "arise mainly from economic or cultural grievances," globally "the most persuasive explanation is that nationalist political entrepreneurs have combined both grievances" in fostering societal anger and resentment.[16] The cases empirically confirm that no single set of grievances are necessary or sufficient to trigger intolerance-based violence, as most violence perpetrators analyzed had multiple distinct motivations for their disruptive actions. Thus this myth corrective suggests that global societal stability requires more comprehensive scrutiny—taking into account the perspectives of angry native citizens or foreign migrants—about when and how a wider variety of grievances become aroused, when and how each type of frustrating grievance is most likely to take precedence, and when and how each type of frustrating grievance is likely to reach a threshold where barbarity is unleashed. In the end, containing such violent disruption "will require both cultural and economic solutions."[17]

Overcoming Overblown Fears

While both native citizens and foreign migrants feel genuine socioeconomic frustrations, the insecurity-enhancing apprehensions of each group about the other may be hyperbolically distorted, as shown in Figure C.2. Each group

NATURE OF PROJECTED NATIVE-FOREIGNER FEARS

Native citizens and foreign migrants each may exaggerate the threat severity posed by the other group, with each group perceived as intent on making the other group's existence miserable

Native citizens and foreign migrants each may exaggerate sinister extremist elements' dominance in the other group, with such elements perceived as characteristic of the entire group

Native citizens and foreign migrants each may exaggerate the rigidity of the other group, with each group perceived as completely set in its ways, unable or unwilling to modify its behavior

Native citizens may exaggerate the extent to which foreigners will overwhelm, degrade, and ultimately destroy their society's economic well-being and dominant culture

Foreign migrants may exaggerate the extent to which everyone within their host societies will never accept them, and will always exhibit severe discrimination and mistreatment toward them

REDUCTION OF PROJECTED NATIVE-FOREIGNER FEARS

Because most native citizens and foreign migrants do not exhibit highly threatening negative characteristics, it is a huge policy mistake to accept mutually overblown characterizations as true

Policy makers must neither dismiss all these fears as completely groundless nor regard them all as representing genuine threats needing immediate attention

Policy makers need to ask which groups fear for their physical security, why these security fears exist, and how this insecurity can be reduced

Remedial policy should start by finding general means to reduce each group's perceived fears and then afterward find specific remedies to tangible cultural or economic frustrations

Better outreach and education to communities/civil society groups is needed to reduce mutual anxieties, advance police-community relations, and improve reporting and data collection

FIGURE C.2: Overcoming Overblown Fears

confidently projects onto the other grossly exaggerated fears and culpability for one's misery, with the overall threat misperception encompassing three distinct dimensions: native citizens and foreign migrants both exaggerate (1) the dangers posed by the other group, seeing it as intent on degrading one's traditional lifestyle; (2) the dominance of extremists with sinister intentions within the other group, viewing fringe elements as characteristic of the entire group; and (3) the rigidity of the other group, characterizing it as completely set in its ways, unable or unwilling to modify its behavior. More specifically, for many native citizens, a highly emotional sense of dread exists that foreigners will overwhelm, degrade, and ultimately destroy their society's economic well-being and dominant culture; and for many foreign migrants, an equally powerful sense of dread exists that they will never be accepted within host societies, and that they will continuously experience severe discrimination and mistreatment, deprived of meaningful opportunities to improve their lot.

Amplifying this mutual sense of threat is inflammatory rhetoric introduced by extremist politicians and one-sided media sources. As with sometimes-voiced but obviously inaccurate comments like "all devout Muslims are dangers to society," "all patriotic Europeans and Americans are racist white supremacists," or "all foreign immigrants are criminals or terrorists," the steadfast refusal by many native citizens or foreign migrants to differentiate in a sensitive way between an extremist minority and a more moderate majority persistently impedes efforts to overcome the stereotypes and to achieve greater mutual understanding and tolerance. It is, of course, psychologically predictable that people would be highly prone to lump all members of another group into a single pattern, mentally saying to themselves "their kind is all like that" and then dismissing any possibility of discussion, cooperation, or compromise. Moreover, preexisting misconceptions can be reinforced both through brief superficial cross-group encounters colored by initial impressions and through electronic communication unable to adequately convey nuance or emotional subtlety.

Because most native citizens and foreign migrants do not exhibit these highly threatening characteristics in their attitudes and behaviors, treating these overblown mutual misperceptions of dread as if they were true is a fundamental mistake in trying to achieve a stable durable societal solution to intolerance-based violence. For example, it is extremely dangerous to fall prey to "taking at face value and even amplifying the dubious stories that nationalist populists tell" as the basis for understanding the relationship between native citizens and foreign migrants, for such nationalist populists "often represent not a silent majority but a very loud minority" within their societies: "by embracing the idea that populists have developed a unique purchase on people's concerns and anxieties, established parties and media organizations have created something akin to a self-fulfilling prophecy."[18] Similarly, media reports of unspeakable migrant misery do not always tell the whole story.

Instead, it seems crucial for policy makers seeking to address native-foreigner violence to take an analytical stance that neither dismisses all fears as completely groundless nor regards them all as genuine threats needing immediate attention.[19] It seems important to ask "which groups fear for their physical security,"[20] why these security fears exist, and how these security fears can be reduced. In addressing passionately held opposing views between native citizens and foreign migrants, remedial policies should generally begin by attempting to reduce each group's perceived insecurity fears and then afterward fix actual cultural discrimination or economic displacement. To assist in dampening overblown mass public anxieties, Human Rights First suggests that national governments experiencing native-foreigner tensions "should conduct outreach and education efforts to communities and civil society groups to reduce fear and assist victims, advance police-community relations, encourage improved reporting of hate crimes to the police and improve the quality of data collection by law enforcement bodies."[21]

Fortress Mentality Dangers

Global intolerance can easily lead to a "fortress mentality," shown in Figure C.3. This mentality accentuates within and across countries isolation, distance, self-sufficiency, and barriers to entry as the primary security focus: "as populist demagogues around the world exploit the churn of economic discontent, the danger is that the politics of engagement could give way to the politics of withdrawal."[22] Consistent with tribalist enclaves' separatist logic, this "out of sight, out of mind" mentality—reflecting a desire to hole up to feel safe—inhibits genuine tolerance between natives and foreigners. If taken too far, this fortress orientation could lead to an overemphasis on security expenditures for internal and external protection: "Europe remains locked into a fortress model of border enforcement that will never be able to do anything more than slow down the pace of migration—unless European governments are prepared to escalate the current level of surveillance and enforcement in ways that would effectively seal the continent off from the outside world and transform much of the continent into panoptic police states of the kind that were only recently thought to have passed into historical obsolescence."[23]

Considering the domestic impact, amid an atmosphere of identified outside threat, native citizens may turn to unorthodox protection efforts, such as private contractors, vigilante groups, or gated communities using armed guards to deny unwanted outsiders entrance. Indeed, "when people feel their culture and way of life threatened, they look to their own for protection";[24] "some of the most violent cities of the developing world have become a mosaic of fortresses, creating

SELF-CENTERED PROTECTION WITHOUT BROADER CONCERN
Embracing tribalist enclaves' separatist logic, this mentality produces "out of sight, out of mind" feelings rather than genuine tolerance of outsiders
Fear-motivated self-interested "everyone for themselves" actions proliferate with no concern for impact on others

ANARCHIC PARANOID COERCIVE SETTING
Greater latitude for individual action could easily lead to uncontrolled lawlessness and violence rather than citizen safety
"Do‑it‑yourself immigration enforcers" and anti-foreigner private groups may disregard traditional government law enforcement rules of engagement

GROWING INTERNAL AND EXTERNAL DISTRUST
Increased arms purchases and other coercive measures for personal or group self-defense can promote internal distrust among citizens
Fortified national boundaries provoke foreign outrage and severely damage security relations with international allies

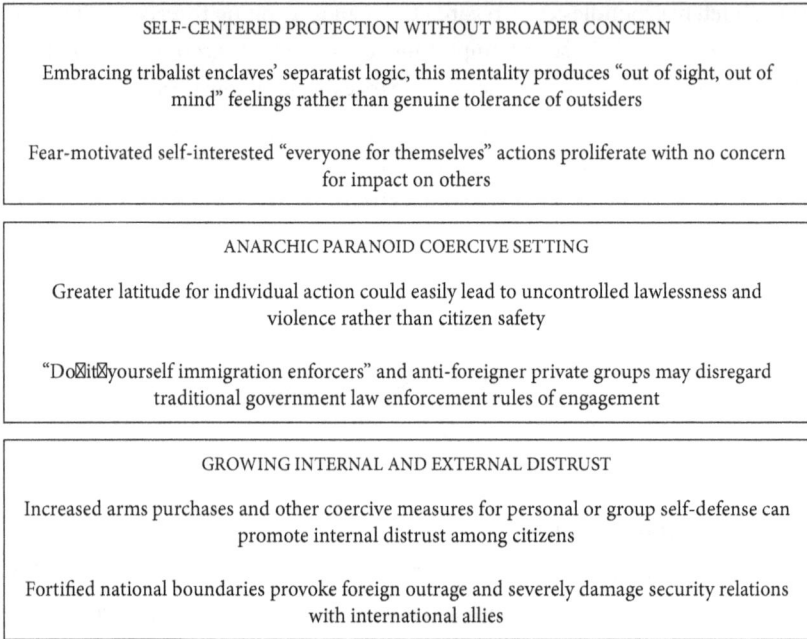

FIGURE C.3: Fortress Mentality Dangers

a fragmented civil society in which families or streets or neighborhoods create their own forms of protection, often relying on armed force."[25] Thus individuals and groups feel greater latitude to take security matters into their own hands (Greece's Golden Dawn is a prime example); and, if the freedom to act is used indiscriminately, the result can be uncontrolled lawlessness and violence rather than citizen safety.[26] In anarchic settings, local security groups may proliferate with arbitrary security limits, such as the groups of "do-it-yourself immigration enforcers" patrolling the southern United States borders for migrants,[27] disregarding state law enforcement rules of engagement. The security outcome can easily degenerate into a competitive race focusing only on "protecting those of one's own kind," creating highly uneven citizen protection within a society.

Regarding the international impact, given identified foreign threat, paranoid national governments using barriers to entry for foreigners—such as through fortifying national borders to preserve just their own lives and culture—can be globally destabilizing. Indeed, isolationism "is no more a solution at the regional and global levels than at the ethnic and national levels";[28] "fortified boundaries may provoke outrage by target states and other affected actors, with significant economic, political, or reputational costs for the builder."[29] For example, recent American discrimination against foreign Hispanics and Muslims has damaged security relations between the United States and both its southern neighbors and Arab Middle Eastern countries.

Thus a world full of societies with a fortress mentality could prove quite dangerous:

> The common thread running through these responses is a desire to protect oneself from an onslaught of danger and destruction, while presumably letting everyone else sink into the muck. The unstated premises here are a fatalistic acceptance that the society as a whole is falling apart, a cynicism that anything on a broad overarching level can be done to stop it, and thus a desperate self-interested move to try to be one of the lucky ones who manages to survive and thrive in such an apocalyptic predicament.[30]

Given that the ideal civil society aspiration is assigning dignity to all people and resolving any differences through peaceful discourse rather than through coercive exclusion or violence, the fortress mentality can be highly problematic both within and across countries in leaving many people highly vulnerable to manipulation and misinterpretation. The long-run security consequences of this mentality—including, for example, "increased arms purchases for self-defense, installation of alarms, moving to gated communities, and the organizing of neighborhood security operations"—seem menacing in terms of the potential for promoting mistrust, intolerance, and discriminatory behavior.[31] Even if such allegedly protective steps do not actually increase protection in today's interpenetrated world, these exclusionary measures usually seem incredibly attractive to citizens filled with fear.

Societal Polarization Dangers

Amplifying global intolerance is the polarization of opposing sides, shown in Figure C.4, despite the reality that today ultranationalists often end up living in the same communities as culturally contrasting foreign migrants.[32] Both sides of the immigration debate fall victim to extremist rhetoric; "the irony, however, is that although critics often charge populists with peddling reductive messages, it is these same critics who now grasp at simple explanations for populism's rise; in doing so, many liberal observers play right into their opponents' hands by taking at face value and even amplifying the dubious stories that nationalist populists tell about their own success."[33]

OVERSIMPLIFIED BLACK-AND-WHITE NATURE OF THE DEBATE
Discussion framed in terms of rigid mutually opposed positions Polarized communication style distorts mutual understanding Both sides induced to resort to extremist rhetoric

DEBILITATING ENMITY RATHER THAN EMPATHY BETWEEN OPPOSING SIDES
Ideological gridlock creates an "empathy wall" between the two sides Enduring enemy images lead to greater polarization of good and evil Cross-group grievances raise risks of violent intrasocietal conflict

MEDIA AMPLIFICATION OF EXISTING DISAGREEMENTS
Internet may reinforce prejudices, allow divisions to fester, and magnify hateful ideologies Even with more consumer choice, partisan media may push the extremes and hollow out the middle Media outlets may adopt nationalist populists' framing and rhetoric, ratifying their messages

DECREASING CHANCES OF EFFECTIVE POLICY SOLUTIONS
Opposing parties double down on extremist remedies One-sided approaches undercut mutual tolerance among diverse groups living side-by-side Extreme political polarization impedes any efforts to find acceptable middle-ground compromises

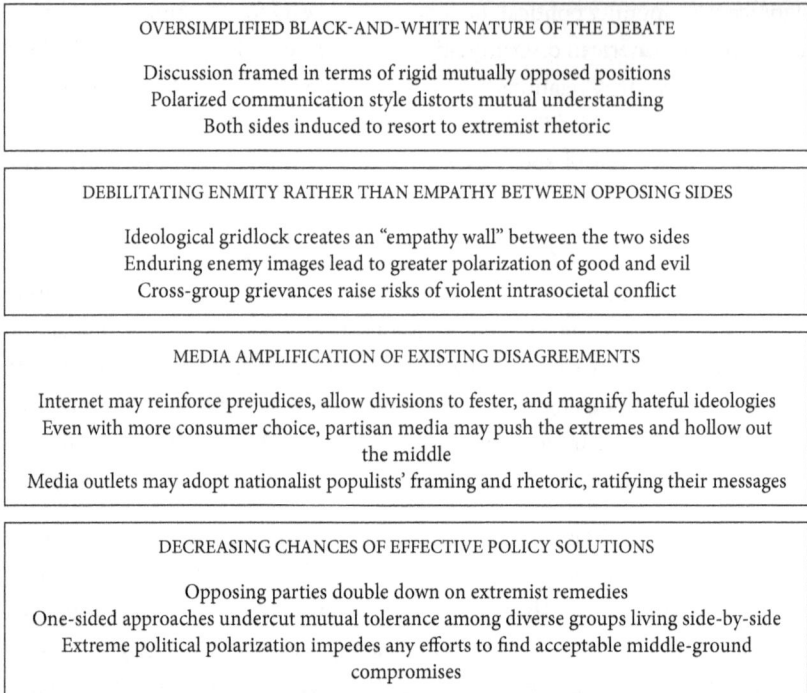

FIGURE C.4: Societal Polarization Dangers

Societal polarization rigidifies opposing positions about migration and—absent appropriate mediation mechanisms—impedes both consensus and compromise. An enduring enemy image linked to foreign immigrant threat can severely disrupt opposing parties' discourse and can ultimately lead to greater polarization of good and evil; "long-standing hostilities and suspicions give rise to habitual response patterns in which each party's activities reinforce laudatory views of the self and negative views of the other."[34] This form of extreme ideological gridlock creates an "empathy wall" in the immigration debate, where people on each side cannot gain deep understanding of the other, escalating mutual hostility and miscommunication.[35] If within diverse societies polarizing intergroup grievances persist and intensify, the risks of intrasocietal violence escalate.[36] In March 2019, Imam Mohamed Magid, a former president of the Islamic Society of North America, stated regarding intolerance-based violence, "I think part of it is polarization—the further this 'us versus them' attitude continues, the more you will see this violence."[37]

Although it is expected that politicians would use manipulation to polarize issues for self-serving purposes, many observers anticipated that the proliferation of news sources thanks to the advent of the Internet would re-duce societal polarization. However, Human Rights First notes that "the on-line world doesn't dissolve tribes—it gives them global reach" because it "offers opinions to reinforce every prejudice"[38] and can end up "allowing divisions to fester and magnifying hateful ideologies."[39] On April 29, 2019, UN secretary-general António Guterres announced that "parts of the Internet are becoming hothouses of hate, as like-minded bigots find each other on-line, and platforms serve to inflame and enable hate to go viral."[40] Because of the ways online book-marks and tracking work, social media make it easier than ever to be exposed only to news feeds from sources confirming preexisting biases: for example, on Facebook, there exists a "red feed" and a "blue feed" with diametrically op-posing interpretation of news stories.[41] Even traditional broadcast media have amplified polarization:

> Just a generation ago, the evening news largely carried the same message no matter which channel you were tuning in to. Now, however, by watching Fox News or MSNBC, one is able to only hear messages reinforcing one's core be-liefs. Alternatively, one could also simply choose not to watch the news. Hence, the partisan media seem to strengthen the extremes, while hollowing out the middle.[42]

So thanks to social media, societal polarization has not been reduced but in-stead has been amplified.

Thus political polarization impedes efforts to find mutually acceptable middle-ground solutions:

> Today political polarization makes compromise seem unlikely. Both illiberal nationalists and cosmopolitan elites have, in their own way, doubled down on one-sided solutions, seeking to rout their opponents rather than reach a durable settlement. Trump calls for a border wall and a ban on Muslim immigration, and his opponents continue to speak as if immigration and refugee policy is a matter of abstract legal and moral commitments rather than a subject for demo-cratic deliberation.[43]

As a result, constructive dialogue about the foreign immigration challenge seems doomed to fail.

Within the United States, polarization over migrants is highly visible and emotional. Overall, "the increasing polarization in American society contrib-utes to nativism's new dawn."[44] Although "immigration has always polarized America," xenophobic views have recently "reached a screaming pitch, fueled

by talk-radio invective, mass protests by immigrants, and sometimes ugly debate over who deserves to be an American."[45] The 2016 American presidential
campaign was filled with hateful rhetoric,[46] with societal venom directed at
Hispanic and Muslim migrants and at Donald Trump and his supporters. Reinforcing this pattern is the reality that "polarization is characteristic of the
economic make-up of the US, as the highest and lowest ends of the spectrum
are the fastest-growing."[47]

Security Outsourcing Dangers

When confronting national border control and immigration pressures, stakeholders often look for outside help. So national governments, native citizens,
and foreign migrants all find outsourcing a convenient way in relieving themselves of sole responsibility for attaining their ends. However, security dangers—highlighted in Figure C.5—lurk behind this approach.

Looking first at native citizens outsourcing monitoring of border control, native citizens may depend heavily on private security contractors, gated

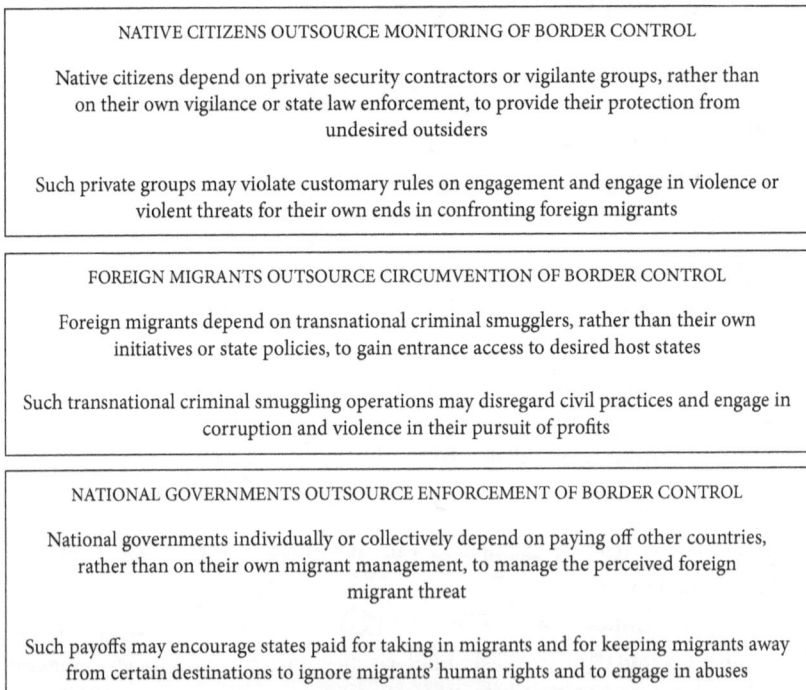

NATIVE CITIZENS OUTSOURCE MONITORING OF BORDER CONTROL

Native citizens depend on private security contractors or vigilante groups, rather than
on their own vigilance or state law enforcement, to provide their protection from
undesired outsiders

Such private groups may violate customary rules on engagement and engage in violence or
violent threats for their own ends in confronting foreign migrants

---

FOREIGN MIGRANTS OUTSOURCE CIRCUMVENTION OF BORDER CONTROL

Foreign migrants depend on transnational criminal smugglers, rather than their own
initiatives or state policies, to gain entrance access to desired host states

Such transnational criminal smuggling operations may disregard civil practices and engage in
corruption and violence in their pursuit of profits

NATIONAL GOVERNMENTS OUTSOURCE ENFORCEMENT OF BORDER CONTROL

National governments individually or collectively depend on paying off other countries,
rather than on their own migrant management, to manage the perceived foreign
migrant threat

Such payoffs may encourage states paid for taking in migrants and for keeping migrants away
from certain destinations to ignore migrants' human rights and to engage in abuses

---

FIGURE C.5: Security Outsourcing Dangers

communities, or vigilante groups, rather than on state law enforcement, to ensure protection of status quo values and existing lifestyle. Such outsourcing represents an abdication of any need for personal responsibility. Aside from causing unequal community protection, contractors and vigilantes may violate customary rules of engagement and engage in violence or threats of violence in confronting foreign migrants for their own ends.

Moving to foreign migrants outsourcing circumvention of border control, because of attractive destinations' increasingly fortified frontiers, migrants find they need outside help getting into these countries. To gain entrance, many migrants depend heavily on transnational criminal smugglers, rather than their own initiatives or state policies. Such transnational criminal smuggling operations may disregard civil practices and engage in corruption and violence in their pursuit of profits, undercutting the security of migrants, native citizens, and national governments alike.

Concluding with national governments outsourcing enforcement of border control, states individually or collectively may depend heavily on paying off other countries to take in migrants rather than managing their own borders. This is exemplified by the EU's payments to Turkey and Morocco, where supposedly enlightened states want to keep migrants away so badly that they give funds to others to handle it rather than figure out how to integrate or peacefully coexist with the newcomers. Then each paid-off society feels no bounds about what it can do to foreign migrants in its midst, ignoring their human rights and engaging in unrestrained abuses.

Tolerance Hypocrisy Dangers

When considering tolerance between native citizens and foreign migrants, there is often a major gap between rhetoric and reality. Expressed compassion and empathy for the other in many cases appear to be largely a charade designed to impress naïve onlookers. Such a hypocritical pattern, depicted in Figure C.6, is often exhibited by national governments and the global community.

Considering first national government hypocrisy proclaiming tolerance of diversity while practicing intolerance, this pattern is a recipe for external regime distrust. Heads of state voice acceptance of foreigners, while in practice they condone or even indirectly promote their mistreatment. This tendency is evident to differing degrees in the Dominican Republic, Morocco, South Africa, Turkey, and Russia. Because many natives share their government's antipathy toward foreigners, this double standard allowing harassment of foreign migrants while protecting native citizens can actually increase political leaders'

National Government Hypocrisy

> PROCLAIMING TOLERANCE OF DIVERSITY WHILE PRACTICING INTOLERANCE
>
> Heads of state voice rhetoric of acceptance of foreigners while in reality being complicit in allowing or indirectly promoting foreign migrant mistreatment
>
> Embedded double standards, allowing foreign migrant harassment alongside native citizen protection, can actually increase political leaders' approval ratings
>
> Persistent contradictions about the treatment of those living within one's borders is a certain recipe for external regime distrust
>
> Such inconsistency, when applied to civil society initiatives, can impede monitoring state policy change, undertaking state policy reform, and state credibility of commitment

Global Community Hypocrisy

> PROCLAIMING INCLUSIVE OPEN TRANSACTIONS WHILE
> PRACTICING EXCLUSIONARY CLOSURE
>
> The international community views cross-border flows of people in a radically more restrictive way than cross-border flows of goods and services
>
> A clash exists between universal enlightened liberal international order principles and policies promoting national identity and control
>
> The avowed global welcoming spirit toward outsiders directly contradicts the on-the-ground national atmosphere of exclusion and rejection
>
> Such inconsistency can obscure foreign migrants' economic benefits to private enterprise and the cultural benefits to local communities

FIGURE C.6: Tolerance Hypocrisy Dangers

approval ratings. Such inconsistency, when applied to civil society initiatives, can significantly impede monitoring state policy change, undertaking state policy reform, and perceived credibility of state commitment.

Concluding with global community hypocrisy proclaiming inclusive open transactions while practicing exclusionary closure, this pattern bizarrely encourages cross-border movement of goods and services but not migrants, highlighting a clash between universal liberal international order principles and national identity and control interests. The international community, evident both in global rules of the game and in nation-state and intergovernmental organization policies, prevents most foreigners from residing permanently abroad while simultaneously courting foreign firms, ideas, and products. The avowed global welcoming spirit toward outsiders directly contradicts the on-the-ground national atmosphere of exclusion and rejection, reflecting considerable selectivity in translating enlightened open and inclusive principles into policy. Such inconsistency can obscure foreign migrants' potential economic benefits to local business and cultural benefits to local communities.

Rethinking National Identity

Considering the pervasiveness of intolerance-based violence, it seems vital to rethink national identity, as displayed in Figure C.7. National identity, which

---

IS NATIONAL IDENTITY STILL RELEVANT?

Do states and their citizens need to possess internal consensus about a distinctive national identity, readily distinguishable from that of others?

Does possession of a strong sense of national identity, and the accompanying patriotic fervor, contribute to a secure, stable, and peaceful world?

Does possessing a distinctive national identity cause high national morale and stabilizing unity and pride, or alternatively virulent nationalism, tribalism, xenophobia, and destabilizing global violence?

What would be the consequence for public officials and private citizens if a state possessed no sense of strong national identity?

WHAT SHOULD CONSTITUTE THE CORE OF NATIONAL IDENTITY?

Should the essence of national identity be loyalty to the state, acceptance of existing national traditions and norms, or racial, ethnic, religious, or national origin heritage?

How can we alter existing notions of national identity within a society, replacing rigid closed notions of national identity with more flexible open ones?

Should we promote an idealistic global citizen identity—since it seems to reduce nationalism and xenophobia—or a less lofty sense of tolerant national citizen identity?

How should national identity resolve the value clash between tolerance of diversity and enforcement of uniformity in determining its core?

HOW IS IT POSSIBLE TO PROPERLY FOSTER NATIONAL IDENTITY?

How can we deal with the reality that in many places citizen loyalties still run strongest to local tribal and ethnic identities, not to central state governments?

How can we avoid expecting new migrants to immediately give up their former national identities and be subject to complete assimilation into the new country's belief system and norms of behavior?

How can we avoid expecting long-standing citizens to immediately embrace cosmopolitan multiculturalism as the new norm and give up their former sense of who they were and what their country represents?

How can we shape national identity so that it still maintains pride in one's own group yet at the same time does not promote separatism, condescension, or intolerance toward other groups?

FIGURE C.7: Rethinking National Identity

appears in differing forms under differing conditions,[48] constitutes an essential bottom-up foundation of societal unity and cohesiveness within states. For example, Europe's refugee crisis intensified a crisis of European identity:

> Do Europeans share a deeper connection to one another based on a common historical and cultural legacy? And if so, what components of that past are relevant to Europe today? Is Europe secular or religious? Is it Christian, Judeo-Christian, or Judeo-Christian-Islamic?[49]

Indeed, "understandings of who forms part of the nation, who may become a member and under what conditions, and who is to be excluded, as well as the contestation of those understandings, are central in grasping the power dynamics underlying immigrant–native relations."[50] Destabilizing confusion often emerges about the core of citizens' national identity; for example, Islamophobia may "not spring directly from a fear of Islam, or a hatred of Muslims, but from ambiguities rooted in our dominant models of citizenship and national belonging."[51] Over time, "appeals to exclusive forms of identity—whether national, racial, or ethnic—have become more salient" and "sow fertile ground for populism, nativism, and nationalism to flourish."[52] Even under liberal internationalism, "in a world where national identity matters greatly, mixing different peoples together . . . is usually a prescription for serious trouble."[53]

To some observers, the ideal identity for international harmony is global citizenship,[54] raising the important question of what would happen if national identity were downplayed. However, although global citizenship might reduce international intolerance,[55] this aspiration is unrealistic in a world where people tend to cling to that which makes their group or country special; as one skeptical analyst quips, "universalistic cosmopolitanism . . . has little purchase outside the philosophy departments of Western universities."[56] So rather than trying to downplay national identity it might be wiser to pursue "tolerant national citizenship" as a goal. To do so, there would be a need to figure out how to replace rigid closed notions of national identity—especially those based on a fixed heritage component requiring racial, ethnic, religious, or national origin roots—with more flexible open ones that still maintain a cohesive and distinctive sense of national self-image. Unfortunately, such a move is often impeded by many societies pursuing the goals of "diversity" and "difference" rather than "colour blindness" and proper integration of people into the broader society[57] based on their potential to contribute. Expecting new migrants to immediately give up their former national identities and be subject to complete assimilation into the new country's belief system and norms of behavior appears to be just as outlandish as expecting long-standing citizens to immediately embrace multiculturalism as the new norm and give up their former sense of who they were and what their country represents.

A key question raised by thinking about national versus global citizenship is whether these two are necessarily directly at odds with one another in a zero-sum relationship. In other words, does one need to "weigh the relative importance of global and local allegiances against each other, as if they were bound to be in competition," or does the most central identity for an individual or group depend completely on the context, with the underlying premise that managing multiple identities "is something everyone has to do"?[58]

Lurking behind this questioning of national identity are worries about glorifying loyalty to the nation-state. For example, in 1996 German chancellor Helmut Kohl asserted that the nation-state "cannot solve the great problems of the twenty-first century."[59] Many analysts consider extreme state patriotism to be just as divisive and intolerance-promoting as extreme attachment to ethnic, racial, or religious identities. Some observers even conclude that the entire nation-state system is atavistic and should be replaced.

Another means of making national identity more tolerance-inducing is broadening its foundation. As discussed earlier, there is an ongoing push to base citizenship on civic loyalty rather than on ethnic background. In order to incorporate the flood of new migrants, within Europe there is talk of coming up with "a definition of inclusion that is as wide and unobjectionable as possible"; however, moving in this direction can cause national values to become "meaninglessly shallow" and unlikely to inspire deep national loyalties.[60] The mixed success of sincere national attempts at multiculturalism highlights such challenges. Some status quo analysts, including Samuel Huntington, even characterize multiculturalism as a major threat—"it is basically an anti-Western ideology."[61]

Does a state need to pursue internal consensus (rare in today's world) about its national identity, readily distinguishable from that of others, in order to be stable and secure in today's world? Possessing a distinctive national identity can raise national morale and stabilizing unity and pride within a country, or alternatively trigger virulent nationalism, xenophobia, tribalism, and destabilizing violence. The underlying controversy here concerns whether—or under what conditions—national identity can be positively channeled.

An important underlying value clash exists between tolerance of diversity and enforcement of uniformity, where critical cultural divides exist about whether homogeneity or heterogeneity is always a virtue or a vice. A key tension exists between the state system and human diversity, for "it was assumed that people—the very entities the state was designed to protect—in the long run would recognize that the authority which possesses the power to protect is the authority with which their loyalty must lie."[62] Today, as in the past, citizen loyalties within many countries still run strongest to local tribal and ethnic identities, not to central state governments. Attempts to transform local identities and allegiances so that they align more with the state have frequently not proven to be very successful, often triggering within-society and cross-society friction. As cultural diversity increases through the entrance of foreign migrants, pressures intensify to downplay state-mandated uniformity in favor of allowing multiculturalism, which can sometimes lead to a loyalty shift downward and thereby undercut overall societal coherence. So the ultimate question is, how can countries shape national identity so that it still maintains pride in one's own group yet at the same time does not promote separatism, condescension, or intolerance toward outside groups?

Rethinking National Control

Intolerance-based violence can fundamentally challenge traditional national control notions, with needed rethinking summarized in Figure C.8. Top-down control typically derives from durable principles, dating back to the Treaty of Westphalia in 1648 establishing the nation-state system, of national sovereignty and self-determination of peoples. Such principles make it legitimate for duly selected government officials to make decisions affecting what transpires within national borders, and illegitimate for foreign groups unilaterally without invitation to alter those rightfully local decisions.

In resisting delegating any control to foreigners, nationalistic elements within societies often vainly try to preserve what they consider to be the status quo, protecting existing power hierarchies and cultural traditions within a society. A notable illustration of this kind of effort is the French Académie Française's 2014 "reconquête de la langue française" push to cleanse the French language of any foreign words.[63] Given such efforts' mixed record of success, partially due to immigration, for quite some time nationalists have bemoaned "the loss of control over borders."[64]

Heads of state like Donald Trump and Viktor Orbán justifiably receive criticism for pursuing national control largely through enforcing exclusion of outsiders. Yet in many other countries, such as Morocco, Russia, and Turkey, rulers

---

IS SOVEREIGN AUTHORITY OVER TERRITORY STILL RELEVANT?

Could national control be gauged by whether its members are thriving, choose to stay within that society, are flexible and adaptable, and get along with each other and neighbors in a civil manner?
Could national control become more responsive, taking into account the full range of valid concerns promoting societal welfare of foreign migrants as well as native citizens?

HOW FEASIBLE IS NATIONAL CONTROL?

Given long-standing principles of sovereignty and the self-determination of peoples, should citizens expect a high level of control over their own destiny once their national identity is established?
How is it possible to maintain control over a strong distinctive national identity and induce its persistence within a globalized interdependent world?

HOW LEGITIMATE IS NATIONAL CONTROL?

Is it legitimate for citizens of a country (or their domestic representatives) to make crucial decisions affecting their fate, and illegitimate for any uninvited foreign group to unilaterally affect those decisions?
Is it legitimate for a society to exert control to maintain the status quo—protecting the existing hierarchy of power and influence—and to prevent foreign-induced influence from changing its culture?

WHAT SHOULD BE SUBJECT TO NATIONAL CONTROL?

Is it most important for national control to prioritize regulation of who gets to enter a country or to prioritize regulation of what immigrants do after they cross the border?
What facets of foreigner migrant behavior—their economic livelihood, their political rights, their cultural expression, or their freedom of movement—are most needy of national control?

WHAT ARE NATIONAL CONTROL'S IMPLEMENTATION LIMITS?

Is it acceptable for national control to incorporate utilitarian calculations about which foreign migrant groups are contributing most to the broader society?
Is it acceptable for national governments to grant to disgruntled groups of foreign migrants some level of autonomy in addressing their internal problems to promote stable peace?

FIGURE C.8: Rethinking National Control

who voice tolerance and acceptance of foreigners are no better, for in reality they are duplicitously complicit in facilitating severe mistreatment of strangers in their midst. Few political leaders have demonstrated a willingness in both principle and practice to exhibit sensitive flexibility about national control over their societies.

Is the most important manifestation of national control regulating who gets to enter a country or alternatively how immigrants fare after crossing the border? Many countries today place far more emphasis on restricting entry through fortifying borders, perhaps because they have not yet discovered ways to effectively integrate foreign migrants and to foster constructive native-foreigner relations once large numbers of outsiders have entered their societies.

Critical controversies surround what facets of foreigner migrant behavior—their economic livelihood, their political rights, their cultural expression, or their freedom of movement—most need control to promote stable civil relations between native citizens and foreign migrants. Too often today native citizens bristle indiscriminately at foreigners' differences, regardless of whether they actually interfere in any tangible way with natives' own freedoms. In considering which foreign migrant groups should be given the greatest freedoms, should there be a utilitarian calculation about which groups are contributing most to, or detracting most from, the broader society, or alternatively about which groups are most and least likely to push for separatist independence? Understandably, widespread wariness exists about performing this kind of cost-benefit analysis, because it often relies on overconfidence about group proclivities (potentially reflecting prejudicial profiling) and underconfidence about group abilities to modify behavior.

Should national governments cease being so obsessed with maintaining state sovereign control and instead consider granting to disgruntled foreign migrant groups living within their borders some level of influence in addressing their own internal problems to increase the chances of societal stability? As discussed in Chapter 6, national political leaders usually vehemently oppose anything that looks like it could become a subnational autonomy movement. However, a large influx of immigrants into an area does not automatically cause a state to lose control over its society,[65] and some national governments overstate the level of control desired by frustrated foreign migrants. In some circumstances, there may need to be softening in the rigid state position that any form of power-sharing with non-native groups constitutes a dangerous concession. For example, it sometimes might make sense for state officials to welcome, within parts of cities with foreign migrant concentrations, newcomers' desire for input into the content of public school curriculum to enhance its relevance for migrant children, or for bottom-up private assistance to public policing in violent areas to enhance community safety.

Interdependence-intolerance tensions may sometimes affect a national government's foreign policy formulation. For example, a leaked 2014 British Ministry of Defence report indicated that because of the United Kingdom's increased diversity and multiculturalism (due to the volume of foreign immigrants), "British military intervention in foreign countries was becoming impossible" thanks to potential strenuous objections from new British citizens emanating from those states.[66] So the mass influx of foreign migrants can sometimes marginally affect a state's national control by constraining a government's sovereign right to determine appropriate foreign policy based on what it thinks it best for the interest of the state and the majority population.

Finally, is the aspiration for sovereign authority over territory still relevant within an interdependent globalized world? The idea of "state control" seems a bit archaic as a primary security goal, because external forces regularly erode state sovereignty and make trying to keep foreigners and foreign ideas out futile. Directly affecting people's lives—with national governments less in control[67]—from above are multinational corporations, foreign states, international organizations, and transnational interest groups; from below are private security contractors, private vigilante groups, and transnational criminal organizations. The frequent involvement of such interfering independent entities can make government political leaders—who normally think that they should be in charge—instead feel like helpless bystanders when it comes to effective immigration regulation.

Instead, is it possible that a more appropriate measure of a society's success and stability could be whether its members are thriving in ways they consider important, whether they choose to stay within that society even when other options are available, whether they are flexible and adaptable in the face of uncontrollable change, and whether they get along with each other and neighbors in a civil manner? Perhaps political leaders' notion of national control needs to be more responsive, taking into account valid concerns both of native citizens and of foreign migrants, and adapting over time to accommodate differing internal and external circumstances.

Confronting Global Intolerance in an Interdependent World

Throughout human history, while "human beings have always lived in a multiplicity of communities and possessed a variety of identifications,"[68] it has seemed quite natural and survival-enhancing for people encountering diversity to want to find ways to distinguish between insiders and outsiders and to strive to become members of higher-status groups. The propensity to separate into tribes exhibiting key commonalities appears to be an almost instinctual pattern, usually providing great comfort, pride, and security to those who do so.

Typically one's sense of self seems bound up with deeply held notions about being part of a desirable group, with its perceived value often a direct function of its exclusivity. Within the popular literature, perhaps the most colorful metaphorical illustration of this seemingly universal tendency is Dr. Seuss's beloved children's story about the "star-bellied sneetches." Nonetheless, there is no inherent reason why these commonplace group predispositions—reflecting "overindulgence in the domestic and international politics of parochialism"[69]— have to translate into violence, especially given crucial mutually recognizable interdependencies.

How people and countries choose to deal with encounters with strangers and alien ideas constitutes a lightning rod of their basic civility. At different periods in history, and across the world at any one point in time, there have been vastly different levels of global intolerance and associated violence. In this context, tolerance would not equate with accepting anyone who wishes to cross national borders, or with forbearance toward any form of behavior undertaken by anyone within one's society; openness to differences means neither that rules of civil expression and interaction are discarded nor that restrictions and punishments for violating these rules are lenient. In contrast, such tolerance entails a pragmatic societal willingness to give those who are very different a fair though by no means guaranteed shot at crossing borders and joining one's group and a fair though by no means guaranteed shot at success once they do so.

Far too frequently, when different nationalities encounter each other, each automatically assumes that it is more civilized, projects its own positive self-image onto the way it thinks others will see it, assumes differences from it others exhibit to be dysfunctional, and greets others with suspicion and hostility and with little attempt at meaningful understanding. Just as it is easier to destroy than to create, it is far easier to harbor fear and hatred of outsiders than it is to try to establish solid bonds of respect and trust with them. Each group often fails to comprehend that others might see it with the same apprehension and confusion as it see others—as strange and bizarre (just as in a famous episode of the television show *Star Trek* where confounded and harassed outer space aliens legitimately viewed humans as "ugly bags of mostly water"). Rather than beginning domestic cross-nationality encounters by intentionally suspending judgment about the justifiability of each side's deep-seated aspirations and grievances, the typical pattern is for both participants in and observers of such interaction to believe from the outset that one side is better and the other is worse. Globally, interdependence has created the widespread recognition of mutual need but not the pervasive emergence of mutual openness or respect.

UN secretary-general António Guterres, upset about rising intolerance-based violent incidents aimed at migrants and "at anyone considered the 'other,'" warns that "as crime feeds on crime, and as vile views move from the fringes to the mainstream, I am profoundly concerned that we are nearing a pivotal moment in battling hatred and extremism."[70] Yet up to this point, globally far too few political leaders have exhibited the courage to take up seriously this major security challenge by focusing on finding legitimate and effective means to promote genuine tolerance.

On the surface, initiating discourse about intolerance under interdependence between native citizens and foreign migrants appears to be a "fool's errand"—inescapably divisive and likely to produce counterproductive finger-pointing. Because of passionate emotions, stubborn misperceptions, and muzzling political correctness, many sober thinkers prudently choose to stay away from this set of issues, figuring that any recommendations derived from dispassionate analysis would make no difference to the heated closed-minded voices on all sides. Nonetheless, the intense trauma created by violence linked to interdependent intolerance makes it crucial for all of us to deepen our understanding of the resulting societal insecurity. Such an effort will be well worth it, for the only alternative is bearing witness to endlessly escalating threat to community survival and global order.

Notes

Introduction

1. Andreas Wimmer, *Nationalist Exclusion and Ethnic Conflict: Shadows of Modernity* (Cambridge, UK: Cambridge University Press, 2002), 268.

2. Pierre Hassner, "Beyond Nationalism and Internationalism: Ethnicity and World Order," in Michael E. Brown, ed., *Ethnic Conflict and International Security* (Princeton, NJ: Princeton University Press, 1993), 131.

3. Colin Crouch, "The Familiar Axes of Politics Are Changing, with Momentous Consequences," *OpenDemocracy* (September 23, 2016), https://www.opendemocracy .net/uk/colin-crouch/familiar-axes-of-politics-are-changing-with-momentous -consequences.

Chapter 1

1. Yi Wang, "Globalization Enhances Cultural Identity," *Intercultural Communication Studies* 16 (2007), 83.

2. International Organization for Migration, *World Migration Report 2018* (Geneva: International Organization for Migration/UN Migration Agency, 2018), 149, https:// publications.iom.int/system/files/pdf/wmr_2018_en.pdf.

3. Carl Hunt and Nancy Chesser, *Deterrence 2.0: Deterring Violent Non-State Actors in Cyberspace* (Arlington, VA: Strategic Multi-Layer Analysis Team for the US Strategic Command Global Innovation and Strategy Center, January 9–10, 2008), 3.

4. Charles L. Glaser, "A Flawed Framework: Why the Liberal International Order Concept Is Misguided," *International Security* 43 (Spring 2019), 58.

5. Daniel Deudney and G. John Ikenberry, "Liberal World: The Resilient Order," *Foreign Affairs* 97 (July/August 2018), 18.

6. Robert Kagan, *The Jungle Grows Back: America and Our Imperiled World* (New York: Knopf, 2018), 4.

7. Dale C. Copeland, *Economic Interdependence and War* (Princeton, NJ: Princeton University Press, 2014), 16–50. See also Thomas L. Friedman, *The World Is Flat: A Brief History of the Twenty-First Century* (New York: Farrar, Straus and Giroux, 2005).

8. Robert O. Keohane and Joseph S. Nye, *Power and Interdependence*, 2nd ed. (New York: HarperCollins, 1989), 21–29.

9. Deudney and Ikenberry, "Liberal World: The Resilient Order," 16.

10. Yael Tamir, "Building a Better Nationalism: The Nation's Place in a Globalized World," *Foreign Affairs* 98 (March/April 2019), 51.

11. Nikil Saval, "Globalisation: The Rise and Fall of an Idea That Swept the World," *The Guardian* (July 14, 2017), https://www.theguardian.com/world/2017/jul/14/globalisation -the-rise-and-fall-of-an-idea-that-swept-the-world.

12. Joseph E. Stiglitz, *Globalization and Its Discontents Revisited* (New York: Norton, 2018), xvii–xviii, xix.

13. Marcos Engelken-Jorge, "The Upsurge of Xenophobic Nationalism—Threat and Opportunity," *OpenDemocracy* (March 10, 2017), https://www.opendemocracy.net/ marcos-engelken-jorge/upsurge-of-xenophobic-nationalism-threat-and-opportunity.

14. Ronald F. Inglehart and Pippa Norris, *Trump, Brexit, and the Rise of Populism: Economic Have-Nots and Cultural Backlash* (Cambridge, MA: Harvard Kennedy School Faculty Research Working Paper Series #RWP16–026, August 2016), 13, https://www .hks.harvard.edu/publications/trump-brexit-and-rise-populism-economic-have-nots -and-cultural-backlash.

15. Kagan, *The Jungle Grows Back*, 105.

16. Nick Mabey, *Security Trends and Threat Misperceptions* (London: E3G, 2007), 5.

17. Kagan, *The Jungle Grows Back*, 127, 128.

18. Stiglitz, *Globalization and Its Discontents Revisited*, 3, 336.

19. Pierre Hassner, "Beyond Nationalism and Internationalism: Ethnicity and World Order," in Michael E. Brown, ed., *Ethnic Conflict and International Security* (Princeton, NJ: Princeton University Press, 1993), 132.

20. John Rennie Short, "Why There's a Globalization Backlash," *US News and World Report* (November 29, 2016), https://www.usnews.com/news/national-news/articles/ 2016-11-29/why-theres-a-globalization-backlash.

21. John J. Mearsheimer, "Bound to Fail: The Rise and Fall of the Liberal International Order," *International Security* 43 (Spring 2019), 11.

22. This section draws heavily from Robert Mandel, *Deadly Transfers and the Global Playground: Transnational Security Threats in a Disorderly World* (Westport, CT: Praeger, 1999).

23. Zeev Maoz, *Paradoxes of War* (Boston: Unwin Hyman, 1990), 327.

24. Max G. Manwaring and Courtney E. Prisk, "The Umbrella of Legitimacy," in Max G. Manwaring, ed., *Gray Area Phenomena: Confronting the New World Disorder* (Boulder, CO: Westview Press, 1993), 90.

25. Mearsheimer, "Bound to Fail," 11.

26. Stiglitz, *Globalization and Its Discontents Revisited*, xxv.

27. Mkotama Katenga-Kaunda, "Xenophobia: A By-Product of Globalization," *International Association for Political Science Students* (April 20, 2015), http://www.iapss.org/wp/2015/04/20/xenophobia-a-by-product-of-globalisation/.

28. Deudney and Ikenberry, "Liberal World: The Resilient Order," 18.

29. Inglehart and Norris, *Trump, Brexit, and the Rise of Populism*, 6.

30. Kagan, *The Jungle Grows Back*, 127–128.

31. Kwame Anthony Appiah, "The Importance of Elsewhere: In Defense of Cosmopolitanism," *Foreign Affairs* 98 (March/April 2019), 20.

32. Tamir, "Building a Better Nationalism," 51.

33. René Cuperus, "The Populist Revolt Against Globalisation," *Perspective Politics* (June 2017), 14, https://www.clingendael.org/pub/2017/3/the-populist-revolt-against-globalisation/.

34. Cuperus, "The Populist Revolt Against Globalisation," 8–9, 14.

35. Daniel Deudney and G. John Ikenberry, "The Nature and Sources of Liberal International Order," *Review of International Studies* 25 (April 1999), 194.

36. Cuperus, "The Populist Revolt Against Globalisation," 14.

37. "The Rise of Nativism in Europe," *Europe Now* (January 31, 2018), https://www.europenowjournal.org/2108/01/31/the-rise-of-nativism-in-europe/.

38. Douglas Murray, *The Strange Death of Europe: Immigration, Identity, Islam* (London: Bloomsbury, 2017), 319.

39. Tamir, "Building a Better Nationalism," 48.

40. Mearsheimer, "Bound to Fail," 7.

41. Stiglitz, *Globalization and Its Discontents Revisited*, 343.

42. Yoeri Maertens, "'America First': Why Has Nativism Resurfaced in the New World?" (master's thesis, Universiteit Gent, 2017), 9, https://lib.ugent.be/fulltxt/RUG01/002/376/009/RUG01-002376009_2017_0001_AC.pdf; and Peter Schrag, *Not Fit for Our Society: Nativism and Immigration* (Berkeley: University of California Press, 2010), 6–7, 21, 57, 108–109, 120, and 214.

43. Jack Snyder, "The Broken Bargain: How Nationalism Came Back," *Foreign Affairs* 98 (March/April 2019), 58.

44. Cas Mudde, *The Relationship Between Immigration and Nativism in Europe and North America* (Washington, DC: Migration Policy Institute, May 2012), 12.

45. James Kirchick, "Is Germany Capable of Protecting Its Jews?," *The Atlantic* (April 29, 2018), https://www.theatlantic.com/international/archive/2018/04/germany-jews-muslim-migrants/558677/.

46. Colin Crouch, "The Familiar Axes of Politics Are Changing, with Momentous Consequences," *OpenDemocracy* (September 23, 2016), https://www.opendemocracy.net/uk/colin-crouch/familiar-axes-of-politics-are-changing-with-momentous-consequences.

47. International Organization for Migration, *World Migration Report 2018*, 13, 150.

48. Arne Seifert, "The Problems of Central Asian Migration to Russia," *International Organization for Migration (IOM)* (January 12, 2018), https://doc-research.org/2018/01/the-problems-of-central-asian-migration-to-russia/.

49. Kerstin Fisk, "Out of the Fire, Into the Frying Pan? Examining Violence Against Foreign Migrants in Africa," in Heather Smith-Cannoy, ed., *Emerging Threats to Human Rights: Resources, Violence, and Deprivation of Citizenship* (Philadelphia: Temple University Press, 2019), 99.

50. Seth M. Holmes and Heide Castañeda, "Representing the 'European Refugee Crisis' in Germany and Beyond: Deservingness and Difference, Life and Death," *American Ethnologist* 43 (January 2016), 12.

51. Pew Charitable Trust, "Europe's Latest Asylum Seekers," *Trend: Transcending Borders* (Summer 2016), 4, https://trend.pewtrusts.org/-/media/post-launch-images/trust-magazine/trend-summer-2016-test/trendsummer2016.pdf.

52. International Organization for Migration, *World Migration Report 2018*, 2.

53. International Organization for Migration, *World Migration Report 2003* (Geneva: International Organization for Migration/UN Migration Agency, 2003), 4.

54. David Henderson, "International Migration: Appraising Current Policies," *International Affairs* 70 (1994), 93–110.

55. Robert Mandel, "Perceived Security Threat and the Global Refugee Crisis," *Armed Forces and Society* 24 (Fall 1997), 77–78.

56. Rogers Brubaker, "Migration, Membership, and the Modern Nation-State: Internal and External Dimensions of the Politics of Belonging," *Journal of Interdisciplinary History* 41 (Summer 2010), 63.

57. Fiona B. Adamson, "Crossing Borders: International Migration and National Security," *International Security* 31 (Summer 2006), 197–198.

58. Short, "Why There's a Globalization Backlash."

59. Adamson, "Crossing Borders: International Migration and National Security," 183.

60. Tomas Faist, *The Migration-Security Nexus: International Migration and Security Before and After 9/11* (Malmö, Sweden: Malmö University School of International Migration and Ethnic Relations, Willy Brandt Series of Working Papers in International Migration and Ethnic Relations, 2004), 9.

61. Fareed Zakaria, "Populism on the March: Why the West Is in Trouble," *Foreign Affairs* 95 (November/December 2016), 14.

62. International Organization for Migration, *World Migration Report 2018*, 2.

63. Michael E. Brown, "Causes and Implications of Ethnic Conflict," in Michael E. Brown, ed., *Ethnic Conflict and International Security* (Princeton, NJ: Princeton University Press, 1993), 17; and Kathleen Newland, "Ethnic Conflict and Refugees," in Brown, *Ethnic Conflict and International Security*, 146–147.

64. Katenga-Kaunda, "Xenophobia."

65. World Bank, *Migration and Development: A Role for the World Bank Group* (Washington, DC: World Bank, 2016), http://documents.worldbank.org/curated/en/690381472677671445/Migration-and-development-arole-for-the-World-Bank-Group.

66. Jayati Ghosh, "Fear of Foreigners: Recession and Racism in Europe," *Race/Ethnicity* 4 (Winter 2011), 184.

67. Demetrios G. Papademetriou, "Migration," *Foreign Policy* 109 (Winter 1997), 22.

68. Philippe Legrain, "Europe Needs to Let Migrants In," *Foreign Policy* (August 24, 2015), http://foreignpolicy.com/2015/08/24/europe-needs-stop-fear-mongering-and-let-migrants-economy/.

69. Kenneth Roth, "The Refugee Crisis That Isn't," *Human Rights Watch* (September 3, 2015), https://www.hrw.org/news/2015/09/03/refugee-crisis-isnt.

70. Eleni Psarrou, "National Identity in the Era of Globalisation" (PhD diss., London School of Economics, 2002), 206, 210, http://etheses.lse.ac.uk/2507/1/U615456.pdf.

71. Mat Staver, "Has the World Become Desensitized?," *Liberty Counsel Connect* (April 23, 2015), http://libertycounsel.com/has-the-world-become-desensitized-lri/.

72. Katenga-Kaunda, "Xenophobia."

73. Tiyanjana Maluwa, "The Refugee Problem and the Quest for Peace and Security in Southern Africa," *International Journal of Refugee Law* 7 (1995), 672.

74. Brown, "Causes and Implications of Ethnic Conflict," 17–18.

75. Ghosh, "Fear of Foreigners," 189.

76. Saval, "Globalisation."

77. Myron Weiner, "Security, Stability, and International Migration," *International Security* 17 (Winter 1992/93), 109.

78. Ana Gonzalez-Barrera and Phillip Connor, "Around the World, More Say Immigrants Are a Strength Than a Burden," *Pew Research Center* (May 18, 2019), https://www.pewresearch.org/global/2019/03/14/around-the-world-more-say-immigrants-are-a-strength-than-a-burden/.

79. Adamson, "Crossing Borders: International Migration and National Security," 197.

80. Katenga-Kaunda, "Xenophobia."

81. Psarrou, "National Identity in the Era of Globalisation," 273.

82. Stiglitz, *Globalization and Its Discontents Revisited*, xxii–xxiii.

83. Manuela Achilles, Kyrill Kunakhovich, and Nicole Shea, "Nationalism, Nativism, and the Revolt Against Globalization," *Europe Now* (February 1, 2018), https://www.europenowjournal.org/2018/01/31/nationalism-nativism-and-the-revolt-against-globalization/.

84. Saval, "Globalisation."

85. Anthony Giddens, *Runaway World: How Globalisation Is Reshaping Our Lives* (London: Profile Books, 1999), 13.

86. Wang, "Globalization Enhances Cultural Identity," 85.

87. Gal Ariely, "Globalization, Immigration and National Identity: How the Level of Globalization Affects the Relations Between Nationalism, Constructive Patriotism and Attitudes Toward Immigrants?," *Group Processes and Intergroup Relations* 15 (2011), 543.

88. Short, "Why There's a Globalization Backlash."

89. Ariely, "Globalization, Immigration and National Identity," 543; and Manuel Castells, *The Power of Identity: The Information Age Economy, Society and Culture* (New York: Wiley-Blackwell, 2004).

90. Anthony Giddens, *Beyond Left and Right: The Future of Radical Politics* (Cambridge, UK: Polity Press, 1994), 5.

91. Anthony F. Heath and James R. Tilley, "British National Identity and Attitudes Toward Immigration," *International Journal on Multicultural Societies* 7 (2005), 121.

92. Irene Bloemraad, Anna Korteweg, and Gökçe Yurdakul, "Citizenship and Immigration: Multiculturalism, Assimilation, and Challenges to the Nation-State," *Annual Review of Sociology* 34 (2008), 154.

93. Alternative governance by violent groups is usually pernicious unless the national government is completely dysfunctional—see Robert Mandel, *Global Security Upheaval: Armed Nonstate Groups Usurping State Stability Functions* (Stanford, CA: Stanford University Press, 2013), 78–80. For further discussion, see Anne L. Clunan and Harold A. Trinkunas, eds., *Ungoverned Spaces: Alternatives to State Authority in an Era of Softened Sovereignty* (Stanford, CA: Stanford University Press, 2010).

94. Phil Williams, "Here Be Dragons: Dangerous Spaces and International Security," in Clunan and Trinkunas, *Ungoverned Spaces*, 44.

95. Katenga-Kaunda, "Xenophobia."

96. Guntram H. Herb, "Power, Territory, and National Identity," in Guntram H. Herb and David H. Kaplan, eds., *Scaling Identities: Nationalism and Territoriality* (Lanham, MD: Rowman and Littlefield, 2018), 8.

97. Yanis Varoufakis, "Globalization Is Stuck in a Trap—What Will It Be When It Breaks Free?" *Globe and Mail* (January 12, 2018), https://www.theglobeandmail.com/opinion/yanis-varoufakis-globalization-stuck-in-a-trap/article37588492/.

98. Manolis Pratsinakis, "Established and Outsider Nationals: Immigrant–Native Relations and the Everyday Politics of National Belonging," *Ethnicities* 18 (2018), 7.

99. Stiglitz, *Globalization and Its Discontents Revisited*, xxv.

100. Pratsinakis, "Established and Outsider Nationals," 14.

101. Eleonore Kofman, "Citizenship, Migration and the Reassertion of National Identity," *Citizenship Studies* 9 (2005), 464.

102. Bloemraad, Korteweg, and Yurdakul, "Citizenship and Immigration," 154, 155.

103. See, for example, Andreas Wimmer, "Why Nationalism Works—And Why It Isn't Going Away," *Foreign Affairs* 98 (March/April 2019), 27.

104. See Christian Joppke, *Immigration and the Nation-State: The United States, Germany and Great Britain* (Oxford, UK: Oxford University Press, 1999); and Christian Joppke, "The Retreat of Multiculturalism in the Liberal State: Theory and Policy," *British Journal of Sociology*, 55 (2004), 237–257.

105. Bloemraad, Korteweg, and Yurdakul, "Citizenship and Immigration," 154.

Chapter 2

1. Ross Hammond and Robert Axelrod, "The Evolution of Ethnocentrism," *Journal of Conflict Resolution* 50 (December 2006), 2.

2. Elizabeth Cashdan, "Ethnocentrism and Xenophobia: A Cross-Cultural Study," *Current Anthropology* 42 (December 2001), 760.

3. Andreas Wimmer, "Why Nationalism Works—And Why It Isn't Going Away," *Foreign Affairs* 98 (March/April 2019), 27.

4. Anthony Smith, *National Identity* (London: Penguin, 1991), 74.

5. See John Higham, *Strangers in the Land* (New Brunswick, NJ: Rutgers University Press, 1955); Robert A. LeVine and Donald T. Campbell, *Ethnocentrism: Theories of Conflict, Ethnic Attitudes, and Group Behavior* (New York: Wiley, 1972), 212–223; and Peter Schrag, *Not Fit for Our Society: Nativism and Immigration* (Berkeley: University of California Press, 2010).

6. Colin Crouch, "The Familiar Axes of Politics Are Changing, with Momentous Consequences," *OpenDemocracy* (September 23, 2016), https://www.opendemocracy.net/uk/colin-crouch/familiar-axes-of-politics-are-changing-with-momentous-consequences.

7. Dani Rodrik, "Populism and the Economics of Globalization," *Journal of International Business Policy* (2018), 13, https://doi.org/10.1057/s42214-018-0001-4.

8. Jürgen Osterhammel, "Nationalism and Globalization," in John Breuilly, ed., *The Oxford Handbook of the History of Nationalism* (New York: Oxford University Press, 2013), 705.

9. Jan-Werner Müller, "False Flags: The Myth of the Nationalist Resurgence," *Foreign Affairs* 98 (March/April 2019), 36.

10. Wimmer, "Why Nationalism Works—And Why It Isn't Going Away," 27.

11. Lars-Erik Cederman, "Blood for Soil: The Fatal Temptations of Ethnic Politics," *Foreign Affairs* 98 (March/April 2019), 61.

12. Manolis Pratsinakis, "Established and Outsider Nationals: Immigrant–Native Relations and the Everyday Politics of National Belonging," *Ethnicities* 18 (2018), 4.

13. Anthony D. Smith, "Nationalism in Decline?," in Mitchell Young, Eric Zuelow, and Andreas Sturm, eds., *Nationalism in a Global Era* (New York: Routledge, 2007), 30.

14. Wimmer, "Why Nationalism Works—And Why It Isn't Going Away," 28, 30–31.

15. Mary Kaldor, "Nationalism and Globalisation," *Nations and Nationalism* 10 (2004), 169.

16. Pierre Hassner, "Beyond Nationalism and Internationalism: Ethnicity and World Order," in Michael E. Brown, ed., *Ethnic Conflict and International Security* (Princeton, NJ: Princeton University Press, 1993), 135.

17. Craig Calhoun, *Nations Matter: Culture, History, and the Cosmopolitan Dream* (London: Routledge, 2007).

18. Pratsinakis, "Established and Outsider Nationals," 10.

19. Leonard Zeskind, "The New Nativism: The Alarming Overlap Between White Nationalists and Mainstream Anti-Immigrant Forces," *American Prospect* 16 (November 2005), A15.

20. Jack Snyder, "Nationalism and the Crisis of the Post-Soviet State," in Michael E. Brown, ed., *Ethnic Conflict and International Security* (Princeton, NJ: Princeton University Press, 1993), 86.

21. Gal Ariely, "Global Identification, Xenophobia and Globalisation: A Cross-National Exploration," *International Journal of Psychology* (2016), 3.

22. Kaldor, "Nationalism and Globalisation," 169.

23. Rodrik, "Populism and the Economics of Globalization," 2.

24. John Garnett, "The Causes of War and the Conditions of Peace," in John Baylis, James J. Wirtz, Colin S. Gray, and Eliot Cohen, eds., *Strategy in the Contemporary World*, 2nd ed. (New York: Oxford University Press, 2007), 34.

25. Hans-Georg Betz, "Xenophobia, Identity Politics and Exclusionary Populism in Western Europe," *Socialist Register* 39 (2003), 205.

26. Kaldor, "Nationalism and Globalisation," 168, 171.

27. Wimmer, "Why Nationalism Works—And Why It Isn't Going Away," 27.

28. See, for example, Daniel Deudney and G. John Ikenberry, "Liberal World: The Resilient Order," *Foreign Affairs* 97 (July/August 2018), 17; and Kaldor, "Nationalism and Globalisation," 169.

29. Cederman, "Blood for Soil," 61.

30. For related insights, see Robert M. Kunovich, "The Sources and Consequences of National Identification," *American Sociological Review* 74 (2009), 573–593; and Gal Ariely, "Globalisation and the Decline of National Identity? An Exploration Across Sixty-Three Countries," *Nations and Nationalism* 18 (2012), 466, 472, 474, 476.

31. Müller, "False Flags," 35.

32. See Sam Keen, *Faces of the Enemy: Reflections of the Hostile Imagination* (New York: Harper and Row, 1986), 17; Jerome D. Frank and Andrei Y. Melville, "The Image of the Enemy and the Process of Change," in Anatoly Gromyko and Martin Hellman, eds., *Breakthrough—Emerging New Thinking: Soviet and Western Challenges Issue a Challenge to Build a World Beyond War* (New York: Walker, 1988), 199; and Katja M. Flückiger,

Xenophobia, Media Stereotyping, and Their Role in Global Insecurity (Geneva: Geneva Centre for Security Policy Brief #21, December 6, 2006), https://www.files.ethz.ch/isn/92736/Brief-21.pdf.

33. Albert F. Eldridge, *Images of Conflict* (New York: St. Martin's Press, 1979), 148.

34. Higham, *Strangers in the Land*, 3, 335.

35. Michael E. Brown, "Causes and Implications of Ethnic Conflict," in Brown, *Ethnic Conflict and International Security* (Princeton, NJ: Princeton University Press, 1993), 14.

36. Joseph E. Stiglitz, *Globalization and Its Discontents Revisited* (New York: Norton, 2018), 43.

37. Fareed Zakaria, "Populism on the March: Why the West Is in Trouble," *Foreign Affairs* 95 (November/December 2016), 15.

38. Human Rights Watch, "Covid-19 Fueling Anti-Asian Racism and Xenophobia Worldwide" (May 12, 2020), https://www.hrw.org/news/2020/05/12/covid-19-fueling-anti-asian-racism-and-xenophobia-worldwide.

39. Vivian Wang and Amy Qin, "As Coronavirus Fades in China, Nationalism and Xenophobia Flare," *New York Times* (April 16, 2020), https://www.nytimes.com/2020/04/16/world/asia/coronavirus-china-nationalism.html.

40. Yasmeen Serhan and Timothy McLaughlin, "The Other Problematic Outbreak," *The Atlantic* (March 13, 2020), https://www.theatlantic.com/international/archive/2020/03/coronavirus-covid19-xenophobia-racism/607816/.

41. Eugene Robinson, "Can You Say, 'Bienvenidos'?," *Washington Post* (June 27, 2006), A21.

42. Gil Loescher, *Beyond Charity: International Cooperation and the Global Refugee Crisis* (New York: Oxford University Press, 1993), 35.

43. Eleni Psarrou, "National Identity in the Era of Globalisation" (PhD diss., London School of Economics, 2002), 206, http://etheses.lse.ac.uk/2507/1/U615456.pdf.

44. Arvind Subramanian, "The Globalization Backlash Paradox," *Project Syndicate* (April 16, 2018), https://www.project-syndicate.org/commentary/globalization-backlash-financial-integration-risks-by-arvind-subramanian-2018-04.

45. Andreas Wimmer, *Nationalist Exclusion and Ethnic Conflict: Shadows of Modernity* (Cambridge, UK: Cambridge University Press, 2002), 217–218.

46. See Ralph K. White, *Nobody Wanted War: Misperception in Vietnam and Other Wars* (Garden City, NY: Doubleday, 1970).

47. Philippe Legrain, "Europe Needs to Let Migrants In," *Foreign Policy* (August 24, 2015), http://foreignpolicy.com/2015/08/24/europe-needs-stop-fear-mongering-and-let-migrants-economy/.

48. Seth M. Holmes and Heide Castañeda, "Representing the 'European Refugee Crisis' in Germany and Beyond: Deservingness and Difference, Life and Death," *American Ethnologist* 43 (January 2016), 18.

49. Human Rights First, *Germany Conflicted: The Struggle Between Xenophobia and Tolerance* (New York: Human Rights First, February 2017), 12, 27, 38.

50. Human Rights First, *Germany Conflicted*, 12, 26.

51. Paul Verryn, "Foreword," in Eric Worby, Shireen Hassim, and Tawana Kupe, eds., *Go Home or Die Here* (Johannesburg: Wits University Press, 2008), vii.

52. Ashley Kirk, "EU Referendum: The Claims That Won It for Brexit, Fact Checked," *The Telegraph* (February 20, 2017), http://www.telegraph.co.uk/news/0/eu-referendum -claims-won-brexit-fact-checked/.

53. Martin Moore and Gordon Ramsay, "Acrimonious and Divisive: The Role the Media Played in Brexit," *LSE Brexit* (May 17, 2017), http://blogs.lse.ac.uk/brexit/2017/05/ 16/acrimonious-and-divisive-the-role-the-media-played-in-brexit/.

54. Piotr Cap, *The Language of Fear: Communicating Threat in Public Discourse* (London: Palgrave Macmillan, 2017), 67.

55. Moore and Ramsay, "Acrimonious and Divisive."

56. Jakub Grygiel, "The Return of Europe's Nation-States: The Upside to the EU's Crisis," *Foreign Affairs* 95 (2016), 97.

57. Jayati Ghosh, "Fear of Foreigners: Recession and Racism in Europe," *Race/Ethnicity* 4 (Winter 2011), 189.

58. Amnesty International, *Amnesty International Report 2017/18: The State of the World's Human Rights* (London: Amnesty International, 2018), 13.

59. Myron Weiner, *The Global Migration Crisis* (New York: HarperCollins, 1994), 139–144; and Cas Mudde, *The Relationship Between Immigration and Nativism in Europe and North America* (Washington, DC: Migration Policy Institute, May 2012), 31–32.

60. Klaus Knorr, "Threat Perception," in Klaus Knorr, ed., *Historical Dimensions of National Security Problems* (Lawrence: University Press of Kansas, 1976), 113.

61. Robert Kagan, *The Jungle Grows Back: America and Our Imperiled World* (New York: Knopf, 2018), 10.

62. Roger Cohen, "Tribalism Here, and There," *New York Times* (March 10, 2008), https://www.nytimes.com/2008/03/10/opinion/10webcohen.html.

63. Benjamin R. Barber, "Jihad vs. McWorld," *The Atlantic* (March 1992), https:// www.theatlantic.com/magazine/archive/1992/03/jihad-vs-mcworld/303882/. See also Benjamin Barber, *Jihad vs. Mcworld: How Globalism and Tribalism Are Reshaping the World* (New York: Corgi, 2003).

64. Phil Williams, *Violent Non-State Actors and National and International Security* (Zurich: Swiss Federal Institute of Technology International Relations and Security Network, 2008), 6. See also Mathew Horsman and Andrew Marshall, *After the Nation State: Citizens, Tribalism and the New World Disorder* (London: HarperCollins, 1995).

65. John Lea and Kevin Stenson, "Security, Sovereignty, and Non-State Governance 'from Below,'" *Canadian Journal of Law and Society* 22 (2007), 15; Clifford Shearing, "Punishment and the Changing Face of the Governance," *Punishment and Society* 3

(2001), 203; and Teresa P. R. Caldeira, "Fortified Enclaves: The New Urban Segregation," *Public Culture* 8 (1996), 303.

66. John Rapley, "The New Middle Ages," *Foreign Affairs* 85 (May/June 2006), 101.

67. Marvin J. Cetron and Owen Davies, *55 Trends Now Shaping the Future of Terrorism* (Washington, DC: Proteus Trends, February 2008), 71.

68. Barber, "Jihad vs. McWorld."

69. Amy Chua, "The Destructive Dynamics of Political Tribalism," *New York Times* (February 20, 2018), https://www.nytimes.com/2018/02/20/opinion/destructive -political-tribalism.html.

70. Cetron and Davies, *55 Trends Now Shaping the Future of Terrorism*, 73, 95.

71. See Robert D. Kaplan, *Balkan Ghosts: A Journey Through History* (New York: Vintage, 1994).

72. Kagan, *The Jungle Grows Back*, 105, 107.

73. Alex Macleod, "Culture, National Identity and Security," presentation prepared for the Toronto Symposium on Human Cultural Security and EU-Canada Relations, Toronto (June 6–7, 2005), 1.

74. Human Rights First, *Combating Xenophobic Violence: A Framework for Action* (New York: Human Rights First, 2011), 1.

75. Jan Scholte, *What Is Happening?* (Cambridge, MA: St. Martin's Press, 2000), 55.

76. Ariely, "Globalisation and the Decline of National Identity?," 462–463.

77. William H. McNeill, "Winds of Change," in Nicholas X. Rizopoulos, ed., *Sea-Changes* (New York: Council on Foreign Relations Press, 1990), 176.

78. Psarrou, "National Identity in the Era of Globalisation," 255.

79. Stiglitz, *Globalization and Its Discontents Revisited*, xxii–xxiii; and Neil Irwin, "Globalization's Backlash Is Here, at Just the Wrong Time," *New York Times* (March 23, 2018), https://www.nytimes.com/2018/03/23/upshot/globalization-pain-and-promise -for-rich-nations.html.

80. Rodrik, "Populism and the Economics of Globalization," 7. See also Claire Cain Miller, "The Long-Term Jobs Killer Is Not China—It's Automation," *New York Times* (December 21, 2016), https://www.nytimes.com/2016/12/21/upshot/thelong-term-jobs -killer-is-not-china-its-automation.html.

81. Mkotama Katenga-Kaunda, "Xenophobia: A By-Product of Globalization," *International Association for Political Science Students* (April 20, 2015), http://www.iapss.org/ wp/2015/04/20/xenophobia-a-by-product-of-globalisation/.

82. Corey Robin, *Fear: The History of a Political Idea* (New York: Oxford University Press, 2004), 2, 25.

83. David Martosko, "Obama Delivers a New Veiled Slap at Trump as He Warns—in Canada—That America Could Descend into 'Extreme Nationalism and Xenophobia and the Politics of Us-Versus-Them,'" *Daily Mail* (June 6, 2017), http://www.dailymail.co

.uk/news/article-4578906/Obama-warns-Trump-s-extreme-nationalism-xenophobia .html.

84. Meredith Hoffman, "Whatever Happened to Arizona's Minutemen?," *Vice* (March 22, 2016), https://www.vice.com/en_us/article/xd7jmn/what-happened-to -arizonas-minutemen.

85. See Robert Mandel, *Global Data Shock: Strategic Ambiguity, Deception, and Surprise in an Age of Information Overload* (Stanford, CA: Stanford University Press, 2019), chap. 3.

86. Müller, "False Flags," 38.

87. Mudde, *The Relationship Between Immigration and Nativism in Europe and North America*, 26–27.

88. L. K. Samuels, "Terrorism, Global Warming and Fear" (June 14, 2007), http:// www.lewrockwell.com/orig7/samuels4.html.

89. David Green, "The Trump Hypothesis: Testing Immigrant Populations as a Determinant of Violent and Drug-Related Crime in the United States," *Social Science Quarterly* 97 (September 2016), 507.

90. Zoltan Dujisin, "Media Complicity in Rising Xenophobia," *Al Jazeera* (June 3, 2011), https://www.aljazeera.com/indepth/features/2011/05/2011523111628194989.html.

91. HansPeter Kriesi, Edgar Grande, Romain Lachat, Martin Dolezal, Simon Bornschier, and Timotheos Frey, "Globalization and the Transformation of the National Political Space: Six European Countries Compared," *European Journal of Political Research* 45 (2006), 921–956.

92. International Organization for Migration, *World Migration Report 2018* (Geneva: International Organization for Migration/UN Migration Agency, 2018), 209, https:// publications.iom.int/system/files/pdf/wmr_2018_en.pdf.

93. International Organization for Migration, *World Migration Report 2018*, 1, 193–194.

94. Pratsinakis, "Established and Outsider Nationals," 13.

95. Helen Dempster, "Evidence Doesn't Work in the Migration Public Debate," *Overseas Development Institute* (October 2, 2017), https://www.odi.org/blogs/10569-evidence -doesn-t-work-migration-public-debate.

96. International Organization for Migration, *World Migration Report 2018*, 193–194.

97. Pratsinakis, "Established and Outsider Nationals," 16.

98. See, for example, Dina Okamoto and Kim Ebert, "Group Boundaries, Immigrant Inclusion, and the Politics of Immigrant–Native Relations," *American Behavioral Scientist* 60 (2016), 227.

99. Bill Kovach and Tom Rosenstiel, *Blur: How to Know What's True in the Age of Information Overload* (Bloomsbury, NJ: Bloomsbury USA, 2011), 7.

100. International Organization for Migration, *World Migration Report 2018*, 195.

101. Müller, "False Flags," 40.

102. See Jack Snyder and Karen Ballentine, "Nationalism and the Marketplace of Ideas," *International Security* 21 (Fall 1996), 5–40.

103. John R. Bowen, "The Myth of Global Ethnic Conflict," *Journal of Democracy* 7 (October 1996), 11.

104. Flückiger, *Xenophobia, Media Stereotyping, and Their Role in Global Insecurity*, 3; and Matt Mogekwu, "The Media's Role in Stoking Xenophobia," *World Policy Journal* (April 26, 2017), https://worldpolicy.org/2017/04/26/the-medias-role-in-stoking-xenophobia/.

105. Mogekwu, "The Media's Role in Stoking Xenophobia."

106. Bernard I. Finel and Kristin M. Lord, "The Surprising Logic of Transparency," *International Studies Quarterly* 43 (June 1999), 320, 335.

107. For an alternative conceptualization, see Rodney Barker, *Making Enemies* (New York: Palgrave Macmillan, 2007), 38.

108. J. Glenn Gray, *The Warriors: Reflections on Men in Battle* (New York: Harper and Row, 1959), 148–149. See also Barker, *Making Enemies*, chap. 8.

109. Stephen Chan, *Out of Evil: New International Politics and Old Doctrines of War* (Ann Arbor: University of Michigan Press, 2005), ix.

110. Barker, *Making Enemies*, 119–120.

111. Brian Michael Jenkins, *Unconquerable Nation: Knowing Our Enemy, Strengthening Ourselves* (Santa Monica, CA: RAND, 2006), 153.

112. Jerome D. Frank, *Sanity and Survival: Psychological Aspects of War and Peace* (New York: Random House, 1967), 124.

113. David J. Finlay, Ole R. Holsti, and Richard R. Fagen, *Enemies in Politics* (Chicago: Rand McNally, 1967), 6–22; and Arthur Gladstone, "The Conception of the Enemy," *Journal of Conflict Resolution*, 3 (June 1959), 132–137.

114. Barker, *Making Enemies*, 8.

Chapter 3

1. Elizabeth Cashdan, "Ethnocentrism and Xenophobia: A Cross-Cultural Study," *Current Anthropology* 42 (December 2001), 760; Cas Mudde, *The Relationship Between Immigration and Nativism in Europe and North America* (Washington, DC: Migration Policy Institute, May 2012), 22–25; and Jonathan Marcus, "Exorcising Europe's Demons: A Far-Right Resurgence?" *Washington Quarterly* 23 (2000), 31–40.

2. Marcos Engelken-Jorge, "The Upsurge of Xenophobic Nationalism—Threat and Opportunity," *OpenDemocracy* (March 10, 2017), https://www.opendemocracy.net/marcos-engelken-jorge/upsurge-of-xenophobic-nationalism-threat-and-opportunity.

3. See, for example, Michael T. Light and Ty Miller, "Does Undocumented Immigration Increase Violent Crime?," *Criminology* 56 (2018), 393–396; and David Green,

"The Trump Hypothesis: Testing Immigrant Populations as a Determinant of Violent and Drug-Related Crime in the United States," *Social Science Quarterly* 97 (September 2016), 521.

4. Steven Pinker, *The Better Angels of Our Nature: Why Violence Has Declined* (New York: Viking, 2011).

5. Jaweed Kaleem, "The New Zealand Mosque Shooting Is Just the Latest in a Trend of Violence Against Houses of Worship," *Los Angeles Times* (March 15, 2019), https:// www.latimes.com/world/la-fg-new-zealand-world-religious-attacks-20190315-story .html; and Doug Stanglin and Joel Shannon, "Police Identify 'Racist' Suspect in New Zealand's Terror Attack That Killed 49," *USA Today* (March 15, 2019), https://www .usatoday.com/story/news/world/2019/03/15/new-zealand-mosque-shooting-police -critical-incident/3172048002/.

6. Steve George, "Easter Attacks Are Just the Latest Chapter in Sri Lanka's History of Violence," *CNN* (April 22, 2019), https://www.cnn.com/2019/04/22/asia/sri-lanka -violence-explainer-intl/index.html.

7. Chris Woodvard, "One Jewish, One Christian: How the California Syna- gogue Shooting Tore Apart Two Congregations," *USA Today* (April 29, 2019), https:// www.usatoday.com/story/news/nation/2019/04/29/poway-synagogue-shooting-two -congregations-torn-apart/3613812002/.

8. David A. Lake and Donald Rothchild, *Ethnic Fears and Global Engagement: The International Spread and Management of Ethnic Conflict* (San Diego: Institute on Global Conflict and Cooperation Policy Paper #20, University of California, San Diego, Janu- ary 1996), 8.

9. Human Rights First, *Combating Xenophobic Violence: A Framework for Action* (New York: Human Rights First, 2011), 1.

10. United Nations, "Amid Rising Xenophobia, Violence, States Must Do More to Protect Migrants' Rights, General Assembly Hears on International Day for Ending Racial Discrimination," Seventy-First Session of the United Nations General Assem- bly, New York (March 21, 2017), https://www.un.org/press/en/2017/ga11895.doc.htm. See also Max Friedrich Steinhardt, *The Impact of Xenophobic Violence on the Integration of Immigrants* (Bonn, Germany: Institute of Labor Economics IZA Discussion Paper #11781, August 2018), 24.

11. Mary Kaldor, "Nationalism and Globalisation," *Nations and Nationalism* 10 (2004), 172.

12. International Organization for Migration, *World Migration Report 2018* (Geneva: International Organization for Migration/UN Migration Agency, 2018), 209, https:// publications.iom.int/system/files/pdf/wmr_2018_en.pdf.

13. Yoeri Maertens, "'America First': Why Has Nativism Resurfaced in the New World?" (master's thesis, Universiteit Gent, 2017), 9, https://lib.ugent.be/fulltxt/RUG01/ 002/376/009/RUG01-002376009_2017_0001_AC.pdf.

14. International Organization for Migration, *World Migration Report 2018*, 213–214.

15. Aristide R. Zolberg, Astri Suhrke, and Sergio Aguayo, *Escape from Violence: Conflict and the Refugee Crisis in the Developing World* (Oxford, UK: Oxford University Press, 1989), 275–278.

16. Myron Weiner, "Security, Stability, and International Migration," *International Security* 17 (Winter 1992/93), 103, 109.

17. Fiona B. Adamson, "Crossing Borders: International Migration and National Security," *International Security* 31 (Summer 2006), 198.

18. Robert S. Leiken, *Bearers of Global Jihad? Immigration and National Security After 9/11* (Washington, DC: Nixon Center, 2004), 6.

19. Department of Justice, *DOJ, DHS Report: Three out of Four Individuals Convicted of International Terrorism and Terrorism-Related Offenses Were Foreign-Born* (Washington, DC: U.S. Department of Justice, Office of Public Affairs, January 16, 2018), https://www.justice.gov/opa/pr/doj-dhs-report-three-out-four-individuals-convicted -international-terrorism-and-terrorism.

20. Ben Thompson, "NATO Commander Says Russia and Syria Are Using Migration as a Weapon," *Christian Science Monitor* (March 2, 2016), http://www.csmonitor .com/World/Global-News/2016/0302/NATO-commander-says-Russia-and-Syria-are -using-migration-as-a-weapon.

21. Seth M. Holmes and Heide Castañeda, "Representing the 'European Refugee Crisis' in Germany and Beyond: Deservingness and Difference, Life and Death," *American Ethnologist* 43 (January 2016), 18.

22. Malcolm Brabant, "Can Security Forces Screen Refugees Arriving in Europe?" *PBS NewsHour* (March 7, 2016), http://www.pbs.org/newshour/bb/can-security-forces -screen-refugees-arriving-in-europe/.

23. John Hayward, "Failure to Stop Muslim Terror Attacks Shows 'European Union Experiment Is Not Working,'" *Breitbart* (March 28, 2016), http://www.breitbart .com/national-security/2016/03/28/armstrong-williams-failure-to-stop-muslim-terror -attacks-show-european-union-experiment-is-not-working/.

24. Thomas L. Friedman, "Lift, Lift, Contain," *New York Times* (June 4, 1995), E15.

25. Tamar Lapin, "Footage Shows Hundreds of Migrants Occupying French Airport Terminal," *New York Post* (May 19, 2019), https://nypost.com/2019/05/19/footage-shows -hundreds-of-migrants-occupying-french-airport-terminal/.

26. Kerstin Fisk, "Out of the Fire, Into the Frying Pan? Examining Violence Against Foreign Migrants in Africa," in Heather Smith-Cannoy, ed., *Emerging Threats to Human Rights: Resources, Violence, and Deprivation of Citizenship* (Philadelphia: Temple University Press, 2019), 100.

27. Weiner, "Security, Stability, and International Migration," 120.

28. Human Rights First, *Combating Xenophobic Violence*, 1, 7.

29. Kathleen Newland, "Ethnic Conflict and Refugees," in Brown, *Ethnic Conflict and International Security*, 146.

30. Michael D. Shear, Miriam Jordan, and Manny Fernandez, "The U.S. Immigration System May Have Reached a Breaking Point," *New York Times* (April 10, 2019), https://www.nytimes.com/2019/04/10/us/immigration-border-mexico.html.

31. Light and Miller, "Does Undocumented Immigration Increase Violent Crime?," 375.

32. Weiner, "Security, Stability, and International Migration," 93.

33. Ron E. Hassner and Jason Wittenberg, "Barriers to Entry: Who Builds Fortified Boundaries and Why?," *International Security* 40 (Summer 2015), 183.

34. Jerome D. Frank and Andrei Y. Melville, "The Image of the Enemy and the Process of Change," in Anatoly Gromyko and Martin Hellman, eds., *Breakthrough— Emerging New Thinking: Soviet and Western Challenges Issue a Challenge to Build a World Beyond War* (New York: Walker, 1988), 201–203.

35. Robert Mandel, *The Changing Face of National Security: A Conceptual Analysis* (Westport, CT: Greenwood Press, 1994), 34; and Myron Weiner, *The Global Migration Crisis* (New York: HarperCollins, 1994), 3.

36. Phil Williams, *Violent Non-State Actors and National and International Security* (Zurich: Swiss Federal Institute of Technology International Relations and Security Network, 2008), 6.

37. Weiner, "Security, Stability, and International Migration," 120.

38. Matthew Carr, *Fortress Europe: Dispatches from a Gated Continent* (New York: New Press, 2012), 6.

39. Giorgos Christidis, Katrin Kuntz, Walter Mayr, Peter Müller, Jan Puhl, and Mathieu von Rohr, "European Crisis Disunity: A De Facto Solution Takes Shape in the Balkans," *Spiegel* (February 26, 2016), http://www.spiegel.de/international/europe/european-response-to-refugee-crisis-fracturing-a-1079547.html.

40. Souad Mekhennet and William Booth, "Migrants Are Disguising Themselves as Syrians to Enter Europe," *Washington Post* (September 23, 2015), https://www.washingtonpost.com/world/europe/migrants-are-disguising-themselves-as-syrians-to-gain-entry-to-europe/2015/09/22/827c6026-5bd8-11e5-8475-781cc9851652_story.html.

41. Mekhennet and Booth, "Migrants Are Disguising Themselves as Syrians to Enter Europe."

42. Jeanne Park, "Europe's Migration Crisis," *Council on Foreign Relations* (September 2, 2015), http://www.cfr.org/migration/europes-migration-crisis/p32874.

43. Daniela Kietz, "Craving for Control: Refugee Screening in the EU and the US," *Europe for Citizens Programme of the European Union* (December 15, 2015), http://reshaping-europe.boellblog.org/2015/12/15/craving-for-control-refugee-screening-in-the-eu-and-the-us/.

44. Mekhennet and Booth, "Migrants Are Disguising Themselves as Syrians to Enter Europe."

45. Cecilia Jacob, "Human Security and the Politics of Protection" (September 2011), 7, http://www.uq.edu.au/isaasiapacific/content/CeciliaJacob3-3.pdf.

46. Lars-Erik Cederman, "Blood for Soil: The Fatal Temptations of Ethnic Politics," *Foreign Affairs* 98 (March/April 2019), 62.

47. James Milner, *Sharing the Security Burden: Towards the Convergence of Refugee Protection and State Security* (Oxford, UK: Refugee Studies Centre, University of Oxford, 2000), 1, http://www.rsc.ox.ac.uk/PDFs/workingpaper4.pdf.

48. Steinhardt, *The Impact of Xenophobic Violence on the Integration of Immigrants*, 25.

49. Achilles, Kunakhovich, and Shea, "Nationalism, Nativism, and the Revolt Against Globalization."

50. Robert Mandel, *Armies Without States: The Privatization of Security* (Boulder, CO: Rienner, 2002), 7.

51. Robert Mandel, *The Global Illusion of Citizen Protection: Transnational Threats and Human Security* (Lanham, MD: Rowman and Littlefield, 2018), 77–78.

52. Dan Caldwell and Robert E. Williams Jr., *Seeking Security in an Insecure World* (Lanham, MD: Rowman and Littlefield, 2012), 210–211.

53. Benjamin Wittes and Gabriella Blum, *The Future of Violence: Robots and Germs, Hackers and Drones* (New York: Basic Books, 2015), 22.

54. Human Rights First, *Combating Xenophobic Violence*, 2.

55. David A. Graham, "Violence Has Forced 60 Million People from Their Homes," *The Atlantic* (June 17, 2015), http://www.theatlantic.com/international/archive/2015/06/refugees-global-peace-index/396122/.

56. Human Rights First, *Combating Xenophobic Violence*, 2.

57. Harriet Sinclair, "White Nationalism Is as Much of a Threat to U.S. as ISIS, FBI'S Open Investigations Show," *Newsweek* (September 27, 2017), http://www.newsweek.com/white-nationalism-much-threat-us-isis-fbis-open-investigations-show-672623.

58. Kaldor, "Nationalism and Globalisation," 162, 168, 171.

59. Peter Lock, "Africa, Military Downsizing and the Growth in the Security Industry," in Jakkie Cilliers and Peggy Mason, eds., *Peace, Profit or Plunder? The Privatisation of Security in War-Torn African Societies* (Johannesburg, South Africa: Institute for Security Studies, 1999), 26.

60. Edward J. Blakely and Mary Gail Snyder, "Places to Hide," *American Demographics* 19 (May 1997), 23–25.

61. Julie Gallagher, "Anti-Social Security," *New Statesman and Society* 8 (March 31, 1995), 22–24.

62. Adam Taylor, "Europe Had a Dream of a Land Without Borders—Now That Dream May Be Turning to Dust," *Washington Post* (September 2, 2015), https://www

.washingtonpost.com/news/worldviews/wp/2015/09/02/europe-had-a-dream-of-a
-land-without-borders-now-that-dream-may-be-turning-to-dust/.

63. Douglas Murray, *The Strange Death of Europe: Immigration, Identity, Islam* (London: Bloomsbury, 2017), 317.

64. Caroline Moorehead, "A Tide That Can't Be Turned: The Refugee Crisis Proves That Fortress Europe Is a Fantasy," *New Statesman* 20 (May 23, 2016), http://www.newstatesman.com/culture/books/2016/05/refugee-crisis-proves-fortress-europe-fantasy.

65. Hassner and Wittenberg, "Barriers to Entry," 158, 190.

66. International Organization for Migration, *World Migration Report 2018*, 167.

67. Hassner and Wittenberg, "Barriers to Entry," 183.

68. Mark J. Miller, "The Sanctioning of Unauthorized Migration and Alien Employment," in David Kyle and Rey Koslowski, eds., *Global Human Smuggling: Comparative Perspectives* (Baltimore: Johns Hopkins University Press, 2001), 321.

69. Robert Harris, *Political Corruption: In and Beyond the Nation State* (London: Routledge, 2003), 192.

70. International Organization for Migration, *World Migration Report 2018*, 160.

71. Weiner, *The Global Migration Crisis*, 5, 8. See also Robert Mandel, *Dark Logic: Transnational Criminal Tactics and Global Security* (Stanford, CA: Stanford University Press, 2011); and Steven Dudley, *Violence Against Migrants* (Washington, DC: Migration Policy Institute, 2012).

72. International Crisis Group, *Mexico's Southern Border: Security, Violence and Migration in the Trump Era* (Brussels, Belgium: International Crisis Group, Latin America Report #66, May 9, 2018), 20.

73. Phil Williams, "Human Commodity Trafficking: An Overview," in Phil Williams, *Illegal Migration and Commercial Sex: The New Slave Trade* (London: Cass, 1999), 4.

74. John Kerry, *The New War: The Web of Crime That Threatens America's Security* (New York: Simon and Schuster, 1997), 135–136.

75. Philippe Legrain, "Europe Needs to Let Migrants In," *Foreign Policy* (August 24, 2015), http://foreignpolicy.com/2015/08/24/europe-needs-stop-fear-mongering-and-let-migrants-economy/.

76. Mekhennet and Booth, "Migrants Are Disguising Themselves as Syrians to Enter Europe."

77. Roberto Saviano, "Italy's War on Migrants Makes Me Fear for My Country's Future," *The Guardian* (June 19, 2018), https://www.theguardian.com/commentisfree/2018/jun/19/italy-war-migrants-fear-civil-rights.

78. Colleen Barry, "Italy, Austria Signal New Hard-Line Axis on Migration," *Fox News* (June 20, 2018), http://www.foxnews.com/world/2018/06/20/italy-austria-signal-new-hard-line-axis-on-migration.html.

79. Salvatore Borghese and Lorenzo Newman, "Xenophobes in Glass Houses," *Slate* (March 1, 2018), https://slate.com/news-and-politics/2018/03/italys-left-has-a-xenophobia-problem.html.

80. Saviano, "Italy's War on Migrants Makes Me Fear for My Country's Future."

81. Park, "Europe's Migration Crisis."

82. Weiyi Cai and Simone Landon, "Attacks by White Extremists Are Growing—So Are Their Connections," *New York Times* (April 3, 2019), https://www.nytimes.com/interactive/2019/04/03/world/white-extremist-terrorism-christchurch.html.

83. Michael E. Brown, ed., *The International Dimensions of Internal Conflict* (Cambridge, MA: MIT Press, 1996), 3.

84. Weiner, "Security, Stability, and International Migration," 104.

85. Ashraf Ghani, Clare Lockhart, and Michael Carnahan, *Closing the Sovereignty Gap: An Approach to State-Building* (London: Overseas Development Institute, September 2005), 4.

Chapter 4

1. Human Rights First, *Combating Xenophobic Violence: A Framework for Action* (New York: Human Rights First, 2011), 2.

2. See Alexander L. George and Andrew Bennett, *Case Studies and Theory Development in the Social Sciences* (Cambridge, MA: MIT Press, 2005).

3. Ginger Thompson, "Immigrant Laborers from Haiti Are Paid with Abuse in the Dominican Republic," *New York Times* (November 20, 2005), https://www.nytimes.com/2005/11/20/world/americas/immigrant-laborers-from-haiti-are-paid-with-abuse-in-the.html.

4. Thompson, "Immigrant Laborers from Haiti Are Paid with Abuse in the Dominican Republic."

5. E. Benjamin Skinner, "A World Enslaved," *Foreign Policy* 165 (2008), 62–67; and Calla Cloud, "Human Rights Abuses Along the Dominican-Haitian Border," 58, https://www.du.edu/korbel/hrhw/researchdigest/latinamerica2/digest-human%20rights%20in%20latin%20america%20vol%202-dominican-haiti.pdf.

6. Thompson, "Immigrant Laborers from Haiti Are Paid with Abuse in the Dominican Republic."

7. Abby Phillip, "The Bloody Origins of the Dominican Republic's Ethnic 'Cleansing' of Haitians," *Washington Post* (June 17, 2015), https://www.washingtonpost.com/news/worldviews/wp/2015/06/16/the-bloody-origins-of-the-dominican-republics-ethnic-cleansing-of-haitians/.

8. Cloud, "Human Rights Abuses Along the Dominican-Haitian Border," 59.

9. "Four Haitians Slain in Dominican Republic," *Latin American Herald Tribune* (October 23, 2009), http://www.laht.com/article.asp?ArticleId=346031&CategoryId=14092.

10. Amanda Taubamanda, "Dominican Republic Strips Thousands of Black Residents of Citizenship, May Now Expel Them," *Vox* (June 18, 2015), https://www.vox.com/2015/6/18/8802587/dominican-republic-haitian-deportation.

11. LaToya A. Tavernier, "The Stigma of Blackness: Anti-Haitianism in the Dominican Republic," *Socialism and Democracy* 22 (November 2008), 98.

12. Thompson, "Immigrant Laborers from Haiti Are Paid with Abuse in the Dominican Republic."

13. Thompson, "Immigrant Laborers from Haiti Are Paid with Abuse in the Dominican Republic."

14. Thompson, "Immigrant Laborers from Haiti Are Paid with Abuse in the Dominican Republic."

15. Jonathan M. Katz, "In Exile," *New York Times* (January 17, 2016), http://www.nytimes.com/2016/01/17/magazine/haitians-in-exile-in-the-dominican-republic.html.

16. Tavernier, "The Stigma of Blackness," 98.

17. Thompson, "Immigrant Laborers from Haiti Are Paid with Abuse in the Dominican Republic."

18. Cloud, "Human Rights Abuses Along the Dominican-Haitian Border," 59.

19. Human Rights First, *Combating Xenophobic Violence*, 3; Mariela Rosario, "Lynching of Haitian Man Highlights Tension in Dominican Republic," *Latina* (November 5, 2009), http://www.latina.com/lifestyle/news-politics/lynching-haitian-man-highlights-tension-dominican-republic; and EFE World News Service, "Haitian Migrant Lynched in the Dominican Republic," *Highbeam Business* (August 16, 2007), http://business.highbeam.com/436103/article-1G1-167631727/haitian-migrant-lynched-dominican-republic.

20. Human Rights First, *Combating Xenophobic Violence*, 17.

21. Taubamanda, "Dominican Republic Strips Thousands of Black Residents of Citizenship, May Now Expel Them."

22. Thompson, "Immigrant Laborers from Haiti Are Paid with Abuse in the Dominican Republic."

23. Thompson, "Immigrant Laborers from Haiti Are Paid with Abuse in the Dominican Republic."

24. Thompson, "Immigrant Laborers from Haiti Are Paid with Abuse in the Dominican Republic."

25. Amnesty International, *Dominican Republic: Submission to the U.N. Universal Periodic Review*, Sixth Session of the UPR Working Group of the Human Rights Council (April 20, 2009), http://www.amnesty.org/en/library/asset/AMR27/002/2009/en/448ee393-3c36-4d36-bd79-1871ef8659f0/amr270022009en.html.

26. Mariela Rosario, "Lynching of Haitian Man Highlights Tension in Dominican Republic," *LATINA* (November 5, 2009), http://www.latina.com/lifestyle/news-politics/lynching-haitian-man-highlights-tension-dominican-republic.

27. U.S. Department of State, *2009 Country Reports on Human Rights Practices: Dominican Republic* (Washington, DC: U.S. Department of State Bureau of Democracy, Human Rights and Labor, March 11, 2010), http://www.state.gov/g/drl/rls/hrrpt/2009/wha/136110.htm; and "Four Haitians Slain in Dominican Republic."

28. Associated Press, "Haitian Boy Killed When Homes Burned in DR," *Fox News* (January 25, 2011), http://www.foxnews.com/world/2011/01/25/haitian-boy-killed-homes-burned-dr/#.

29. Julia Wilde, "Why Dominican Republic Hates Haiti," *Seeker* (February 23, 2015), https://www.seeker.com/why-dominican-republic-hates-haiti-1792546817.html.

30. "Couple's Murder Stokes Violence at Haiti-Dominican Republic Border," *Dominican Today* (March 13, 2018), https://dominicantoday.com/dr/local/2018/03/13/couples-murder-stokes-violence-at-haiti-dominican-republic-border/.

31. Taubamanda, "Dominican Republic Strips Thousands of Black Residents of Citizenship, May Now Expel Them."

32. Thompson, "Immigrant Laborers from Haiti Are Paid with Abuse in the Dominican Republic."

33. Thompson, "Immigrant Laborers from Haiti Are Paid with Abuse in the Dominican Republic."

34. Taubamanda, "Dominican Republic Strips Thousands of Black Residents of Citizenship, May Now Expel Them."

35. Cloud, "Human Rights Abuses Along the Dominican-Haitian Border," 60.

36. Tavernier, "The Stigma of Blackness," 99.

37. Jonathan M. Katz, "What Happened When a Nation Erased Birthright Citizenship," *The Atlantic* (November 12, 2018), https://www.theatlantic.com/ideas/archive/2018/11/dominican-republic-erased-birthright-citizenship/575527/.

38. Thompson, "Immigrant Laborers from Haiti Are Paid with Abuse in the Dominican Republic."

39. Phillip, "The Bloody Origins of the Dominican Republic's Ethnic 'Cleansing' of Haitians."

40. Taubamanda, "Dominican Republic Strips Thousands of Black Residents of Citizenship, May Now Expel Them."

41. Thompson, "Immigrant Laborers from Haiti Are Paid with Abuse in the Dominican Republic."

42. Thompson, "Immigrant Laborers from Haiti Are Paid with Abuse in the Dominican Republic."

43. Thompson, "Immigrant Laborers from Haiti Are Paid with Abuse in the Dominican Republic."

44. Katz, "What Happened When a Nation Erased Birthright Citizenship."

45. Cloud, "Human Rights Abuses Along the Dominican-Haitian Border," 60.

46. Thompson, "Immigrant Laborers from Haiti Are Paid with Abuse in the Dominican Republic."

47. Human Rights First, *Combating Xenophobic Violence*, 17.

48. Thompson, "Immigrant Laborers from Haiti Are Paid with Abuse in the Dominican Republic."

49. Tavernier, "The Stigma of Blackness," 101.

50. European Parliament, "Egypt: Violence Against Sudanese Refugees" (Brussels: Egyptian Resolution P6_TA(2006)0031, January 19, 2006), http://eur-lex.europa.eu/LexUriServ/LexUriServ.do?uri=OJ:C:2006:287E:0331:0333:EN:PDF.

51. United Nations High Commissioner for Refugees, "2011 UNHCR Country Operations Profile—Egypt" (Geneva: UNHCR, 2011), http://www.unhcr.org/cgi-bin/texis/vtx/page?page=49e486356.

52. Human Rights First, *Combating Xenophobic Violence*, 3; and Kelsy Yeargain, "No Protection: Egypt's Refugees and Migrants," *Muftah* (February 2, 2011), http://muftah.org/?p=716.

53. Amnesty International, *Amnesty International Report 2017/18: The State of the World's Human Rights* (London: Amnesty International, 2018), 155.

54. Samy Magdy, "Fleeing War, Poverty, African Migrants Face Racism in Egypt," *Star Tribune* (January 2, 2020), https://www.startribune.com/fleeing-war-poverty-african-migrants-face-racism-in-egypt/566643141/.

55. Joseph El-Cassabgui, "Egypt's Sudanese Migrants: Caught Between the Devil and the Deep Blue Sea," *Huffington Post* (April 7, 2017), https://www.huffingtonpost.com/entry/egypts-sudanese-migrants-caught-between-the-devil_us_58e79af1e4b0acd784ca5750.

56. El-Cassabgui, "Egypt's Sudanese Migrants."

57. "Migrants and Refugees in Egypt: 'They Do Not Find the Security or the Human Dignity They Hoped For,'" *AlarmPhone* (December 4, 2017), https://alarmphone.org/en/2017/12/04/migrants-and-refugees-in-egypt-they-do-not-find-the-security-or-the-human-dignity-they-hoped-for/.

58. "Egypt: Refugees Hit by Discrimination, Violence amid Heightened Nationalism," *IRIN News* (November 24, 2011), http://www.irinnews.org/report.aspx?reportid=94294.

59. Yeargain, "No Protection."

60. Michael Slackman, "After Cairo Police Attack, Sudanese Have Little but Rage," *New York Times* (January 3, 2006), https://www.nytimes.com/2006/01/03/world/africa/after-cairo-police-attack-sudanese-have-little-but-rage.html; and Human Rights Watch, "Sinai Perils: Risks to Migrants, Refugees, and Asylum Seekers in Egypt and Israel" (November 12, 2008), 18, http://www.hrw.org/en/node/75941/section/1.

61. Human Rights Watch, "Sinai Perils," 18–19.

62. "Migrants and Refugees in Egypt."

63. Jane Freedman and Bahija Jamal, *Violence Against Migrant and Refugee Women in the Euromed Region* (Copenhagen: Euro-Mediterranean Human Rights Network, December 2008), 62, 64.

64. "Migrants and Refugees in Egypt."

65. Tom Rollins, "Sudanese Refugees on Egypt's Border," *Atlantic Council* (December 1, 2015), http://www.atlanticcouncil.org/blogs/menasource/sudanese-refugees-on-egypt-s-border; and Human Rights Watch, "Sinai Perils," 1.

66. Kareem Fahim, "Egypt: Forces Kill 5 Sudanese at Border," *New York Times* (November 23, 2015), https://www.nytimes.com/2015/11/24/world/middleeast/egypt-forces-kill-5-sudanese-at-border.html.

67. El-Cassabgui, "Egypt's Sudanese Migrants."

68. Engy Magdy, "Sudanese Refugees in Egypt Suffer Discrimination, Poverty," *The Tablet* (September 19, 2018), https://thetablet.org/sudanese-refugees-in-egypt-suffer-discrimination-poverty/; and Magdy, "Fleeing War, Poverty, African Migrants Face Racism in Egypt."

69. Human Rights First, *Combating Xenophobic Violence*, 17.

70. El-Cassabgui, "Egypt's Sudanese Migrants."

71. "Migrants and Refugees in Egypt."

72. Magdy, "Fleeing War, Poverty, African Migrants Face Racism in Egypt."

73. Valentina Primo, "'They Call Us Black and Filthy': Sudanese Refugees in Egypt, Trapped Between Racism and Violence," *Cairo Scene* (May 6, 2017), http://www.cairoscene.com/In-Depth/They-Call-Us-Black-and-Filthy-Sudanese-Refugees-in-Egypt-Trapped-Between-Racism-and-Violence.

74. Magdy, "Sudanese Refugees in Egypt Suffer Discrimination, Poverty."

75. Human Rights Watch, "Sinai Perils," 3.

76. "Egypt: Refugees Hit by Discrimination, Violence amid Heightened Nationalism."

77. Human Rights First, *Combating Xenophobic Violence*, 17–18; and Fred Pleitgen and Mohamed Fadel Fahmy, "Refugees Face Organ Theft in the Sinai," *CNN* (November 3, 2011), http://www.cnn.com/2011/11/03/world/meast/pleitgen-sinai-organ-smugglers/index.html.

78. Human Rights Watch, "Sinai Perils," 22.

79. Freedman and Jamal, *Violence Against Migrant and Refugee Women in the Euromed Region*, 62, 64.

80. El-Cassabgui, "Egypt's Sudanese Migrants."

81. El-Cassabgui, "Egypt's Sudanese Migrants."

82. El-Cassabgui, "Egypt's Sudanese Migrants."

83. Human Rights Watch, "Sinai Perils," 19.

84. Freedman and Jamal, *Violence Against Migrant and Refugee Women in the Euromed Region*, 68.

85. "Migrants and Refugees in Egypt."

86. El-Cassabgui, "Egypt's Sudanese Migrants."

87. Rollins, "Sudanese Refugees on Egypt's Border."

88. Jayati Ghosh, "Fear of Foreigners: Recession and Racism in Europe," *Race/Ethnicity* 4 (Winter 2011), 183, 189.

89. Seth M. Holmes and Heide Castañeda, "Representing the 'European Refugee Crisis' in Germany and Beyond: Deservingness and Difference, Life and Death," *American Ethnologist* 43 (January 2016), 12.

90. Human Rights First, *Combating Xenophobic Violence*, 7.

91. James Kirchick, "Is Germany Capable of Protecting Its Jews?," *The Atlantic* (April 29, 2018), https://www.theatlantic.com/international/archive/2018/04/germany-jews-muslim-migrants/558677/.

92. "Germany: Migrants 'May Have Fuelled Violent Crime Rise,'" *BBC News* (January 3, 2018), https://www.bbc.com/news/world-europe-42557828.

93. Kirchick, "Is Germany Capable of Protecting Its Jews?"

94. Anthony Faiola and Stephanie Kirchner, "Germany Confirms Asylum Seekers Are Suspected in New Year's Eve Assaults," *Washington Post* (January 8, 2016), https://www.washingtonpost.com/world/europe/asylum-seekers-suspected-in-rash-of-new-years-eve-assaults/2016/01/08/af1ed4c8-b584-11e5-8abc-d09392edc612_story.html.

95. Melissa Eddy, "Reports of Attacks on Women in Germany Heighten Tension over Migrants," *New York Times* (January 5, 2016), https://www.nytimes.com/2016/01/06/world/europe/coordinated-attacks-on-women-in-cologne-were-unprecedented-germany-says.html.

96. Eddy, "Reports of Attacks on Women in Germany Heighten Tension over Migrants."

97. Eva Quadbeck, "New Year's Perpetrators Came with a Wave of Refugees in the Country," *RP Online* (June 9, 2016), https://rp-online.de/politik/deutschland/berlin/silvester-nacht-von-koeln-taeter-kamen-mit-fluechtlingswelle-ins-land_aid-9233833.

98. Eddy, "Reports of Attacks on Women in Germany Heighten Tension over Migrants."

99. Eddy, "Reports of Attacks on Women in Germany Heighten Tension over Migrants."

100. Eddy, "Reports of Attacks on Women in Germany Heighten Tension over Migrants."

101. Eddy, "Reports of Attacks on Women in Germany Heighten Tension over Migrants."

102. Eddy, "Reports of Attacks on Women in Germany Heighten Tension over Migrants."

103. Eddy, "Reports of Attacks on Women in Germany Heighten Tension over Migrants."

104. Riham Alkousaa, "Afghan Migrant Gets Life Sentence for Raping, Murdering German Student," *Reuters* (March 22, 2018), https://www.reuters.com/article/us-germany-trial/afghan-migrant-gets-life-sentence-for-raping-murdering-german-student-idUSKBN1GY1LK.

105. Julie Vitkovskaya and Jennifer Hassan, "Berlin Attack: What We Know So Far," *Washington Post* (December 21, 2016), https://www.washingtonpost.com/news/worldviews/wp/2016/12/20/berlin-attack-how-the-events-unfolded/; and Alison Smale, Gaia Pianigiani, and Carlotta Gall, "Anis Amri, Suspect in the Berlin Truck Attack: What We Know," *New York Times* (December 23, 2016), https://www.nytimes.com/2016/12/22/world/europe/anis-amri-suspect-in-the-berlin-truck-attack-what-is-known.html.

106. Katrin Bennhold, "A Girl's Killing Puts Germany's Migration Policy on Trial," *New York Times* (January 17, 2018), https://www.nytimes.com/2018/01/17/world/europe/germany-teen-murder-migrant.html.

107. Bennhold, "A Girl's Killing Puts Germany's Migration Policy on Trial."

108. Katrin Bennhold, "A Girl's Killing Shakes Germany's Migration Debate," *New York Times* (June 8, 2018), https://www.nytimes.com/2018/06/08/world/europe/germany-susanna-murder-migration.html.

109. Melissa Eddy, "Iraqi Refugee Is Convicted in Germany of Raping and Murdering Teenage Girl," *New York Times* (July 10, 2019), https://www.nytimes.com/2019/07/10/world/europe/iraqi-refugee-germany-rape-murder.html.

110. "Germany: Migrants 'May Have Fuelled Violent Crime Rise.'"

111. "Germany: Migrants 'May Have Fuelled Violent Crime Rise.'"

112. Human Rights First, *Germany Conflicted: The Struggle between Xenophobia and Tolerance* (New York: Human Rights First, February 2017), 12.

113. Manuela Achilles, Kyrill Kunakhovich, and Nicole Shea, "Nationalism, Nativism, and the Revolt Against Globalization," *Europe Now* (February 1, 2018), https://www.europenowjournal.org/2018/01/31/nationalism-nativism-and-the-revolt-against-globalization/.

114. Hugh Williamson, "German Judge Takes Stand Against Xenophobic Violence: Court Finds Anti-Refugee Group Members Guilty of Terrorism, Attempted Murder," *Human Rights Watch* (March 8, 2018), https://www.hrw.org/news/2018/03/08/german-judge-takes-stand-against-xenophobic-violence#.

115. Justin Huggler, "Angela Merkel says Germany Has Lost Control of the Refugee Crisis amid Public Anger over Cologne Sex Attacks," *National Post* (January 11, 2016), https://nationalpost.com/news/world/angela-merkel-says-germany-has-lost-control-of-the-refugee-crisis-amid-public-anger-over-cologne-sex-attacks; and James Rothwell, "Cologne Sex Attacks: Mob Attacks Group of Migrants in 'Manhunt' for Suspects," *The Telegraph* (January 11, 2016), https://www.telegraph.co.uk/news/worldnews/europe/germany/12092354/Cologne-sex-attacks-New-Years-Eve-cases-rise-to-more-than-500.html.

116. "The Self-Proclaimed Guardians of Dusseldorf," *Frankfurter Allgemeine* (July 1, 2016), http://www.faz.net/aktuell/politik/bildung-einer-buergerwehr-die-selbsternannten -aufpasser-von-duesseldorf-14002759.html.

117. Williamson, "German Judge Takes Stand Against Xenophobic Violence."

118. "Far-Right 'Street Patrol' in German Town After Migrant Violence," *Times of Israel* (January 3, 2019), https://www.timesofisrael.com/far-right-street-patrol-in-german -town-after-migrant-violence/; "Germany: Asylum-Seekers Agree to Confess to Assaulting Strangers," *Deutsche Welle* (April 23, 2019), https://www.dw.com/en/germany -asylum-seekers-agree-to-confess-to-assaulting-strangers/a-48440305;   and   Melissa Eddy, "German Man Is Suspected of Attacking Foreigners, Using Car as Weapon," *New York Times* (January 1, 2019), https://www.nytimes.com/2019/01/01/world/europe/ germany-foreigners-attack.html.

119. Kate Connolly, "German Far-Right Party AfD Accused of Fuelling Hate After Hanau Attack," *The Guardian* (February 21, 2020), https://www.theguardian.com/world/ 2020/feb/21/german-far-right-party-afd-hanau-attack.

120. Malcolm Brabant, "Crime Spike in Germany Puts Pressure on Immigration Policy," *PBS NewsHour* (February 7, 2018), https://www.pbs.org/newshour/show/crime -spike-in-germany-puts-pressure-on-immigration-policy#transcript.

121. Katrin Bennhold, "Germany Has Been Unified for 30 Years—Its Identity Still Is Not," *New York Times* (November 8, 2019), https://www.nytimes.com/2019/11/08/world/ europe/germany-identity.html.

122. Kirchick, "Is Germany Capable of Protecting Its Jews?"

123. Rick Noack, "Multiculturalism Is a Sham, Says Angela Merkel," *Washington Post* (December 14, 2015), https://www.washingtonpost.com/news/worldviews/wp/2015/12/ 14/angela-merkel-multiculturalism-is-a-sham/.

124. Brabant, "Crime Spike in Germany Puts Pressure on Immigration Policy."

125. Katrin Bennhold, "A Girl's Killing Shakes Germany's Migration Debate."

126. Brabant, "Crime Spike in Germany Puts Pressure on Immigration Policy."

127. Brabant, "Crime Spike in Germany Puts Pressure on Immigration Policy."

128. Bennhold, "A Girl's Killing Puts Germany's Migration Policy on Trial."

129. Eddy, "Reports of Attacks on Women in Germany Heighten Tension over Migrants."

130. Brabant, "Crime Spike in Germany Puts Pressure on Immigration Policy."

131. Judith Mischke, "Germany Passes Controversial Migration Law," *Politico* (June 7, 2019), https://www.politico.eu/article/germany-passes-controversial-migration-law/.

132. "Germany: Migrants 'May Have Fuelled Violent Crime Rise.'"

133. Shari Miller, "German City Bans Any More Refugees as Violence by Asylum Seekers and Right-Wing Extremists Escalates," *Daily Mail* (January 21, 2018), http:// www.dailymail.co.uk/news/article-5294141/German-city-BANS-new-refugees-amid -anti-migrant-violence.html.

134. Bennhold, "A Girl's Killing Puts Germany's Migration Policy on Trial."

135. Katrin Bennhold and Melissa Eddy, "'Politics of Hate' Takes a Toll in Germany Well Beyond Immigrants," *New York Times* (February 21, 2020), https://www.nytimes.com/2020/02/21/world/europe/germany-mayors-far-right.html.

136. Human Rights First, *Combating Xenophobic Violence*, 3; Samsideen Iddrisu and Andriana Mardaki, "Racism in Greece: ENAR Shadow Report 2008," *European Network Against Racism* (2009), http://cms.horus.be/files/99935/MediaArchive/national/Greece - SR 2008.pdf; Hellenic League for Human Rights and Association Européenne pour la Défense des Droits de l'Homme, "The Asylum Crisis and the Rise of Racist Violence in Greece," press release (June 3, 2009), http://www.hlhr.gr/press/Statement%20asylum%20and%20racist%20violence%20in%20Greece%20EN.pdf; and BBC, "Immigrants Hurt in Greek Violence," *BBC News* (May 10, 2009), http://news.bbc.co.uk/2/hi/8042409.stm.

137. Human Rights Watch, *Hate on the Streets: Xenophobic Violence in Greece* (New York: Human Rights Watch, July 2012), 6, https://www.hrw.org/report/2012/07/10/hate-streets/xenophobic-violence-greece.

138. Lena Karamanidou, "Violence Against Migrants in Greece: Beyond the Golden Dawn," *Ethnic and Racial Studies* 39 (2016), 2002.

139. Liz Alderman, "Greek Far Right Hangs a Target on Immigrants," *New York Times* (July 11, 2012), https://www.nytimes.com/2012/07/11/world/europe/as-golden-dawn-rises-in-greece-anti-immigrant-violence-follows.html.

140. Alderman, "Greek Far Right Hangs a Target on Immigrants."

141. Patrick Strickland, "Anti-Migrant Attacks Surge in Greece's Piraeus," *Al Jazeera* (January 5, 2018), https://www.aljazeera.com/news/2018/01/anti-migrant-attacks-surge-greece-piraeus-180105112319244.html.

142. Sylvia Poggioli, "Violence at Both Ends of Political Spectrum Threatens Greece," *NPR News* (February 4, 2013), https://www.npr.org/2013/02/04/170849432/violence-at-both-ends-of-political-spectrum-threatens-greece.

143. Timothy Garton Ash, "The Crisis of Europe: How the Union Came Together and Why It's Falling Apart," *Foreign Affairs* 91 (September/October 2012), 14.

144. Liz Alderman, "Bomb Attacks in Greece Raise Fear of Radicalism," *New York Times* (January 20, 2013), http://www.nytimes.com/2013/01/21/world/europe/bomb-attacks-in-greece-raise-fear-of-revived-radicalism.html.

145. Alderman, "Bomb Attacks in Greece Raise Fear of Radicalism."

146. Dimitris Dalakoglou, "The Crisis Before 'The Crisis': Violence and Urban Neoliberalization in Athens," *Social Justice* 39 (March 2013), 33.

147. Associated Press, "Greece: Nationalist Mobs Attack Immigrants in Athens," *New York Times* (May 13, 2011), http://www.nytimes.com/2011/05/14/world/europe/14briefs-Greece.html.

148. "Immigrants Coming Under Attack in Greece," *International Business Times* (May 13, 2011), http://www.ibtimes.com/articles/145543/20110513/greece-athens-immigrants-attacks.htm.

149. "Immigrants Coming Under Attack in Greece."

150. Poggioli, "Violence at Both Ends of Political Spectrum Threatens Greece."

151. AthensLive News, "In 2018, the Recorded Racist Violence in Greece Was Increased: Refugees and Migrants Were Targeted for One More Year," *Medium* (April 19, 2019), https://medium.com/athenslivegr/in-2018-the-recorded-racist-violence-in-greece-was-increased-34a376d97ab2.

152. AthensLive News, "In 2018, the Recorded Racist Violence in Greece Was Increased."

153. Human Rights First, *Combating Xenophobic Violence*, 18.

154. BBC, "Immigrants Hurt in Greek Violence."

155. BBC, "Immigrants Hurt in Greek Violence."

156. Human Rights Watch, *Hate on the Streets*, 4, 42.

157. Human Rights First, *Combating Xenophobic Violence*, 18; Associated Press, "Greece: Extremist Attack Migrants in Athens," *mail.com international* (May 12, 2011), http://www.msnbc.msn.com/id/43002483; Associated Press, "Greece: Nationalist Mobs Attack Immigrants in Athens"; "Immigrants Coming Under Attack in Greece"; and Asteris Masouras, "Greece: Wave of Racist Attacks on Immigrants in Athens," *Global Voices* (May 13, 2011), http://globalvoicesonline.org/2011/05/13/greece-wave-of-racist-attacks-on-immigrants-in-athens/.

158. Amnesty International USA, "Greece: Horrific Knife Attack Targets Migrants in Crete," *States News Service* (August 14, 2013), https://www.amnesty.org/en/latest/news/2013/08/greece-horrific-knife-attack-targets-migrants-crete/.

159. Strickland, "Anti-Migrant Attacks Surge in Greece's Piraeus."

160. Strickland, "Anti-Migrant Attacks Surge in Greece's Piraeus."

161. Helena Smith, "Greek Police Accused of Beating Migrants Trying to Enter from Turkey," *The Guardian* (December 18, 2018), https://www.theguardian.com/world/2018/dec/18/greek-police-accused-beating-migrants-trying-to-enter-from-turkey.

162. Niki Kitsantonis, "'One of the Hardest Nights': Violence Erupts Between Greeks and Migrants," *New York Times* (April 24, 2018), https://www.nytimes.com/2018/04/24/world/europe/greece-lesbos-refugees.html.

163. "Violence Flares at Greek Island Protest over Migrants," *Deutsche Welle* (March 5, 2018), https://www.dw.com/en/violence-flares-at-greek-island-protest-over-migrants/a-43647656.

164. Kitsantonis, "'One of the Hardest Nights.'"

165. "Violence Flares at Greek Island Protest over Migrants."

166. Poggioli, "Violence at Both Ends of Political Spectrum Threatens Greece."

167. Kitsantonis, "'One of the Hardest Nights.'"

168. Poggioli, "Violence at Both Ends of Political Spectrum Threatens Greece."

169. "Violence Flares at Greek Island Protest over Migrants."

170. Karamanidou, "Violence Against Migrants in Greece," 2003.

171. BBC, "Immigrants Hurt in Greek Violence."

172. Associated Press, "Greece: Nationalist Mobs Attack Immigrants in Athens."

173. Alderman, "Bomb Attacks in Greece Raise Fear of Radicalism."

174. Kitsantonis, "'One of the Hardest Nights.'"

175. Alderman, "Greek Far Right Hangs a Target on Immigrants."

176. Matina Stevis-Gridneff, Patrick Kingsley, Haley Willis, Sarah Almukhtar, and Malachy Browne, "'We Are Like Animals': Inside Greece's Secret Site for Migrants," *New York Times* (March 10, 2020), https://www.nytimes.com/2020/03/10/world/europe/greece-migrants-secret-site.html.

177. Karamanidou, "Violence Against Migrants in Greece," 2014.

178. Georgi Voynov, Hana Franková, Anikó Bakonyi, Marta Górczyńska, and Miha Nabergoj, *Denial of Access to Asylum in Eastern EU Member States* (Budapest, Hungary: Hungarian Helsinki Committee, 2017), 12.

179. Annastiina Kallius, Daniel Monterescu, and Prem Kumar Rajaram, "Immobilizing Mobility: Border Ethnography, Illiberal Democracy, and the Politics of the 'Refugee Crisis' in Hungary," *American Ethnologist* 43 (February 2016), 3.

180. Andrew Byrne, "Hungary's Anti-Migrant Campaign Takes Root as Villagers Vent Fury," *Financial Times* (October 5, 2017), https://www.ft.com/content/4ae32ad0-a9cb-11e7-ab55-27219df83c97.

181. Byrne, "Hungary's Anti-Migrant Campaign Takes Root as Villagers Vent Fury."

182. Holmes and Castañeda, "Representing the 'European Refugee Crisis' in Germany and Beyond," 18.

183. Johann Pall Astvaldsson, "Iceland Plans to Ban Circumcision," *Iceland Review* (March 29, 2018) http://icelandreview.com/news/2018/03/29/focus-iceland-plans-ban-circumcision

184. Matthew Weaver, "Burqa Bans, Headscarves and Veils: A Timeline of Legislation in the West," *The Guardian* (May 31, 2018), https://www.theguardian.com/world/2017/mar/14/headscarves-and-muslim-veil-ban-debate-timeline.

185. "Arabic, Muslim Symbols Ordered Taken Down in China's Capital," *Al Jazeera* (July 31, 2019), https://www.aljazeera.com/news/2019/07/arabic-muslim-symbols-ordered-china-capital-190731072007867.html.

186. Kallius, Monterescu, and Rajaram, "Immobilizing Mobility," 1.

187. Kallius, Monterescu, and Rajaram, "Immobilizing Mobility," 2.

188. Rachel Roberts, "European Border Forces 'Frequently Abuse' Refugees and Migrants, Report Finds," *The Independent* (April 6, 2017), https://www.independent.co.uk/

news/world/western-border-forces-abuse-migrants-refugee-crisis-serbia-macedonia
-hungary-asylum-seekers-a7671201.html.

189. Kallius, Monterescu, and Rajaram, "Immobilizing Mobility," 2.

190. Paul Peachey, "Hungary's Muslims Fear Fallout from Anti-Islam Rhetoric," *The National* (March 10, 2018), https://www.thenational.ae/world/europe/hungary-s -muslims-fear-fallout-from-anti-islam-rhetoric-1.711823.

191. Médecins Sans Frontières, "Hungary: Widespread Violence Against Migrants and Refugees at Border," *Doctors Without Borders* (March 8, 2017), https://www .doctorswithoutborders.org/what-we-do/news-stories/news/hungary-widespread -violence-against-migrants-and-refugees-border.

192. Nóra Köves, "Serious Human Rights Violations in the Hungarian Asylum System" (May 10, 2017), https://www.boell.de/en/2017/05/10/serious-human-rights -violations-hungarian-asylum-system.

193. Human Rights Watch, "Hungary: Migrants Abused at the Border" (July 13, 2016), https://www.hrw.org/news/2016/07/13/hungary-migrants-abused-border.

194. Amnesty International, *Stranded Hope: Hungary's Sustained Attack on the Rights of Refugees and Migrants* (London: Amnesty International, September 2016), 24–27.

195. Köves, "Serious Human Rights Violations in the Hungarian Asylum System."

196. Roberts, "European Border Forces 'Frequently Abuse' Refugees and Migrants, Report Finds."

197. Médecins Sans Frontières, "Hungary: Widespread Violence Against Migrants and Refugees at Border."

198. Amnesty International, *Amnesty International Report 2017/18*, 188.

199. Peachey, "Hungary's Muslims Fear Fallout from Anti-Islam Rhetoric."

200. Jon Stone, "UN Sounds Alarm over Hungary's Far-Right Government Starving Rejected Asylum Seekers of Food: Asylum Seekers Deprived of Food for up to Five Days, Humanitarian Office Suggests," *The Independent* (May 3, 2019), https://www .independent.co.uk/news/world/europe/un-hungary-asylum-seekers-food-far-right -orban-human-rights-a8897906.html.

201. Kallius, Monterescu, and Rajaram, "Immobilizing Mobility," 1.

202. Byrne, "Hungary's Anti-Migrant Campaign Takes Root as Villagers Vent Fury."

203. Byrne, "Hungary's Anti-Migrant Campaign Takes Root as Villagers Vent Fury."

204. Roberts, "European Border Forces 'Frequently Abuse' Refugees and Migrants, Report Finds."

205. Roberts, "European Border Forces 'Frequently Abuse' Refugees and Migrants, Report Finds."

206. Peachey, "Hungary's Muslims Fear Fallout from Anti-Islam Rhetoric."

207. Amnesty International, *Stranded Hope*, 5.

208. Köves, "Serious Human Rights Violations in the Hungarian Asylum System."

209. Human Rights Watch, "Hungary: Migrants Abused at the Border."

210. Chris Stevenson, "Far-Right Party in Hungary Forms Uniformed 'Self-Defence' Force in Spirit of Outlawed Vigilante Group," *The Independent* (May 14, 2019), https://www.independent.co.uk/news/world/europe/hungary-far-right-group-national-legion-laszlo-toroczkai-jobbik-a8914021.html.

211. Byrne, "Hungary's Anti-Migrant Campaign Takes Root as Villagers Vent Fury."

212. "How to Make a Migrant Crisis Worse," *New York Times* (September 9, 2017), https://www.nytimes.com/2017/09/08/opinion/hungary-is-making-europes-migrant-crisis-worse.html.

213. Daniel Nolan and Shaun Walker, "Hungarian Journalists Admit Role in Forging Anti-Migrant 'Atmosphere of Fear,'" *The Guardian* (April 13, 2018), https://www.theguardian.com/world/2018/apr/13/hungary-journalists-state-tv-network-migrants-viktor-orban-government; and Ishaan Tharoor, "Hungary's Leader Says He's Defending Christian Europe," *Washington Post* (April 10, 2018), https://www.washingtonpost.com/news/worldviews/wp/2018/04/10/the-popes-challenge-to-orban-and-europes-far-right/.

214. Nolan and Walker, "Hungarian Journalists Admit Role in Forging Anti-Migrant 'Atmosphere of Fear.'"

215. Megan Specia, "Hungary Pulls Out of U.N. Global Migration Agreement," *New York Times* (July 19, 2018), https://www.nytimes.com/2018/07/18/world/europe/hungary-migration-united-nations.html.

216. Stone, "UN Sounds Alarm over Hungary's Far-Right Government Starving Rejected Asylum Seekers of Food."

217. "How to Make a Migrant Crisis Worse."

218. "Austria's Sebastian Kurz Backs Viktor Orban Against EU Migrant Quotas," *Deutsche Welle* (January 3, 2018), https://www.dw.com/en/austrias-sebastian-kurz-backs-hungarys-viktor-orban-against-eu-migrant-quotas/a-42373709.

219. Salvatore Borghese and Lorenzo Newman, "Xenophobes in Glass Houses," *Slate* (March 1, 2018), https://slate.com/news-and-politics/2018/03/italys-left-has-a-xenophobia-problem.html.

220. Human Rights Watch, *Everyday Intolerance: Racist and Xenophobic Violence in Italy* (New York: Human Rights Watch, March 21, 2011), http://www.hrw.org/sites/default/files/reports/italy0311WebRevised.pdf.

221. Giulia Segreti and Philip Pullella, "Murder and Abuse: Italy's Migrants Fear Future After Election," *Sydney Morning Herald* (March 7, 2018), https://www.smh.com.au/world/europe/murder-and-abuse-italy-s-migrants-fear-future-after-election-20180306-p4z2z3.html.

222. Human Rights Watch, *Everyday Intolerance*, 5.

223. Médecins Sans Frontières, "Italy: Migrants and Refugees on the Margins of Society," *Doctors Without Borders* (February 8, 2018), https://www.msf.org/italy-migrants-and-refugees-margins-society.

224. Lorenzo Tondo, "Italy's Intelligence Agency Warns of Rise in Racist Attacks: Agency Says Increase in Attacks on Migrants Is Likely Before European Elections in May," *The Guardian* (February 28, 2019), https://www.theguardian.com/world/2019/feb/28/italys-intelligence-agency-warns-of-rise-in-racist-attacks.

225. Pietro Castelli Gattinara and Francis O'Connor, "An Italian Neo-Fascist Shot 6 Immigrants—So Why Won't Italy's Political Parties Condemn Xenophobia?," *Washington Post* (February 9, 2018), https://www.washingtonpost.com/news/monkey-cage/wp/2018/02/09/an-italian-neo-fascist-shot-6-migrants-how-does-this-play-into-the-upcoming-elections/.

226. Human Rights First, *Combating Xenophobic Violence*, 3; and Human Rights Watch, *Everyday Intolerance*, 10.

227. Tondo, "Italy's Intelligence Agency Warns of Rise in Racist Attacks."

228. Borghese and Newman, "Xenophobes in Glass Houses."

229. Cedric Gerome, "Anti-Immigrant Violence and Riots Explode Against the Background of Economic Crisis," *SocialistWorld.net* (January 19, 2010), http://www.socialistworld.net/doc/4019; "Racist and Xenophobic Violence in Italy Condemned," *Africa-News* (January 28, 2011), http://www.theafricanews.com/news-italy/1701-racist-and-xenophobic-violence-in-italy-condemned-.html; Human Rights Watch, *Everyday Intolerance*; and U.S. Department of State, *2009 Country Reports on Human Rights Practices: Italy* (Washington, DC: U.S. Department of State Bureau of Democracy, Human Rights and Labor, March 11, 2010), http://www.state.gov/g/drl/rls/hrrpt/2009/eur/136038.htm.

230. Amnesty International, *Amnesty International Report 2017/18*, 212.

231. Gattinara and O'Connor, "An Italian Neo-Fascist Shot 6 Immigrants."

232. Segreti and Pullella, "Murder and Abuse."

233. Tondo, "Italy's Intelligence Agency Warns of Rise in Racist Attacks."

234. "Desirée Mariottin, "Killing: Migrants Held in Italy over Girl's Death," *BBC News* (October 25, 2018), https://www.bbc.com/news/world-europe-45976450; and "Italy Arrests 3 in Teen's Slaying That Fuels Migrant Debate," *AP News* (October 25, 2018), https://apnews.com/18055a786dc742a8ae41962ffc7125bc.

235. Human Rights Watch, *Everyday Intolerance*, 6–7.

236. Borghese and Newman, "Xenophobes in Glass Houses"; and Crispian Balmer, "Rape Cases Fuel Anti-Migrant Angst in Italy Ahead of Election," *Reuters* (September 13, 2017), https://www.reuters.com/article/us-italy-rapes/rape-cases-fuel-anti-migrant-angst-in-italy-ahead-of-election-idUSKCN1BO23C.

237. Segreti and Pullella, "Murder and Abuse."

238. Ghosh, "Fear of Foreigners," 183.

239. Silvia Marchetti, "Fearing Migrant Crime, Italians Go Vigilante," *OZY* (March 5, 2017), https://www.ozy.com/fast-forward/fearing-migrant-crime-italians-go-vigilante/75161.

240. Segreti and Pullella, "Murder and Abuse."

241. Human Rights Watch, *Everyday Intolerance*, 10–12.

242. Council of Europe Commissioner for Human Rights, "Report by Thomas Hammarberg, Commissioner for Human Rights of the Council of Europe, Following His Visit to Italy on 13–15 January 2009," Report # CommDH(2009)16 (April 16, 2009), https://wcd.coe.int/wcd/ViewDoc.jsp?id=1428427.

243. Gattinara and O'Connor, "An Italian Neo-Fascist Shot 6 Immigrants."

244. Human Rights Watch, *Everyday Intolerance*, 2, 3.

245. Human Rights Watch, *Everyday Intolerance*, 2.

246. Gattinara and O'Connor, "An Italian Neo-Fascist Shot 6 Immigrants."

247. Gattinara and O'Connor, "An Italian Neo-Fascist Shot 6 Immigrants."

248. Human Rights First, *Combating Xenophobic Violence*, 19–20; and Human Rights Watch, *Everyday Intolerance*, 2–3, 58–61.

249. Human Rights Watch, *Everyday Intolerance*, 3.

250. Human Rights Watch, *Everyday Intolerance*, 8–9.

251. Segreti and Pullella, "Murder and Abuse."

252. Gattinara and O'Connor, "An Italian Neo-Fascist Shot 6 Immigrants."

253. Stephanie Kirchgaessner, "Italy's Salvini Warns EU to 'Defend Its Border' Against Migrants," *The Guardian* (June 20, 2018), https://www.theguardian.com/world/2018/jun/20/italys-salvini-warns-eu-to-defend-its-border-against-migrants.

254. Kirchgaessner, "Italy's Salvini Warns EU to 'Defend Its Border' Against Migrants."

255. Roberto Saviano, "Italy's War on Migrants Makes Me Fear for My Country's Future," *The Guardian* (June 19, 2018), https://www.theguardian.com/commentisfree/2018/jun/19/italy-war-migrants-fear-civil-rights.

256. Segreti and Pullella, "Murder and Abuse."

257. Gattinara and O'Connor, "An Italian Neo-Fascist Shot 6 Immigrants."

258. Médecins Sans Frontières, "Italy: Migrants and Refugees on the Margins of Society."

259. Human Rights First, *Combating Xenophobic Violence*, 4; and United Nations Human Rights Council, "Item 3: Interactive Dialogue with the Working Group on Arbitrary Detention," Oral Statement by Temme Lee, Asian Forum for Human Rights and Development (FORUM-ASIA)" (March 7, 2011), http://english.cpiasia.net/index.php?option=com_content&view=article&id=2142:arbitrarydetention-laws-in-malaysia-another-call-for-repeal&catid=186:suaram&Itemid=161.

260. Seth Mydans, "A Growing Source of Fear for Migrants in Malaysia," *New York Times* (December 10, 2007), https://www.nytimes.com/2007/12/10/world/asia/10malaysia.html.

261. John West, "Malaysia's Abuse of Migrants' Rights," *Asian Century Institute* (August 30, 2014), http://asiancenturyinstitute.com/migration/190-malaysia-s-abuses-of-migrants-rights.

262. Matthew Abbey, "Myanmar Migrants Face Malaysian Violence," *Asia Sentinel* (January 11, 2017), https://www.asiasentinel.com/econ-business/myanmar-migrants -face-malaysia-violence/.

263. Amnesty International, *Abused and Abandoned: Refugees Denied Rights in Malaysia* (New York: Amnesty International Report # ASA 28/010/2010, June 2010), https://www.amnesty.org/download/Documents/36000/asa280102010en.pdf; United Nations High Commissioner for Refugees, "2011 UNHCR Country Operations Profile— Malaysia" (Geneva: UNHCR, 2011), http://www.unhcr.org/cgi-bin/texis/vtx/page?page =49e4884c6; and West, "Malaysia's Abuse of Migrants' Rights."

264. Pete Pattisson, "Violence, Prejudice, Low Pay: All in a Day's Work for Migrants in Malaysia," *The Guardian* (February 2, 2017), https://www.theguardian.com/global -development/2017/feb/02/violence-prejudice-low-pay-migrant-workers-malaysia.

265. Abbey, "Myanmar Migrants Face Malaysian Violence."

266. Abbey, "Myanmar Migrants Face Malaysian Violence."

267. Abbey, "Myanmar Migrants Face Malaysian Violence."

268. Mydans, "A Growing Source of Fear for Migrants in Malaysia."

269. Amnesty International, *Abused and Abandoned*, 9.

270. National Coalition Government of the Union of Burma, "Burma Human Rights Yearbook 2008," *Burma Library* (November 2009), http://www.burmalibrary .org/docs08/HRYB2008.pdf; and Mydans, "A Growing Source of Fear for Migrants in Malaysia."

271. U.S. Committee for Refugees and Immigrants, "World Refugee Survey 2008: Malaysia," *USCRI* (June 19, 2008), http://www.unhcr.org/refworld/docid/485f50c385 .html.

272. Amnesty International, "Malaysia Should Halt Expansion of Security Force Ac- cused of Abuses," press release (August 19, 2010), http://www.amnesty.org/en/news-and -updates/malaysia-should-halt-expansion-security-forceaccused-abuses-2010-08-19; and Human Rights First, *Combating Xenophobic Violence*, 21.

273. P. Gunasegaram, "Volunteer Corps Still Rela-vant?," *The Star* (May 30, 2012), https://www.thestar.com.my/opinion/columnists/question-time/2012/05/30/volunteer -corps-still-relevant/.

274. U.S. Committee for Refugees and Immigrants, "World Refugee Survey 2009: Malaysia," *USCRI* (2009), http://www.refugees.org/resources/refugeewarehousing/ archived-world-refugee-surveys/2009-wrs-country-updates/malaysia.html.

275. Nyein Nyein, "Pair of Burmese Migrants Slashed to Death in Malaysia," *The Ir- rawaddy* (September 18, 2014), https://www.irrawaddy.com/news/burma/pair-burmese -migrants-slashed-death-malaysia.html.

276. Abbey, "Myanmar Migrants Face Malaysian Violence."

277. Pattisson, "Violence, Prejudice, Low Pay."

278. Steven Sim, "We Need to Strengthen Protection for Migrant Labour in Malaysia," *Malaysian Insight* (February 12, 2018), https://www.themalaysianinsight.com/s/37517.

279. Beh Lih Yi, "'Silent in Fear': Refugee Women in Malaysia Unprotected Against Violence," *Reuters* (January 7, 2018), https://www.reuters.com/article/us-malaysia-refugees-women/silent-in-fear-refugee-women-in-malaysia-unprotected-against-violence-idUSKBN1EX00F.

280. West, "Malaysia's Abuse of Migrants' Rights."

281. Amy Gunia, "Human Traffickers Accused of 'Crimes Against Humanity' in Thailand and Malaysia," *Time* (March 28, 2019), https://time.com/5560095/malaysia-thailand-rohingya-crimes-against-humanity/.

282. Pattisson, "Violence, Prejudice, Low Pay."

283. Human Rights First, *Combating Xenophobic Violence*, 20.

284. Pattisson, "Violence, Prejudice, Low Pay."

285. Sim, "We Need to Strengthen Protection for Migrant Labour in Malaysia."

286. Pattisson, "Violence, Prejudice, Low Pay."

287. Abbey, "Myanmar Migrants Face Malaysian Violence."

288. Yi, "'Silent in Fear.'"

289. West, "Malaysia's Abuse of Migrants' Rights."

290. Tula Connell, "Malaysia: Widespread Forced Labor, Abuse of Migrants," *Solidarity Center* (July 10, 2015), https://www.solidaritycenter.org/malaysia-widespread-forced-labor-abuse-of-migrants/.

291. Amnesty International, *Abused and Abandoned*, 7.

292. Yi, "'Silent in Fear.'"

293. Sim, "We Need to Strengthen Protection for Migrant Labour in Malaysia."

294. Abbey, "Myanmar Migrants Face Malaysian Violence."

295. Abbey, "Myanmar Migrants Face Malaysian Violence."

296. Pattisson, "Violence, Prejudice, Low Pay."

297. Amnesty International, *Abused and Abandoned*, 8.

298. Human Rights First, *Combating Xenophobic Violence*, 21.

299. A. Ananthalakshmi, "More Than 100 Die in Malaysian Immigration Detention Camps in Two Years," *Reuters* (March 30, 2017), https://www.reuters.com/article/us-malaysia-detention-deaths/exclusive-more-than-100-die-in-malaysian-immigration-detention-camps-in-two-years-idUSKBN1710GR.

300. Abbey, "Myanmar Migrants Face Malaysian Violence."

301. Zsombor Peter, "Myanmar Workers Bound for Malaysia Stuck with Stifling Fees," *The Irrawaddy* (April 5, 2019), https://www.irrawaddy.com/news/burma/malaysiamyanmar-workers-bound-for-malaysia-stuck-with-stifling-fees.html.

302. Abbey, "Myanmar Migrants Face Malaysian Violence."

303. Médecins Sans Frontières, *Violence, Vulnerability and Migration: Trapped at the Gates of Europe* (Geneva, Switzerland: Doctors Without Borders, March 2013), 3, https://www.msf.org.uk/sites/uk/files/Migration_Morocco_2013_201303132441.pdf.

304. Lily Jay, "Deaths, Deportations and Arrests: Violence Against Migrants in Morocco," *OpenDemocracy* (December 12, 2016), https://www.opendemocracy.net/5050/lily-jay/deaths-deportations-and-arrests-violence-against-migrants-in-morocco.

305. Paul Raymond, "African Migrants in Morocco Are Trapped in a Cycle of Violence," *Vice* (February 10, 2014), https://www.vice.com/en_uk/article/kw9eym/african-migrants-in-morocco-are-trapped-in-a-spiral-of-violence-and-despair.

306. Obinna Anyadike, "Morocco: The Forgotten Frontline of the Migrant Crisis," *IRIN News* (July 29, 2015), http://newirin.irinnews.org/extras/2015/7/28/morocco-the-forgotten-front-line-of-the-migrant-crisis.

307. Jay, "Deaths, Deportations and Arrests."

308. Anyadike, "Morocco: The Forgotten Frontline of the Migrant Crisis."

309. Jay, "Deaths, Deportations and Arrests."

310. Gillian Coyne, "'Migrants Don't Exist': Morocco Struggles with Migration Issues Despite Reforms," *Middle East Eye* (April 1, 2018), http://www.middleeasteye.net/news/migrants-dont-exist-morocco-struggles-migration-issues-despite-reforms-998281491.

311. Jay, "Deaths, Deportations and Arrests."

312. Human Rights First, *Combating Xenophobic Violence*, 21; Parastou Hassouri, "Refugees or Migrants? Difficulties of West Africans in Morocco," *ReliefWeb* (September 12, 2017), https://reliefweb.int/report/morocco/refugees-or-migrants-difficulties-west-africans-morocco; and Human Rights Watch, *Abused and Expelled: Ill-Treatment of Sub-Saharan African Migrants in Morocco* (New York: Human Rights Watch, February 2014), 15–17.

313. Aida Alami, "African Migrants in Morocco Tell of Abuse," *New York Times* (November 29, 2012), http://www.nytimes.com/2012/11/29/world/middleeast/african-migrants-in-morocco-tell-of-abuse.html.

314. Aida Alami, "Morocco Unleashes a Harsh Crackdown on Sub-Saharan Migrants," *New York Times* (October 22, 2018), https://www.nytimes.com/2018/10/22/world/africa/morocco-crackdown-sub-saharan-migrants-spain.html.

315. Raymond, "African Migrants in Morocco Are Trapped in a Cycle of Violence."

316. "GADEM Condemns Racist Attacks in Morocco," *December18* (August 24, 2010), http://www.december18.net/article/gadem-condemns-racist-attacksmorocco.

317. Daan Bauwens, "African Refugees Targeted," *IPS* (June 23, 2009), http://www.ipsnews.net/2009/06/morocco-african-refugees-targeted/.

318. Angela Li Rosi and Alanna Ryan, *Refugee Protection and International Migration: A Review of UNHCR's Role and Activities in Morocco* (Geneva: UNHCR, March 2010), http://www.unhcr.org/4ba8ce896.html.

319. Médecins Sans Frontières, *Violence, Vulnerability and Migration*, 14.

320. Anyadike, "Morocco: The Forgotten Frontline of the Migrant Crisis."

321. Jay, "Deaths, Deportations and Arrests"; and Anyadike, "Morocco: The Forgotten Frontline of the Migrant Crisis."

322. Anyadike, "Morocco: The Forgotten Frontline of the Migrant Crisis."

323. Alami, "Morocco Unleashes a Harsh Crackdown on Sub-Saharan Migrants."

324. Alami, "Morocco Unleashes a Harsh Crackdown on Sub-Saharan Migrants."

325. Human Rights First, *Combating Xenophobic Violence*, 4; and Smahane Bouyahia, "Racism Towards Blacks in Morocco and Maghreb, a Taboo Topic," *AFRIK-News* (July 29, 2010), http://www.afriknews.com/article18043.html; and Bauwens, "African Refugees Targeted."

326. Jay, "Deaths, Deportations and Arrests."

327. Rosi and Ryan, *Refugee Protection and International Migration*; and Groupe Antiraciste de Defense et d'Accompagnement des Etrangers et Migrants (GADEM), "Note on Racial Discrimination Against Foreigners in Morocco" (August 2010), http://www.jsf-jwb-migrants.org/documents%20-%20all/GADEM%20rapport%20CERD%20final-2-4%20ENG.pdf.

328. GADEM, "Note on Racial Discrimination Against Foreigners in Morocco"; Bouyahia, "Racism Towards Blacks in Morocco and Maghreb"; and Bauwens, "African Refugees Targeted."

329. Alami, "Morocco Unleashes a Harsh Crackdown on Sub-Saharan Migrants."

330. Médecins Sans Frontières, *Violence, Vulnerability and Migration*, 3, 12.

331. Médecins Sans Frontières, *Violence, Vulnerability and Migration*, 11.

332. Fabíola Ortiz, "The Dark Reality for Women Migrants in Morocco," *Huffington Post* (February 23, 2017), https://www.huffingtonpost.com/entry/dark-reality-for-women-migrants-in-morocco_us_58af46obe4b060480e05fb62.

333. Anyadike, "Morocco: The Forgotten Frontline of the Migrant Crisis."

334. Médecins Sans Frontières, *Violence, Vulnerability and Migration*, 3.

335. Human Rights Watch, *Abused and Expelled*, 20.

336. Coyne, "'Migrants Don't Exist.'"

337. Alami, "Morocco Unleashes a Harsh Crackdown on Sub-Saharan Migrants."

338. Human Rights Watch, *Abused and Expelled*, 15.

339. Alami, "African Migrants in Morocco Tell of Abuse."

340. Alami, "African Migrants in Morocco Tell of Abuse."

341. Anyadike, "Morocco."

342. Médecins Sans Frontières, *Violence, Vulnerability and Migration*, 3.

343. Médecins Sans Frontières, *Violence, Vulnerability and Migration*, 9.

344. Médecins Sans Frontières, *Violence, Vulnerability and Migration*, 9.

345. Jay, "Deaths, Deportations and Arrests."

346. Alami, "African Migrants in Morocco Tell of Abuse."

347. GADEM, "Note on Racial Discrimination Against Foreigners in Morocco"; and Human Rights First, *Combating Xenophobic Violence*, 21.

348. Médecins Sans Frontières, *Violence, Vulnerability and Migration*, 9, 11, 19.

349. Alami, "African Migrants in Morocco Tell of Abuse."

350. Alami, "African Migrants in Morocco Tell of Abuse."

351. Alami, "African Migrants in Morocco Tell of Abuse."

352. Alami, "African Migrants in Morocco Tell of Abuse."

353. Coyne, "'Migrants Don't Exist.'"

354. Jay, "Deaths, Deportations and Arrests."

355. Raymond, "African Migrants in Morocco Are Trapped in a Cycle of Violence."

356. Alami, "African Migrants in Morocco Tell of Abuse."

357. Jane Freedman, "Analysing the Gendered Insecurities of Migration: A Case Study of Female Sub-Saharan African Migrants in Morocco," *International Feminist Journal of Politics* 14 (March 2012), 40.

358. Faras Ghani, "Morocco's Migrants Treatment Under Spotlight After UN Conference," *Al Jazeera* (December 11, 2018), https://www.aljazeera.com/news/2018/12/spotlight-morocco-defends-treatment-migrants-181212033244311.html.

359. Médecins Sans Frontières, *Violence, Vulnerability and Migration*, 14.

360. Anyadike, "Morocco."

361. Leonid Ragozin, "Russia Wants Immigrants the World Doesn't," *Bloomberg* (March 13, 2017), https://www.bloomberg.com/news/features/2017-03-14/russia-s-alternative-universe-immigrants-welcome; and Pete Cobus, "For Migrants in Russia, Shattered Dreams and Uncertain Futures," *Voice of America* (February 4, 2019), https://www.voanews.com/europe/migrants-russia-shattered-dreams-and-uncertain-futures.

362. Andrea Ó Súilleabháin, "Discrimination, Often Violent, Impacts Thousands of Central Asian Migrants in Russia," *International Peace Institute Global Observatory* (February 20, 2013), https://theglobalobservatory.org/2013/02/discrimination-often-violent-impacts-thousands-of-central-asian-migrants-in-russia/.

363. Ragozin, "Russia Wants Immigrants the World Doesn't"; and Cobus, "For Migrants in Russia, Shattered Dreams and Uncertain Futures."

364. Isabel Gorst, "Russia's Migrants Living on the Edge," *Financial Times* (December 16, 2011), https://www.ft.com/content/0d1569a0-2607-11e1-856e-00144feabdco.

365. United Nations High Commissioner for Refugees, "2011 UNHCR Country Operations Profile—Russia" (Geneva: UNHCR, 2011), http://www.unhcr.org/pages/49e48d456.html.

366. Institute of Oriental Studies of the Russian Academy of Sciences, *Causes and Motives of Radicalisation Among Central Asian Labour Migrants in the Russian Federation* (Moscow: IOS RAS, 2017), 32.

367. Arne Seifert, "The Problems of Central Asian Migration to Russia," *International Organization for Migration (IOM)* (January 12, 2018), https://doc-research.org/2018/01/the-problems-of-central-asian-migration-to-russia/.

368. Ragozin, "Russia Wants Immigrants the World Doesn't."

369. Human Rights First, *Combating Xenophobic Violence*, 4.

370. Khristina Narizhnaya, "Russia's Xenophobia Problem," *Public Radio International* (April 29, 2012), https://www.pri.org/stories/2012-04-29/russias-xenophobia-problem.

371. Ó Súilleabháin, "Discrimination, Often Violent, Impacts Thousands of Central Asian Migrants in Russia."

372. Natalia Yudina, "Xenophobia in Figures: Hate Crime in Russia and Efforts to Counteract It in 2017," *SOVA* (December 2, 2018), https://www.sova-center.ru/en/xenophobia/reports-analyses/2018/02/d38830/#_ftnref1; and Natalia Yudina, "Far Right and Arithmetic: Hate Crime in Russia and Efforts to Counteract It in 2018," *SOVA* (April 2, 2019) https://www.sova-center.ru/en/xenophobia/reports-analyses/2019/02/d40603/.

373. Human Rights First, *Combating Xenophobic Violence*, 4; and Galina Kozhevnikova, "The Phantom of Manezhnaya Square: Radical Nationalism and Efforts to Counteract It in 2010," *SOVA* (May 5, 2011), http://www.sova-center.ru/en/xenophobia/reports-analyses/2011/05/d21561/.

374. Yoshiko M. Herrera and Nicole M. Butkovich Kraus, "Pride Versus Prejudice: Ethnicity, National Identity, and Xenophobia in Russia," *Comparative Politics* 48 (April 2016), 293.

375. Human Rights First, *Combating Xenophobic Violence*, 21.

376. Human Rights First, *Combating Xenophobic Violence*, 22; and SOVA Center for Information and Analysis, "Napadenie na Urozhentsa Kongo v Moskve" (January 14, 2011), http://www.sova-center.ru/racismxenophobia/news/racism-nationalism/2011/01/d20724/.

377. Office of the Prosecutor General, Investigative Committee of the Russian Federation, "V Sankt-Peterburge Vozbuzhdeno Ugolovnoe delo ob Ubijstve Grazhdanina Tadzhikistana," press release (March 3, 2011), http://www.sledcomspb.ru/node/2323.

378. Gabriela Baczynska and Igor Belyatski, "Over 1,600 Migrants Rounded Up After Ethnic Riots in Moscow," *Reuters* (October 14, 2013), https://www.reuters.com/article/us-russia-migrants/over-1600-migrants-rounded-up-after-ethnic-riots-in-moscow-idUSBRE99D0A320131014.

379. Baczynska and Belyatski, "Over 1,600 Migrants Rounded Up After Ethnic Riots in Moscow."

380. Yudina, "Xenophobia in Figures."

381. Yudina, "Far Right and Arithmetic."

382. Gorst, "Russia's Migrants Living on the Edge."

383. Seifert, "The Problems of Central Asian Migration to Russia."

384. Edward Lemon and John Heathershaw, "How Can We Explain Radicalisation Among Central Asia's Migrants?," *OpenDemocracy* (2017), http://www.opendemocracy .net/od-russia/edward-lemon-john-heathershaw/can-we-explain-radicalisation -amongcentral-asia-s-migrants; and International Organization for Migration, *World Migration Report 2018* (Geneva: International Organization for Migration/UN Migration Agency, 2018), 219, https://publications.iom.int/system/files/pdf/wmr_2018_en.pdf.

385. "Siberian City Holds Unauthorized Protest After Rape Blamed on Migrants," *Moscow Times* (March 18, 2019), https://www.themoscowtimes.com/2019/03/18/siberian -city-holds-unauthorized-protest-after-rape-blamed-on-migrants-a64841.

386. Lemon and Heathershaw, "How Can We Explain Radicalisation Among Central Asia's Migrants?"; and International Organization for Migration, *World Migration Report 2018*, 219.

387. Institute of Oriental Studies of the Russian Academy of Sciences, *Causes and Motives of Radicalisation Among Central Asian Labour Migrants in the Russian Federation*, 31.

388. Mohammed S. Elshimi, *Understanding the Factors Contributing to Radicalisation Among Central Asian Labour Migrants in Russia* (London: Royal United Services Institute for Defence and Security Studies Occasional Paper, April 2018), ix.

389. Ragozin, "Russia Wants Immigrants the World Doesn't."

390. Narizhnaya, "Russia's Xenophobia Problem."

391. Herrera and Kraus, "Pride Versus Prejudice," 308–309.

392. Gorst, "Russia's Migrants Living on the Edge."

393. Gorst, "Russia's Migrants Living on the Edge."

394. Ragozin, "Russia Wants Immigrants the World Doesn't."

395. Cobus, "For Migrants in Russia, Shattered Dreams and Uncertain Futures."

396. Cobus, "For Migrants in Russia, Shattered Dreams and Uncertain Futures."

397. Gorst, "Russia's Migrants Living on the Edge."

398. Ragozin, "Russia Wants Immigrants the World Doesn't."

399. Ó Súilleabháin, "Discrimination, Often Violent, Impacts Thousands of Central Asian Migrants in Russia."

400. Gorst, "Russia's Migrants Living on the Edge."

401. Ragozin, "Russia Wants Immigrants the World Doesn't."

402. Elshimi, *Understanding the Factors Contributing to Radicalisation Among Central Asian Labour Migrants in Russia*, x–xi, 63.

403. Herrera and Kraus, "Pride Versus Prejudice," 293–294; and Frederick Soit, "Diversionary Nationalism: Economic Inequality and the Formation of National Pride," *Journal of Politics* 73 (July 2011), 821–830.

404. Gorst, "Russia's Migrants Living on the Edge."

405. Shaun Walker, "St Petersburg Bomb Suspect Identified as 22-Year-Old Born in Kyrgyzstan," *The Guardian* (April 4, 2017), https://www.theguardian.com/world/2017/apr/04/st-petersburg-metro-bombing-suspect-kyrgyzstan-akbarzhon-jalilov-says-security-service; and "St. Petersburg Attack: What We Know," *BBC News* (April 19, 2017), https://www.bbc.com/news/world-europe-39481067.

406. Elshimi, *Understanding the Factors Contributing to Radicalisation Among Central Asian Labour Migrants in Russia*, 63.

407. Gorst, "Russia's Migrants Living on the Edge."

408. Ó Súilleabháin, "Discrimination, Often Violent, Impacts Thousands of Central Asian Migrants in Russia."

409. Seifert, "The Problems of Central Asian Migration to Russia."

410. Jean Pierre Misago, Tamlyn Monson, Tara Polzer, and Loren Landau, "Violence Against Foreign Nationals in South Africa," *University of the Witwatersrand's Forced Migration Studies Programme (FMSP) and Consortium for Refuges and Migrants in South Africa (CoRMSA)* (April 2010), http://www.cormsa.org.za/wpcontent/uploads/2009/05/may-2008-violence-against-foreign-nationals-in-south-africa.pdf.

411. Kevin Sieff, "In South Africa, Violence Follows a Surge in Xenophobia," *Washington Post* (February 24, 2017), https://www.washingtonpost.com/world/in-south-africa-a-surge-in-xenophobia-leads-to-violence/2017/02/24/dbf8d864-fecf-4d14-b6f5-3a25d8c46b61_story.html.

412. Faith Karimi, "What's Behind Xenophobic Attacks in South Africa?," *CNN* (April 19, 2015), http://www.cnn.com/2015/04/18/africa/south-africa-xenophobia-explainer/index.html.

413. United Nations High Commissioner for Refugees, "2011 UNHCR Country Operations Profile—South Africa" (Geneva: UNHCR, 2011), http://www.unhcr.org/pages/49e485aa6.html; U.S. Department of State, *2009 Country Reports on Human Rights Practices: South Africa* (Washington, DC: U.S. Department of State Bureau of Democracy, Human Rights and Labor, March 11, 2010), http://www.state.gov/g/drl/rls/hrrpt/2009/af/135977.htm; and Human Rights Watch, "World Report 2010: South Africa" (January 2010), http://www.hrw.org/en/node/87452.

414. Sieff, "In South Africa, Violence Follows a Surge in Xenophobia."

415. Tamerra Griffin, "South Africa Has an Anti-Immigration Problem, and It Looks a Lot Like America's," *BuzzFeed* (May 4, 2019), https://www.buzzfeednews.com/article/tamerragriffin/south-africa-election-xenophobia.

416. Loren B. Landau and Tamlyn Monson, "Immigration and Subterranean Sovereignty in South African Cities," in Anne L. Clunan and Harold A. Trinkunas, eds., *Ungoverned Spaces: Alternatives to State Authority in an Era of Softened Sovereignty* (Stanford, CA: Stanford University Press, 2010), 159.

417. Annsilla Nyar, "'What Happened?': A Narrative of the May 2008 Xenophobic Violence," *Atlantic Philanthropies* (2010), 2, https://www.atlanticphilanthropies.org/wp -content/uploads/2010/07/4_What_happened_c.pdf.

418. Karimi, "What's Behind Xenophobic Attacks in South Africa?"

419. Griffin, "South Africa Has an Anti-Immigration Problem, and It Looks a Lot Like America's."

420. Nyar, "'What Happened?,'" 1.

421. Lynsey Chutel, "South Africa's Election Season Rhetoric Has Sparked Fresh Xenophobic Attacks on African Migrants," *Quartz Africa* (April 2, 2019), https://qz.com/africa/1585736/xenophobic-attacks-on-africans-in-south-africa-ahead-of-elections/.

422. Amnesty International, "South Africa: Ten Years After Xenophobic Killings, Refugees and Migrants Still Living in Fear" (May 11, 2018), https://www.amnesty.org/en/latest/news/2018/05/south-africa-ten-years-after-xenophobic-killings-refugees-and -migrants-still-living-in-fear/.

423. Misago, Monson, Polzer, and Landau, "Violence Against Foreign Nationals in South Africa."

424. Karimi, "What's Behind Xenophobic Attacks in South Africa?"

425. Jean Pierre Misago, Loren B. Landau, and Tamlyn Monson, *Towards Tolerance, Law and Dignity: Addressing Violence Against Foreign Nationals in South Africa* (Pretoria: International Organisation for Migration, 2009).

426. Nyar, "'What Happened?,'" 3.

427. Human Rights First, *Combating Xenophobic Violence*, 23.

428. United Nations Office for the Coordination of Humanitarian Affairs, "More Than 2,000 Zimbabweans Flee, Fearing Attacks," *IRIN News* (November 17, 2009), http://www.irinnews.org/Report.aspx?ReportId=87090.

429. United Nations Office for the Coordination of Humanitarian Affairs, "More Than 2,000 Zimbabweans Flee, Fearing Attacks."

430. BBC, "South Africa: Foreigners Injured in Xenophobia Clashes," *BBC News* (July 20, 2010), http://www.bbc.co.uk/news/world-africa-10696292.

431. Human Rights First, *Combating Xenophobic Violence*, 22.

432. Amnesty International, "South Africa: Ten Years After Xenophobic Killings, Refugees and Migrants Still Living in Fear."

433. Karimi, "What's Behind Xenophobic Attacks in South Africa?"

434. Karimi, "What's Behind Xenophobic Attacks in South Africa?"

435. Amnesty International, "South Africa: Ten Years After Xenophobic Killings, Refugees and Migrants Still Living in Fear"; Norimitsu Onishi, "South Africa Anti-Immigrant Protests Turn Violent," *New York Times* (February 24, 2017), https://www.nytimes.com/2017/02/24/world/africa/immigrant-protests-south-africa.html; and Sieff, "In South Africa, Violence Follows a Surge in Xenophobia."

436. Amnesty International, *Amnesty International Report 2017/18*, 333.

437. Thuso Khumalo, "South Africa: Xenophobic Violence Resurfaces," *Deutsche Welle* (September 7, 2018), https://www.dw.com/en/south-africa-xenophobic-violence-resurfaces/a-45399481.

438. "South Africa: Attacks on Foreign Nationals—Rise in Xenophobic Violence as Elections Near," *Human Rights Watch* (April 15, 2019), https://www.hrw.org/news/2019/04/15/south-africa-attacks-foreign-nationals.

439. Karimi, "What's Behind Xenophobic Attacks in South Africa?"

440. "Refugees in South Africa: 'Give Us a Place Where We Can Be Safe,'" *BBC News* (February 3, 2020), https://www.bbc.com/news/world-africa-51284576.

441. Onishi, "South Africa Anti-Immigrant Protests Turn Violent."

442. Griffin, "South Africa Has an Anti-Immigration Problem, and It Looks a Lot Like America's."

443. Karimi, "What's Behind Xenophobic Attacks in South Africa?"

444. Paul Verryn, "Foreword," in Eric Worby, Shireen Hassim, and Tawana Kupe, eds., *Go Home or Die Here* (Johannesburg: Wits University Press, 2008), vii.

445. Nyar, "'What Happened?,'" 1–2.

446. Griffin, "South Africa Has an Anti-Immigration Problem, and It Looks a Lot Like America's."

447. Amnesty International, "South Africa: Ten Years After Xenophobic Killings, Refugees and Migrants Still Living in Fear."

448. Nyar, "'What Happened?,'" 3.

449. Karimi, "What's Behind Xenophobic Attacks in South Africa?"

450. Nyar, "'What Happened?,'" 8.

451. Landau and Monson, "Immigration and Subterranean Sovereignty in South African Cities," in Clunan and Trinkunas, *Ungoverned Spaces*, 162.

452. Human Rights First, *Combating Xenophobic Violence*, 11.

453. Amnesty International, "South Africa: Ten Years After Xenophobic Killings, Refugees and Migrants Still Living in Fear."

454. Karimi, "What's Behind Xenophobic Attacks in South Africa?"

455. Amnesty International, "South Africa: Ten Years After Xenophobic Killings, Refugees and Migrants Still Living in Fear."

456. Amnesty International, *Amnesty International Report 2017/18*, 335.

457. Griffin, "South Africa Has an Anti-Immigration Problem, and It Looks a Lot Like America's."

458. Khumalo, "South Africa: Xenophobic Violence Resurfaces."

459. "South Africa: Attacks on Foreign Nationals—Rise in Xenophobic Violence as Elections Near."

460. Dewa Mavhinga, "South Africa Launches Plan to Combat Xenophobia and Racism: Crucial Step in South Africa's Path to Justice and Equality," *Human Rights*

Watch (March 25, 2019), https://www.hrw.org/news/2019/03/25/south-africa-launches
-plan-combat-xenophobia-and-racism.

461. Karimi, "What's Behind Xenophobic Attacks in South Africa?"

462. Karimi, "What's Behind Xenophobic Attacks in South Africa?"

463. Umar Farooq and Kiran Nazish, "Clashes Erupt in Istanbul Between Turks and Migrants Whose Lives Remain on Hold," *Los Angeles Times* (May 20, 2017), http://www
.latimes.com/world/la-fg-turkey-migrants-violence-20170520-story.html.

464. Patrick Kingsley, "Refugee Crisis: What Does the EU's Deal with Turkey Mean?" *The Guardian* (March 18, 2016), https://www.theguardian.com/world/2016/mar/18/eu
-deal-turkey-migrants-refugees-q-and-a.

465. "Turkey Says Millions of Migrants May Head to EU," *BBC News* (March 2, 2020), https://www.bbc.com/news/world-europe-51707958.

466. International Crisis Group, *Turkey's Syrian Refugees: Defusing Metropolitan Tensions* (Brussels, Belgium: International Crisis Group Europe Report #248, January 29, 2018), 1.

467. "Turkey Says Millions of Migrants May Head to EU"; and Stephen Starr, "Syrians in Turkey Face Anger and Violence," *Irish Times* (November 7, 2018), https://www
.irishtimes.com/news/world/europe/syrians-in-turkey-face-anger-and-violence-1
.3688674.

468. Farooq and Nazish, "Clashes Erupt in Istanbul Between Turks and Migrants Whose Lives Remain on Hold."

469. Dogus Simsek, "Anti-Syrian Racism in Turkey," *OpenDemocracy* (January 27, 2015), https://www.opendemocracy.net/en/north-africa-west-asia/antisyrian-racism-in
-turkey/.

470. International Crisis Group, *Turkey's Syrian Refugees*, i.

471. Starr, "Syrians in Turkey Face Anger and Violence."

472. Human Rights First, *Combating Xenophobic Violence*, 4; and Helsinki Citizens' Assembly-Turkey and Organization for Refugee, Asylum and Migration, "Unsafe Haven: The Security Challenges Facing Lesbian, Gay, Bisexual and Transgender Asylum Seekers and Refugees in Turkey" (June 2009), http://www.hyd.org.tr/staticfiles/files/unsafe_latest.pdf.

473. International Crisis Group, *Turkey's Syrian Refugees*, i.

474. International Crisis Group, *Turkey's Syrian Refugees*, i, 4.

475. Howard Eissenstat, "Refugees in Turkey: Unsafe Harbor," *Human Rights Now Blog* (August 23, 2011), http://blog.amnestyusa.org/justice/refugees-in-turkeyunsafe
-harbor/.

476. Simsek, "Anti-Syrian Racism in Turkey."

477. Simsek, "Anti-Syrian Racism in Turkey."

478. Farooq and Nazish, "Clashes Erupt in Istanbul Between Turks and Migrants Whose Lives Remain on Hold."

479. Farooq and Nazish, "Clashes Erupt in Istanbul Between Turks and Migrants Whose Lives Remain on Hold."

480. International Crisis Group, *Turkey's Syrian Refugees*, 5.

481. Starr, "Syrians in Turkey Face Anger and Violence."

482. Starr, "Syrians in Turkey Face Anger and Violence."

483. Yasemin Mert, "Dangerous Journeys: Violence Against Women Migrants in Turkey," *OpenDemocracy* (December 8, 2016), https://www.opendemocracy.net/5050/yasemin-mert/dangerous-journeys-women-migrants-in-turkey.

484. International Crisis Group, *Turkey's Syrian Refugees*, 4.

485. Simsek, "Anti-Syrian Racism in Turkey."

486. International Crisis Group, *Turkey's Syrian Refugees*, 1.

487. International Crisis Group, *Turkey's Syrian Refugees*, 6–7.

488. International Crisis Group, *Turkey's Syrian Refugees*, 3.

489. International Crisis Group, *Turkey's Syrian Refugees*, 12.

490. Roy Gutman, "Europe's Migrants, Turkey's Problem," *Politico* (April 4, 2016), https://www.politico.eu/article/europes-migrants-turkeys-problem/.

491. International Crisis Group, *Turkey's Syrian Refugees*, 8.

492. Simsek, "Anti-Syrian Racism in Turkey."

493. Human Rights First, *Combating Xenophobic Violence*, 23.

494. Human Rights First, *Combating Xenophobic Violence*, 23; and European Commission Against Racism and Intolerance, "Fourth Report on Turkey," Report # CRI (2001)5 (February 8, 2011), http://www.coe.int/t/dghl/monitoring/ecri/Country-by-country/Turkey/TUR-CBC-IV-2011-005-ENG.pdf.

495. Gutman, "Europe's Migrants, Turkey's Problem."

496. Phillip Connor and Gustavo López, "5 Facts About the U.S. Rank in Worldwide Migration," *Pew Research Center* (May 18, 2016), http://www.pewresearch.org/fact-tank/2016/05/18/5-facts-about-the-u-s-rank-in-worldwide-migration/.

497. International Organization for Migration, *World Migration Report 2018*, 18.

498. Gustavo López and Kristin Bialik, "Key Findings About U.S. Immigrants." *Pew Research Center* (May 3, 2017), http://www.pewresearch.org/fact-tank/2017/05/03/key-findings-about-u-s-immigrants/.

499. Michael T. Light and Ty Miller, "Does Undocumented Immigration Increase Violent Crime?," *Criminology* 56 (2018), 370.

500. Dan Caldwell and Robert E. Williams Jr., *Seeking Security in an Insecure World* (Lanham, MD: Rowman and Littlefield, 2006), 170.

501. Robert Mandel, *Global Threat: Target-Centered Assessment and Management* (Westport, CT: Praeger Security International, 2008), 25.

502. Caroline Freund, "Anti-Globalization or Xenophobia?" *Peterson Institute for International Economics* (April 28, 2016), https://piie.com/blogs/realtime-economic-issues-watch/anti-globalization-or-xenophobia.

503. David A. Shirk, *The Drug War in Mexico: Confronting a Shared Threat*, Council on Foreign Relations Special Report #60 (March 2011), 5.

504. John Higham, *Strangers in the Land* (New Brunswick, NJ: Rutgers University Press, 1955), 301.

505. Peter Schrag, *Not Fit for Our Society: Nativism and Immigration* (Berkeley: University of California Press, 2010), 14.

506. Khaled A. Beydoun, *American Islamophobia: Understanding the Roots and Rise of Fear* (Berkeley: University of California Press, 2018), 4.

507. "The New Nativism," *The Nation* 283 (August 28/September 4, 2006), 5.

508. Héctor Tobar, "Latinos Feel the Sting of Trump's Presidency," *New Yorker* (March 8, 2017), https://www.newyorker.com/news/news-desk/latinos-feel-the-sting-of -trumps-presidency.

509. Douglas S. Massey and Kristin E. Espinosa, "What Is Driving Mexico-U.S. Migration? A Theoretical, Empirical, and Policy Analysis," *American Journal of Sociology* 102 (January 1997), 989–990.

510. Edward D. Murphy, "Anti-Immigrant Bias Assessed in New Study," *Portland Press Herald* (June 20, 2011), http://www.pressherald.com/news/antiimmigrant-bias -assessed-in-new-study_2011-06-20.html; "Refugees in NY Attacked," *APFA News. com* (July 14, 2009), http://www.apfanews.com/stories/refugees-in-ny-attacked/; Sarah Palermo, "Concord Police Investigate Graffiti on Refugees' Homes," *Concord Monitor* (September 19, 2011), http://www.concordmonitor.com/blogentry/280790/refugee -families-attacked-with-graffiti; and Shawne K. Wickam, "'Love Your Neighbor' Rally Draws 300," *New Hampshire Sunday News* (September 25, 2011), http://www.unionleader .com/article/20110925/NEWS03/709259971.

511. Patrick J. Buchanan, *State of Emergency: The Third World Invasion and Conquest of America* (New York: Dunne, 2006).

512. "Here's Donald Trump's Presidential Announcement Speech," *Time* (June 16, 2015), http://time.com/3923128/donald-trump-announcement-speech/.

513. The Leadership Conference on Civil and Human Rights, "Hate Crimes Against Hispanics" (2009), http://www.civilrights.org/publications/hatecrimes/hispanics.html; and U.S. Department of Justice, *Hate Crime Statistics* (Washington, DC: U.S. Department of Justice, Federal Bureau of Investigation, Criminal Justice Information Services Division, November 18, 2011), http://www.fbi.gov/about-us/cjis/ucr/hate-crime/2010.

514. Southern Poverty Law Center, "Hate Group Numbers Up by 54% Since 2000," press release (February 26, 2009), http://www.splcenter.org/getinformed/news/hate -group-numbers-up.

515. Amnesty International, *Amnesty International Report 2017/18*, 385.

516. Jessica Weiss, "Six Months of Hate: How Anti-Immigrant Sentiment Is Affecting Latinos in the United States," *Univision News* (June 14, 2017), https://www

.univision.com/univision-news/united-states/six-months-of-hate-how-anti-immigrant
-sentiment-is-affecting-latinos-in-the-united-states.

517. Will Carless and Aaron Sankin, "The Hate Report: The State of Anti-Immigrant Hate, 2018," *Center for Investigative Reporting* (June 8, 2018), https://www.revealnews .org/blog/the-hate-report-the-state-of-anti-immigrant-hate-2018/.

518. Lauren Turner, "Texas Walmart Shooting: El Paso Attack 'Domestic Terrorism,'" *BBC News* (August 5, 2019), https://www.bbc.com/news/world-us-canada-49226573.

519. Robert Gearty, "Illegal Immigrant Linked to Nevada Killing Spree Was from El Salvador, According to ICE," *Fox News* (January 22, 2019), https://www.foxnews.com/ us/illegal-immigrant-linked-to-nevada-killing-spree-was-from-el-salvador-according -to-ice.

520. See Pamela Geller, *Stop the Islamization of America: A Practical Guide to the Resistance* (Washington, DC: WND Books, 2011); Wajahat Ali, Eli Clifton, Matthew Duss, Lee Fang, Scott Keyes, and Faiz Shakir, *Fear, Inc.: The Roots of the Islamophobia Network in America* (Washington, DC: Center for American Progress, 2011); and Beydoun, *American Islamophobia*.

521. Yoeri Maertens, "'America First': Why Has Nativism Resurfaced in the New World?" (master's thesis, Universiteit Gent, 2017), 36, https://lib.ugent.be/fulltxt/ RUG01/002/376/009/RUG01-002376009_2017_0001_AC.pdf.

522. Eric D. Gould and Esteban F. Klor, "The Long-Run Effect of 9/11: Terrorism, Backlash, and the Assimilation of Muslim Immigrants in the West," *Economic Journal* 126, (2016), 2091.

523. Beydoun, *American Islamophobia*, 13.

524. Human Rights First, *Germany Conflicted*, 8.

525. Gould and Klor, "The Long-Run Effect of 9/11," 2064–2065.

526. Brian Levin, "Islamophobia in America: Rise in Hate Crimes Against Muslims Shows What Politicians Say Matters," *Newsweek* (July 21, 2017), http://www .newsweek.com/islamophobia-america-rise-hate-crimes-against-muslims-proves-what -politicians-640184.

527. International Organization for Migration, *World Migration Report 2018*, 217.

528. Levin, "Islamophobia in America."

529. Katayoun Kishi, "Assaults Against Muslims in U.S. Surpass 2001 Level," *Pew Research Center* (November 15, 2017), http://www.pewresearch.org/fact-tank/2017/11/15/ assaults-against-muslims-in-u-s-surpass-2001-level/.

530. Human Rights First, *Germany Conflicted*, 44.

531. Bill Berkowitz, "Nativists Declare Open Season on Undocumented Immigrants" (May 4, 2006) http://www.workingforchange.com/article.cfm?itemid=20748.

532. Pew Research Center, "U.S. Muslims Concerned About Their Place in Society, but Continue to Believe in the American Dream," *Pew Research Center* (July 26,

2017), http://www.pewforum.org/2017/07/26/findings-from-pew-research-centers-2017
-survey-of-us-muslims/.

533. *Communities on Fire: Confronting Hate Violence and Xenophobic Political Rhetoric* (Washington, DC: South Asian Americans Leading Together (SAALT), 2018), 24. See also Suman Raghunathan, "Trump's Xenophobic Vision of America Is Inciting Racist Violence," *The Nation* (January 27, 2018), https://www.thenation.com/article/trumps-xenophobic-vision-of-america-is-inciting-racist-violence/.

534. Nicole Chavez, Emanuella Grinberg, and Eliott C. McLaughlin, "Pittsburgh Synagogue Gunman Said He Wanted All Jews to Die, Criminal Complaint Says," *CNN* (October 31, 2018), https://www.cnn.com/2018/10/28/us/pittsburgh-synagogue-shooting/index.html.

535. Chavez, Grinberg, and McLaughlin, "Pittsburgh Synagogue Gunman Said He Wanted All Jews to Die, Criminal Complaint Says"; and Chris Woodvard, "One Jewish, One Christian: How the California Synagogue Shooting Tore Apart Two Congregations," *USA Today* (April 29, 2019), https://www.usatoday.com/story/news/nation/2019/04/29/poway-synagogue-shooting-two-congregations-torn-apart/3613812002/.

536. Achilles, Kunakhovich, and Shea, "Nationalism, Nativism, and the Revolt Against Globalization."

537. "The New Nativism," 5.

538. Nikil Saval, "Globalisation: The Rise and Fall of an Idea That Swept the World," *The Guardian* (July 14, 2017), https://www.theguardian.com/world/2017/jul/14/globalisation-the-rise-and-fall-of-an-idea-that-swept-the-world.

539. Ronald F. Inglehart and Pippa Norris, *Trump, Brexit, and the Rise of Populism: Economic Have-Nots and Cultural Backlash* (Cambridge, MA: Harvard Kennedy School Faculty Research Working Paper Series #RWP16–026, August 2016), 5, https://www.hks.harvard.edu/publications/trump-brexit-and-rise-populism-economic-have-nots-and-cultural-backlash.

540. Freund, "Anti-Globalization or Xenophobia?"

541. Alan M. Kraut, "Nativism, An American Perennial," *Center for Migration Studies* (February 8, 2016), http://cmsny.org/publications/kraut-nativism/.

542. Cas Mudde, *The Relationship Between Immigration and Nativism in Europe and North America* (Washington, DC: Migration Policy Institute, May 2012), 14.

543. "Hillary Clinton Calls Half of Trump Supporters Bigoted 'Deplorables,'" *The Guardian* (September 10, 2016), https://www.theguardian.com/us-news/2016/sep/10/hillary-clinton-trump-supporters--bigoted-deplorables.

544. Mudde, *The Relationship Between Immigration and Nativism in Europe and North America*, 15.

545. *Communities on Fire: Confronting Hate Violence and Xenophobic Political Rhetoric*, 3.

546. Human Rights First, *Germany Conflicted*, 38.

547. Samuel P. Huntington, "The Hispanic Challenge," *Foreign Policy* 141 (March/April 2004), 32.

548. Rasmussen Reports, "Voters Like Trump's Proposed Muslim Ban" (December 10, 2015), http://www.rasmussenreports.com/public_content/politics/current_events/immigration/december_2015/voters_like_trump_s_proposed_muslim_ban.

549. Mudde, *The Relationship Between Immigration and Nativism in Europe and North America*, 11.

550. Meredith Hoffman, "Whatever Happened to Arizona's Minutemen?," *Vice* (March 22, 2016), https://www.vice.com/en_us/article/xd7jmn/what-happened-to-arizonas-minutemen.

551. Mudde, *The Relationship Between Immigration and Nativism in Europe and North America*, 24; and Jesse McKinley and Malia Wollan, "New Border Fear: Violence by a Rogue Militia," *New York Times* (June 26, 2009), https://www.nytimes.com/2009/06/27/us/27arizona.html.

552. Karla Zabludovsky, "Hunting Humans: The Americans Taking Immigration into Their Own Hands," *Newsweek* (July 23, 2014), https://www.newsweek.com/2014/08/01/texan-ranchers-hunt-daily-illegal-immigrants-260489.html.

553. Hoffman, "Whatever Happened to Arizona's Minutemen?."

554. Simon Romero, "Militia in New Mexico Detains Asylum Seekers at Gunpoint," *New York Times* (April 18, 2019), https://www.nytimes.com/2019/04/18/us/new-mexico-militia.html. See also "How Armed Vigilante Groups Are Detaining Migrants on US-Mexico Border," *The Independent* (April 25, 2019) https://www.independent.co.uk/news/long_reads/us-mexico-border-militia-vigilante-migrants-united-constitutional-patriots-a8886186.html.

555. International Organization for Migration, *World Migration Report 2018*, 203.

556. Tobar, "Latinos Feel the Sting of Trump's Presidency."

557. Dina Okamoto and Kim Ebert, "Group Boundaries, Immigrant Inclusion, and the Politics of Immigrant–Native Relations," *American Behavioral Scientist* 60 (2016), 225.

558. Light and Miller, "Does Undocumented Immigration Increase Violent Crime?," 372.

559. Maertens, "'America First,'" 35.

560. Michael D. Shear, Miriam Jordan, and Manny Fernandez, "The U.S. Immigration System May Have Reached a Breaking Point," *New York Times* (April 10, 2019), https://www.nytimes.com/2019/04/10/us/immigration-border-mexico.html.

561. Levin, "Islamophobia in America: Rise in Hate Crimes Against Muslims Shows What Politicians Say Matters."

562. Marina Fang and Willa Frej, "Here's How the Trump Administration Will Implement Its Travel Ban," *Huffington Post* (June 29, 2017), http://www.huffingtonpost.com/entry/travel-ban-implementation-supreme-court_us_5954f318e4b05c37bb7c624d.

563. Light and Miller, "Does Undocumented Immigration Increase Violent Crime?," 396.

564. John Roberts, "DHS Orders Creation of VOICE Office to Help Victims of Criminal Aliens," *Fox News* (February 21, 2017), http://insider.foxnews.com/2017/02/21/dhs-orders-creation-voice-office-work-behalf-victims-criminal-aliens.

565. David Nakamura, "Trump Administration Moving Quickly to Build Up Nationwide Deportation Force," *Washington Post* (April 12, 2017), https://www.washingtonpost.com/politics/trump-administration-moving-quickly-to-build-up-nationwide-deportation-force/2017/04/12/7a7f59c2-1f87-11e7-be2a-3a1fb24d4671_story.html.

566. For more details on recent American immigrants' significant deportation anxieties and tribulations, see Beth C. Caldwell, *Deported Americans: Life After Deportation to Mexico* (Raleigh, NC: Duke University Press, 2019).

567. Shear, Jordan, and Fernandez, "The U.S. Immigration System May Have Reached a Breaking Point."

568. W. J. Hennigan, "Trump's Cuts to Central American Aid Won't Slow Migration," *Time* (April 5, 2019), http://time.com/5564653/donald-trump-central-american-aid/.

569. Carless and Sankin, "The Hate Report."

570. Weiss, "Six Months of Hate."

571. Shear, Jordan, and Fernandez, "The U.S. Immigration System May Have Reached a Breaking Point."

572. David Kyle and Rey Koslowski, eds., *Global Human Smuggling: Comparative Perspectives* (Baltimore: Johns Hopkins University Press, 2001), 8.

573. Catherine Rampell, "America Has Always Been Hostile to Immigrants," *Washington Post* (August 28, 2015), https://www.washingtonpost.com/opinions/from-benjamin-franklin-to-trump-the-history-of-americas-nativist-streak/2015/08/27/d41f9f26-4cf9-11e5-84df-923b3ef1a64b_story.html.

Chapter 5

1. Elizabeth Cashdan, "Ethnocentrism and Xenophobia: A Cross-Cultural Study," *Current Anthropology* 42 (December 2001), 763.

2. Mikael Hjerm, "National Identities, National Pride and Xenophobia: A Comparison of Four Western Countries," *Acta Sociologica* 41 (1998), 344.

3. Anthony F. Heath and James R. Tilley, "British National Identity and Attitudes Toward Immigration," *International Journal on Multicultural Societies* 7 (2005), 131.

4. Jeanne Park, "Europe's Migration Crisis," *Council on Foreign Relations* (September 2, 2015), http://www.cfr.org/migration/europes-migration-crisis/p32874.

5. Gordon W. Allport, *The Nature of Prejudice* (Cambridge, UK: Addison-Wesley, 1954); and Human Rights First, *Germany Conflicted: The Struggle Between Xenophobia and Tolerance* (New York: Human Rights First, February 2017), 24.

6. Fred Halliday, *The World at 2000* (Hampshire, UK: Palgrave, 2001), 12.

7. Eleni Psarrou, "National Identity in the Era of Globalisation" (PhD diss., London School of Economics, 2002), 238, http://etheses.lse.ac.uk/2507/1/U615456.pdf.

8. See Samuel Huntington, *The Clash of Civilizations and the Remaking of World Order* (New York: Simon and Schuster, 1996).

9. Psarrou, "National Identity in the Era of Globalisation," 142.

10. Katja M. Flückiger, *Xenophobia, Media Stereotyping, and Their Role in Global Insecurity* (Geneva: Geneva Centre for Security Policy Brief #21, December 6, 2006), 3, https://www.files.ethz.ch/isn/92736/Brief-21.pdf.

11. Caroline Freund, "Anti-Globalization or Xenophobia?" *Peterson Institute for International Economics* (April 28, 2016), https://piie.com/blogs/realtime-economic-issues -watch/anti-globalization-or-xenophobia.

12. Jayati Ghosh, "Fear of Foreigners: Recession and Racism in Europe," *Race/Ethnicity* 4 (Winter 2011), 189.

13. Myron Weiner, *The Global Migration Crisis* (New York: HarperCollins, 1994), 3.

14. Jürgen Osterhammel, "Nationalism and Globalization," in John Breuilly, ed., *The Oxford Handbook of the History of Nationalism* (New York: Oxford University Press, 2013), 704.

15. Cemal Eren Arbatli, Quamrul H. Ashraf, Oded Galor, and Marc Klemp, *Diversity and Conflict* (Cambridge, MA: National Bureau of Economic Research Working Paper #21079, November 2018), http://www.nber.org/papers/w21079.

16. José G. Montalvo and Marta Reynal-Querol, "Ethnic Polarization, Potential Conflict, and Civil Wars," *American Economic Review* 95 (2005), 796.

17. John R. Bowen, "The Myth of Global Ethnic Conflict," *Journal of Democracy* 7 (October 1996), 10.

18. Manolis Pratsinakis, "Established and Outsider Nationals: Immigrant–Native Relations and the Everyday Politics of National Belonging," *Ethnicities* 18 (2018), 4.

19. Matina Stevis-Gridneff, "Diverting Europe's Asylum Seekers, This Time to Rwanda," *New York Times* (September 8, 2019), section A, 8.

20. Stevis-Gridneff, "Diverting Europe's Asylum Seekers, This Time to Rwanda," 8.

21. Patrick Kingsley and Haley Willis, "Latest Tactic to Push Migrants from Europe? A Private, Clandestine Fleet," *New York Times* (April 30, 2020), https://www.nytimes .com/2020/04/30/world/europe/migrants-malta.html.

22. "The New Nativism," *The Nation* 283 (August 28/September 4, 2006), 5.

23. Human Rights First, *Combating Xenophobic Violence: A Framework for Action* (New York: Human Rights First, 2011), 6–7.

24. Griff Witte, "Along the Migrant Trail, Pressure Grows to Close Europe's Open Borders," *Washington Post* (November 2, 2015), https://www.washingtonpost.com/ world/europe/along-the-migrant-trail-pressure-grows-to-close-europes-open-borders/ 2015/11/02/31fdfc30-7cc2-11e5-bfb6-65300a5ff562_story.html.

25. Douglas Murray, *The Strange Death of Europe: Immigration, Identity, Islam* (London: Bloomsbury, 2017), 1.

26. Human Rights First, *Germany Conflicted*, 27.

27. Human Rights First, *Germany Conflicted*, 36–37.

28. Brian Levin, "Islamophobia in America: Rise in Hate Crimes Against Muslims Shows What Politicians Say Matters," *Newsweek* (July 21, 2017), http://www.newsweek.com/islamophobia-america-rise-hate-crimes-against-muslims-proves-what-politicians-640184.

29. Ghosh, "Fear of Foreigners, 183.

30. Matt Mogekwu, "The Media's Role in Stoking Xenophobia," *World Policy Journal* (April 26, 2017), https://worldpolicy.org/2017/04/26/the-medias-role-in-stoking-xenophobia/.

31. Peter Schrag, *Not Fit for Our Society: Nativism and Immigration* (Berkeley: University of California Press, 2010), 206.

32. John J. Mearsheimer, "Bound to Fail: The Rise and Fall of the Liberal International Order," *International Security* 43 (Spring 2019), 31.

33. Mkotama Katenga-Kaunda, "Xenophobia: A By-Product of Globalization," *International Association for Political Science Students* (April 20, 2015), http://www.iapss.org/wp/2015/04/20/xenophobia-a-by-product-of-globalisation/.

34. Dina Okamoto and Kim Ebert, "Group Boundaries, Immigrant Inclusion, and the Politics of Immigrant–Native Relations," *American Behavioral Scientist* 60 (2016), 226–227.

35. Myron Weiner, "Security, Stability, and International Migration," *International Security* 17 (Winter 1992/93), 113.

36. Yoeri Maertens, "'America First': Why Has Nativism Resurfaced in the New World?" (master's thesis, Universiteit Gent, 2017), 11, https://lib.ugent.be/fulltxt/RUG01/002/376/009/RUG01-002376009_2017_0001_AC.pdf.

37. Heath and Tilley, "British National Identity and Attitudes Toward Immigration," 131.

38. Amnesty International, *Stranded Hope: Hungary's Sustained Attack on the Rights of Refugees and Migrants* (London: Amnesty International, September 2016), 4.

39. Eric Kaufmann, "Levels or Changes? Ethnic Context, Immigration and the UK Independence Party Vote," *Electoral Studies* 48 (2017), 57–69.

40. Amnesty International, *Amnesty International Report 2017/18: The State of the World's Human Rights* (London: Amnesty International, 2018), 234–235.

41. See Robert Wuthnow, *Be Very Afraid: The Cultural Response to Terror, Pandemics, Environmental Devastation, Nuclear Annihilation, and Other Threats* (New York: Oxford University Press, 2010); and Lydia Khalil, "Public Perception and Homeland Security," in James J. F. Forest, ed., *Homeland Security: Protecting America's Targets*, vol. 2, *Pub-*

lic Spaces and Social Institutions (Westport, CT: Praeger Security International, June 1, 2006), 312–313.

42. Nicole Goodkind, "Donald Trump Is Right, There Is a Border Crisis: Here's What Caused It and What's Being Done About It," *Newsweek* (April 5, 2019), https://www.newsweek.com/border-crisis-donald-trump-immigration-1387585.

43. For an early general discussion of this issue, see Leo Postman and Jerome S. Bruner, "Perception Under Stress," *Psychological Review* 55 (November 1948), 314–323.

44. For theoretical explanations of the breakdown of decision making under crisis conditions, see Irving L. Janis, *Groupthink* (New York: Free Press, 1982); Herbert A. Simon, "Rational Choice and the Structure of the Environment," *Psychological Review*, 63 (1966), 129–138; and Yaacov Y. I. Vertzberger, *The World in Their Minds: Information Processing, Cognition, and Perception in Foreign Policy Decisionmaking* (Stanford, CA: Stanford University Press, 1990).

45. Maertens, *"America First": Why Has Nativism Resurfaced in the New World?*, 7.

46. David H. Bennett, *The Party of Fear: From Nativist Movements to the New Right in American History* (Raleigh, NC: University of North Carolina Press, 1988), 11.

47. Wuthnow, *Be Very Afraid*, 217.

48. Lars-Erik Cederman, "Blood for Soil: The Fatal Temptations of Ethnic Politics," *Foreign Affairs* 98 (March/April 2019), 63–64.

49. Pratsinakis, "Established and Outsider Nationals," 16.

50. Michael T. Light and Ty Miller, "Does Undocumented Immigration Increase Violent Crime?," *Criminology* 56 (2018), 372.

51. Pratsinakis, "Established and Outsider Nationals," 9.

52. Cederman, "Blood for Soil," 64.

53. Pratsinakis, "Established and Outsider Nationals," 8.

54. Christiane Amanpour and Thom Patterson, "Passport Linked to Terrorist Complicates Syrian Refugee Crisis," *CNN* (November 15, 2015), http://www.cnn.com/2015/11/15/europe/paris-attacks-passports/index.html; "The Paris Attacks Have Put Europe's Refugee Crisis Under Renewed Scrutiny," *Time* (November 16, 2015), http://time.com/4114009/paris-attacks-migrant-crisis-refugees-eu/; and Akbar Shahid Ahmed, "Don't Judge Today's Refugee Screening Process by Past Failures, Says Official," *Huffington Post* (November 19, 2015), http://www.huffingtonpost.com/entry/refugee-screening-process_us_564df3c1e4b00b7997f97e0a.

55. International Organization for Migration, *World Migration Report 2018* (Geneva: International Organization for Migration/UN Migration Agency, 2018), 216, https://publications.iom.int/system/files/pdf/wmr_2018_en.pdf.

56. Anna Getmansky, Tolga Sınmazdemir, and Thomas Zeitzoff, "Refugees, Xenophobia, and Domestic Conflict: Evidence from a Survey Experiment in Turkey," *Journal of Peace Research* 55 (February 15, 2018), 504.

57. Human Rights First, *Germany Conflicted*, 26.

58. Christopher J. Lyons, María B. Vélez, and Wayne A. Santoro, "Neighborhood Immigration, Violence, and City-Level Immigrant Political Opportunities," *American Sociological Review* 78 (2013), 604–632.

59. Kerstin Fisk, "Out of the Fire, Into the Frying Pan? Examining Violence Against Foreign Migrants in Africa," in Heather Smith-Cannoy, ed., *Emerging Threats to Human Rights: Resources, Violence, and Deprivation of Citizenship* (Philadelphia: Temple University Press, 2019), 111.

60. For a detailed discussion of humiliation and enemy images, see Evelin Lindner, *Making Enemies: Humiliation and International Conflict* (Westport, CT: Praeger, 2006).

61. International Organization for Migration, *World Migration Report 2018*, 185.

62. Jane Freedman, "Analysing the Gendered Insecurities of Migration: A Case Study of Female Sub-Saharan African Migrants in Morocco," *International Feminist Journal of Politics* 14 (March 2012), 51.

63. Jane Freedman and Bahija Jamal, *Violence Against Migrant and Refugee Women in the Euromed Region* (Copenhagen: Euro-Mediterranean Human Rights Network, December 2008), 13–14.

64. See, for example, Ginger Thompson, "Immigrant Laborers from Haiti Are Paid with Abuse in the Dominican Republic," *New York Times* (November 20, 2005), https://www.nytimes.com/2005/11/20/world/americas/immigrant-laborers-from-haiti-are-paid-with-abuse-in-the.html; Voice of Chin Refugees, "Refugee Woman Savagely Assaulted in Delhi," *VOCR News* (March 30, 2010), http://vocrnews.blogspot.com/2010/03/refugee-woman-savagely-assaulted-in.html; Beh Lih Yi, "'Silent in Fear': Refugee Women in Malaysia Unprotected Against Violence," *Reuters* (January 7, 2018), https://www.reuters.com/article/us-malaysia-refugees-women/silent-in-fear-refugee-women-in-malaysia-unprotected-against-violence-idUSKBN1EX00F; Fabíola Ortiz, "The Dark Reality for Women Migrants in Morocco," *Huffington Post* (February 23, 2017), https://www.huffingtonpost.com/entry/dark-reality-for-women-migrants-in-morocco_us_58af46obe4b060480e05fb62; and Yasemin Mert, "Dangerous Journeys: Violence Against Women Migrants in Turkey," *OpenDemocracy* (December 8, 2016), https://www.opendemocracy.net/5050/yasemin-mert/dangerous-journeys-women-migrants-in-turkey.

Chapter 6

1. John Chapman, "Managing the Politics of Parochialism," in Michael E. Brown, ed., *Ethnic Conflict and International Security* (Princeton, NJ: Princeton University Press, 1993), 260.

2. Nick Mabey, *Security Trends and Threat Misperceptions* (London: E3G, 2007), 13.

3. Douglas Murray, *The Strange Death of Europe: Immigration, Identity, Islam* (London: Bloomsbury, 2017), 103.

4. Lars-Erik Cederman, "Blood for Soil: The Fatal Temptations of Ethnic Politics," *Foreign Affairs* 98 (March/April 2019), 67.

5. Kwame Anthony Appiah, "The Importance of Elsewhere: In Defense of Cosmopolitanism," *Foreign Affairs* 98 (March/April 2019), 24.

6. Murray, *The Strange Death of Europe*, 311.

7. Jan-Werner Müller, "False Flags: The Myth of the Nationalist Resurgence," *Foreign Affairs* 98 (March/April 2019), 41.

8. See, for example, Joseph H. Carens, "Aliens and Citizens: The Case for Open Borders," *Review of Politics* 49 (Spring 1987), 251–273; Adi Gaskell, "Making the Case for Open Borders," *Forbes* (May 17, 2019), https://www.forbes.com/sites/adigaskell/2019/05/17/making-the-case-for-open-borders/#c136aa6577e8; Farhad Manjoo, "There's Nothing Wrong with Open Borders," *New York Times* (January 16, 2019), https://www.nytimes.com/2019/01/16/opinion/open-borders-immigration.html; and Jeffrey Miron, "Forget the Wall Already, It's Time for the U.S. to Have Open Borders," *USA Today* (July 31, 2018), https://www.usatoday.com/story/opinion/2018/07/31/open-borders-help-economy-combat-illegal-immigration-column/862185002/.

9. Jeff Eggers, "The Cost of Fear-Based Policy," *New America Weekly* (September 10, 2015), https://www.newamerica.org/weekly/the-cost-of-fear-based-policy/.

10. Gerasimos Tsourapas, "Labor Migrants as Political Leverage: Migration Interdependence and Coercion in the Mediterranean," *International Studies Quarterly* 62 (2018), 385, 386.

11. W. J. Hennigan, "Trump's Cuts to Central American Aid Won't Slow Migration," *Time* (April 5, 2019), http://time.com/5564653/donald-trump-central-american-aid/.

12. Human Rights First, *Combating Xenophobic Violence: A Framework for Action* (New York: Human Rights First, 2011), 1.

13. Jack Snyder, "The Broken Bargain: How Nationalism Came Back," *Foreign Affairs* 98 (March/April 2019), 60.

14. Chua, "The Destructive Dynamics of Political Tribalism."

15. Jeanne Park, "Europe's Migration Crisis," *Council on Foreign Relations* (September 2, 2015), http://www.cfr.org/migration/europes-migration-crisis/p32874.

16. Caroline Moorehead, "A Tide That Can't Be Turned: The Refugee Crisis Proves That Fortress Europe Is a Fantasy," *New Statesman* 20 (May 23, 2016), http://www.newstatesman.com/culture/books/2016/05/refugee-crisis-proves-fortress-europe-fantasy.

17. Human Rights First, *Germany Conflicted: The Struggle between Xenophobia and Tolerance* (New York: Human Rights First, February 2017), 36.

18. Tamba François Koundouno, "The Complex Lives of Sub-Saharan Migrants in Morocco: Beyond News Headlines and Politicians' Simplifications, Migration Is Complex and Multifaceted," *Morocco World News* (December 28, 2018), https://www.moroccoworldnews.com/2018/12/261760/sub-saharan-migrants-morocco-migration/.

19. Mary Kaldor, "Nationalism and Globalisation," *Nations and Nationalism* 10 (2004), 171.

20. Matt Mogekwu, "The Media's Role in Stoking Xenophobia," *World Policy Journal* (April 26, 2017), https://worldpolicy.org/2017/04/26/the-medias-role-in-stoking-xenophobia/.

21. Chua, "The Destructive Dynamics of Political Tribalism."

22. Manuela Achilles, Kyrill Kunakhovich, and Nicole Shea, "Nationalism, Nativism, and the Revolt Against Globalization," *Europe Now* (February 1, 2018), https://www.europenowjournal.org/2018/01/31/nationalism-nativism-and-the-revolt-against-globalization/.

23. Linda Bordoni, "Xenophobic Violence Fueled by Corruption in South Africa," *Vatican News* (April 5, 2019), https://www.vaticannews.va/en/world/news/2019-04/south-africa-corruption-xenophobia-violence-elections.html.

24. Human Rights First, *Germany Conflicted*, 36.

25. Tiyanjana Maluwa, "The Refugee Problem and the Quest for Peace and Security in Southern Africa," *International Journal of Refugee Law*7, (1995), 655.

26. Andreas Wimmer, *Nationalist Exclusion and Ethnic Conflict: Shadows of Modernity* (Cambridge, UK: Cambridge University Press, 2002), 220.

27. International Organization for Migration, *World Migration Report 2018* (Geneva: International Organization for Migration/UN Migration Agency, 2018), 1, https://publications.iom.int/system/files/pdf/wmr_2018_en.pdf.

28. Anna Getmansky, Tolga Sınmazdemir, and Thomas Zeitzoff, "Refugees, Xenophobia, and Domestic Conflict: Evidence from a Survey Experiment in Turkey," *Journal of Peace Research* 55 (February 15, 2018), 504.

29. Human Rights First, *Combating Xenophobic Violence*, 13; and Human Rights First, *Germany Conflicted*, 28–37.

30. Human Rights First, *Germany Conflicted*, 35.

31. See, for example, Katja M. Flückiger, *Xenophobia, Media Stereotyping, and Their Role in Global Insecurity* (Geneva: Geneva Centre for Security Policy Brief #21, December 6, 2006), 10, https://www.files.ethz.ch/isn/92736/Brief-21.pdf.

32. Martin Rogers, "Why the World Cup Is a Great Advertisement for Immigration," *USA Today* (July 10, 2018), https://www.usatoday.com/story/sports/columnist/martin-rogers/2018/07/10/world-cup-immigration-france-belgium-england/771277002/.   See support for this kind of approach in International Organization for Migration, *World Migration Report 2018*, 198.

33. Appiah, "The Importance of Elsewhere," 22.

34. Human Rights First, *Germany Conflicted*, 41.

35. Kerstin Fisk, "Out of the Fire, Into the Frying Pan? Examining Violence Against Foreign Migrants in Africa," in Heather Smith-Cannoy, ed., *Emerging Threats to Hu-*

man Rights: Resources, Violence, and Deprivation of Citizenship (Philadelphia: Temple University Press, 2019), 111.

36. Human Rights First, *Combating Xenophobic Violence*, 13; and Human Rights First, *Germany Conflicted*, 28–37.

37. Human Rights First, *Combating Xenophobic Violence*, 13; and Human Rights First, *Germany Conflicted*, 28–37.

38. Brian Levin, "Islamophobia in America: Rise in Hate Crimes Against Muslims Shows What Politicians Say Matters," *Newsweek* (July 21, 2017), http://www.newsweek.com/islamophobia-america-rise-hate-crimes-against-muslims-proves-what-politicians-640184.

39. International Organization for Migration, *World Migration Report 2018*, 205.

40. René Cuperus, "The Populist Revolt Against Globalisation," *Perspective Politice* (June 2017), 13, https://www.clingendael.org/pub/2017/3/the-populist-revolt-against-globalisation/.

41. Robert Sapolsky, "This Is Your Brain on Nationalism: The Biology of Us and Them," *Foreign Affairs* 98 (March/April 2019), 47.

42. Dina Okamoto and Kim Ebert, "Group Boundaries, Immigrant Inclusion, and the Politics of Immigrant–Native Relations," *American Behavioral Scientist* 60 (2016), 242.

43. See, for example, Human Rights Watch, *Abused and Expelled: Ill-Treatment of Sub-Saharan African Migrants in Morocco* (New York: Human Rights Watch, February 2014), 47–52.

44. Andreas Wimmer, "Why Nationalism Works—And Why It Isn't Going Away," *Foreign Affairs* 98 (March/April 2019), 34.

45. Stephen Grootes, "The Awful Politics of Xenophobia," *Daily Maverick* (February 27, 2017), https://www.dailymaverick.co.za/article/2017-02-27-analysis-the-awful-politics-of-xenophobia/#.WyrOl6dKjmE.

46. Amnesty International, *Amnesty International Report 2017/18: The State of the World's Human Rights* (London: Amnesty International, 2018), 14.

47. James Milner, *Sharing the Security Burden: Towards the Convergence of Refugee Protection and State Security* (Oxford, UK: Refugee Studies Centre, University of Oxford, 2000), 16, http://www.rsc.ox.ac.uk/PDFs/workingpaper4.pdf.

48. Snyder, "The Broken Bargain," 60.

49. For a review of some existing efforts in this direction, see Flückiger, *Xenophobia, Media Stereotyping, and Their Role in Global Insecurity*, 6–8.

50. Fisk, "Out of the Fire, Into the Frying Pan?," 111.

51. Fisk, "Out of the Fire, Into the Frying Pan?," 112.

52. Tsourapas, "Labor Migrants as Political Leverage," 383, 393.

53. International Organization for Migration, *World Migration Report 2018*, 220.

54. International Organization for Migration, *World Migration Report 2018*, 215.

55. Manolis Pratsinakis, "Established and Outsider Nationals: Immigrant–Native Relations and the Everyday Politics of National Belonging," *Ethnicities* 18 (2018), 16.

56. Jane Freedman, "Analysing the Gendered Insecurities of Migration: A Case Study of Female Sub-Saharan African Migrants in Morocco," *International Feminist Journal of Politics* 14 (March 2012), 50.

57. Nazli Choucri, "Migration and Security: Some Key Linkages," *Journal of International Affairs* 56 (Fall 2002), 117.

58. Cederman, "Blood for Soil," 68.

59. Jayati Ghosh, "Fear of Foreigners: Recession and Racism in Europe," *Race/Ethnicity* 4 (Winter 2011), 189.

60. Will Carless and Aaron Sankin, "The Hate Report: The State of Anti-Immigrant Hate, 2018," *Center for Investigative Reporting* (June 8, 2018), https://www.revealnews .org/blog/the-hate-report-the-state-of-anti-immigrant-hate-2018/.

61. Magdalena Adriana Duvenage, *Intelligence Analysis in the Knowledge Age: An Analysis of the Challenges Facing the Practice of Intelligence Analysis* (master's thesis, Stellenbosch University, 2010), 50.

62. Oikonomakis Panagiotis, *Strategic Military Deception: Prerequisites of Success in Technological Environment* (Athens: Research Institute for European and American Studies, Research Paper No. 171, August–September 2016), 26, http://www.rieas.gr/ images/publications/rieas171.pdf.

63. Richards J. Heuer, *Psychology of Intelligence Analysis* (Washington, DC: Central Intelligence Agency Center for the Study of Intelligence, 1999), 70, 181.

64. Yi Wang, "Globalization Enhances Cultural Identity," *Intercultural Communication Studies* 16 (2007), 85.

65. James Kirchick, "Is Germany Capable of Protecting Its Jews?," *The Atlantic* (April 29, 2018), https://www.theatlantic.com/international/archive/2018/04/germany -jews-muslim-migrants/558677/.

66. See Ayumi Takenaka, "Secondary Migration: Who Re-Migrates and Why These Migrants Matter," *Migration Information Source* (April 26, 2007), https://www .migrationpolicy.org/article/secondary-migration-who-re-migrates-and-why-these -migrants-matter.

67. Cederman, "Blood for Soil," 64.

68. Natalie Sabanadze, *Globalization and Nationalism* (Budapest: Central European University Press, 2010), 177.

69. Richard Rousseau, "Globalization, Democracy, and Civil Society: An Assessment," *Diplomatic Courier* (November/December 2014), https://www.diplomaticourier .com/globalization-democracy-and-civil-society-an-assessment/.

70. Benjamin H. Friedman, "Managing Fear: The Politics of Homeland Security," *Political Science Quarterly* 126 (2011), 79.

71. Khadija Patel and Azad Essa, "South Africa Under Scrutiny for 'State Xenophobia,'" *Al Jazeera* (May 14, 2015), https://www.aljazeera.com/news/2015/05/south-africa-scrutiny-state-xenophobia-150514062325847.html.

72. Andrew Goldsmith, "Policing Weak States: Citizen Safety and State Responsibility," *Policing and Society* 13 (2002), 6.

73. See, for example, Human Rights First, *Germany Conflicted*, 26.

74. Roland Bleiker and Emma Hutchison, "Fear No More: Emotions and World Politics," *Review of International Studies* 34 (January 2008), 119; and Corey Robin, *Fear: The History of a Political Idea* (New York: Oxford University Press, 2004), 145–146.

75. Cederman, "Blood for Soil," 68.

Conclusion

1. See, for example, the United Nations High Commissioner for Refugees placing responsibility squarely on host state governments, as mentioned in Kerstin Fisk, "Out of the Fire, Into the Frying Pan? Examining Violence Against Foreign Migrants in Africa," in Heather Smith-Cannoy, ed., *Emerging Threats to Human Rights: Resources, Violence, and Deprivation of Citizenship* (Philadelphia: Temple University Press, 2019), 111.

2. See, for example, Lars-Erik Cederman, "Blood for Soil: The Fatal Temptations of Ethnic Politics," *Foreign Affairs* 98 (March/April 2019), 62.

3. Weiyi Cai and Simone Landon, "Attacks by White Extremists Are Growing—So Are Their Connections," *New York Times* (April 3, 2019), https://www.nytimes.com/interactive/2019/04/03/world/white-extremist-terrorism-christchurch.html.

4. René Cuperus, "The Populist Revolt Against Globalisation," Perspective Politice (June 2017), 9, https://www.clingendael.org/pub/2017/3/the-populist-revolt-against-globalisation/. See also Klaus von Beyme, "Right-Wing Extremism in Post-War Europe," *West European Politics* 11 (1988), 1–18.

5. "European Migration: Fear of Foreigners," *The Economist* (November 22, 2007), http://www.economist.com/node/10177918.

6. Caroline Freund, "Anti-Globalization or Xenophobia?" *Peterson Institute for International Economics* (April 28, 2016), https://piie.com/blogs/realtime-economic-issues-watch/anti-globalization-or-xenophobia. See also Jarret T. Crawford and Jane M. Pinlanski, "Political Intolerance, Right and Left," *Political Psychology* 35 (2014), 849; Jayati Ghosh, "Fear of Foreigners: Recession and Racism in Europe," *Race/Ethnicity* 4 (Winter 2011), 189; Cas Mudde, *The Relationship Between Immigration and Nativism in Europe and North America* (Washington, DC: Migration Policy Institute, May 2012), 11; Jan-Werner Müller, "False Flags: The Myth of the Nationalist Resurgence," *Foreign Affairs* 98 (March/April 2019), 36; and Yael Tamir, "Building a Better Nationalism: The Nation's Place in a Globalized World," *Foreign Affairs* 98 (March/April 2019), 51.

7. Andreas Wimmer, "Why Nationalism Works—And Why It Isn't Going Away," *Foreign Affairs* 98 (March/April 2019), 28.

8. Tamir, "Building a Better Nationalism," 51.

9. David Adler, "Meet Europe's Left Nationalists," *The Nation* (January 10, 2019), https://www.thenation.com/article/meet-europes-left-nationalists/.

10. Tamir, "Building a Better Nationalism," 51.

11. Müller, "False Flags," 40, 41.

12. Eugene Robinson, "Can You Say, 'Bienvenidos'?," *Washington Post* (June 27, 2006), A21.

13. Robert Kagan, *The Jungle Grows Back: America and Our Imperiled World* (New York: Knopf, 2018), 128.

14. Mudde, *The Relationship Between Immigration and Nativism in Europe and North America*, 31.

15. Ronald F. Inglehart and Pippa Norris, *Trump, Brexit, and the Rise of Populism: Economic Have-Nots and Cultural Backlash* (Cambridge, MA: Harvard Kennedy School Faculty Research Working Paper Series #RWP16-026, August 2016), 13, 29, 30, https://www.hks.harvard.edu/publications/trump-brexit-and-rise-populism-economic-have-nots-and-cultural-backlash.

16. Jack Snyder, "The Broken Bargain: How Nationalism Came Back," *Foreign Affairs* 98 (March/April 2019), 58.

17. Wimmer, "Why Nationalism Works—And Why It Isn't Going Away," 34.

18. Müller, "False Flags," 37, 38, 40.

19. Myron Weiner, "Security, Stability, and International Migration," *International Security* 17 (Winter 1992/93), 104.

20. Barry R. Posen, "The Security Dilemma and Ethnic Conflict," in Michael E. Brown, ed., *Ethnic Conflict and International Security* (Princeton, NJ: Princeton University Press, 1993), 119.

21. Human Rights First, *Combating Xenophobic Violence: A Framework for Action* (New York: Human Rights First, 2011), 30.

22. Kwame Anthony Appiah, "The Importance of Elsewhere: In Defense of Cosmopolitanism," *Foreign Affairs* 98 (March/April 2019), 26.

23. Matthew Carr, *Fortress Europe: Dispatches from a Gated Continent* (New York: New Press, 2012), 248.

24. Kagan, *The Jungle Grows Back*, 128.

25. Diane E. Davis, "Irregular Armed Forces, Shifting Patterns of Commitment, and Fragmented Sovereignty in the Developing World," *Theory and Society* 39 (2010), 397-413.

26. Benjamin Wittes and Gabriella Blum, *The Future of Violence: Robots and Germs, Hackers and Drones* (New York: Basic Books, 2015), 228, 229-230, 232.

27. Michael C. LeMay, *Guarding the Gates: Immigration and National Security* (Westport, CT: Praeger Security International, 2006), 260.

28. Pierre Hassner, "Beyond Nationalism and Internationalism: Ethnicity and World Order," in Michael E. Brown, ed., *Ethnic Conflict and International Security* (Princeton, NJ: Princeton University Press, 1993), 135.

29. Ron E. Hassner and Jason Wittenberg, "Barriers to Entry: Who Builds Fortified Boundaries and Why?," *International Security* 40 (Summer 2015), 183.

30. Robert Mandel, *Deadly Transfers and the Global Playground: Transnational Security Threats in a Disorderly World* (Westport, CT: Praeger Publishers, 1999), 4.

31. Catalina Smulovitz, "Citizen Insecurity and Fear: Public and Private Responses in Argentina," in Hugo Frühling and Joseph L. Tulchin, eds., *Crime and Violence in Latin America: Citizen Security, Democracy, and the State* (Baltimore, MD: Johns Hopkins University Press, 2003), 146–147.

32. Appiah, "The Importance of Elsewhere," 24.

33. Müller, "False Flags," 37.

34. David J. Finlay, Ole R. Holsti, and Richard R. Fagen, *Enemies in Politics* (Chicago: Rand McNally, 1967), 21, 23.

35. See Arlie Russell Hochschild, *Strangers in Their Own Land: Anger and Mourning on the American Right* (New York: New Press, 2016), 5–8.

36. See Joan Esteban, Laura Mayoral, and Debraj Ray, "Ethnicity and Conflict: An Empirical Study," *American Economic Review*, 102 (2012), 1310–1342; and José G. Montalvo and Marta Reynal-Querol, "Ethnic Polarization, Potential Conflict, and Civil Wars," *American Economic Review* 95 (2005), 796–816.

37. Jaweed Kaleem, "The New Zealand Mosque Shooting Is Just the Latest in a Trend of Violence Against Houses of Worship," *Los Angeles Times* (March 15, 2019), https://www.latimes.com/world/la-fg-new-zealand-world-religious-attacks-20190315-story.html.

38. Roger Cohen, "Tribalism Here, and There," *New York Times* (March 10, 2008), https://www.nytimes.com/2008/03/10/opinion/10webcohen.html.

39. Human Rights First, *Germany Conflicted: The Struggle between Xenophobia and Tolerance* (New York: Human Rights First, February 2017), 26.

40. "Secretary-General's Statement on Intolerance and Hate-Based Violence," *United Nations* (April 29, 2019), https://www.un.org/sg/en/content/sg/statement/2019-04-29/secretary-generals-statement-intolerance-and-hate-based-violence.

41. "Blue Feed, Red Feed: See Liberal Facebook and Conservative Facebook, Side by Side," *Wall Street Journal*, (January 29, 2017), http://graphics.wsj.com/blue-feed-red-feed/.

42. Yoeri Maertens, "'America First': Why Has Nativism Resurfaced in the New World?" (master's thesis, Universiteit Gent, 2017), 29, https://lib.ugent.be/fulltxt/RUG01/002/376/009/RUG01-002376009_2017_0001_AC.pdf. See also Matt Levendusky, "Are Fox and MSNBC Polarizing America?" *Washington Post* (February 3, 2014), https://

www.washingtonpost.com/news/monkey-cage/wp/2014/02/03/are-fox-and-msnbc
-polarizing-america.

43. Snyder, "The Broken Bargain," 59–60.

44. Maertens, *"America First": Why Has Nativism Resurfaced in the New World?*, 29.

45. John M. Broder, "Immigration, from a Simmer to a Scream," *New York Times* (May 21, 2006), 1.

46. Human Rights First, *Germany Conflicted*, 38.

47. Maertens, *'America First': Why Has Nativism Resurfaced in the New World?*, 29.

48. Jack Snyder, "Nationalism and the Crisis of the Post-Soviet State," in Michael E. Brown, ed., *Ethnic Conflict and International Security* (Princeton, NJ: Princeton University Press, 1993), 86.

49. Carr, *Fortress Europe*, 208–209.

50. Manolis Pratsinakis, "Established and Outsider Nationals: Immigrant–Native Relations and the Everyday Politics of National Belonging," *Ethnicities* 18 (2018), 18.

51. Andrew J. Shryock, "Attack of the Islamophobes: Religious War (and Peace) in Arab/Muslim Detroit," in Carl W. Ernst, ed., *Islamophobia in America: The Anatomy of Intolerance* (New York: Palgrave Macmillan, 2013), 167.

52. Rebecca Friedman Lissner and Mira Rapp-Hooper, "The Day After Trump: American Strategy for a New International Order," *Washington Quarterly* 41 (Spring 2018), 16.

53. John J. Mearsheimer, "Bound to Fail: The Rise and Fall of the Liberal International Order," *International Security* 43 (Spring 2019), 37.

54. See, for example, Gal Ariely, "Global Identification, Xenophobia and Globalisation: A Cross-National Exploration," *International Journal of Psychology* (2016), 1.

55. Ariely, "Global Identification, Xenophobia and Globalisation," 1–10.

56. Wimmer, "Why Nationalism Works—And Why It Isn't Going Away," 34.

57. Douglas Murray, *The Strange Death of Europe: Immigration, Identity, Islam* (London: Bloomsbury, 2017), 315.

58. Appiah, "The Importance of Elsewhere," 21, 22.

59. Murray, *The Strange Death of Europe*, 6.

60. Murray, *The Strange Death of Europe*, 7–8.

61. Samuel P. Huntington, *Who Are We?* (New York: Simon and Schuster, 2005), 171.

62. Troy S. Thomas, Stephen D. Kiser, and William D. Casebeer, *Warlords Rising: Confronting Violent Non-State Actors* (Lanham, MD: Lexington Books, 2005), 5. See also John Herz, *The Nation-State and the Crisis of World Politics* (Philadelphia, PA: McKay, 1976).

63. Joanna Rubery, "Can the Académie Française Stop the Rise of Anglicisms in French?," *OUPblog—Oxford University Press Blog* (March 21, 2014), https://blog.oup.com/2014/03/academie-francaise-french-anglicisms/.

64. LeMay, *Guarding the Gates*, 239.

65. Fiona B. Adamson, "Crossing Borders: International Migration and National Security," *International Security* 31 (Summer 2006), 175.

66. Murray, *The Strange Death of Europe*, 314.

67. Hassner, "Beyond Nationalism and Internationalism," 132.

68. Anthony D. Smith, "The Ethnic Sources of Nationalism," in Brown, *Ethnic Conflict and International Security*, 28.

69. Chapman, "Managing the Politics of Parochialism," 237.

70. "Secretary-General's Statement on Intolerance and Hate-Based Violence."

Index

The authorized representative in the EU for product safety and compliance is:
Mare Nostrum Group
B.V Doelen 72
4831 GR Breda
The Netherlands

www.ingramcontent.com/pod-product-compliance
Lightning Source LLC
Chambersburg PA
CBHW031357270326
41929CB00010BA/1220